World Economic Performance

Dedicated to the memory of

Angus Maddison

*scholar, mentor, great friend and a well wisher
who sadly passed away during the preparation of the
manuscript*

Angus Maddison, 1926–2010

*Friend or stranger, stop and shed a tear:
Gentle Angus Maddison lies here.
Joining the social sciences with art,
He took human misery to heart
And mixed time, space and math to set men free
From want. Angus hated poverty.*

*A poem by
Roger Dickinson-Brown*

World Economic Performance
Past, Present and Future

Essays in celebration of the life and work of Angus Maddison

Edited by

D.S. Prasada Rao

School of Economics
The University of Queensland
Brisbane, Australia

Bart van Ark

The Conference Board
New York, USA

Faculty of Economics and Business
University of Groningen
Groningen, The Netherlands

Edward Elgar
Cheltenham, UK • Northampton, MA, US

Published by
Edward Elgar Publishing Limited
The Lypiatts
15 Lansdown Road
Cheltenham
Glos GL50 2JA
UK

Edward Elgar Publishing, Inc.
William Pratt House
9 Dewey Court
Northampton
Massachusetts 01060
USA

A catalogue record for this book
is available from the British Library

Library of Congress Control Number: 2012930566

This book is available electronically in the ElgarOnline.com
Economics Subject Collection, E-ISBN 978 1 78195 355 6

ISBN 978 1 84844 848 3

Printed and bound by MPG PRINTGROUP, UK

Contents

Contributors

Bart van Ark
Chief Economist, The Conference Board, New York, USA and Professor of Economics, Groningen Growth and Development Centre, University of Groningen, Groningen, Netherlands.

Derek Blades
Consultant in economic statistics and statistical office management, Blades Consultancy Services, 28 Bd. Eugène Tripet, 06400 Cannes, France.

Pierre van der Eng
School of Management, Marketing & International Business, College of Business and Economics, The Australian National University, Canberra, Australia.

Kyoji Fukao
Professor, Institute of Economic Research, Hitotsubashi University, Kunitachi City, Tokyo, Japan.

Ross Garnaut
Professor of Economics, Research School of Pacific and Asian Studies, The Australian National University, Canberra, Australia.

Robert J. Gordon
Stanley G. Harris Professor of the Social Sciences, Northwestern University, Evanston, Illinois, USA; NBER, Cambridge, MA, USA and CEPR, London, UK.

André A. Hofman
Economic Commission for Latin America and the Caribbean, Santiago, Chile.

Deepak Lal
James S. Coleman Professor of International Development Studies, University of California, Los Angeles, USA.

Angus Maddison
As the Manuscript was prepared, Angus Maddison, Visiting Professor, United Nations University (MERIT), Maastricht, Netherlands and Professor Emeritus, University of Groningen, Groningen, Netherlands, sadly passed away on 27th April 2010.

Stanislav Menshikov
Moscow School of Economics, Moscow State University, Moscow, U.S.S.R.

Mary O'Mahony
Professor of International Industrial Economics, Birmingham Business School, University House, Birmingham, U.K.

D.S. Prasada Rao
Professor of Economics, The University of Queensland, Brisbane, Australia.

Osamu Saito
Institute of Economic Research, Hitotsubashi University, Kunitachi City, Tokyo, Japan.

Adam Szirmai
Professorial Fellow, UNU-MERIT and Professor of Development Economics, Maastricht Graduate School of Governance, Maastricht University, Maastricht, The Netherlands.

Marcel P. Timmer
Professor of Economics, Groningen Growth and Development Centre, University of Groningen, Groningen,The Netherlands.

Francisco Villarreal
Economic Commission for Latin America and the Caribbean, Santiago, Chile.

Harry X. Wu
Professor of Economics, Institute of Economic Research, Hitotsubashi University, Tokyo, Japan.

Justin Yifu Lin
Senior Vice President, Development Economics, and Chief Economist, The World Bank, Washington DC, USA.

Acknowledgements

Our sincere thanks are due to all the contributors to this volume for the time and effort they have put into the preparation and subsequent revisions of their chapters. But this book would not have been possible without constant encouragement and involvement by Late Professor Angus Maddison who was involved in this project right from the conception stage. We are deeply sorry that Angus has not lived to see the completion of the project and the manuscript in print. We sincerely hope that the completed version would have met with his approval. We are also thankful to the Publisher, Edward Elgar, for making it possible to include additional material on the Life and Work of Angus Maddison, and to Managing Editors of *The Review of Income and Wealth* for allowing us to reprint Angus' obituary by Derek Blades, Harry X. Wu and Bart van Ark. Our sincere thanks are due to Roger Dickinson-Brown, a long time friend of Angus, for writing the poem. Finally, we thank Visala Rao who has persevered with the difficult job of formatting and proof reading of various chapters.

D.S. Prasada Rao
Bart van Ark
Editors

1. Introduction

D.S. Prasada Rao and Bart van Ark

1.1   BACKGROUND

What was the world's average per capita income in the year 1 AD? Why could China's expansion not last beyond the 13th century? Why and when did the West get rich? Why did Sub–Saharan Africa not take off? Why is India still poor? While Angus Maddison will probably be most widely known for his long term series on gross domestic product and per capita income, going back many centuries, he more than anyone else used it to develop an immense research portfolio which shed light on those and other fundamental questions.

Angus Maddison was an example of this rare brand of scholars who didn't shy away from the big issues in economic development and growth. On 24 April 2010 he died at the age of 83. It was the end of a fascinating life and an impressive and internationally acclaimed career in reconstructing and studying the history of economic performance. Angus' work has been widely acclaimed and he has been honored both during his lifetime and since he passed away.

This book represents one of those honors. It is a collection of revised versions of a set of core papers which were presented at mini-conferences held in Groningen and Brisbane on the occasion of Angus Maddison's 80th birthday in 2006. The Groningen meeting focused on the long term growth performance in the Western Hemisphere, whereas the Brisbane meeting had prime focus on Asia.

1.2   OVERVIEW

This introduction briefly summarizes the papers published in this volume. All papers in this volume highlight the importance of institutions, and other ultimate causes of growth such as policy actions and changes in the international order. The more qualitative and historical discussion of ultimate causality highlight the deeper forces which explain the proximate causes of growth. The latter represent the primary factors of production, such as increased supply of labour and capital, and improved quality of labour and physical capital, but also structural change and total factor productivity.

The Chinese economic performance over the last two decades has been spectacular and the envy of the world. There is considerable debate as to when China will overtake the US as the world's largest economy. In Chapter 2, Angus Maddison examines the Chinese performance over a period spanning more than a millennium covering the period 960 to 2005 and presents forecasts to 2030. The chapter identifies six phases of the Chinese economy. Maddison's analysis starts with the Sung dynasty from 960 to 1280 AD which is identified as the first phase of economic transformation. During this period China experienced rapid population growth as well as an increase in real per capita income by a third and at the same level as that in Western Europe. The second phase, 1700 to 1840, is considered to be a period of stagnation and one of isolation from outside the world. The third phase spanning 1840–1950 witnessed internal conflicts and foreign intrusions and a decline in real per capita income by a third. During the fourth phase of the Maoist period of 1950 to 1978 there was a modest recovery in per capita income. A spectacular recovery in the Chinese economic performance started during the fifth phase during 1978 to 2008 a period characterized by pragmatic reforms and impressive growth rates in GDP well above those observed in the rest of the world. Chinese share in the world GDP increased to 16.8 per cent by 2006. Maddison's analysis projects growth in real per capita income around 4.5 to 5.6 per cent per annum during the period 2006 to 2030 which will make China the largest economy by 2030 with a share of 25 per cent of the world GDP.

Justin Lin's chapter follows on from Chapter 2 as it analyses the economic performance of China since the Sung Dynasty with the prime objective of offering credible answers to the Weber Question and the Needham Puzzle and the question as to why the industrial revolution did not originate in China despite the existence of a number of favourable preconditions. These are framed in the form of the Needham puzzle which asks why China had been so far in advance of other civilizations and despite its position why China has lagged behind the rest of the world. In this fascinating chapter, Lin critically evaluates a number of arguments and counter arguments in this debate and offers his own explanation. In particular, he concludes that the incentive system embedded in the civil-service examination system in the pre-modern times made Chinese talents to focus on Confucian classics, prevented them from accumulating human capital in other areas which in turn deprived China from the opportunity of indigenous scientific and industrial revolutions. His main conclusion is that if China maintains its transition to market economy and continues to tap into the Gerschenkronian growth potential of "the advantage of backwardness" it is likely that China will maintain a dynamic GDP growth rate for several more decades.

Chapter 4 by Deepak Lal focuses on India, the second most populous country, which has posted consistent and impressive growth rates over the last decade. Lal traces the history of economic policy in India and assesses its growth performance since its independence in 1947. The post-independent India posted a low but consistent Hindu rate of growth of 3.5 per cent against a population growing at 2.2 per cent until the 1980s. Lal traces the first steps towards liberalization and reform in the mid-1980s and the resumption of these policies in the early 1990s by the current prime minister and the then finance minister, Dr. Manmohan Singh. During the period 1993–99 the output per worker grew at a rate of 5.8 per cent which may be considered as a turning point. Lal identifies agricultural growth based on the Green revolution as a major source in the first two decades since independence. Though there has been an increase in manufacturing employment and output, the fastest growth since the 1980s has been in the services sector spanning both the modern and traditional service thus making Indian growth somewhat atypical of the international growth patterns. In looking to the next two decades, Lal argues that if the recent strong growth in savings, around 35 per cent, is maintained then a growth rate of 10 per cent in the foreseeable future would be possible even without further reforms.

In contrast to the chapters on China and India, Stanislav Menshikov's Chapter 5 on Russia focuses on the recent transition period since 1991. The chapter looks at the initial shock and decline and the subsequent stagnation during the period 1991 to 1998 and contrasts it with the overall growth performance since 1998. Menshikov studies the anatomy of the crisis, beginning in 1991, and identifies spectacular contractions in personal and government consumption as the major drivers with strong increases in net exports providing a cushion. An equally impressive recovery in the Russian economy since 1999 is attributed to a substantive devaluation of the ruble and sharp increases in the prices of exported oil and natural gas. Menshikov's calculations suggest that domestic demand accounted for nearly 75 per cent of total GDP growth during 1998–2005 while 25 per cent is attributed to net external demand. Using the growth in capital, labour, reductions in unused capacity and estimates of TFP growth during the period 1998 to 2005 and making a few plausible assumptions, Menshikov projects annual growth rates of 7 and 5.5 per cent respectively in the periods 2003–2015 and 2015–2030. These growth rates compare well with projected growth rates for 14 other nations including China, Brazil and India. Menshikov predicts that Russia will be the fifth largest economy in 2030 with an estimated share of 5.5 per cent of world GDP.

Japanese post-war growth and economic performance and the deceleration in growth since the oil crisis in 1973 have been the subject matter of considerable research. In Chapter 6, Kyoji Fukao and Osamu Saito examine the main features of Japanese growth performance since the Meiji period in 1868. During the early period Japan successfully exploited the Grechenkronian situation of being in a materially and institutionally backward state compared to the Western countries. During the period from 1850 to 1950, Japan kept pace with the world average while performing well below Western Europe. The accelerated growth performance from 1955 to 1973 and the processes underlying the dramatic transformation of Japan form the core of the chapter by Fukao and Saito. Limited opportunities for TFP growth in the manufacturing sector after catching-up with the United States and a decline in the working-age population and the relatively high saving levels are listed as some of the main factors for the stagnation over the last two decades. The authors tend to concur with the projections made by Angus Maddison of a modest GDP per capita growth of 1.3 per cent during the period 2003 to 2030. The authors conclude that unless a new and promising regime of productivity growth in the service sector emerges, growth prospects for Japan appear to be limited.

In Chapter 7 Ross Garnaut examines the prospects for global economic performance in the next two decades and more importantly discusses the institutional structures to the trading systems and environments required to sustain economic growth. Garnaut's chapter briefly reviews the salient features of growth performance of nations in the Golden Age, 1950–73, in the Silver Age spanning the period 1973 to the end of the twentieth century and then assesses the projections made by Maddison in Chapter 2 of this book. The author argues that the growth rates for China and India by Maddison are conservative and concludes that global growth rates during the period 2003–2030 dubbed as the Platinum Age would exceed those experienced during the Golden age. The author stresses the need for adequate management of international public goods including international security, focus on the problems arising out of increasing global inequality; the importance of external environmental costs of economic growth; and, finally, the need to dismantle barriers to free trade.

In Chapter 8 Pierre van der Eng provides revised estimates of economy wide TFP growth rates for Indonesia over the period 1950 to 2005. The chapter demonstrates the importance of checking the accuracy of the national accounts figures before using them for TFP growth estimation. Using meticulously constructed series of GDP, capital stock and education-adjusted labour force figures along with estimated labour shares, the chapter shows that TFP growth over the whole period was a negative 0.1 per cent and its contribution to GDP growth was found to be a negligible 2 per cent. In fact the only period during which TFP growth was found to be positive was the more recent decade 2000–2010 with a growth of 1.6 per cent which contributed 30 per cent to the overall GDP growth during the decade. A major innovation in the chapter is its attempt to conduct analyses to determine the validity of the key assumptions that underpin the TFP computations such as perfect markets and efficient production practices and concludes that the positive TFP growth observed during 2000–10 is due to improvements in efficiency rather than technical change. The general conclusion is that Indonesian data supports the Krugman hypothesis for growth in Indonesia during the study period, 1950 to 2000.

Chapter 9 by Adam Szirmai takes a holistic view of the process of economic development and examines the sources of growth. Noting the failure of mono-causal explanations, the author embarks on a detailed examination of the proximate, intermediate and ultimate sources of growth. Absorptive capacity and ability and willingness to tap into global technology are identified as key sources of catch-up for developing countries. The Greschenkronian advantages of backwardness allow countries to profit from technological advance without having to bear many of the costs and risks. The main conclusion of the chapter is that countries need to go all out to acquire and assimilate international technology or otherwise risk stagnation.

Chapter 10 by André Hofman and Francisco Villarreal explores the medium-term growth prospects for countries in Latin America. The authors pursue a rigorous econometric approach to measure the performance and to forecast future performance. The chapter uses a production function approach with time-varying trend which makes it possible to characterize long-term potentital output and to forecast its future evolution using a parametric model. The model is then expressed in the state-space form. The authors use estimated econometric models in assessing growth performance of a selected set of countries in Latin America under several scenarios. Under the baseline scenario which assumes that capital accumulation and multifactor productivity will continue to grow at current trends and with population growth projected to decline over the medium term, the chapter reports that Brazil will experience an average annual growth rate of 1.6 per cent over the period 2005–2030 compared to a projected growth rate of 4.3 for Chile and 2.6 for Argentina.

Chapter 11 by Bart van Ark, Mary O'Mahony and Marcel Timmer places Europe's growth experience since WWII in a comparative perspective with the United States. The authors provide a breakdown of Europe's output and productivity into the contributions of labor, capital and multifactor productivity. They conclude that following several decades of catching up on the U.S., Europe saw a widening of the productivity gap since the mid 1990s. The failure to realize the potential productivity gains of information and communication technology (ICT) in the services sector is identified as a major cause. The authors conclude from a range of growth scenarios that that the chances of accelerating future growth by way of a strengthening of manufacturing productivity, or through an acceleration in services productivity has limited scope for success, in part due to the region's demographic burden of a rapidly aging population, and the difficulty to realize a deepening of Europe's single market for services.

In Chapter 12, Robert Gordon discusses the prospects for growth in the United States in the light of the historical growth performance during the long century from 1891 to 2007. Building on his previous work, the author revisits the latest quarterly, annual and long term estimates of U.S. productivity growth. The extraordinarily rapid productivity growth during the "one big wave" from 1929–1950 period, caused by the major technological and institutional inventions of that era, is contrasted with the sources of growth for the next 20 years. Gordon argues that the productivity gains during the first decade of the 21st century were primarily the result of declines in working hours and "cost cutting" which strengthened profits but cannot sustain long term growth. Taking this pessimistic view on the prospects for technology to take over as the leading source of growth, Gordon's results imply that American GDP per capita is unlikely to grow at more than 1.5 per cent for the next 20 years, which is far below the 2.17 per cent of the previous 80 years.

1.3   EPILOGUE

After the sad demise of Angus Maddison, as editors we have decided to include an epilogue consisting of reprints of Angus' own memoirs which was published in the *Banco Nazionale del Lavoro*; a hitherto unpublished overview of his research objectives, which he wrote in the early 2000s, and his obituary published in *The Review of Income and Wealth* in September 2010.

The chapters in this volume are a tribute to Angus Maddison's contribution to the economics profession which was spread over a period of more than half century. To continue the scholarly work on the analysis of the sources of economic growth and stagnation, his unique data series will be an indispensable tool. A group of scholars, including several of the authors that contributed to this volume, have recently founded and joined The Maddison Project http://www.ggdc.net/maddison/maddison-project/ index. htm. This is a coordinated effort to gradually build upon Angus' work to extend and update his data series. It will remain a crucial tool for the analysis of long term economic growth. Angus Maddison will be missed. But his legacy will stay, and many will continue the work in his spirit.

2. Six Transformations in China: 960–2030

Angus Maddison

2.1 INTRODUCTION

In world perspective China's performance has been exceptional. In the thirteenth century, it was the world's leading economy in terms of per capita income. It outperformed Europe in levels of technology, the intensity with which it used its natural resources, and capacity for administering a huge territorial empire. By 1500, western Europe had overtaken China in per capita real income, technological and scientific capacity. From the 1840s to the middle of the twentieth century, China's performance actually declined in a world where economic progress elsewhere was very substantial. In the past 60 years, China has been resurrected in a catch-up process which seems likely to continue in the next quarter century. By 2030 Chinese per capita income will be well above the world average. In terms of GDP, it will very probably have overtaken the USA as the world's biggest economy around 2015 (see Figure 2.1 and Tables 2.1, 2.2 and 2.3).

2.1.1 Six Transformations

One can identify six major phases in economic performance of China in the past millennium.

1) **The first transformation** saw *intensive* and *extensive* growth in the Sung dynasty 960-1280, when per capita income rose by a third and population almost doubled. There was a major shift in the centre of gravity of the economy. In the eighth century three-quarters of the population lived in North China, where the main crops were wheat and millet. By the end of the thirteenth, three-quarters lived south of the Yangtse. This area had been swampy and lightly-settled, but with irrigation and early ripening seeds, it provided an ideal opportunity for massive development of rice cultivation. There was also a significant opening to the world economy in the southern Sung, Yuan and early Ming dynasties (1130 to 1433), which

ended abruptly when China withdrew from world trade, at a time when its
maritime technology was superior to that of Europe.

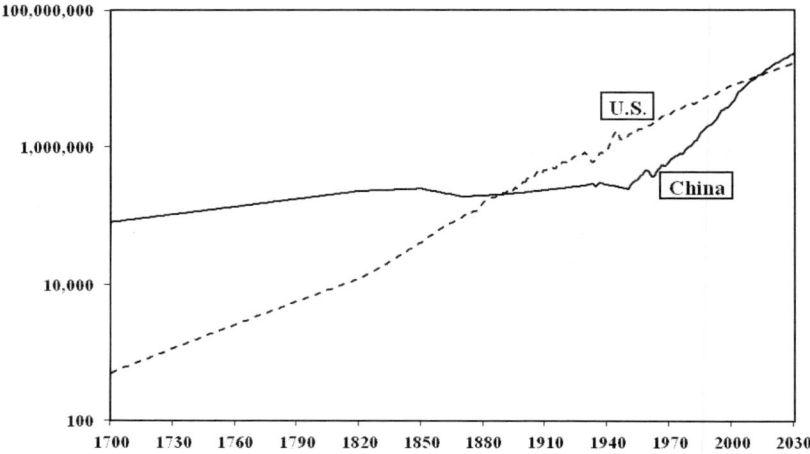

*Figure 2.1   Comparative levels of GDP, China and USA, 1700–2030
(million 1990 International dollars)*

*Table 2.1   Population of China, Western Europe and the USA, 960–2030
AD (million)*

	960	1280	1700	1840	1952	1978	2006	2030
China	55	100	138	412	569	956	1,311	1,462
W. Europe	20	55	81	157	309	366	400	406
USA	1.3	2.0	1.8	17	158	223	298	374

*Table 2.2   Levels of Chinese, West European and US GDP per capita, 960–
2030 AD (1990 $)*

	960	1280	1700	1840	1952	1978	2006	2030
China	450	600	600	600	538	978	6,048	17,394
W. Europe	422	595	997	1,437	4,952	12,576	21,203	31,030
USA	400	400	527	1,588	10,316	18,373	31,049	45,446

Table 2.3   China's share of world GDP, 1000–2030 (per cent)

1000	1280	1700	1840	1952	1978	2006	2030
22.1	33.2	22.3	31.2	5.2	4.9	16.8	25.0

Source for Tables 2.1, 2.2, and 2.3:   See Maddison website: www.ggdc.net/Maddison.

2) After a long period of mediocre progress and episodic setbacks, the **second transformation** occurred between 1700 and 1840, when population rose nearly threefold (much faster than in Europe and Japan), with no fall in per capita income. This achievement was possible because of accelerated use of dry-land crops from the Americas (maize, sweet potatoes, Irish potatoes and peanuts), which could be grown in hilly, sandy and mountainous areas. There was also a huge expansion of the national territory and closer control of docile tributary states. China remained isolated from the outside world and repudiated British efforts to establish diplomatic relations at the end of the eighteenth century.

3) Because of technological backwardness, and weakness of governance, there was a **third transformation** from 1840 to 1950. China suffered from internal conflict and collusive foreign intrusions on its territory and sovereignty. The economic results were disastrous. Chinese GDP fell from a third to a twentieth of the world total, and per capita income fell in a period when it rose threefold in Japan, fourfold in Europe and eightfold in the USA.

4) The **fourth transformation** in the Maoist period (1950–78), saw a significant recovery of per capita income, but growth was interrupted by disastrous economic and social experiments, wars with Korea, India and Vietnam, and long years of almost complete autarchy.

5) In the **fifth transformation** (1978–2008), China dropped the Maoist policies and adopted a pragmatic reformism which was successful in sparking off growth much faster than in all other parts of the world economy. There were large, once-for-all, gains in efficiency in agriculture, an explosive expansion of foreign trade and accelerated absorption of foreign technology through large-scale foreign direct investment.

6) In the **sixth transformation** (2006–2030), catch-up will continue, but the pace of progress will slacken as China gets nearer to the technological frontier. I have assumed that per capita income will grow at an average rate of 4.5 per cent a year between 2006 and 2030, but that the rate of advance will taper off over the period. Specifically, I assume a per capita growth rate of 5.6 per cent a year to 2010, 4.6 per cent between 2010 and 2020, and a little more than 3.6 per cent a year from 2020 to 2030. By

then, it will have reached the per capita level of Western Europe and Japan around 1990. As it approaches this level, technical advance will be more costly as imitation is replaced by innovation. China will overtake the USA as number one economy in terms of GDP, will produce a quarter of world GDP by 2030. Its geopolitical leverage will certainly be greater then than now.

2.2   THE SUNG TRANSFORMATION AND IDIOSYNCRATIC CHARACTERISTICS OF TRADITIONAL CHINA

China was a pioneer in bureaucratic governance. In the tenth century, it was already administered by professionally trained public servants, recruited by examination on a meritocratic basis. The bureaucracy, schooled in the Confucian classics, was the main instrument for imposing social and political order in a unitary state over a huge area. It had no challenge from a landed aristocracy, established church, judiciary, dissident intellectuals, or an urban bourgeoisie, and only rarely from the military. They used a written language common to all of China, and the official Confucian ideology was deeply ingrained in the education system. This system was relatively efficient and cheap to operate compared with the multilayered structure of governance in feudal Europe and Japan.

In Tokugawa Japan, the shogunal, daimyo and samurai households were about 6 per cent of the population compared with 3 per cent for the imperial household, bureaucracy, military, and degree-holding gentry who composed the ruling elite in China. At that time, fiscal levies accounted for 5 per cent of GDP in China compared with 25 per cent in Japan. However, the Chinese bureaucracy augmented their official income substantially by 'customary charges' and non-fiscal exactions and the gentry had rental incomes. Altogether, the income of the Chinese elite was probably about 15 per cent of GDP. In the West, recruitment of professionally trained public servants on a meritocratic basis was initiated by Napoleon, a millennium later, but European bureaucrats never had the social status and power of the Chinese literati. Within each European country power was fragmented between a much greater variety of countervailing forces. Europe had a system of independent nation-states in close propinquity. They were outward looking, had significant trading relations and relatively easy intellectual interchange. This benign fragmentation stimulated competition and innovation to a degree not possible in China.

Between the eighth and the thirteenth centuries there was a major shift in the centre of gravity of the economy. In the eighth century three-quarters of the population lived in North China, where the main crops were wheat and millet. By the end of the thirteenth, three-quarters lived south of the Yangtse. This area had been swampy and lightly-settled, but with irrigation and early ripening seeds, it provided an ideal opportunity for massive development of rice cultivation, and an increase in per capita income by a third. Thereafter, from the thirteenth to the beginning of the nineteenth century, China was able to accommodate a fourfold increase in population whilst maintaining average per capita income as more or less stable. Its capacity for *extensive* growth was most clearly demonstrated in the eighteenth century when its GDP grew faster than that of Western Europe. However, European per capita income grew by a fifth.

The economic impact of the Chinese bureaucracy was very positive for agriculture. Like the Physiocrats, they thought it was the key sector from which they could squeeze a surplus in the form of taxes and compulsory levies. They nurtured it with hydraulic works. Thanks to the precocious development of printing (500 years before Europe) they were able to diffuse best practice techniques by widespread distribution of illustrated agricultural handbooks. They settled farmers in promising new regions. They developed a public granary system to mitigate famines. They fostered innovation by introducing early ripening seeds which eventually permitted double or triple cropping. They promoted the introduction of new crops - tea in the Tang dynasty, cotton in the Sung, sorghum in the Yuan, new world crops such as maize, potatoes, sweet potatoes, peanuts and tobacco in the Ming.

Land shortage was compensated by the intensive use of labour, irrigation and natural fertilisers. Land was under continuous cultivation, without fallow. Because of land scarcity, serfdom and slavery were not necessary. Land was cultivated by working proprietors, tenants who paid rents, and landless peasants who worked for wages. The need for fodder crops and grazing land was minimal. Livestock was concentrated on scavengers (pigs and poultry). Beef, milk and wool consumption were rare. The protein supply was augmented by widespread production of fish and ducks in small scale aquaculture. Improved land productivity permitted denser settlement, reduced transport cost, raised the proportion of farm output which could be marketed, released labour for rural handicraft activity, particularly the spinning and weaving of cotton, which provided more comfortable, more easily washable, and healthier clothing. Because of land shortage, there was no need to tie labour to the land by slavery or serfdom.

Outside agriculture the bureaucratic system had negative effects. The bureaucracy and the associated gentry were quintessential rent-seekers. They prevented the emergence of an independent commercial and industrial bourgeoisie on the European pattern. Entrepreneurial activity was insecure in a framework where legal protection for private business activity was exiguous. Any activity that promised to be lucrative was subject to bureaucratic squeeze. Larger undertakings were limited to state or publicly licensed monopolies.

2.2.1   Limited Exposure to the World Economy

The most striking example of the adverse effect of bureaucratic regulation was the virtual closure of China to international trade early in the fifteenth century, and the subsequent disappearance of its sophisticated shipbuilding industry.

In view of the historic importance of this withdrawal, it is worth retracing Chinese experience from the thirteenth to the early fifteenth century when China was the most dynamic force in Asian trade.

China's exposure to world trade was greatly enhanced when the Sung were driven out of North China and relocated their capital at Hangzhou, south of the Yangtse. It was a prosperous and densely populated region of rice cultivation. It was not necessary to bring food supplies from distant areas, and the Sung had deliberately sabotaged the dykes of the Grand Canal. They relied more heavily on commercial taxes than most Chinese dynasties and fostered the development of ports and foreign trade. Their major port was Ch'üan-chou, about 600 kilometres north of Canton. They fostered large scale production techniques for ceramics and other new products for the export market. As a result the kilns of Ching-te-chen (in Kiangsi) prospered greatly.

In order to defend the Yangtse and coastal areas against Mongol attacks the first Chinese professional navy was created in 1232. The ships included treadmill operated paddle-wheelers with protective armour plates for service on the Yangtse. These were armed with powerful catapults to fling heavy stones or other missiles at enemy ships.

After the Sung were defeated, the Yuan (Mongol) dynasty (1279–1368) enlarged shipbuilding for grain transport to Peking, for maritime commerce with Asia and for naval operations. They reopened overland commerce to Europe and the Middle East on the silk route. They also launched two unsuccessful maritime invasions of Japan in 1274 and 1281. The first attempt involved a fleet of 900 ships. The second was much larger and carried an invasion force of a quarter of a million.

As in the Sung, a large proportion of the trading community in the Yuan dynasty were immigrants from all parts of the Muslim world. This is clear from the observations of Marco Polo, the Venetian who came to China in the last quarter of the thirteenth century, and Ibn Battuta from Morocco more than 50 years later. Both left striking testimony to the vigour of the international trade of China at that time.

Early in the Ming dynasty (1368–1644), China embarked on a series of naval expeditions into the 'Eastern' and 'Western Oceans'. They were initiated by the Yung-lo emperor, the third ruler of the Ming dynasty (1402–1424). He was a usurper, who had deposed his nephew in a successful military rebellion. The naval ventures were intended to display China's power and wealth and enhance his own legitimacy. They were also intended to extend Chinese suzerainty over a much wider area. Korea was a permanent member of the Chinese system of tributary relationships and Yung-lo persuaded Japan to accept a similar status in 1404 (which lasted with a brief interruption until 1549). In the tribute system, there was an initial exchange of 'gifts' (consisting on the Chinese side of specialties such as silk, gold lacqueur and porcelain) and the other side were permitted to reciprocate with goods of lower value.

These tributary relations were conceived as a vehicle for asserting China's moral and cultural superiority, to act as a civilising force on barbarians at the frontiers, and thereby enhance China's security. For this reason the government expected to play a leading role in developing and supervising exchange relationships, and private trade was prohibited. The underlying idea was not to create a colonial empire, but to assert China's benign hegemony. This traditional view of Chinese relations with the outside world was very different from that of the succeeding Mongol dynasty whose objective was world conquest. In the Ming dynasty the Yung-lo emperor felt the need to re-establish a more attractive image of Chinese civilisation.

Seven expeditions between 1405 and 1433 penetrated very deep into the 'Western Oceans'. They were commanded by Admiral Cheng-Ho, a member of the emperor's household since he was 15 years old who had become a comrade in arms. Cheng-Ho was a eunuch. There were thousands of eunuchs in the Ming imperial household and emperors of this dynasty used them as a trusted and loyal counterweight to the power of the bureaucracy. Most of the latter regarded the expeditions as a waste of money, at a time when there were very large commitments in moving the Ming capital from Nanking to Peking and in rebuilding the Grand Canal. These involved very heavy fiscal burdens, and special levies on the coastal provinces. Yung-lo augmented his revenues by printing massive quantities of paper money. The resulting inflation led to a disappearance of paper money transactions in the private economy. From the 1430s, silver became the predominant instrument for commercial exchange and tax payment.

Under the Yung-lo emperor, the Ming navy consisted of 2,700 patrol vessels and combat ships attached to guard stations or island bases, 400 large warships stationed near Nanking and 400 grain transport freighters (see Needham, 1971, p. 484). Another 317 ships were built for the Cheng-Ho expeditions at the Longjiang shipyards near Nanking which had seven very

large dry-docks. The biggest vessels in the maritime expeditions to the
Western Oceans were 'treasure ships'. Cheng-Ho's flagship was one of these
and had a much bigger capacity than Columbus' ship the Santa Maria. Xi and
Chalmers (2004) estimated it to have been 120–125 metres long, about 50
metres wide and 12 meters deep, and the Santa Maria to have been 34 meters
long, 7.9 metres wide and 4 metres deep (see Figure 2.2).

Sources: Louise Levathes (1994), *When China Ruled the Seas*, Simon & Schuster, New York,
p. 21. Here Levathes compares the size of a Chinese treasure ship with the much smaller Santa
Maria of Columbus. See also Xi and Chalmers (2004).

Figure 2.2   Size of Cheng-Ho's 1405 and Columbus' 1492 flagships

   Chinese ships differed substantially from those in Europe or Asian vessels
in the Indian Ocean. The treasure ships had nine masts, and smaller ships also
had multiple masts. Transverse laths of bamboo attached to the sail fabric
permitted precise stepwise reefing. When sails were furled, they fell
immediately into pleats. When sails were torn, the area affected was
restricted by the lathing. Big ships had 15 or more watertight compartments,
so a partially damaged ship would not sink and could be repaired at sea. They
also had up to 60 cabins so the crew quarters were much more comfortable
than in European ships. European watertight compartments were first
introduced into the British navy in 1795 (see Xi and Chalmers, 2004).

Table 2.4   Chinese naval diplomacy: Voyages to the 'Western' and 'Eastern' oceans, 1405–33

Date	Number of ships	Number of naval, military & other personnel	Places visited in Western Oceans	Places visited in Eastern Oceans
1405–7	62 large, 255 small	27,000	Calicut	Champa, Java, Sumatra
1407–9	Small number	n.a.	Calicut, Cochin	Siam, Sumatra, Java
1409–11	48	30,000	Malacca, Quilon	Sumatra
1413–15	63	29,000	Hormuz, Red Sea, Maldives, Bengal	Champa, Java, Sumatra
1417–19	n.a.	n.a.	Hormuz, Aden, Mogadishu, Malindi	Java, the Ryukyu islands, Brunei
1421–2	41	n.a.	Aden, East Africa	Sumatra
1431–33	100	27,500	Ceylon, Calicut, Aden, Hormuz, Jedda, Malindi	Vietnam, Sumatra, Java, Malacca

Sources: Needham (1971) and Levathes (1994). The detailed official records of these trips were destroyed by the bureaucracy which was opposed to renewal of such expeditions. The evidence is based on the writings of participants and later imperial histories.

Table 2.4 shows the characteristics of the six naval expeditions of the Yung-lo emperor, and the seventh which sailed after his death. The first three had India and its spices as their destination. The last three explored the East Coast of Africa, the Red Sea and the Persian Gulf. The fleets were very large and the big ships were intended to overawe rulers of the countries visited. The intentions were peaceful but the military force was big enough to deal effectively with attacks on the fleet, which occurred on only three occasions.

A major purpose of these voyages was to establish good relations by presentation of gifts and escort of ambassadors or rulers to or from China. There was no attempt to establish bases for trade or for military objectives. There was a search for new plants for medical purposes, and one of the missions was accompanied by 180 medical personnel. There was also an interest in types of African livestock which were unknown in China. The expeditions brought back ostriches, giraffes, zebras, elephant tusks and rhinoceros horns. However, these were exotica. The international interchange of flora and fauna was negligible compared to what occurred after the European encounter with the Americas.

Cheng-Ho died at sea on the seventh voyage and support for distant diplomacy evaporated. The broadening of China's tributary relations with countries of the 'Western Oceans' had not enhanced China's security and the naval expeditions had exacerbated a situation of fiscal and monetary crisis. The meritocratic bureaucracy had always opposed a venture which promoted the eunuch interest. They terminated these ventures and destroyed the official records of the expeditions. There was increasing concern to defend the new Ming capital at Peking against potential invasion from Mongolia or Manchuria. The new capital's food supply was guaranteed by the Grand Canal which was reopened in its full length in 1415 (2,300 kilometres, equal to the distance from Paris to Istanbul). It functioned better than ever before because of new locks which made it operational on a full-time basis. Grain shipments by sea to the capital had already ceased, sea-going grain ships were replaced by canal barges, and the naval commitments to coastal defence were relaxed.

2.2.2   China Turned its Back on the World Economy, 1450–1840

As oceanic diplomacy ended, there was no longer a need for treasure ships. Coastal defences were reduced and by 1474 the fleet of large warships had been cut from 400 to 140. Most of the shipyards were closed, and naval manpower was reduced by retrenchment and desertions. Tributary arrangements for countries within the Eastern Ocean (Burma, Nepal, Siam, Indochina, Japan, Korea, and the Ryukyus) continued, but the ban on private trade continued, and sea-going junks with more than two masts were prohibited.

China turned its back on the world economy when its maritime technology was superior to that of Europe. During large parts of the Ming and Ch'ing dynasties, it virtually cut itself off from foreign commerce. However, there was a large illicit export of Japanese silver to China in exchange for silk (see table 2.5). The main beneficiaries were Chinese and Japanese pirates, and the Portuguese who were allowed to establish a base in Macao in 1557, which they kept until 1999.

China's attitude to the world economy was different to the imperialist drive which characterised European countries from 1500 onwards. With the exception of the Mongol dynasty, the Chinese elite regarded their country as special 'Middle Kingdom', ringed by friendly tributary states which acknowledged their sovereignty and were linked by non-exploitative gift relationships. Confucianism reinforced the Chinese elite's belief in the superiority of their place in the world order. Yung-lo's naval expeditions were regarded as a deviation by the traditional bureaucracy. These views were reinforced by the success of the bureaucracy in feeding and supplying the capital city with canal transport.

Table 2.5   Chinese imports of silver from Japan, Portugal and the Philippines, 1550–1700 (metric tons)

	Shipments from Japan	Portuguese shipments via Macao	Shipments of Mexican silver via the Philippines	Total
1550–1600	1,280	380	584	2,244
1601–40	1,968	148	719	2,835
1641–85	1,586	0	108	1,694
1685–1700	41	0	137	178
Total 1550–1700	4,875	428	1,548	6,951

Note: From 1571, when the Spanish installed themselves in the Philippines, Mexican silver was shipped from Acapulco to Manila, but Spaniards played little part in the Manila–China trade. The overseas Chinese population of Manila acted as intermediaries for Chinese ships.

Source: von Glahn (1996), pp.140 and 232.

2.3   EXTENSIVE GROWTH IN CHINA, 1700–1820

After a long period of mediocre progress and episodic setbacks, there was vigorous *extensive* growth in China from 1700 to 1820, when population rose nearly threefold (much faster than in Europe and Japan), with no fall in per capita income. This achievement was possible because of an accelerated use of dry-land crops from the Americas (maize, sweet potatoes, Irish potatoes and peanuts), which could be grown in hilly, sandy and mountainous areas. There was also a huge expansion of the national territory and closer control of docile tributary states. Because of the disdain and indifference of the bureaucratic elite towards things-foreign China isolated itself from the outside world and repudiated British efforts to establish diplomatic and commercial relations at the end of the eighteenth century.

2.3.1   Chinese Disdain of the West and its Consequences

China failed to react adequately to the Western technological challenge until the middle of the twentieth century, mainly because the ideology, mindset and education system of the bureaucracy promoted an ethnocentric outlook, indifferent to developments outside China. There were Jesuit scholars in Peking for nearly two centuries; some of them like Ricci, Schall and Verbiest had intimate contact with ruling circles, but there was little curiosity amongst the Chinese elite about intellectual or scientific development in the West. In 1792–93, Lord Macartney spent a year carting 600 cases of presents from George III. They included a planetarium, globes, mathematical instruments, chronometers, telescopes, measuring instruments, plate glass, copperware and other miscellaneous items. After he presented them to the Ch'ien-lung Emperor, the official response was: 'there is nothing we lack.... We have never set much store on strange or ingenious objects, nor do we need any more of your country's manufactures'. These deeply engrained mental attitudes helped prevent China from emulating the West's protocapitalist development from 1500 to 1800, and from participation in much more dynamic processes of economic growth thereafter. It did not start establishing embassies or legations abroad until 1877.

Chinese indifference to the west was very different from the situation in Japan, whose first western contact occurred in 1543, when Portuguese sailors were shipwrecked on Tanegashima Island. They had firearms unknown in Japan. The potential of this new weaponry was quickly appreciated by the military who managed to copy the guns and manufacture them in Japan. Japanese were also interested in Portuguese ships, maps, and navigation techniques. The Dutch had a small Japanese outpost in Deshima from 1638 to 1853. In the course of their long stay they had a significant impact in transmitting knowledge of European science and technology to Japan.

2.4   THE THIRD TRANSFORMATION (1820–1950): THE WORLD ECONOMY EXPANDS, CHINA CONTRACTS

Between 1820 and 1950, the world economy made enormous progress by any previous yardstick. World product rose eightfold, and world per capita income 2.6 fold. US per capita income rose eightfold, European income fourfold and Japanese threefold. In other Asian countries except Japan, economic progress was very modest but in China per capita product actually fell by 10 per cent and its share of world GDP fell from a third to one twentieth. Its real per capita income fell from 90 to 20 per cent of the world average. Most Asian countries had problems similar to those of China, i.e. indigenous institutions which hindered modernisation, and foreign colonial intrusion. But these problems were worse in China, and help to explain why its performance was exceptionally disappointing.

2.4.1 Internal Forces Undermining the Manchu Regime

Chinese development was interrupted by internal causes and by foreign intrusion. Internal disorder took a heavy toll on population and economic welfare (see Table 2.6). The Taiping rebellion (1850–64) affected more than half of China's provinces and did extensive damage to its richest areas. In the five provinces most affected, population in the early 1890s was 50 million lower than it had been 70 years earlier. Parts of the same area bore the main brunt of the Yellow river floods in 1855. Due to governmental neglect of irrigation works it burst its banks and caused widespread devastation in Anhwei and Kiangsu. It had previously flowed to the sea through the lower course of the Huai river but after 1855, it flowed from Kaifeng to the Shantung peninsula, more than 400 km north of its previous channel. There were Muslim rebellions in Shensi, Kansu and Sinkiang, where population fell due to brutal repression in the 1860s and 1870s. In the Republican era there were two decades (1927–1949) of civil war between the Kuo Ming Tang (KMT) forces of Chiang Kai Shek and the communists led by Mao Tse Tung.

Table 2.6   China's population by province, 1819–1953 (million)

	1819	1893	1953
Provinces most affected by Taiping rebellion[a]	153.9	101.8	145.3
Provinces affected by Muslim rebellions[b]	41.3	26.8	43.1
Ten Other Provinces of China Proper[c]	175.6	240.9	338.6
Three Manchurian Provinces[d]	2.0	5.4	41.7
Sinkiang, Mongolia, Tibet, Ningsia, Tsinghai	6.4	11.8	14.0
Total	379.4	386.7	582.7

Notes: [a] Anhwei, Chekiang, Hupei, Kiangsi, Kiangsu.
[b] Kansu, Shensi, Shansi.
[c] Fukien, Honan, Hopei, Hunan, Kwangsi, Kwangtung, Kweichow, Shantung, Szechwan, Yunnan.
[d] Heilungkiang, Kirin, Liaoning.

Source: Maddison (1998), p. 47

2.4.2 The Impact of Collusive Imperialism

Colonial penetration began with the capture of Hong Kong by British gunboats in 1842. The immediate motive was to guarantee free access to Canton to exchange Indian opium for Chinese tea. A second Anglo–French attack in 1858–60 destroyed the summer palace of the Emperor in Peking. The subsequent treaty opened access to the interior of China via the Yangtse and the huge network of internal waterways which debouched at Shanghai.

This was the era of free trade imperialism. Western traders were individual firms, not monopoly companies. In sharp contrast to their hostile and mutually exclusive trade regimes in the merchant capitalist epoch, the British and French had made their Cobden–Chevalier Treaty to open European commerce on a most-favoured-nation basis. European countries acted collusively in applying the same principle in treaties imposed on China. Hence 12 other European countries, Japan, the USA, and three Latin American countries acquired the same trading privileges before the first world war.

The treaties forced China to maintain low tariffs. They legalised the opium trade and gave foreigners extra-territorial rights and consular jurisdiction in 92 'treaty ports' opened between 1842 and 1917. Some of these 'ports' were far inland, e.g. Harbin in the middle of Manchuria, and Chungking 1,400 km. up the Yangtse. Six territories were 'leased' to Britain, France, Germany, Japan and Russia. To monitor the Chinese commitment to low tariffs, a Maritime Customs Inspectorate was created (with Sir Robert Hart as Inspector General from 1861 to 1908) to collect tariff revenue for the Chinese government. A large part of this was earmarked to pay the 'indemnities' which the colonialists demanded to defray the costs of their attacks on China. The treaty port system was not terminated until 1943.

In addition to these 'port' arrangements, China also suffered large territorial losses and the dismantlement of its network of tributary states. In 1860, 82 million hectares of land and a huge stretch of Pacific coast were ceded to Russia, where it constructed its new port, Vladivostok. In the 1860s, the khanates of Tashkent, Bokhara, Samarkand, Khiva and Khokand became part of the Russian empire. In 1882, the Ryukyus were lost to Japan. In 1885, Indochina was ceded to French suzerainty and in 1886 Burma to British. In 1895, Taiwan was lost to Japan which also got suzerainty over Korea. In 1911, Tibet proclaimed its independence and expelled its Chinese population. In 1915, Russia gained suzerainty over Outer Mongolia. In 1931–3, Japan took over China's Manchurian provinces and Jehol to create its puppet state of Manchukuo. The reaction to these intrusions was feeble and ineffective, and serious Chinese resistance did not start until the Japanese attack in 1937.

The centre of this multilateral colonial regime was the international settlement in Shanghai. The British picked the first site in 1843 north of the 'native city'. The French, Germans, Italians, Japanese and Americans had neighbouring sites along the Whangpoo River opposite Pudong, with extensive grounds for company headquarters, the cricket club, country clubs, tennis clubs, swimming pools, the race course, the golf club, movie theatres, churches, schools, hotels, hospitals, cabarets, brothels, bars, consulates and police stations of the colonial powers. There were similar facilities, on a smaller scale, in Tientsin and Hankow. Most of the Chinese allowed into these segregated settlements were servants.

Foreigners were the main beneficiaries of this brand of free trade imperialism and extra-territorial privilege. The treaty ports were glittering islands of modernity, but the character of other Chinese cities did not improve, and those which had been damaged by the massive Taiping rebellion of 1850–64 had deteriorated. Chinese agriculture was not significantly affected by the opening of the economy.

The continued expansion in treaty port facilities and the freedom which foreigners obtained in 1895 to manufacture in China contributed substantially to the growth of the modern sector, including railways, banking, commerce, industrial production and mining. There was also an associated growth of Chinese capitalist activity, which had its origins mainly in the *compradore* middlemen of the Treaty ports. There was an inflow of capital from overseas Chinese who had emigrated in substantial numbers to other parts of Asia.

Table 2.7 Comparative economic performance of Japan and its former colonies, 1820–2006 (annual average compound growth of real GDP)

	1820–70	1870–1913	1913–41	1941–55	1955–90	1990–2006
Japan	0.4	2.4	4.0	1.1	6.6	1.3
Korea	0.1	1.0	3.7	0.0	8.0	5.5
Manchukuo	n.a.	n.a.	3.8[a]	n.a.	n.a.	n.a.
Taiwan	0.3	1.6	4.5	2.1	8.4	5.2
China	−0.4	0.6	0.7[b]	1.2[c]	5.3	8.6
India	0.4	0.8	0.4	1.3	4.1	6.2
Indonesia	1.1	2.0	2.5	−0.3	4.9	7.3
U.K.	2.1	1.9	1.7	0.8	2.8	2.5

Notes: [a] 1924–41; [b] 1913–38; [c] 1938–55.

Sources: Manchukuo from Chao (1982), p. 258; other countries from Maddison (2007 b) updated in www.ggdc.net/Maddison.

The share of exports in Chinese GDP was small (0.7 per cent of GDP in 1870, 1.2 per cent in 1913) - much smaller than in India, Indonesia and Japan. China regained its tariff autonomy in 1928 and there was some relaxation of other constraints on its sovereignty in the treaty ports. In the first half of the twentieth century, China ran a significant trade deficit, quite unlike the situation in India and Indonesia which had large surpluses.

Remittances from some of the 9 million overseas Chinese to their families covered part of the deficit and there was a large outflow of silver in the 1930s following the US devaluation in 1932 and China's switch from a silver currency to paper in 1935.

From the 1860s onwards, the most dynamic areas in the Chinese economy were Shanghai and Manchuria. Manchuria had been closed to ethnic Chinese settlement by the Manchu dynasty until 1860. They became interested in promoting Han Chinese settlement after they had been forced to cede the very thinly settled territory north of the Amur River to Russia. Between 1860 and 1930 the Manchurian population grew tenfold – from 3.3 to 31.3 million.

Shanghai rose to prominence because of its location at the mouth of a huge system of waterways.

> The total of inland waterways navigable by junks in nearly all seasons was nearly 30,000 miles. To this must be added an estimated half million miles of canals or artificial waterways in the delta area. It is not surprising therefore that between 1865 and 1936, Shanghai handled 45 to 65 per cent of China's foreign trade. (Eckstein et al., 1968, pp.60–61)

It was already an important coastal port earlier in the Ch'ing dynasty with a population of 230,000 in the 1840s. By 1938 this had risen to 3.6 million and Shanghai was the biggest city in China. It now has a population of 16 million.

The Ch'ing regime collapsed in 1911, after seven decades of major internal rebellion, and humiliating foreign intrusions. The bureaucratic gentry elite were incapable of achieving serious reform or modernisation, because of a deeply conservative attachment to a thousand year old polity on which their privileges and status depended. After its collapse there were nearly four decades in which political power was taken over by the military. They too were preoccupied with major civil wars, and faced more serious foreign aggression than the Ch'ing. They did little to provide a new impetus for economic change and the five-tier political structure of the KMT government was far from democratic. The treaty-port form of colonialism was not ended until 1943. The limited modernization of the economy came mainly in the treaty ports and in Manchuria, where foreign capitalist enterprise penetrated and the sprouts of Chinese capitalism burgeoned.

2.5   THE FOURTH TRANSFORMATION: ECONOMIC PERFORMANCE IN THE MAOIST PERIOD, 1949–78

The establishment of the People's Republic marked a sharp change in China's political elite and mode of governance (see Box 2.1 below).

Box 2.1   China's emergence from international isolation, 1949–2001

1949 Oct	People's Republic of China created. Diplomatic recognition by Burma, India and communist countries in 1949, by Afghanistan, Denmark, Finland, Israel, Norway, Pakistan, and the United Kingdom in 1950.
1950 Feb	USSR agreed to provide financial and technical assistance – eventually $1.4 billion in loans and 10,000 technicians. China acknowledged the independence of Outer Mongolia, agreed to joint Soviet–Chinese operation of Manchurian railways, Soviet military bases in Port Arthur and Dairen, and Soviet mining enterprises in Sinkiang.
1950 June 25	North Korea invaded South, penetrating deeply to Pusan.
1950 June 27	US changed its neutral line on Taiwan, sent in 7th Fleet.
1950 Oct	China sent 'volunteers' (eventually 700,000) to N. Korea to push back UN forces advancing towards the Chinese border on Yalu River.
1950–1	China took over Tibet.
1953 July	Korean armistice.
1954	India ceded former British extraterritorial claims to Tibet.
1958	China menaced Taiwan in Quemoy and Matsu incidents. Khrushchev retracted offer of nuclear aid.
1959	Revolt in Tibet, Dalai Lama fled to India.
1960	USSR withdrew Soviet experts, abandoned unfinished projects.
1962	Border clash with India over Aksai-chin road from Sinkiang to Tibet.
1964	First Chinese atom bomb test, 1969 first hydrogen bomb test.
1963–69	Border clashes with USSR in Manchuria. China questioned legitimacy of Soviet/Chinese boundaries in Manchuria and Sinkiang.
1971 April	US lifted trade embargo on China.
1971 Oct	China entered the United Nations, Taiwan ousted.
1972 Feb	President Nixon visited China.
1972 Sep	Visit of Prime Minister Tanaka normalised diplomatic relations with Japan.
1973	US and China established *de facto* diplomatic relations.
1978 Dec	US established formal diplomatic relations, derecognised Taiwan.
1979 Feb–Mar	Border war with Vietnam after expulsion of ethnic Chinese and Vietnamese destruction of Khmer Rouge regime in Cambodia.
1980	China became a member of the World Bank and IMF, 1986 entered Asian Development Bank.
1997	Hong Kong restored to China; 1999, Macao restored to China.
2001	China admitted to the World Trade Organisation.

Sources: MacFarquhar and Fairbank (1987 and 1991).

   The degree of central control reached to the lowest levels of government, to the workplace, to farms, and to households. The party maintained detailed oversight of the regular bureaucratic apparatus. The military were tightly integrated into the system. Propaganda for government policy and ideology was diffused through mass movements under party control. Landlords' national and foreign capitalist interests were eliminated by expropriation of private property. China became a command economy on the Soviet pattern.

After a century of surrender or submission to foreign incursions and aggression, the new regime was a ferocious and successful defender of China's national integrity, willing to operate with minimal links to the world economy. For most of the Maoist period there was little contact with the outside world. From 1952 to 1973 the United States applied a comprehensive embargo on trade, travel and financial transactions, and from 1960 onwards the USSR did the same.

In the Maoist era, its version of communism involved risky experimentation on a grand scale. It brought the economic and political system close to collapse during the Great Leap Forward (1958–60), and again in the Cultural Revolution (1966–76) when education and the political system were deeply shaken. Allocation of resources was extremely inefficient. China grew more slowly than other communist economies. Nevertheless, economic performance was a great improvement over the past. GDP trebled, per capita real product rose by 80 per cent and labour productivity by 60 per cent from 1952 to 1978. The economic structure was transformed. In 1952, industry's share of GDP was one sixth of that of agriculture. By 1978, it was bigger than the agricultural share. China achieved this in spite of its political and economic isolation, hostile relations with both the United States and the Soviet Union, and wars with South Korea and India.

2.6 THE FIFTH TRANSFORMATION: CHINA'S RESURRECTION IN THE REFORM PERIOD SINCE 1978

After 1978, there was a major political shift to pragmatic reformism which relaxed central political control and modified the economic system profoundly. These changes brought a more stable path of development and a great acceleration of economic growth. From 1978 to 2006 GDP rose 7.9 per cent a year, population growth decelerated and per capita real income rose 6.7 per cent a year. Growth was faster than in any Asian country. A major reason was exceptionally high and accelerating investment.

The other main reason for growth acceleration was increased efficiency in resource allocation. Collective agriculture was abandoned and production decisions reverted to individual peasant households. Small scale industrial and service activities were freed from government control and their performance greatly outpaced that of the state sector. Exposure to foreign trade and investment were greatly enhanced. These changes strengthened market forces and introduced consumers to a wide variety of new goods.

Table 2.8 Basic Growth Accounts, China, Japan, the USA and South Korea, 1952–2003 (annual average compound - growth rates)

	China		Japan		United States		South Korea	
	1952–78	1978–2003	1952–78	1978–2003	1952–78	1978–2003	1952–78	1978–2003
			Macroeconomic Performance					
Population	2.02	1.20	1.10	0.41	1.34	1.07	1.34	1.07
GDP	4.39	7.85	7.86	2.53	3.61	2.94	3.61	2.94
Per Capita GDP	2.33	6.57	6.69	2.11	2.24	1.85	2.24	1.85
Labour input	2.57	1.89	1.12	0.07	1.12	1.10	1.12	1.10
Education	4.49	2.63	1.19	1.12	1.12	1.20	1.12	1.20
Quality adjusted labour input	4.87	3.23	1.72	0.63	1.69	1.61	1.69	1.61
Non-Residential Capital	7.72	7.73	9.57	5.03	3.39	3.23	3.39	3.23
Labour Productivity	1.78	5.85	6.67	2.46	2.47	1.82	2.47	1.82
Capital Productivity	-3.09	0.11	-1.56	-2.39	0.22	-0.38	0.22	-0.38
Capital per Person Engaged	5.02	5.73	7.97	4.38	1.85	1.81	1.85	1.81
Total Factor Productivity	-1.37	2.95	3.32	0.36	1.28	0.69	1.28	0.69
Export Volume	2.6	14.42	13.17	4.09	5.19	5.91	5.19	5.91

Source: Population and GDP for all countries from Maddison www.ggdc.net/Maddison. Hours, education and capital stock for Japan and USA mainly from Maddison (1995a p.253–4) updated in Maddison (2007b). See also Maddison (1995b, p.150–156), for details of capital stock estimation for Japan and USA; for these two countries I assumed that non-residential structures had a life of 29 years and machinery and equipment 14 years. Korean labour input and education 1952–78 from Maddison (1998, p.66). Growth of Korean productive fixed capital stock 1952–78 from van Ark and Timmer, 2002, p.239–240. Korean labour input 1978–2003 from Groningen Growth and Development Centre database; capital stock 1978–2003 from Pyo et al. (2006, p.108). China employment, education and capital stock from Maddison (1998) updated. I was unable to break down the Chinese capital stock between non-residential structures and machinery, and assumed an average asset life for the two assets combined of 25 years. Labour input for Japan, Korea, and the United States refers to total hours worked, and to employment for China. Labour quality is improved by increases in the average level of education of the population of working age; it was assumed that the impact on the quality of labour input was half the rate of growth of education. In calculating total factor productivity growth, labour input was given a weight of 0.65, education 0.325 and capital 0.35.

Table 2.9   Comparative levels of economic performance in 14 countries

	2006 GDP per capita in 1990 (int. $)	2006 Population (million)	2003 Energy consumption (million tons of oil equivalent)	2006 Exports (billion US$)
China	6,048	1,311.0	1,409	969
Hong Kong	29,481	6.9	17	317
India	2,598	1,111.7	553	120
Indonesia	4,029	221.7	162	99
Japan	22,462	127.5	517	650
Singapore	26,162	4.5	22	272
South Korea	18,356	48.1	205	326
Taiwan	19,860	22.8	99	224
Australia	24,343	20.5	113	123
France	22,786	63.3	271	485
Germany	19,993	82.4	347	1,126
Russia	7,831	142.1	640	305
UK	23,013	60.6	232	371*
USA	31,049	298.4	2,281	1,038

Note: *2005

Sources: Per capita GDP and population from www.gdc.net/Maddison; Energy from International Energy Agency, *Energy Balances of Non–OECD Countries, 2002–2003*; and *Energy Balances of OECD Countries, 2002–2003*, OECD, Paris 2005. Exports from IMF, *International Financial Statistics*, April 2006.

The new Chinese policies were indigenously generated and quite out of keeping with the prescriptions for 'transition' which were proffered and pursued by the USSR. The contrast between Chinese and Soviet performance in the reform period is particularly striking. As China prospered, the Soviet economy collapsed and the USSR disintegrated. In 1978 Chinese per capita income was 15 per cent of that of the former Soviet Union. In 2006 it was 89 per cent of its level.

The reform period was one of much reduced international tension. China's geopolitical standing, stature and leverage were greatly increased. It became the world's second largest economy, overtaking Japan by a respectable margin and the former USSR by a very large margin. China took back Hong Kong and Macao peacefully, and inaugurated a 'two systems' policy designed to attract Taiwan back into the national fold.

The rigid monopoly of foreign trade and the policy of autarkic self-reliance were abandoned after 1978. Foreign trade decisions were decentralised. The yuan was devalued and China became highly competitive. Special enterprise zones were created as free trade areas. In response to the greater role for market forces, competition emerged, resource allocation improved, and consumer satisfaction increased. There was a massive increase in interaction with the world economy through trade (see Tables 2.8 and 2.9), large inflows of foreign direct investment, opportunities for study and travel abroad, and for foreigners to visit China. At the same time, China was prudent in retaining control over the more volatile types of international capital movement and has built up massive foreign exchange reserves of $2 trillion. Although it had to wait 15 years to be admitted to the World Trade Organisation, it is now, including Hong Kong, the world's largest exporter.

2.6.1 Why China did Better than Russia in Moving Towards a Market Economy

China has had very much greater success than Russia since it abandoned the communist command economy. Table 2.10 compares its GDP growth performance since 1990 with that of Russia, India, Japan and the USA. It has grown more rapidly than all these countries, but the contrast with Russia is by far the most striking. In 1990, Chinese GDP was less than twice as big as Russian, but by 2006 it was seven times as large. It is therefore worth summarising the reasons for the difference in China's performance:

1) Chinese reformers gave first priority to agriculture. They ended Mao's collectivist follies and offered individual peasant households the opportunity to raise their income by their own efforts. Russian reformers more or less ignored agriculture, and the potential for individual peasant household enterprise had been killed off by Stalin in the 1920s. The Chinese government encouraged small-scale manufacturing production in township and village enterprises. Local officials and party elite got legal opportunities for greatly increasing their income if they ran the enterprises successfully.

2) The Chinese state did not disintegrate as the USSR did. The proportion of ethnic minorities was very small by comparison with the USSR, and the political system did not collapse. By patient diplomacy and creating capitalist enclaves it reintegrated Hong Kong and Macao as special administrative regions.

3) In the reform era, China benefited substantially from the great number of overseas Chinese. A large part of foreign investment and foreign entrepreneurship has come from Hong Kong, Singapore, Taiwan and Chinese in other parts of the world.

Table 2.10 Comparative GDP of China, Russia, Japan, India and the USA, 1978–2030

	(GDP levels in billion 1990 PPP dollars)					(China as per cent of)			
	Russia	Japan	China	USA	India	Russia	Japan	USA	India
1978	993	1,446	935	4090	626	94	65	23	149
1990	1,151	2,321	2,124	5,803	1,098	185	92	37	199
1991	1,093	2,399	2,264	5,792	1,112	207	94	39	204
1992	935	2,422	2,484	5,985	1,169	266	103	42	212
1993	854	2,428	2,724	6,146	1,238	319	112	44	220
1994	745	2,455	2,997	6,396	1,328	402	122	47	226
1995	715	2,504	3,450	6,558	1,426	483	138	53	242
1996	689	2,590	3,521	6,804	1,537	511	136	52	229
1997	699	2,636	3,707	7,110	1,611	530	141	52	230
1998	662	2,559	3,717	7,413	1,716	561	145	50	217
1999	704	2,553	3,961	7,746	1,820	563	155	51	218
2000	774	2,628	4,319	8,032	1,900	558	164	54	227
2001	814	2,634	4,781	8,093	2,009	587	182	59	238
2002	852	2,640	5,374	8,224	2,080	631	204	65	258
2003	914	2,686	6,188	8,431	2,257	677	230	73	273
2006	1,113	2,864	7,928	9,266	2,888	712	277	86	275
2030	1,758	3,732	25,422	16,974	12,198	1,446	681	150	208

Source: www.ggdc.net/Maddison

4) China started from a very low level of productivity and income. In 1978, when the reform era began, per capita income was less than 15 per cent of that in the USSR and its degree of industrialisation was much smaller. If the right policies are pursued, backwardness is a favourable position for a nation which wants to achieve rapid catch-up. The very fact that the Chinese income level was so much lower than that of Hong Kong, Japan, Malaysia, South Korea, Singapore and Taiwan made it easier to capture the advantages of backwardness, and make big structural changes. It meant that its period of super-growth could stretch further into the future than theirs.

5) Chinese family planning policy reduced the birth rate and changed the population structure in a way that promoted economic growth. In 1978–2003 the population of working age rose from 54 to 70 per cent. In China, life expectation has risen. In Russia it has fallen.

6) The leadership was very sensitive to the dangers of hyper-inflation which China had experienced when the KMT were in charge. Instead of destroying private savings as in Russia, they were encouraged and have increased enormously. They are the main reason that it has been feasible to raise investment to such high levels. In Russia, the reform process involved a period of hyper-inflation, large-scale capital flight, currency collapse and default on foreign debt. The Chinese government has been internationally creditworthy with negligible capital flight.

7) The state sector was not privatised, but waned by attrition. There are now many wealthy entrepreneurs in China and some have enjoyed official favours, but China did not create super-rich oligarchs by selling off state enterprises at knock-down prices as Russia did.

8) China has made massive strides to integrate into the world economy. It gave high priority to promotion of manufactured exports, setting up tax-free special enterprise zones near the coast. Exports were also facilitated by maintaining an undervalued currency. The rebound in the Russian economy since 1998 has been largely driven by the rise in the price of its exports of oil and natural gas. If Hong Kong is included, China is now the biggest exporter, accounting for nearly 11 per cent of the world total. In 2006, exports were $1,286 billion including Hong Kong, Germany was second, with $1,126, USA third with $1,038, Japan fourth with $650 billion, Russia was seventh with $305 billion (see IMF, April, 2007, *International Financial Statistics*).

2.7   THE SIXTH TRANSFORMATION, THE OUTLOOK
TO 2030

In 1998, I made projections for Chinese growth from 1995 to 2015. At that time it seemed that China faced three big domestic problems: a) to shut down a very large number of loss-making state enterprises; b) to transform its financial system which operated with an important and increasing proportion of non-performing assets; and c) to strengthen the weak fiscal position of central government. However, China was more successful in solving or significantly mitigating these problems than I expected and its integration into the world economy much more rapid.

It is difficult to be pessimistic about the economic growth prospects for an economy which has shown such dynamism in the last quarter century, but China still has important problems of another kind.

2.7.1   Inequality

(a) The degree of regional inequality is extreme, with average household income nearly ten times as high in Shanghai as in Guizhou, the poorest province; (b) rural-urban differentials in income, education, health and employment opportunity are a major cause of discontent; and (c). there are also big intra-urban inequalities. The household registration system penalises immigrant workers who can only get unregistered work in urban areas. They are denied public health and education services, have difficulty in getting housing, get low wages for long hours, their wages are often in arrears, and sometimes fail to be paid. Sicular et al. (2007) estimate that unregistered households are about 17 per cent of the urban population and that their average income is 60 per cent lower than that of registered urban households.

2.7.2   The Legal System and Private Property Rights

China has made giant strides in moving towards a market economy, and its legal system allows private enterprise to flourish. Property rights have recently been strengthened, but are a good deal weaker and more ambiguous than they would be in a capitalist economy. Paradoxically for a socialist country, property rights are weaker for ordinary citizens than they are for domestic or foreign capitalists. Urban developers find it easier than would be the case in a capitalist country to expropriate land of peasants or poor urban residents, and demolish their homes without adequate compensation. Influential party officials are able to enrich themselves by conniving in such transactions. These problems have led to increased public protests, and punishment of party officials for corruption. The equity and efficiency of the economy would benefit if property rights were strengthened and the judiciary were less subject to official pressure.

2.7.3   Energy and the Environment

The Chinese economy has expanded very fast and energy consumption has risen a good deal. Electricity production increased tenfold between 1978 and 2005, and its availability at rather low prices transformed living conditions in many urban households, with the spread of electric light, television, washing machines, microwaves, fans and air conditioners. Car ownership has also risen, and is likely to be the most dynamic element in private consumption. In 2006, there were about 19 million passenger cars in circulation (one for every 70 persons). Judging by the average west European relationship of car ownership to per capita income, it seems likely there will be 300 million passenger cars in China (one for every 5 persons) in 2030.

Per capita energy consumption has doubled since 1973. There was a surprisingly large improvement in the efficiency with which energy is used. In 1973, 0.64 tons of oil equivalent were used per thousand dollars of GDP, by 2003, this had fallen to 0.22 tons. The International Energy Agency (IEA) projects a further fall to 0 11 tons in 2030. Energy efficiency was better in China than in the USA in 2003 and this is expected to be true in 2030.

However, the environmental impact of energy use in China is particularly adverse because its dependence on coal is unusually large, and carbon emissions are proportionately much bigger from coal than those from oil or gas. In 2003, 60 per cent of energy consumption came from coal, compared to 23 per cent in the USA, 17 per cent in Russia and 5 per cent in France. This means that the ratio of carbon emissions to energy consumption is higher in China than in most countries. In the IEA's A scenario, China is expected to emit 0.8 tons of carbon per ton of energy used in 2030, compared with 0.63 in the USA, and a world average of 0.60 (see Table 2.11).

Chinese coal is particularly dirty, sulfur dioxide and sooty particles released by coal combustion have polluted the air in its major cities and created acid rain which falls on 30 per cent of its land mass. There are more than 20,000 coal mines, and nearly six million miners, whose productivity is low and working conditions are dangerous. Several thousand are killed every year in mining accidents.

World Economic Performance

*Table 2.11   Energy use and carbon emissions, China, USA, and World
1973–2030 (energy in million metric tons of oil equivalent;
carbon emissions in million tons)*

	1973	1990	2003	2030A	2030R
		China			
Total Energy Use	**472**	**880**	**1,409**	**2,630**	**2,971**
tons per capita	0.54	0.78	1.09	1.80	2.04
tons/$1000 GDP	0.64	0.41	0.22	0.11	0.13
Carbon Emissions	**244**	**615**	**1,043**	**2,100**	**2,487**
per capita emissions	0.28	0.52	0.81	1.44	1.71
emission/energy use	0.52	0.70	0.74	0.80	0.83
		USA			
Total Energy Use	**1,736**	**1,928**	**2,281**	**2,889**	**3,131**
tons per capita	8.19	7.71	7.86	7.94	8.61
tons/$1000 GDP	0.49	0.33	0.27	0.17	0.19
Carbon Emissions	**1,283**	**1,321**	**1,562**	**1,828**	**2,081**
per capita emissions	6.05	5.28	5.38	5.02	5.72
emission/energy use	0.74	0.69	0.68	0.63	0.66
		World			
Total Energy Use	**6,248**	**8,811**	**10,760**	**14,584**	**16,203**
tons per capita	1.60	1.68	1.71	1.78	1.98
tons/$1000 GDP	0.39	0.32	0.26	0.15	0.17
Carbon Emissions	**4,271**	**5,655**	**6,736**	**8,794**	**10,447**
per capita emissions	1.09	1.08	1.07	1.08	1.28
emission/energy use	0.68	0.64	0.63	0.60	0.64

Sources: Primary energy consumption, 1973–2003, from International Energy Agency, *Energy Balances of OECD and Non-OECD Countries,* 2005 edition, OECD, Paris. Carbon emissions, 1990–2003, from International Energy Agency, *CO2 Emissions from Fuel Combustion, 1971– 2003,* 2005 edition, 1973 supplied by IEA. I converted CO2 to carbon by dividing by 3.667 (the molecular weight ratio of carbon dioxide to carbon). Projections for 2030 were derived from the 'alternative scenario' of IEA for that year in *World Energy Outlook 2006,* pp. 528–9, 534–5 and 552–3. I adjusted the IEA projections for 2030 by the difference between their GDP projections and mine (a downward coefficient of 0.875 for China, 1.069 upward for the USA, and .9478 downward for the world). The 'alternative A scenario' takes account of energy-efficiency policies countries might reasonably be expected to adopt over the projected period; the IEA 'reference R scenario' (pp. 492–517) provides a 'baseline vision' of how energy demand would evolve if governments do nothing beyond their present commitments. GDP in 1990 Geary– Khamis PPP dollars and population from www.ggdc.net/Maddison.

Table 2.12 Per capita GDP, world and major regions, 1950–2030

| | 1990 Geary–Khamis dollars | | | | | Annual % change | |
	1950	1973	1990	2006	2030	1990–2006	2006–2030
W. Europe	4,568	11,380	15,905	21,203	31,030	1.8	1.6
USA	9,561	16,689	23,201	31,049	45,446	1.8	1.6
Other W. Offshoots	7,424	13,399	17,906	24,215	35,443	1.9	1.6
Japan	1,921	11,434	18,789	22,462	32,877	1.1	1.6
RICH	**5,643**	**13,060**	**18,748**	**24,911**	**37,162**	**1.79**	**1.68**
E. Europe	2,111	4,988	5,427	7,689	12,367	2.0	2.0
Russia	3,086	6,582	7,779	7,831	14,164	0.04	2.5
other USSR	2,520	5,468	5,962	5,830	8,334	-0.14	1.5
Latin America	2,510	4,518	5,065	6,444	9,212	1.5	1.5
China	448	838	1,871	6,048	17,394	7.6	4.5
India	619	853	1,309	2,598	7,472	4.4	4.5
Other Asia	913	2,034	3,052	4,803	7,723	2.9	2.0
Africa	891	1,391	1,429	1,666	2,115	1.0	1.0
REST	**1,091**	**2,065**	**3,139**	**4,469**	**8,864**	**2.23**	**2.9**
WORLD	**2,109**	**4,080**	**5,143**	**7,224**	**12,108**	**2.15**	**2.18**

Table 2.12 provides a comparative perspective on China's growth prospects over the next quarter century. In the reform period, changes in age structure made it possible to raise the activity rate substantially. Because of the low starting point, the average educational level of the labour force was multiplied by a factor of five from 1952 to 1995. These big changes cannot be repeated. For per capita GDP growth, I assume a sizeable slowdown – from 7.6 per cent a year in 1990–2006 to 4.5 per cent in 2006–2030. Some slowdown can be expected as the average technological level gets closer to the frontier in the advanced countries. Technical advance will be more costly as imitation is replaced by innovation. Specifically, I assume a rate of 5.6 per cent a year to 2010, 4.6 per cent between 2010 and 2020, and a little more than 3.6 per cent a year from 2020 to 2030. By then, in our scenario, per capita income will have reached a slightly better level than Western Europe in 1996, and of Japan in 1988, when their catch-up process had ceased. As it approaches this level, technical advance will be more costly as imitation is replaced by innovation. However, by 2030 the technical frontier will have moved forward, so there will still be some scope for catch-up thereafter.

Even on my rather conservative assumptions, China would again become the world's biggest economy around 2015, and the USA would take second place. The average per capita level would be well below that of the USA, Western Europe and Japan, but it would be well above the world average.

REFERENCES

Chao, K. (1982), *The Economic Development of Manchuria: The Rise of a Frontier Economy*, Michigan Papers in Chinese Studies, 43, Ann Arbor.

Eckstein A., W. Galenson and T.C. Liu (eds) (1968), *Economic Trends in Communist China*, Chicago: Aldine.

EU, IMF, OECD, UN, World Bank (1993), *System of National Accounts, 1993*, Brussels, New York, Paris, Washington DC.

Fogel, R. (2007), 'Capitalism & Democracy in 2040', *Daedalus, Journal of the American Academy of Arts & Sciences*, **136** (3), 87–95.

Goldman Sachs (2003), 'Dreaming with BRICS: the Path to 2050', *Global Economics Paper*, no. 99, New York.

Huang, Y. (2008), *Capitalism with Chinese Characteristics*, Cambridge: Cambridge University Press.

IEA (International Energy Agency) (2005), *Energy Balances of OECD and Non–OECD Countries*, Paris.

IEA (International Energy Agency) (2005), *CO2 Emissions from Fuel Combustion, 1971–2003*, Paris.

IEA (International Energy Agency) (2006), *World Energy Outlook*, Paris.

IMF (International Monetary Fund) (2007), *International Financial Statistics*, Washington DC.

Kravis, I.B. Heston and R. Summers (1982), *World Product and Income:*

International Comparisons of Real Gross Product, Baltimore and London: Johns Hopkins University Press.

Levathes, L. (1994), *When China Ruled the Seas*, New York: Simon and Schuster.

Maddison, A. (1995a), *Monitoring the World Economy, 1820–1992*, Paris: OECD.

Maddison, A. (1995b), *Explaining the Economic Performance of Nations: Essays in Time and Space*, Aldershot/LM, UK and Brookfield, USA: Elgar, Aldershot.

Maddison, A. (1998a), *Chinese Economic Performance in the Long Run*, first edition, Paris: OECD.

Maddison, A. (2007a), *Contours of the World Economy, 1–2030 AD: Essays in Macroeconomic History*, Oxford: Oxford University Press.

Maddison, A. (2007b), *Chinese Economic Performance in the Long Run, 960–2030*, second edition, Paris: OECD.

Maddison, A., D.S. Prasada Rao and W.F. Shepherd (eds) (2002), *The Asian Economies in the Twentieth Century*, Cheltenham, UK and Northampton, MA, USA: Elgar.

Maddison, A. (2003), *The World Economy: Historical Statistics*, OECD, Paris.

Maddison, A. and H. X. Wu (2008), Measuring China's Economic Performance, *World Economics*, **9** (2), 13–44.

MacFarquhar, R. and J.K. Fairbank, (1987), *The People's Republic, Part 1: The Emergence of Revolutionary China, 1949–1965*, volume 14, The Cambridge History of China, Cambridge University Press.

MacFarquhar, R. and J.K. Fairbank, (1991), *The People's Republic, Part 2: Revolutions within the Chinese Revolution, 1966–1982*, volume 15, The Cambridge History of China, Cambridge University Press.

Needham, J. (1971), *Science and Civilisation in China*, vol. 4, part III, *Civil Engineering and Nautical Technology*, Cambridge: Cambridge University Press.

Perkins, D.H. and T.C. Rawski (2007), 'Forecasting China's Economic Growth over the Next Two Decades', chapter 20, in Brandt, L.and T.C. Rawski, (eds.), *China's Great Transformation*, Cambridge: Cambridge University Press.

Pyo, H.K., K.H. Rhee, and B. Ha (2006), '*Estimates of Labor and Total Factor Productivity by 72 Industries in Korea*', OECD Workshop, Paris.

Ren, R (1997), *China's Economic Performance in an International Perspective*, OECD, Paris.

Sicular, T., X. Yue, B. Gustavsson and S. Li (2007), 'The Urban–Rural Income Gap and Inequality in China', *Review of Income and Wealth*, **53** (1), 60–92.

UN (United Nations) (1993), *System of National Accounts*, New York.

Van Ark, B. and M.P. Timmer (2002), 'Realising Growth Potential, South Korea and Taiwan, 1960 to 1998', in Maddison, A., Rao, D.S. Prasada and Shepherd, W.F. (eds.), *The Asian Economies in the Twentieth Century*, Cheltenham, UK and Northampton, MA, USA: Elgar, pp. 226–244.

Von Glahn, R. (1996), *Fountain of Fortune: Money and Monetary Policy in China, 1000–1700*, University of California Press.

World Bank (2008), *Global Purchasing Power Parities and Real Expenditures: 2005 International Comparison Program*, Washington DC.

Wu, H.X. (2007), Measuring Productivity Performance by Industry in China in 1980–2005, *International Productivity Monitor*, Fall, 55–74.

Xi, L. and D.W. Chalmers (2004), 'The Rise and Decline of Chinese Shipbuilding in the Middle Ages', *International Journal of Maritime Engineering*, Royal Institute of Naval Architects.

Xu, X and Y. Ye (2000), *National Accounts for China: Sources and Methods*, Paris: OECD.

APPENDIX

A.2.1   Comparison of Maddison Projections of Chinese Performance in 2030 with those of Goldman Sachs (2003), Perkins and Rawski (2007), and Robert Fogel (2007)

My projections of Chinese growth are based on a careful scrutiny of catch-up surges elsewhere over the past six decades. All of these have slackened off or, in the Japanese case, stopped, as these countries approached the technological frontier. This historical perspective is probably the reason why my projections are more conservative than two of the others cited here.

Goldman Sachs projections are for 2050. In the benchmark estimates for 2000, GDP in national currency is converted to US dollars at the exchange rate, rather than PPP (purchasing power parity). GDP growth is projected for every year in real terms, and Goldman Sachs also assume that the initial exchange rate will gradually converge to something like a PPP level. Here I ignore this second component and use their 'real growth' estimates on p. 21. Their population estimates are the same as mine. They also project gradually decelerating per capita GDP growth, as I do using my numeraire (1990 Geary Khamis PPP dollars) they project a per capita level of $17,964, very similar to my $17,394 for 2030.

Perkins and Rawski cover the period 2005–2025. They use a detailed set of growth accounts to illuminate their judgement. They revise the official Chinese estimates of past GDP growth very slightly, from 9.6 to 9.4 per cent a year for 1978–2003. My much more detailed adjustment shows slower growth of 7.9 per cent a year. They consider two growth paths, one near to past performance, with 9 per cent annual GDP growth, which they reject as implausible, and they opt for a lower rate of 6 per cent (they do not taper this rate as I and Goldman Sachs do). For 2005–2025, their population estimates are virtually the same as mine. They project a per capita growth of 5.5 per cent a year (compared with my 4.7 per cent a year for their period). Hence they project somewhat faster growth than Goldman Sachs and I do. Their view of the past may have given their projections some upward bias, but they clearly expect growth to decelerate as China moves closer to the technological frontier.

Fogel's projections are for 2040. His benchmark estimates for 2000 are in 2000 PPP dollars, though the provenance of the PPPs is not shown. He projects per capita GDP growth of 8.2 per cent over 40 years, giving a per capita income of $85,000 in 2040, more than twice what he projects for the EU. Interpolating his estimate, and using my numeraire, gives a per capita GDP of $36,490 for 2030, compared with my $17,394. Fogel's forecast seems quite implausible. He projects the official estimate of past GDP growth four decades forward, with no tapering off as China nears the technological frontier.

A.2.2   Measuring Chinese GDP Level compared with that of the USA

My level estimates were made internationally comparable by converting China's GDP using a PPP (purchasing power parity) converter, rather than the exchange rate. As the Chinese currency is greatly undervalued, the difference between PPP and exchange rate conversion is unusually large.

Estimation of my PPP converter for China is described in Maddison (2007a) Appendix C, pp. 154–5. It was derived from a binary China/US expenditure comparison for 1986 of Ren Rouen (1997, p. 37). The estimates were updated and converted into 1990 multilateral Geary–Khamis dollars which is the numeraire I used for all other countries in international comparisons in Maddison (1995, 2001, 2003, 2007 and www.ggdc.net/Maddison)

The World Bank (2008) has recently made multilateral PPP comparisons for 2005 which include China for the first time. They show Chinese performance much worse than I estimate, with GDP in 2005 only 43 per cent of the US level, whereas my estimate for 2005 is nearly 82 per cent. Their per capita GDP estimate for China for 2005 is only 9.8 per cent of the US level, mine is 18.3 per cent (see Appendix Table A.2.1). China is the extreme case, but there is also a downward bias in the Bank's estimates for India, Indonesia, Korea, Thailand and Vietnam. There is good reason to be sceptical about the World Bank estimates: a) it used the results of five regional studies and linked them using the EKS method of aggregation. This means that the ranking of countries within each region could not be modified in the linking process, because the regions insisted on 'fixity'. The EKS method produces a lower relative standing of low income countries than the Geary–Khamis method which I used. In the 1982 study of Kravis, Heston and Summers, p. 96, their average Geary–Khamis GDP result for the lowest income group was 16 per cent higher than the EKS measure; b) China provided the World Bank with price estimates for 11 cities. There was a disproportionate selection of items at the higher end of the product range taken from the more expensive outlets in the cities selected. China aimed at comparability with advanced countries, but failed to give an adequate representation of average Chinese consumption; and c) the World Bank did not crosscheck the plausibility of its results. For several years the World Bank's own *Development Indicators* contained estimates for China derived from Ren Rouen quite similar to mine.

Table A.2.1 Maddison and World Bank GDP per capita relatives in 2005

	Maddison (1990 GK $)		W. B. ICP (2005 EKS $)	
		% of USA		% of USA
USA	30,474	100.0	41,674	100.0
Canada	24,485	80.3	35,078	84.2
Australia	24,064	79.0	32,798	78.7
New Zealand	18,078	59.3	24,554	58.9
4 W. Offshoots	*29,413*	*96.5*	*40,360*	*96.8*
Austria	22,049	72.4	34,108	81.8
Belgium	22,131	72.6	32,077	77.0
Denmark	24,130	79.2	33,626	80.7
Finland	22,169	72.7	30,469	73.1
France	21,513	70.6	29,644	71.1
Germany	19,434	63.8	30,496	73.2
Greece	14,841	48.7	25,520	61.2
Ireland	26,606	87.3	38,058	91.3
Italy	19,303	63.3	27,750	66.6
Luxembourg	37,177	122.0	70,014	168.0
Netherlands	22,819	74.9	34,724	83.3
Norway	27,384	89.9	47,551	114.1
Portugal	14,093	46.2	20,006	48.0
Spain	18,197	59.7	27,270	65.4
Sweden	23,292	76.4	31,995	76.8
Switzerland	23,215	76.2	35,520	85.3
UK	22,438	73.6	31,580	75.8
30 W. Europe	*20,497*	*67.3*	*30,137*	*72.3*
12 E. Europe	7,255	23.6	12,260	29.4
15 Former USSR	6,311	20.7	9,646	22.4
Argentina	9,019	29.6	11,063	26.5
Brazil	5,750	18.9	8,596	20.6
Mexico	7,486	24.6	11,317	27.2
Iran	5,737	18.8	10,692	25.7
Turkey	7,699	25.3	7,786	18.7
15 West Asia	6,123	20.1	9,738	23.4
Japan	21,978	72.1	30,290	72.7

Table A.2.1 (Continued)

	Maddison (1990 GK $)	% of USA	W. B. ICP (2005 EKS $)	% of USA
Hong Kong	27,771	91.1	35,680	85.6
Taiwan	19,018	62.4	26,069	62.6
Singapore	24,510	80.8	41,479	99.5
S. Korea	17,526	57.5	21,342	51.2
China	5,575	18.3	4,091	9.8
India	2,419	7.9	2,126	5.1
Pakistan	2,084	6.8	2,396	5.7
Indonesia	3,868	12.7	3,234	7.8
Thailand	7,878	25.9	6,869	16.5
Vietnam	2,456	8.1	2,148	5.1
11 Asia–Pacific	5,183	17.0	4,895	11.7
53 Africa	*1,694*	*5.3*	*2,223*	*5.3*

Sources: The two right-hand columns are from World Bank (2008), *Global Purchasing Power Parities and Real Expenditure in 2005*. The 130 countries covered in the table represent about 95 per cent of world GDP. The two left-hand columns are from the March 2009 version of www.ggdc.net/Maddison: My total for West Asia includes 15 countries: Turkey and Israel which the World Bank includes in the OECD group, Iran which the World Bank includes in Asia/Pacific, and Palestinian territory in the West Bank and Gaza which the World Bank ignores. The other countries are Bahrain, Iraq, Jordan, Kuwait, Lebanon, Oman, Qatar, Saudi Arabia, Syria, United Arab republics and Yemen. I have adjusted the World Bank total for West Asia to include Iran, Israel and Turkey, and excluded Egypt which the World Bank includes in both West Asia and Africa.

There were five previous ICP global studies. These are dismissed by the World Bank (p. 13) as being 'based on very old and very limited data', implying that any discrepancy with earlier findings cannot cast doubt on its weird results for China, India and some other Asian countries. Kravis, Heston and Summers (1982) contained a detailed sophisticated analysis explaining the sensitivity of PPP results to different measurement techniques which is completely lacking in the recent World Bank study; World Bank results for China are highly implausible when one considers their intertemporal implications. My growth estimate shows Chinese per capita income increasing 12.5-fold between 1950 and 2005. If we merge the WB level estimate for 2005 with my growth estimate, one gets a per capita GDP $4,091 in 2005, and $326 (well below subsistence) in 1950. If one believes the official estimate of per capita GDP growth (21–fold over 55 years), the 1950 level would be $196.

For these reasons I stick to my own estimates of Chinese performance and reject those of the World Bank (see Appendix Table A.2.1).

A.2.3 Maddison–Wu Adjustments to the Official Growth Estimates

Figure A.2.1 provides a confrontation of the official and my alternative GDP measure for 1952–2003. Our GDP measure shows slower growth than the official. Generally, the contours are similar, but there is a kink in our curve in 1996–1999, where we show significantly slower growth than the official estimates, and faster growth thereafter. This suggests that the official estimates for these years were deliberately smoothed.

I reconstructed Chinese GDP by industry of origin. For agiculture, I made my own estimates for 125 crop and livestock items from FAO sources, adjusted for farm and non-farm inputs. I found approximately the same rate of growth as the official estimates for 1952–1990. In view of the close congruence with the official estimates up to 1990, the official estimates were used to update the Maddison estimates from 1991 to 2003.

Two major adjustments were made to the official estimates.

1) For industry, Wu's 2007 estimates of gross value added were used. He constructed a volume index, with detailed time series on physical output and prices from the *China Industrial Economic Statistical Yearbook*. Value added was derived from the official input-output table. Wu's sample covered 117 products, with detailed time series showing annual movement for 15 branches of manufacturing as well as mining and utilities. His growth rate was 10.1 per cent a year for industry as a whole for 1952–78, compared to the official 11.5 per cent; and 9.75 per cent a year for 1978–2003 compared to the official 11.5 per cent.

2) I made a major adjustment to growth in 'non-material services' (banking, insurance, housing services, administration of real estate, social services, health, education, entertainment, personal services, R & D activities, the armed forces, police, government and party organisations). I assumed zero productivity growth in these services and used employment as a proxy measure of output. I did this because it is the recommended procedure in the international standardised *System of National Accounts* (UN, 1993, p. 134). In OECD countries, average productivity growth in this sector is very small, (about 0.3 per cent a year), but NBS assumed Chinese productivity growth of 5.1 per cent a year from 1978 to 2003 (faster than labour productivity growth in the rest of the service sector).

The official estimate of average annual GDP growth in 1952–78 was 4.7 per a year. The Maddison–Wu estimates show GDP growth of 4.4 per cent a year for this period. For 1978–2003 official growth was 9.59 per cent a year; after adjustment it falls to 7.85 per cent. The zero productivity assumption for services reduced it by 0.82 per cent; the amendment for industry reduced it a further 0.79 per cent; a small reduction of 0.03 per cent was due to differences in sectoral weights between my estimates and the official measures.

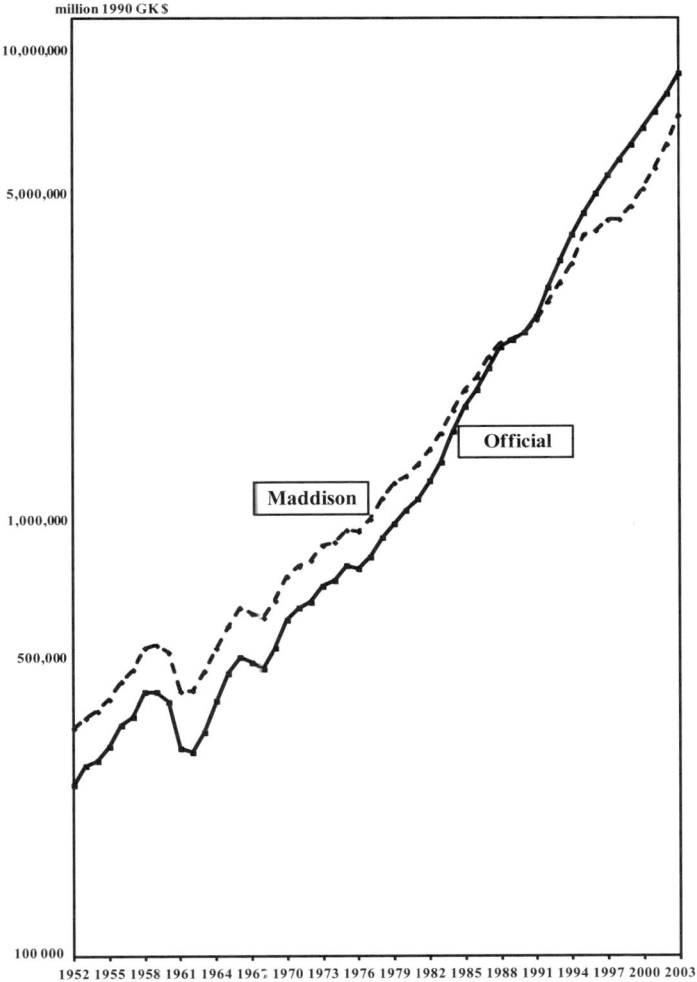

Figure A.2.1   Confrontation of official and Maddison–Wu estimates of GDP Level, 1952–2003

3. The Needham Puzzle, the Weber Question and China's Miracle: Long Term Performance since the Sung Dynasty[1]

Justin Yifu Lin

3.1 INTRODUCTION

Since the start of reform and open–door policy in 1978, the Chinese economy has achieved a miraculous GDP growth of 9.6 per cent annually. Such an economic success has aroused world–wide interest. However, it is worth mentioning that China had also achieved great success in ancient times. According to the estimation of Maddison, in the first century A.D. the development of Han Dynasty in China was on the same level as that of the Roman Empire.[2] Until 1820, Chinese economy had maintained its status as the largest economy in the world. Its GDP accounted for 32.4 per cent of the world total (Maddison, 1998, p.40). However, after Chinese economy reached its peak in the Sung Dynasty, its per capita income remained stagnant ever after.[3] While Chinese economy remained stagnant, through the

---

[1] This chapter was originally prepared as a Paper for the 'World Economic Performance: Past, Present and Future – Long Term Performance and Prospects of Australia and Major Asian Economies', Seminar on the Occasion of Angus Maddison's 80th Birthday, 5–6 December, 2006 at School of Economics, University of Queensland, Australia. I am grateful for the help of Shengyu Yi and Yong Chen in the preparation of the paper.
[2] Based on Goldsmith's work (Goldsmith, 1984), Maddison estimated that in 50 A.D. the per capita GDP in China was at about the same level of that in Europe (Maddison, 1998, p.25).
[3] Many scholars agree that Chinese economy reached its peak in the Song Dynasty (960 A.D.–1280 A.D.). In the period, economic activities were very lively (Hartwell, 1962, 1966 and 1967; Shiba, 1970; Elvin, 1973; Gernet, 1982; Jones, 1988 and 2003). According to the estimation by Maddison, Chinese per capita

Renaissance that started in the fourteenth century, the Europe gradually walked out of the darkness of the medieval age. In the eighteenth century, the industrial revolution first broke out in the Great Britain, which led to a rapid increase in per capita income. According to the Purchasing Power Parity (PPP), the aggregate GDP of the European countries comprised 26.6 per cent of the world total in 1820; in 1890, the ratio increased to 40.3 per cent. Their average annual growth rate of GDP per capita increased from 0.22 per cent in 1700–1820 to 1.03 per cent in 1820–1952. The percentage of Chinese GDP in the world total, however, dropped dramatically to 13.2 per cent in 1890 (Maddison, 1998, p.40). Moreover, during its whole period of modern history (1840–1949), the Chinese economy had been stagnant. Its per capita GDP even dropped during the period of 1820–1952. During the same period, its GDP as a percentage of the world total decreased from 32.4 per cent to 5.2 per cent.

In the whole century after the Opium War in 1840, social turbulence was the major reason for Chinese economic stagnation. However, after the People's Republic of China was established in 1949, there had been no major wars fought in China, but its economic development had not gone smoothly, despite the strenuous efforts of a whole generation that were devoted to the industrialization and modernization and despite of all the efforts and plans of the government. Its GDP per capita on average increased only 2.34 per cent annually, which was lower than the 2.56 per cent world average at the time. The percentage of its GDP in the world total decreased slightly from 5.2 per cent in 1952 to 5 per cent in 1978. Its economic growth rate was not only far lower than the 6.66 per cent rate of Japan but also lower than that of the Four Little Dragons (South Korea, Singapore, Chinese Taiwan and Chinese Hong Kong). The miraculous economic growth of China started at the end of 1978 when Chinese government adopted its reform and open–door policy. During the 27 years between 1978 and 2005; its GDP increased 11.7 fold, and its average annual growth rate was as high as 9.6 per cent. According to the official exchange rate, its GDP reached US$2,225.7 billion in 2005, ranked the fourth in the world. Its per capita GDP increased from US$220 in 1978 to US$1,730. Its total value of foreign trade reached US$ 1421.9 billion in 2005, and its ranking in the world jumped from the 27th in 1978 to the 3rd. It has become and will continue to be a major driving force of the world economy (NBSC, 2006). During its rapid economic growth in the reform period, a series of problems also emerged, which could possibly jeopardize

---

income level in 960 A.D. was about the same as that in 50 A.D, but in Song Dynasty, it increased by approximately one third. During the long period between 1280 A.D. and 1820 A.D. there had been essentially no growth at all (see Maddison, 1998, p. 25).

its development. Such problems include cyclic economic fluctuation (which is also occurring in the developed countries), the slow reform in the state–owned enterprises, the fragile financial system, the widening income disparities and so on. All these problems could possibly lead to sudden emergence of crisis. Will Chinese economy survive all these problems, accomplish its transition to a market economy and maintain its rapid economic growth? Will it be as predicted by Prof. Maddison in his preface to the Chinese version of *The World Economy: A Millennial Perspective*? That is: by 2015, Chinese GDP will reach the level of US and account for 20 per cent of the world total and it will continue to grow rapidly after that. Will it gradually regain its status in the world as happened in the ancient history?

The rest of chapter is organized as follows: Section 2.2 discusses Chinese long economic stagnation since the Sung Dynasty and explores the reasons why it quickly lagged behind western countries since the 1800s; Section 2.3 explains why the industrialization and modernization led by Chinese government in 1949–1978 failed to narrow the gap between China and developed countries. It also discusses the coexistence of Chinese rapid economic growth and the various social and economic problems; Section 2.4 is a brief summary, which also discusses whether China will continue its rapid economic growth in the future.

The basic argument in this chapter goes as follows: long term economic growth depends on the continuous technological innovation. For countries at the technical frontier, innovation can only be achieved through invention on their own. Before the industrial revolution in the eighteenth century, technological innovations were mainly realized through accidental discoveries in production process by craftsmen and peasants. Because China had a large population, it had a large number of craftsmen and peasants. Because of this, China had advantages in this kind of experience–based technological innovations. This is the major reason that China was more developed than western countries in pre–industrial times. However, as technology gradually improved, the room for such technological innovations gradually shrunk. The speed of such technological innovation eventually slowed down and the economy became stagnant. In the western countries, scientific revolution occurred at around fifteenth–sixteenth century. At the mid eighteenth century, the traditional experience–based technological inventions began to be replaced by science–cum–experiment based inventions. Because of this, the rate of technological innovation accelerated, so did their economic growth. At the same time, China failed to realize such a transformation. Therefore, in a relatively short period, its technology lagged behind western countries, as did its international economic status. In 1949, the People's Republic of China was founded. For the first time in a 100 years, it was possible for China to develop its economy in a relatively peaceful environment. Compared with the technological level of developed countries, that in China was very backward. With the 'advantage of backwardness' in technology, China could have accelerated its technological innovation and promoted rapid economic growth through borrowing technologies from the outside world. However, in order to overtake the developed countries, China chose to adopt a comparative–advantage–defying (CAD) strategy. It hoped to first develop advanced capital–intensive industries, which were the comparative advantages of developed countries. Because this was inconsistent with the comparative advantages determined by its endowment structure at the time, the enterprises in these industries were not viable in a free and open market. It became indispensable that government distorted factor prices to lower the costs of construction and operation of the nonviable enterprises and allocated resources through administrative means directly to those enterprises. On the one hand, such a planned economic system helped to build up a modern industrial system on a basis of extreme poverty and backwardness. On the other hand, it also led to low resource–allocation efficiency, insufficient working incentives and poor economic performance. At the end of 1978, China began to its gradual reform and introduced a double–track pricing system. On the one hand, the necessary subsidies for non–viable enterprises in capital–intensive industries were continued. In accordance with the progress of reform and other coordinating conditions, these distortions under traditional system were gradually reformed. The continuation of these traditional practices contributed to the maintenance of economic stability. On the other hand, in order to provide workers and peasants with more working incentives, the government increased the resources that could be freely disposed by peasants and enterprises. At the same time, it relaxed the restrictions on the entrance of labor–intensive industries in which China had a comparative advantage but had long been suppressed. These measures have contributed to the rapid economic growth in China. However, this gradual reform inevitably led to institutional incompatibility between two economic systems (the traditional planned economic system and the market economic system). Such institutional incompatibility was the main reason for many economic problems, such as the cyclic economic fluctuations, the fragile financial system and the deteriorating income disparities. In order to complete the transition to a market economy, China needs to completely abandon the CAD strategy and reform nonviable enterprises in industries that serve this goal. Only in this way, China will be able to eliminate the roots of all its distorted institutions and measures, accelerate capital accumulation and upgrade its endowment structure rapidly. If during the change of its comparative advantages, China, as a developing country, is able to utilize 'the advantage of backwardness', relying on borrowing of technology from the developed countries as the main mechanism for its technological innovations, it will, as Prof. Maddison has predicted, be able to maintain its rapid economic growth for another couple of decades and regain its economic status as in the pre–modern times by the mid of this century.

3.2   THE NEEDHAM PUZZLE, THE WEBER QUESTION AND THE DRAMATIC DECLINE OF CHINA SINCE THE EIGHTEENTH CENTURY

In the 1000 years before the industrial revolution, China had always been the country with most advanced technology and most prosperous economy.[4] From the ninth century onward, the area of cultivated land increased rapidly, as large amounts of population migrated from the north to areas south of Yangtze River[5] and new production technologies (such as the use of farm cattle and crop rotation) were invented. At the beginning of the eleventh century, a new variety of rice with high productivity was introduced from Vietnam, along with innovations in the cropping system and instruments.[6] Chinese agricultural productivity remained as the highest in the world until the thirteenth century. The high agricultural surplus provided the industrial and commercial development with raw materials, labor and funds. The

---

[4] Please refer to Needham (1954, 1969, 1981, 1986) and Elvin (1973) for supporting evidences. Maddison doubts whether the economic and technological level in China's Han Dynasty (206 BC–AD 220) was higher than that in Europe in the fifth Century before the collapse of West Roman Empire (Maddison, 1998, P.38). But we are confident that at least in the 1000 years between the fifth and fifteenth century, while the Europe was in the dark medieval times, China had a more advanced technology. It is worth noting that, according to Francis Bacon (1561–1626), gunpowder, magnetic compass, paper and printing were the most important inventions that facilitated the transformation of Europe from the Dark Ages to the modern world. What he did not know was that these inventions all originated from China (Jones, 2003, p. 58).

[5] According to Balazs' estimates, at the mid eighth century (the early period of Tang Dynasty), only 24 per cent of Chinese population lived in the south of Yangtze River (Balazs, 1931, p. 20). By the end of thirteenth century, the ratio increased to 85 per cent (Elvin, 1973, p. 204).

[6] Because the newly introduced rice was drought–resistant and early maturing, its cultivation area could be easily extended. As for the innovations in farm–tools induced by this shift from dry–land farming to the cultivation of paddy, please refer to Chao, 1986. It is worth mentioning that many of the elements of Arthur Young's scientific (conservation) agriculture, which led to the agricultural revolution in England in the eighteenth century, had become standard practices in China before the thirteenth century (Tang, 1979).

industrial sector in China developed quite well since its Han Dynasty and reached its peak in the Sung Dynasty.[7] Take the utilization of iron, a fundamental material for industrial development, as an example, Chinese output of iron reached 150,000 tons by the end of eleventh century, whose per capita level was 5–6 times larger than that in Europe.[8] The well salt industry and textile industry were also quite prosperous. For instance, the water–powered spinning machine was already used in the production of linen thread in the thirteenth century, whose technology was not inferior to the similar machines used in Europe in 1700 (Elvin, 1973, p.195; Jones, 2003, p.202). Because of the highly developed agriculture, industry and commerce, Chinese urban prosperity in the thirteenth century astonished even the Venetian, Marco Polo, who came from a place famous for its prosperity in commerce (Elvin, 1973, p.177). The market economic system was established in China as early as 300 B.C. in the Period of Warring States. Such a market economic system included private ownership and free trade of land, highly specialized and mobile labor and highly developed product and factor markets (Chao, 1986, p.2–3). Most scholars believe that, as early as the early period of Ming Dynasty (fourteenth century), China had acquired all the major elements that were essential for the British industrial revolution in the eighteenth century (Eberhard, 1956; Evlin, 1973; Tang, 1979; Needham, 1981; Chao, 1986). However, the industrial revolution occurred in Britain instead of China. The Chinese economy was quickly overtaken and lagged behind western countries. Why did the industrial revolution not originate in China, the place that first acquired all the major conditions? This is the Weber Question,[9] which was reinterpreted by Joseph Needham in the following paradox: First, why had China been so far in advance of other civilizations? Second, why is China not now ahead of the rest of the world? (Needham, 1986, p.6)

---

[7] For a brief discussion on the technological achievements in the industrial sector during this period, please refer to Elvin (1973, p. 179).

[8] See Jones, 2003, p.202. Hartwell believes that, in the Song Dynasty (806 A.D–1078 A.D.), the output of iron increased nine times and its per capita level increase 6 times. Because of this, he regards it as an 'early industrial revolution' (Hartwell, 1966, p.29). However, Maddison was suspicious about the validity of his estimation, because it was based only on the iron production in the capital of Song Dynasty (Maddison, 1998, p.37).

[9] See Weber, 'Confucian Politics in China and the Sprout of Capitalism in China: Cities and Industrial Associations' from *Collected Works of Max Weber: The Historical Steps of Civilizations*, Shanghai, Shanghai Sanlian Bookstore. 1997. and Max Weber, *The Religion of China: Confucianism and Daoism*, Translated from the German and Edited by Hans H. Gerth with an Introduction by C.K. Yang (Paperback edition; New York and London: Free Press, 1968)

Several hypotheses have been proposed by many scholars. A widely accepted hypothesis is called 'high level equilibrium trap'.[10] It attributes the stagnancy in Chinese technological innovation to the unfavorable man–to–land ratio. According to this hypothesis, in the pre–modern society, China's early acquisition of advanced social, economic system and scientific technology enabled it to achieve a high level of economic prosperity. However, under the influence of Confucian school, the Chinese family's obsession with male heirs to extend the family lineage encouraged early marriage and high fertility, resulting in a rapid expansion of population. But the possibility for continued expansion of the amount of cultivated land was limited. This led to the continuous decrease in the man–to–land ratio. As labor became cheaper, the demand for labor–saving technology declined. Because of this, although China reached the threshold for industrial revolution as early as in the fourteenth century, its 'population had grown to the point where there was no longer any need for labor–saving devices' (Chao, 1986, p.227). Meanwhile, the rising man–to–land ratio also reduced surplus per capita. As a result, China did not have the surplus to be tapped for sustained industrialization (Tang, 1979, p.7). On the contrary, Europe enjoyed a favorable man–to–land ratio and a legacy of unexploited, traditional economic potential. By the time sufficient knowledge was accumulated to the threshold of an industrial revolution, 'a strong need to save labor was still acutely felt', and a large agricultural surplus was still available to serve 'as the principal means of financing industrialization' (Tang, 1979, p.19).

However, the above logic is intrinsically flawed. The argument that 'as population increases and man–to–land ratio decreases, the labor will become relatively cheaper and per capita surplus will reduce' is based on the assumption that technology is fixed or improving at a very slow rate. With a continuously improving technology, the above argument does not hold. Furthermore, the hypothesis is not supported by the empirical evidence. It is true that many labor–saving tools were invented before the twefth century and only a few later (Chao, 1986, Chapter 9). However, empirical evidence shows that the area of cultivated land per capita in the fourteenth, fifteenth and seventeenth century was significantly higher than that in the eleventh century.[11] According to this hypothesis, the demand for labor–saving

---

[10] This hypothesis was first proposed by Elvin (1973) and was further elaborated by Tang (1979) and Chao (1986). Elvin and Tang emphasized on the insufficient agricultural surplus for accumulation, while Chao put more emphasis on the insufficient demand for labor–saving technology.

[11] Population in China continued to grow until around 1200 A.D.; declined between 1200 A.D. and 1400 A.D.; recovered to the level of 1200 A.D. at around 1500 A.D. In period of 1600 A.D. – 1650 A.D., the population decreased again. Therefore, the

technologies should have been stronger in the above mentioned periods; and the per capita surplus should have also been higher. It should have been particularly so in the peaceful 1368 A.D., when the Ming Dynasty was just established. What we can observe in data, however, is only the population growth, instead of a surge of labor–saving technologies. In addition, in the early decades of the 20th century, although man–to–land ratio was even more unfavorable, labor resources were far from adequate. In the irrigated parts of southern China, there were hardly any periods during the year which farming households were not fully occupied in agricultural activities (Buck, 1964). Therefore, Chao's (1986) argument that 'population has grown to the point where there was no longer any need for labor–saving devices' does not hold. According to the estimation of Riskin (1975), about one third of Chinese GDP in 1933 could potentially be allocated to investment, which was much higher than the 11 per cent of GDP for investment considered by Rostow and other economists as the threshold for getting out of 'the equilibrium trap' and starting economic take–off (Rostow, 1960). During the First Five–Year Plan in China (1953–1958), agricultural technology was still traditional (Perkins and Shahid, 1984, Chapter 4), but the annual accumulation rate was as high as 24.2 per cent (NBSC, 1988, p.60). This puts into question the argument that Chinese agricultural production cannot provide sufficient surplus for accumulation. Finally, from fourteenth century onward, technological innovations in China had not been completely stagnant. The period between fourteenth and early twentieth century still had many new inventions (Elvin, 1973, p.289). Without technological innovations, it is impossible that per unit yield of grains could have doubled in the period from the end of tenth century to the early nineteenth century.[12] Therefore, the arguments for the 'high level

---

estimated per capita acreage in the fourteenth, fifteenth, and seventeenth century should be higher than that in the eleventh century. As for the trend of Chinese population growth, please see Feuerwerker, 1990, p.227. As for historical evidence for the area of cultivated land per capita, please see Chao, 1986, p.89.

[12] During this period, population increased 5–6 times, and output of grains increased accordingly. The contribution of the increase in the per unit yield was just as important as the increase in the area of cultivated land. This indicates that per unit yield of grains should at least double in the period. See Perkins, 1969, p.13–17. Furthermore, based on the materials provided by Chao (1986, p.89), from the end of the tenth century to the end of the fourteenth century, both the area of cultivated land and population had doubled; in the period from the end of the fourteenth century to the nineteenth century, the area of cultivated land doubled again, while the population increased by 6 times. If we adopt the hypothesis of Perkins (1969) that the ratio between the per capita consumption of grains and the area of grain–growing land was basically unchanged, the above evidences show that the per unit yield of grains should at least double in the period from the fourteenth century to the nineteenth century.

equilibrium trap' (that is, the unfavorable man–to–land ratio led to insufficient agricultural surplus and insufficient demand for labor–saving technology, which then led to technological stagnancy) is logically inconsistent and invalidated by empirical evidence.[13]

If technological innovation in China had not been completely stagnant after the fourteenth century, why did it quickly lag far behind the western countries? The key fact lies in the change in the relative pace of technological innovations. After the fourteenth century, technological innovations in China slowed down while in Europe they accelerated rapidly. The change in the way to create technological innovations was the key (Lin, 1995).

In both the pre–modern and modern society, the mechanism of technological innovation is essentially the same: through 'trial and error'. Before the industrial revolution, in both China and the western countries, new technologies were mainly invented by peasants and craftsmen through accidental deviations from routines during their daily work. After the industrial revolution, technological innovations were mainly provided by inventors who did experiments in the laboratory through intentional 'trials and errors'. Since the nineteenth century, the traditional experience–based inventions were replaced by science–cum–experiment based inventions.

Before the industrial revolution, the experience of craftsmen and peasants was the major source of technological innovations. Innovation was a byproduct of the production process and was not done intentionally. Neither was it a result driven by economic motives. The innovation was mainly the minor modification of existing technology (Musson, 1972, p.58; Cipolla, 1993, p.149). In terms of probability, if a country has a larger population, the number of random 'trial and error' experiments done by the craftsmen and peasants will be higher. Its rate of technological innovations will be faster than a country with less population, so will be its economic development (Simon, 1986, Chapter 1). The quality of soil in China was not the richest compared with drainage areas of other rivers (Ho, 1969). However, because it had a topography that had higher elevation in the west and lower elevation in the east, and because the precipitation brought by the monsoon from the Pacific Ocean concentrated between March and October when the light and heat conditions were favorable, the land in China could produce high–yielding grains to support a larger population, if the right farming tools and

---

[13] Although changes in the man–to–land ratio may influence the type of technological innovations, it cannot explain the slow–down of the overall innovation activities in the whole economy. In fact, bottle–neck constraint imposed by the increased man–to–land ratio also occurred in the Europe. The boycott of labor–saving technologies was first recorded in Europe (Cipolla, 1993, p. 140, 198). It could be due to the insufficient supply of technological innovations instead of insufficient demand (Schultz, 1964).

technologies were applied (Temple, 1986). Because of this, Chinese population had been far larger than that of Europe. Such a larger population put China in an advantageous position in the development of technologies in pre–modern periods. The mobility of government officials in ancient China, the print and distribution of agricultural books and the circulation of products and labor in a free market also helped to disseminate new technologies (Maddison, 1998, p.23). During the eight century to twelfth century, as people in northern China continued to migrate on large scale to the south where there were more rains and a wetter climate, the major transportation vehicle shifted from horses to boats, and the major type of grains changed from sorghum and millet to rice. Major transportation vehicles and production tools were changed accordingly. Because of this, the rate of technological innovation and economic growth were quite fast in that period (Chao, 1986, p.224). For the same reason, China maintained its lead in the world civilizations for more than 1000 years. However, the room for this traditional type of technological innovation (based mainly on experience) became smaller and smaller as technological level was upgraded. Eventually, both technological innovation and economic growth stagnated.

In pre–modern society, because Europe had a smaller population size than China, the number of craftsmen and peasants and the corresponding working experiences were relatively less. It was in a disadvantageous position in the technological innovation in pre–modern society. However, after the scientific revolution in the fifteenth and sixteenth century, the experimental method became widely used (Mathias, 1972). The number of 'trials and errors' were no longer constrained by the numbers of craftsmen and peasants in the production process and thus increased dramatically. More importantly, science and technology became more and more closely related. By the mid 1800s, science began to play a crucial role in the inventions of new technologies (Cameron and Neil, 1989: p.165). When there were bottle–necks for technological innovations, efforts in scientific research increased people's knowledge of nature, helped to overcome the bottle–neck and expanded the scope of new technological innovations. This made it possible to maintain an ever accelerating speed of technological innovation (Kuznets, 1966, p.10–11; Hicks, 1932, p.145).

By the mid eighteenth century, after the British industrial revolution, technological innovation in western countries had gradually become an intentional practice: experiments were done with specific goals in mind. This kind of experiment was more costly and economic consideration of cost and benefit was necessary. In this sense, the institutional setups in Europe to protect private properties and commercial interests might have encouraged these experiment–based technological innovations. However, without the scientific revolution in the fifteenth and sixteenth centuries, the advantage brought about by the change in the method of technological innovation could not have lasted for long. As the technological level upgraded, the room for further inventions would have become narrower and narrower. Without the help of scientific research that broke down the bottle–necks in technological innovation, the accelerating speed of technological innovation in Europe after the industrial revolution would have gradually died away as it had occurred in other civilizations; and the technological innovation and economic growth would have become stagnant in the end. Therefore, the key reason for the sudden decline of China was that scientific revolution occurred in the Europe at around fifteenth and sixteenth century, but it had not occurred in China.

Science is a systematic knowledge of the natural phenomena. The primitive sciences before the fifteenth and sixteenth centuries originated from observations of curious scientists. Scientific revolution is itself a revolution of methodology. After the fifteenth and sixteenth centuries, scientists became curious about natural phenomena and began to formalize their hypothesis about nature into 'mathematical' forms. They also began to test inductions derived from their mathematical models through controlled experiments (Needham, 1969, p.15). This revolution in scientific methodology accelerated the elimination of false hypotheses and facilitated the dissemination and accumulation of hypotheses that had not been invalidated. The knowledge of nature exploded after this methodological revolution. However, before the nineteenth century, scientific research was mainly driven by the curiosity felt by the scientists. The new scientific discoveries had not been directly used in the innovations of new technologies. Its contribution to the advances in technology and economic growth was limited. Thus, the scientific revolution was different from the industrial revolution in that there were no apparent economic incentives. Curiosity should be an innate endowment just like intelligence and therefore should be distributed equally in the population. Since China had a larger population, the number of people with high curiosity should have been higher than that in Europe. In pre–modern times, Chinese scientific achievements were not inferior to those of Europe. Moreover, China had a relatively higher mathematical achievement and a relatively more systematic method for experiments in ancient times (Needham, 1969, p.211). Why did the many curious geniuses in China fail to initiate a scientific revolution, formalize their hypothesis in mathematical forms, and test hypotheses under controlled experiments, so as to explore the nature and satiate their curiosity more effectively?

Joseph Needham believed that because Chinese bureaucratic system emphasized agricultural production and discriminated against merchants and artisans, it failed to combine its craftsmen's technology with scholars' mathematical and logical inference. He believed that this was the reason for the absence of a scientific revolution in China (Needham, 1969, p.211). Qian and others held that it was China's imperial and ideological unification that prohibited the growth of modern science (Qian, 1985; Boulding, 1976; Feuerwerker, 1990). However, discrimination against merchants and artisans and the politico–ideological authority in pre–modern China was not absolute. The political environment in Europe right before the scientific revolution was no better than that in China (Monter, 1985): Copernicus, Kepler, Galileo, and other pioneers of the Scientific Revolution in Europe had to contend with schoolmen who upheld the dogma of the authority and omniscience of the classics, and even risk their lives in religious courts.[14] I believe the real reason for the absence of scientific revolution was not due to the adverse political environment that prohibited the creativity of Chinese intellectuals, but due to the special incentives provided by the civil service examination system. Because of this examination system, curious geniuses were diverted from learning mathematics and conducting controllable experiments. Because of this system, the geniuses could not accumulate crucial human capital that was essential for the scientific revolution. As a result, the discoveries of natural phenomena could only be based on sporadic observations, and could not be upgraded into modern science which was built upon mathematics and controlled experiments.

Since Qin unified China in 221 B.C., the bureaucratic system of provinces, prefectures and counties (system of local administration) was established. Government officials of all levels were selected from non–hereditary bureaucrats. During the several hundred years from the Han Dynasty, the recommendation system was used in the selection of government officials. During the selection of government officials, the pool of candidates was determined by the recommendations from government officials of all levels. In the ideal case, they should have recommended individuals with both talent and virtue, which could include both their relatives and their foes. In reality, nepotism inevitably became a major factor for the recommendations of officials at all levels and lost the crucial element for the selection of talents: fair competition. Furthermore, through this recommendation system, it was

---

[14] In the early period of Han Dynasty, merchants were treated equally (Ho, 1962, p.42). During the medieval times in China, those young men who were not interested in books and learning but had an adventurous type of personality could find socially–approved outlet in commerce (Eberhard, 1956). During the Ming and Qing Dynasty, it even became a common practice for people to 'donate' money in exchange for a position in government (Ho, 1962, p.51). The ideology in China was not absolutely rigid: Wang Yangming's revolutionary challenge of the official Neo–Confucian philosophy by Zhu Xi left a permanent imprint on the development of Chinese Confucianism (Ho, 1962, p.198–202). In ancient China, no one was persecuted as in Europe because they proposed a view about a natural phenomenon that was different from his contemporaries.

possible for some powerful families to acquire enough strength to even threaten the throne of the emperor. Sui Dynasty (589–618) established the civil service examination system, which selected talents through fair and impartial examination. This system was continued until the end of Qing Dynasty and was abolished in 1904 (Ho, 1962, p.32).

In the early period of the Tang Dynasty (618–906), the civil service examination tested different knowledge and skills for people with different specialties. For instance, examination of 'Ming Suan' was to select people with strong mathematical skills, examination of 'Xiu Cai' was intended to select people with unusual capabilities. In addition, it was also possible that people with comprehensive talents could be recommended through other channels (Ho, 1962, p.12). But soon the examination became focused on the contents of 'Jing Shi' (Miyazaki, 1976 p.9; Chaffee, 1985: p.184; Liu and Li, 2004, p.156). [15] This civil service examination system was further improved in the Sung Dynasty. The coverage of the tests was limited only to the teaching of the Confucian school, basically its most fundamental readings: the Four Books and the Five Classics. [16] The contents that had to be memorized included 431,286 Chinese characters, not to mention the annotations which were several times longer, and other related historical, literary classics (Miyazaki, 1976, p.16). But memorization was not the most difficult part of this examination. The real difficulties lay in the ability to write creatively, this constituted the intellectual contest element of the

---

[15] Ho (1962, p.13–16) listed many reasons for the narrowing down of examination contents. For instance, the examination of 'Xiu Cai' set too high a standard compared to the reality; the examination on knowledge of mathematics and laws were too specialized for the selection of government officials; the examination of 'Ming Jing' was too focused on memorization and was relatively too simple, and so on. But the key reason was that the examination of 'Jing Shi' tested their literary attainments and their familiarity with the wisdom of ancient sages. These two elements were considered closest to the ethnic and intellectual standards specified by Confucianism as essential talents necessary for the management of state affairs. Moreover, compared with other specialties, these two elements could most effectively facilitate the administration of government officials. Finally, compared with the recommendation system, it was much more objective and fair.

[16] After Han Wu Emperor (156 B.C.–87 B.C.) promoted only the Confucian school and rejected all other schools of philosophy, Confucianism became the orthodox philosophy for Chinese bureaucratic system (Ho, 1962). According to Confucianism, society in essence is hierarchical (James, 1960, p.132). A country should be administered by intelligent and virtuous people. In order to find such people, equal educational opportunities should be provided to all the population and use their educational performances as an indicator for their talents. In this way, it believed that social hierarchy could be maintained. This concept was widely accepted as early as in the Period of Warring States (Ho, 1962, p.7).

exam.[17] Only those with outstanding talents and who devoted most of their efforts into the Confucian study could stand out in the rounds and rounds of competition.[18] Generally, twenty years were needed simply to participate in all these examination.[19] Although the process was long and painful, students still had enough incentive to devote their efforts into it. This was because government officials were regarded as the most honorable and had the most profitable occupation.[20] Traditionally, being a government official was regarded as the shortest path to the upper class (Ho, 1962, p.92). At the same time, the civil service examination system also provided students with strong incentives: students who passed examinations could receive special treatment in accordance with the level of exam they passed.[21] Government also took various measures and create a variety of channels to attract capable people to participate in the civil service examination and become a government

---

[17] Ho (1962, p.14) believed that the most difficult part in the examination of 'Jing Shi' was the requirement of creative writing. During the Ming Dynasty, the civil service examination gradually established a tradition of 'eight–part essay'. To write a beautiful article following a strict format was a highly skillful game. It was believed that this kind of examination could test the intelligence of people and thus considered as the ideal form of civil service examination (Liu and Li, 2004, p.350–352).

[18] The civil service examination system reached its highest prosperity in the Ming and Qing Dynasties. A complete set of civil service examinations included: preliminary stage, county examination, prefecture examination, academy examination, provincial examination, state examination and final imperial examination. In addition, there were many qualification exams before state examinations and additional exams after country examination and metropolitan examinations. Those who passed the preliminary stage were called 'Tongsheng'; those who passed the prefectual examination were called 'Shengyuan'; those who passed the provincial examination were called 'Juren'; and those who passed the final imperial examination were called 'Jinshi' (Miyazaki, 1976).

[19] Elementary education for the civil service examination usually began when children were three years old. They entered school at the age of eight and finished the study on the classics of Confucianism. The learning process was extremely boring and exhausting (Miyazaki, 1976, p.14–16). This was only the preparatory stage for civil service examination. According to Zhang (1991), in the late Qing Dynasty, the average age of : 'Shengyuan' was 24; that of 'Juren' was 31, and 'Jinshi' 34. This means that it generally took 26 years from entering school to become a 'Jinshi'. Although a couple of extremely talented people could become 'Jinshi' at an earlier age (Qian, 2004, p.128–130), the above figures were quite representative. In the Ming Dynasty, the average age of 'Jinshi' was around 30 years old (Qian, 2004, p.132).

[20] In the western countries, bureaucrats never enjoyed such a high social status and authority as in China (Maddison, 1988, p.22).

[21] For the special treatment of 'Xiucai', 'Juren' and 'Jinshi', please see Miyazaki, 1976, p. 36, 59, 83–92; Liu and Li, 2004, p. 283, 287, 293.

official.[22] Governments even publicly advocated the benefits that could be gained through civil service examination, so as to create a wide enthusiasm in the society for the examination.[23]

Such a special incentive structure created a human resource distribution that was only observed in China. It is unique not only because the final success of the few scholars who acquired the high ranking office was achieved at the expense of the enormous amount of time and effort of those who failed.[24] More importantly, the fierce competition for this high profitability made numerous ingenious minds devote all their time and efforts to memorize Confucian classics and acquire literary skills. They were so obsessed with the civil service examination that they had no time for the other branches of knowledge, like mathematics and other useful techniques in real life (Liu and Li, 2004, p.317, 404). Because China was a large and populous country, there were numerous intermediate ranks from the lowest local government officials to a minister, the highest ranking official. Those who were lucky to pass the exams and acquire government positions still had to behave in accordance with Confucian teachings so as to be promoted. Therefore, even winners in the civil service examination had no time for the

---

[22] When the Song Dynasty was first established (970 A.D.), in order to win over the support from the scholars, a special examination was carried out for those who have failed continuously. In this way, it hoped to encourage their continued efforts in the preparation for the civil service examination. In the early period of Tang, Song, and Qing Dynasties, special examinations were carried out to select people with various specialties, as a supplement for 'Jinshi' (Liu and Li, 2004, p. 158, 387).

[23] The 'Quan Xue Poem' by Emperor Zhenzong of Song Dynasty, which has been read through all ages, induced people to participate in civil service examination by direct resort to money, beauties and social status. See Miyazaki, 1976, p.17; Liu and Li, 2004, p.163.

[24] When the empire entered a period of social stability, vacancies for government officials could not increase further. Ho (1962, p.259) estimated that between the sixteenth century and the first half of the 17th century, the total amount of government officials were ranged between 10,000 and 14,000. Therefore, there was a severe surplus in the supply of scholars taking the civil service examination. The admission ratio in the Ming Dynasty was 4 per cent in the provincial examination and around 10 per cent in state examination. For a 'Shengyuan', he only had a 1/3,000 probability ever became a 'Jingshi'. Under the level of 'Shengyuan', there were a still a far larger population who received no government subsidies. Because the civil service examination tested only one particular branch of knowledge, most of the scholars could barely make a living on their own (Qian, 2004, p. 68, 110, 209). At the end of Ming Dynasty, the population of 'Shenyuan' was about 500,000, comprising 0.33 per cent of the national population (Qian, 2004, p.137), which was far larger than the population of government officials.

exploration for other knowledge.[25] As a result, there were only a few scientists in China during the period.[26]

In summary, because the civil service examination system focused only on the Confucianism and the literary skills, most of the talented people in China were fully devoted to either the civil service examination or the research of humanities. They lacked the incentives to learn and accumulate skills in mathematics and controlled experiment, not to mention the ability to combine the two, formalize the knowledge in mathematical forms and test through experiments. As a result, scientific revolution could not spontaneously take place in China, even though China had satisfied many of the crucial conditions for the industrial revolution and capitalism had sprouted as early as in the fourteenth century. Without scientific revolution, the development of its science and technology could not break up the bottle–necks for further development once they reached certain level. Thus its technology could not continue to progress and its capitalism could not be deepened. The further development of capitalist production relation was suppressed. At the same time, after industrial revolution took place in the Europe in the eighteenth century, capitalism developed rapidly in Europe. When the door of China was knocked open by warships and cannons in the nineteenth century, China was still in the embryonic stage of capitalism.

With the help of scientific and industrial revolution, the science and technology developed rapidly in the following century; whereas in China, because it had experienced neither scientific nor industrial revolution, the once glorious country was quickly lagged behind both economically and politically. The international status between China and western countries was quickly reversed. In 1840, the British army forced China opened its door with bombardment of cannons and warships. After that, under the threat of western powers, treaties of forfeiting sovereignty and national humiliation

---

[25] The incentive mechanism of the civil service examination had an extremely important impact on the structure of Chinese human capital. In particular, it led to the lack of talents devoted to the exploration of natural sciences. The comment by Sung Ying–Hsing (Song Yingxing), author of the famous 1637 technology book *T'ien–kung k'ai–wu* (*A Volume on the Creations of Nature and Man*), to his book is the best footnote to this point. He wrote: 'An ambitious scholar will undoubtedly toss this book onto his desk and give it no further thought: it is a work that is in no way concerned with the art of advancement in officialdom.'

[26] According to the studies of Shen and Du (2006), there were a total of 51,561 'Jinshi' in Ming and Qing Dynasty, among which only 925 were considered as the top elites (the first four in the final imperial examination and the first in the state exam). During the same period, the best experts in all areas were estimated to be 1,000, among which only 86 were scientists and philosophers. Although there is concern for the reliability and comparability of the data, the estimates can roughly reflect the situation in the period.

were signed one after another. The cession of territory and payment of indemnities became routine.[27] Grown up under the nurture of Confucianism, Chinese scholars had always regarded the well–being of the country as their own responsibility. Faced with the cruel reality and realizing the weakness and fragility of China, they began to introspect Chinese culture. As their introspection went deeper and deeper, the focus of social movements gradually shifted from the surface of Chinese culture to its intrinsic institutions and kernel values.[28]

The Opium War made the Chinese realize that the tools of western countries were far more advanced, but they still had a fond illusion of Chinese culture's superiority. Guided by the principle of 'maintaining the Chinese culture as the body and learning the western technology to improve the function',[29] many government officials in the Qing Dynasty initiated the Westernization Movement. They purchased guns, cannons, warships and other more advanced instruments from the western countries, established modern enterprises, and hoped to 'learn from the westerners and use their technology to defeat them'. However, the dream was completely crashed in the Sino–Japanese War of 1894–1895. Chinese scholars realized that China was not only backward in technologies, but also in institutions and organizations.[30] Because of this, constitutionalists initiated the Reform Movement of 1898 so as to establish constitutional monarchy in China.[31] In 1911, the capitalist revolutionist initiated the revolution of 1911 in the hope to establish democratic republicanism in China. However, such efforts to change Chinese institutions failed to change the backwardness of China. China was still continuously defeated by western countries. Although the Qing Dynasty was overthrown in 1912, and the Republic of China was

---

[27] For Chinese modern history, please read Maddison 1998, Chapter 2, or *The Cambridge History of China, v. 10–13*.

[28] According to the definition of Malinowski, (translated by Fei, 2002), culture consisted of three integrated layers: tools, organizations, values.

[29] It held that Confucianism was still superior to the western culture, but its technology was not as good as that of the western countries. Therefore, Chinese people should learn the advanced technologies from the western countries.

[30] Chinese political and cultural influence on Japan had been profound for hundreds of years. However, after its Meiji restoration, it began to learn comprehensively from the western countries in all areas, including both the technology and institutions. This process strengthened its power and defeated China in the Sino–Japanese War of 1894–1895.

[31] The Reform Movement of 1898 took the maintenance of imperial authority as a prerequisite. It was intended to establish a new educational system, create a modern administrative system and develop modern industries. However, it was soon defeated by the bureaucrats in power. This movement is also called Hundred Days of Reform.

founded, it was soon obsessed with the war among warlords. Chinese people were driven into a more destitute state. Inflicted by the humiliation of the Treaty of Versailles (1919),[32] for the first time in history, Chinese people realized that the backwardness was not only in the technology and institutions, but also in the ethics and values.

In 1928, although the Nationalist Party nominally unified the China, it suffered from factions and cliques. It was faced with numerous internal conflicts. Since the September eighteenth Incident in 1931, China began to suffer from the Japanese invasion. In 1937, the national war against Japan began. After eight years' struggle, China finally won the war. However, China soon involved in its domestic war, which lasted for another three years. Amidst the flames of wars, Chinese people were driven homeless; China was still unable to get out of the trap of poverty and backwardness.[33]

The 100 years' humiliation inflicted on China brought about an anti–western complex among many Chinese people.[34] Chinese intellectuals also observed the many social economic problems in the early stage of capitalist development in the western powers, like the cyclic economic fluctuations, unemployment, income disparities, and slums in urban areas and so on. They realized that although the capitalist system in the western countries was superior to Chinese traditional system, it was far from perfect. Many Chinese intellectuals were still pursuing a more advanced system that would lead them toward a society with great harmony, a dream they had hoped for thousands of years. They hoped that such a system could make China strong and prosperous, and at the same time, make the nation belong to the people.[35] Because of this, when the Russian Revolution succeeded in 1917, socialism rapidly spread over China, because of its pursuit of prosperity and equality. At the same time, the Soviet Union unilaterally abolished all the unequal treaties and declined all the privileges in China. It also helped the Chinese Nationalist Party to carry out the national revolution. With the socialist planned economy, the Soviet Union rapidly realized industrialization and became a major industrial country in the world. This transition occurred

---

[32] During the Paris Peace Conference of 1919, the concession Qingdao was transferred from Germany to Japan instead of returning to China, although China was among the victorious nations.

[33] The long–standing wars cut the Chinese per capita GDP in 1952 down to the level of 1890. See Maddison, 1998, p.48.

[34] Some people held that China should learn from the western countries, some even believed that China should abandon all its traditions and embrace every aspect of western society. In practice, it is simply impossible for Chinese people to completely abandon its traditional culture.

[35] That is, the concept of fair and justice is well accepted by everyone. The life of every individual was intended for the interest of all the people in the nation.

while the capitalist world was experiencing the great depression in the 1930s. Under such a background, more and more Chinese people accepted socialism. In 1921, the Communist Party was established in China and finally won the support of the majority of Chinese people and defeated the Nationalist Party. In 1949, the People's Republic of China was founded.

In retrospect of this one hundred year history of China, despite all the attempts of Westernization Movement, the Reform Movement of 1898 and the capitalist revolution, none of the administrations adopted effective measures to deal with the challenges of the western advanced technology. The modernization of Chinese economic structure was slow (Maddison, 1998, p.48–49). Wars and foreign aggressions deprived China of many economic sovereignty rights (such as tariffs and railroads) and caused vast damage to its economy; the huge amount of war indemnities further depleted its capital.[36] Wars also caused huge damages on labor resources. Poverty and lack of education formed a vicious cycle and led to low human quality (Maddison, 1998, pp.47, 63). Throughout this one hundred–year history, Chinese economy lacked a stable and peaceful social environment which was crucial for its development.[37] In short, economic growth was deterred by the backward technology, war damages, war indemnities and foreign aggressions. A peaceful environment came only after the founding of the People's Republic of China in 1949. For the first time in the one hundred years, China could promote its industrialization and modernization under a relatively peaceful environment.

3.3   SUCCESSES AND FAILURES OF PLANNED ECONOMY AND THE ECONOMIC MIRACLE AFTER THE REFORM AND OPEN–UP

The founding of the People's Republic of China ended the turbulent times of modern China. In 1949, China was still a poor backward agricultural country with a spectacle of devastation everywhere (Maddison, 1998, p.56). At the time, all developed countries had strong heavy industries, which were commonly regarded as a sign and goal for a strong and prosperous nation.[38]

---

[36] As for the estimation on the amount of war indemnities, please see Xiao, 2004, p.12. Because of scarcity of government revenues (Young, 1971, p.146), government had to default on the foreign debt (Maddison, 1998, p.49).

[37] In its modern history (1840–1949), China experienced 12 major wars. That is, on average, there was one major war in every nine years. See Xiao, 2004, p.7.

[38] Hoffman (1958) proposed to distinguish the industrialization level according to the ratio between light and heavy industry. He discovered that in countries with higher industrialization level, the heavy industries had a higher ratio in the economy.

The success of the Soviet Union in the 1930s under its highly concentrated planned economic system provided Chinese leaders with an attractive example and a strong incentive to follow its step. It was believed a country comprised of mainly poor agricultural population could not provide sufficient demand for industrialization and that the self–servicing and circulation properties of the heavy industry could help to overcome this problem.[39] Because of the Korean War (1950–1953), the western countries began their boycott and economic punishment of China. This put China in a dying thirst for its own independent heavy industry, especially its own national defense and military industrial system. Right after the Korean War, the development strategy that prioritized the development of heavy industries was accepted as the guiding principle for the first Five–Year Plan (1953–1957).[40]

However, developing heavy industries had the following disadvantages: the construction period was long;[41] large amount of equipment had to be imported (especially the key equipments in the early period); the lump–sum investment was huge. These features were in exact conflict with Chinese endowment structure at the time. At that time, China had a severe scarcity of capital,[42] limited exports (so the amount of available foreign exchanges was

---

[39] Before the implementation of its economic plans that prioritized the development of heavy industry, in the Soviet Union, agricultural production constitutes a major part of its economy, which was similar in China. It was believed that through its own accumulation, it was difficult for the Soviet Union to accelerate its capital formation. Because of this, some Soviet economists constructed economic growth models where heavy industries could form a close circulation (See Domar, 1983; Jones, 1976).

[40] The development of heavy industry was the focus of the first Five–Year Plan (CPCCC, 1955, p.160–161). The first Five–Year Plan was built around the heavy industry projects supported by the Soviet Union. The infrastructure investment in heavy industry accounted for 85 per cent of the total industrial investment, and 72.9 per cent of the total infrastructure investment in both agriculture and industry (NBSC, 1992, p.158).

[41] The construction period of light industry projects usually need 1–2 years, whereas that for heavy industries is generally longer. For instance, construction period of metallurgical plant on average took 7 years, chemical plant 5–6 years, machine tool plant 3–4 year. See Li and Zheng, 1989, p.170.

[42] Right after 1949, China was still a backward agricultural country. Agriculture still comprised 58.6 per cent of its GDP (Maddison, 1998, p.56). In 1952, its per capita income was only RMB¥ 104. Even based on the official exchange at the time (US$ 1 = RMB¥ 2.23), it was still less than US$ 50. Capital was in extreme scarcity. In the early 1950s, the market annual interest rate was 30 per cent (monthly rate was 2–3 per cent). Under this interest rate, every RMB¥ 1 investment in heavy industry, should produce a repayment of at least RMB¥ 3.71 in 5 years and RMB¥ 13.79 in 10 years. Such a high interest rate severely impeded the development of heavy industries. See Lin et al., 2003, p.38.

limited),[43] social funds were scarce and dispersed.[44] In order to overcome these difficulties, interest rate and exchange rate had to be lowered so as to reduce the cost of heavy industry investment and import. At the same time, prices of raw materials and wages had to be lowered so as to reduce the cost of heavy industry inputs and increase its rate of return and accumulation. The price of daily necessities also had to be lowered to ensure that workers in the urban areas could make a living with their suppressed wage rates.[45] These comprised the macropolicy environment for the comparative–advantage defying (CAD) strategy that prioritized heavy industry. These policies led to a shortage of capital, foreign exchange, raw materials and daily necessities.[46] In order to insure that resources could effectively flow into the prioritized heavy industries, the government monopolized the supply of resources and distributed them through administrative planning. It also transformed private enterprises into state–owned, so as to prevent them from investing in light industries and affecting the implementation of CAD strategy.[47] Because the market allocation system was distorted in all aspects, profit could no longer be an effective criterion for the economic performance. Under information asymmetry, managers of state–owned enterprises could pursue their personal benefits at the cost of national interests and harm the development of heavy industries. In order to prevent this from happening, managers were deprived

---

[43] In 1950, export was only 1.9 per cent of Chinese GDP, its per capita value was less than US$12 (based on the 1990 fixed price) (Maddison, 1995, p.38, 115, 237). To develop heavy industries in large scale requires large scale import of technologies and instruments. The limited foreign exchange gained through export could in no way meet the large demand of import.

[44] At the time, there were very few funds, the agricultural surplus was dispersed, but the construction of heavy industry required continuous and large amount of capital input. In 1952, the total asset in state–owned banks was only RMB¥ 11.88 billion, the balance of deposit was only RMB¥ 9.33 billion, comprised only 20.2 per cent and 15.8 per cent of the GDP in 1952 (Sheng and Feng, 1991, p.521).

[45] Rural residents could not enjoy the cheap services provided in urban areas, like the cheap consumption goods, housing, medical and educational services. In essence, these policies transformed agricultural surplus into industrial accumulation. For the implementation of low interest rate, low exchange rate, low wage rate and low price for consumption goods, please see Lin et al., 2003, p.41–45.

[46] Shortage of commodities does not only occur in the socialist countries, which is a fact acknowledged by Kornai (1986, p.12), an expert on the shortage economy of socialist countries, but in any countries with price depressions.

[47] These practices were not originated from the socialist doctrines of public ownership, but from the practical incentives. Even though numerous distortional macro policies were implemented to favor the development of heavy industries, the period needed to make profit was still 4–5 times longer than that of light industries (Li, 1983, p.37). Because of this, for private enterprises, investment in light industries was their optimal choice.

of the autonomy in all aspects, including the employment of workers, the use of profits and materials, the plan of production, the supplies of inputs, and the marketing of their products.[48] Because agricultural products were both daily necessities and raw materials for industrial production, the state monopolized the procurement and marketing of agricultural products.[49] Moreover, because agricultural products were the major source of export and therefore generated most of the foreign exchanges at the time,[50] the government initiated the collectivization movement in agricultural production, in order to increase its production capacity without increasing capital investment. On the one hand, the government built water conservancy projects through large–scale labor inputs; on the other hand, it increased the unit yield through the application of traditional methods like close planting, weed control, increase fertilization and so on. The collectivization also facilitated the implementation of the procurement system that government controlled the procurement and the distribution of agricultural goods (Luo, 1985).[51] In order to accumulate more social surplus for the investment in heavy industry, it was necessary to have more and more agricultural surplus transferred into industrial investment. As a result, the government accelerated the pace and enlarged the scale of collectivization of agricultural sector, which finally gave birth to the huge people's communes (Lin 1990). With all these measures, the planned economic system (characterized by the trinity of macro–policy environment, resource allocation system and the micro–management institution) was

---

[48] The production goods and capital were rationed to enterprises according to the government plans; product circulation was under state control; the profits and deficits of enterprises were included into the government financial budget; the employment of workers and the distribution of wages were all implemented according to the national plan. During the early reforms in 1978–1981, enterprises were granted part of autonomous right, which soon affected the profit turned over to the state because firms were overpaying their workers (Lin et al., 2003 p. 55, 151).

[49] In order to maintain the low price of agricultural supplies in urban area, a planned allocation system had to be implemented in the urban areas (Lin et al., 2003, p.51). In order to secure cheap supplies of agricultural products for urban low–price rationing, a compulsory procurement policy was imposed in the rural areas since 1952. This policy obliged peasants to sell certain quantities of their produce to the State at government–set prices (Perkins 1966, chap. 4).

[50] Agricultural products comprised 40 per cent of total export in 1950's. If processed agricultural products are included, it comprised more than 60 per cent of exports until 1970s (Lin, 2004, p.21).

[51] Through the collectivization movement in agriculture, the government could more directly control the agricultural production. It also facilitated government's procurement of large amount of agricultural products at low prices.

established in China to promote the development of heavy industries in an agricultural economy with scarcity in capital.[52]

This development strategy had mobilized resources to the largest possible extent, which was evident through the changes of industrial structure. The average annual accumulation rate was as high as 29.5 per cent in 1952–1978. During the first Five–Year–Plan period, investment in heavy industries was 5.7 times as much as that in light industries; in 1976–1978, it increased to 8.4 times in 1953–1979, the average growth rate of heavy industries was 1.47 times that of light industries. The proportion of industry in GDP increased from 12.6 per cent in 1949 to 46.8 per cent in 1978. This shows that China had increased the proportion of manufacturing industries in its economy even though its per capita income was still low (Lin et al., 2003, p.70–77). This high ratio of manufacturing industries also contributed to China's possession of atom and hydrogen bombs in the 1960s and its successful launch of a man–made satellite in 1970s. In terms of mobilizing all available resources to establish and accelerate the development of heavy industries in a poor agrarian economy, Chinese planned economic system implemented after 1952 was successful.

However, such a success was only achieved at a huge cost. China was abundant in labor but scarce in capital. With this endowment structure, labor–intensive industries were consistent with its comparative advantages, and thus had a lower cost and were more competitive. The development strategy that prioritized heavy industries, on the contrary, was in conflict with Chinese comparative advantage and impaired the competitiveness of the whole economy. Moreover, because the micro–agents lacked the autonomous discretion and sufficient working incentives,[53] production was actually inside

---

[52] Many other developing countries also implemented strategies that prioritized the development of heavy industries (some explicitly stated the priority of heavy industries, some called import substitution but essentially required the development of heavy industries). These economies had similar features as in China: such as distorted macro–policy environment, highly controlled resource allocation system and so on. This shows that the economic system in China was not necessarily unique to socialist countries. Therefore, the analysis of Chinese development strategy and economic system has some general implications. For detailed discussion, please see Lin et al., 2003 p.60–67.

[53] Wage rate of state–owned enterprises was not based on worker's performance, but on education, age, position and other national criteria (Lin, 2004, p.21). In the people's communes, although wages were distributed according on the actual work days, because of the high supervision cost (this is because agricultural production usually involves peasants working in a large area, with long production period, and with output easily affected by various factors), the distribution in reality had to be based on egalitarianism. Because peasants were forced to join the people's communes and were deprived of the right to withdraw, their working incentives

the production frontier. Eecause of this, such a development strategy in effect suppressed China's economic growth (Lin et al., 2003, p.79–80), and the efficiency in resources allocation and production were low.[54] In 1952–1981, the average annual growth of total factor productivity was only 0.5 per cent even based on the most favorable estimation, comprising only one fourth of the average of the 19 developing countries under study (World Bank, 1985a). If only the state–owned enterprises were considered, the figure became negative (World Bank, 1985b). In 1978, the per capita GNP in China was only US$210, less than the cut-off level of low–income developing countries (US$265).[55] Most of the labor force was held–up in rural areas,[56] the urbanization level was far lower than the normal level.[57] The economy became less and less open.[58] In fact, all the countries that adopted the CAD strategy were facing similar problems: a low economic growth rate, a distorted economic structure, low efficiency, loss of social welfare, a deterioration of government finance, inflation and so on (Lin et al., 2003, p.92–95).

At the end of the World War II, the economies of Japan and the Four Little Dragons were at a similar level of other developing countries. However, they

---

were severely dampened (Lin, 1988). Lin (1990) holds that the big decrease in the agricultural production after 1959 was closely related to such an allocation system, which initiated a debate in the American academia (See *Journal of Comparative Economics*, vol. 17, June, 1993).

[54] The consumption of energy and raw materials per unit of GDP in China were not only significantly higher than developed countries, but also higher than India, Korea and Brazil. So was the volume of good transported and the amount of working capital used per unit GDP in China. See World Bank, 1985a.

[55] World Bank (1992, p.184) estimated that Chinese per capita GNP was $220. The US$265 (US dollar in 1975) criterion was set up by the United Nations Industrial Development Organization (UNIDO, 1980, p.49).

[56] In 1952–1978, the proportion of agriculture in GNP reduced by 25 per cent, while the proportion of agricultural labor in the total labor force reduced only 10 per cent. Because of the strategy that prioritized the development of heavy industries, economic growth could not absorb as much agricultural laborers into non–agricultural sectors.

[57] In 1980, the urbanization rate in China was 19.4 per cent, only 6.9 per cent higher than that in 1952, which was lower than the general prediction of Chenery and Syrquin (1988).

[58] The value of foreign trade as a proportion of total value of agricultural and industrial output decreased from 8.16 per cent in 1952–1954 to 5.89 per cent in 1976–1978. The priority given to the development of heavy industries reduced the import of capital goods. At the same time, although the labor–intensive industries had the comparative advantages, they did not have sufficient resources for production and the export of these labor–intensive products also decreased. As a result, the total value of import and export decreased relatively and the economy became less and less open (Lin et al., 2003, p.83).

managed to maintain a rapid economic growth for several decades and became newly industrialized economies. Their economies have reached or become close to the level of developed countries. Their goals of catching–up with the developed countries had been realized (World Bank, 1993). What makes their economic performance so much better than countries that adopted CAD strategies? Economists have proposed three classes of hypotheses: success of free market economy (World Bank, 1993; James et al., 1987); success of government intervention (Johnson, 1982; Amsden, 1989; Wade, 1990); success of export–oriented development policy (Krueger, 1992). These hypotheses have indeed grasped different aspects of the real story. However, the most essential reason for their successes is that these economies had successfully utilized their comparative advantages at each stage of their development processes. Except for Hong Kong, these economies also adopted a CAD type of import–substitution oriented policy in the first place. However, because of either small population size or scarcity of per capita resources, such a policy could not be sustained in these countries.[59] Because their governments soon abandoned the CAD strategy with government interventions along with government subsidies, enterprises in these economies had to act in accordance with their comparative advantages so as to increase their competitiveness. Namely, in the selection of industries and technologies, they started from the labor–intensive industries. As capital accumulated, the economic endowment structure was upgraded, and the industries were gradually upgraded to capital– and technology–intensive ones accordingly. This mode of economic development can be called as 'comparative–advantage–following strategy' (CAF Strategy) (Lin 2003).

The malpractices of the CAD strategy all originated from the fact that the enterprises in the priority sectors of a CAD strategy lack the viability. Viability refers to 'the ability of a normally–managed enterprise to obtain a socially–accepted level of normal profits in a free, open and competitive market, without outside subsidies or protections' (Lin, 2003). In a free, open and competitive market, the viability of a firm depends on whether its selection of technology, product and industry is consistent with the comparative advantages determined by the endowment structure in the economy. For countries with low level of economic development, the endowment structure is characterized by the relative scarcity of capital and relative abundance in labor or natural resources. Therefore, viable firms in

---

[59] As will be discussed below, because CAD strategy defies the comparative advantages to develop the heavy industry, resource requirement per unit GDP is high and the economic efficiency is low. The sustainability of such a policy depends on the relative abundance in per capita resources (the extent to which natural resources could be exploited freely) and population size (the per capita share of the waste of resources).

these countries are those in labor– or natural resource–intensive industries. As the economy develops, only after the economic endowment structure is upgraded, will the enterprises in the relatively capital–or technology–intensive industries become viable (Lin, 2003). In socialist countries that adopted CAD strategies as in other developing countries, because the government defied the comparative advantages of the economy and tried to establish capital–intensive industries, the enterprises lacked the viability.[60] Their investment and operation had to rely on the government's subsidies or protections through various intervention measures, such as the distortion in relative prices, the administrative allocation of resources, the provision of direct subsidies, favorable taxation policies, creation of trade barriers and monopolies. Furthermore, because this lack of viability was due to the fact that these enterprises were asked to shoulder the policy burdens of the government (such as achieve the goal of 'catching–up with the developed countries'), government was accountable for their losses and obliged to provide them with various subsidies. Under information asymmetry, the government could not distinguish losses due to policy burdens from those due to mis–management. Because of this, these enterprises had incentives to ask for more protection and subsidies, which then led to the rent–seeking activities and soft–budget problems[61] (Lin and Tan, 1999). At the same time, enterprises in labor–intensive industries that were competitive in both domestic and international market could not fully develop because they could not get sufficient capital and other resources, even though they were in sectors consistent with the comparative advantages determined by the economy's endowment structure. The implementation of this CAD strategy led to low economic efficiency and slow economic growth.

The only way for a developing country to catch up with developed countries in terms of industrial structure and per capita income is to upgrade its endowment structure and narrow the gap in this respect. Because it is difficult to change the endowment structure of natural resources and because the growth rate of labor force does not differ significantly from country to country, the upgrade of endowment structure mainly lies in the speed of capital accumulation, which depends on the surplus and accumulation rate of the economy in every production period. When economic development follows the comparative advantages of the economy, a normally–managed

---

[60] According to Heckshire–Ohlin model (Ohlin, 1968), countries abundant in labor have comparative advantages in labor–intensive industries. Therefore, when resources are allocated by the market mechanism, it is difficult for the capital–intensive enterprise to acquire the average profit that is socially acceptable.

[61] Losses due to rent–seeking activities were probably larger than the losses due to inappropriate resource allocation, just as the estimation of Brazil in 1967 (Griffin, 1992, p.153).

firm will select the technology, product and industry in accordance with the comparative advantages determined by the endowment structure of the economy. Such a choice will make the firm viable in a free and competitive market. It will be able to produce at the minimum cost, earn the maximum surplus and get the highest marginal rate of return of capital. Consequently, the economy will be able to accumulate capital, upgrade its endowment structure and narrow the industrial and technological gap with the developed countries at the fastest speed.

Firm's selection of technology, product and industry depend on the relative price of the product and production factors. In order to make enterprises follow the principle of comparative advantage, the relative price of production factors should fully reflect the relative scarcity of factors in the endowment structure. This can only be achieved through competition of supply and demand and where all the prices are determined by the market. Therefore, a well–functioning market system is a prerequisite for the implementation of comparative–advantage–following strategy.

Based on the experiences of East Asian countries, a developing country that follows its comparative advantages in the development process has a better economic performance. Its upgrade of endowment structure is fast, so are its upgrade of industrial, product and technological structure. As the economy undergoes such changes, it is necessary that informational and coordinate services be provided to individual firms. Because the successes and failures of these upgrades in individual firms have externalities over the decision of other firms, in addition to the maintenance of social and economic order, government should provide information and coordination for firms through its industrial policies. Some taxation or financial support might be necessary to address the externality problem during the upgrade.[62]

Following its comparative advantages, a country will mainly import products that they do not have comparative advantages. As its resources are mainly used to develop industries with comparative advantages, its export of the corresponding product will also increase. Compared with countries that defy their comparative advantages, both its import and export will be higher and thus the economy is more open. In fact, the amount of import and export is endogenously determined by the comparative advantages of the economy.

The above analysis shows that the three characteristics of the 'East Asian

---

[62] The demarcation between an industrial policy that follows comparative advantages and that defies them lies in the viability of firms that are supported by these policies. Although both policies have subsidies, the amount necessary for these subsidies differs. For the former kind of policy, subsidies are only intended to compensate externality involve, thus the amount is limited. For the latter kind, subsidies are to address the viability of firms, thus a large amount of subsidies are necessary.

Miracle' are actually the consequences of the fact that their economic development follows their comparative advantages (Lin, 2003).

The achievement of Chinese economy since 1979 is exactly due to the shift from a CAD strategy to a CAF strategy.[63] In 1978, revolutionaries like Deng Xiaoping, Chen Yun and others, who were sidelined during the Cultural Revolution, regained leadership after the defeat of the 'Gang of Four'. They initiated the reform so as to accelerate economic development and improve people's living standards. At the beginning, there was no well–defined blueprint for the reform (Perkins, 1988, p.601). The reform started from the micro–level and took a gradual approach through the introduction of a dual–track system (McKinnon, 1995).

At that time, the immediate and observable reason for the poor economic performance was the lack of autonomy in micro–management units and the resultant inadequate working incentives among workers and peasants. Because of this, the reform started from micro–management. It was intended to improve the economic performance by increasing the autonomy of micro–agents and therefore increase their working incentives. The most important change in the micro–management system was the replacement of collective farming with a household–based system in rural areas, now known as the household responsibility system. This household responsibility system granted the peasants with claims over the residuals,[64] which provided them with great working incentives and led to huge improvement in their economic performance (Lin, 1988, 1992). In the urban areas, the reform of the state–owned enterprises was characterized by the increase in the autonomy and the introduction of profit retention, which allowed the enterprises to enjoy part of its incremental profits. Until now, the reform of state–owned enterprises has undergone three phases. In the first phase (1979–1983), the reform introduced profit retention and performance–related bonuses; and enterprises involved in exports were allowed to retain part of their foreign exchange earnings for use at their own discretion.[65] In the second stage (1984–1992),

---

[63] Before 1978, China had also carried out some reforms on its planned economic system. Those reforms were mainly restricted in the decentralization and recentralization of administrative authorities among different government divisions and local governments. Because they had not changed the CAD strategy, they were not successful (Wu and Zhang, 1993, p.65–67).

[64] It was commonly phrased as: 'turn over an enough amount for the state procurement, retain a sufficient amount for the collective, and the rest are all one's own'. For detailed description of its implementation, please see Xiao, 2004, p.210.

[65] However, because of the distortion in macro–policy environment, the problem of soft–budget constraint still existed. The increase in the autonomy led to activities that sacrificed state interests such as understatement of outputs, failure to achieve the planned production target and excessive distribution of bonuses (Lin et al., 2003, p.151).

the reform was mainly focused on the establishment of contract responsibility system for firms.[66] In 1984, state–owned enterprises were allowed to sell output in excess of quotas at negotiated prices and to plan their output accordingly, which led to the introduction of the dual–track price and resource–allocation system. In the third phase (1993–present), it privatizes small–and–medium–sized state–owned enterprises. At the same time, it tries to establish a modern corporate system of large state–owned–enterprises, some of which have been listed on the domestic and/or international capital markets.[67] During the process, government intervention has been gradually reduced and autonomous right of enterprises has been gradually increased.

The reform of micro–management has greatly improved economic efficiency. In 1978–1984, Chinese agricultural production experienced an unprecedented high annual growth rate of 7.7 per cent, almost half of which were due to the increased working incentives brought about by the household responsibility system (Fan 1991; Huang and Rozelle 1996; Wen 1993; Lin 1992; McMillan, et al. 1989).[68] Meanwhile, the productivity of state–owned enterprises also improved significantly (Chen et al. 1988; Gordon and Li 1991; Dollar 1990; Jefferson et al. 1992; Groves et al. 1994; Li 1997).[69] These reforms in the micro–management improved production efficiency and created a large amount of new resources. Because these measures increased the total amount of available resources (just like increasing the size of a cake), they facilitated economic growth and further reforms.

In urban areas, because state–owned enterprises were allowed to produce and sell their product in excess of quotas so as to acquire more profits, additional resources had to be allocated to the enterprises outside the planned channels. This forced the government to gradually relax its control over the resource allocation process, such as in the supply of goods and materials and in the sales of various products. This gradually reduced the planned track of resource allocation and enlarged the market track. The proportion of market–allocated resources gradually increased. In rural areas, the implementation of household responsibility system created large amount of new economic

---

[66] This was related to the thriving of town–and–village enterprises. In order to compete for the scarce resources, it was necessary that state plans be reduced and state–owned–enterprises be given more autonomy so as to make a better use of comparative advantages.

[67] The modern corporate system is characterized by: 'clear definition of property rights, unequivocal specification of authorities and responsibilities, separation of government and enterprises, and scientific management'. See Xiao, 2004, p.288.

[68] Similar improvement in economic performance was also observed in the agricultural reform in Vietnam. See Pingali and Xuan, 1992.

[69] Similar improvement in economic performance was also observed in the reform of state–owned enterprises in Vietnam. See Sun, 1997, p.3–4.

surpluses. At the same time, relaxing state control over resource allocation provided non–state–owned enterprises with access to raw materials and gave them great market opportunities. All these facilitated the development of town–and–village enterprises and other non–state–owned enterprises. The investment of these non–state–owned enterprises was mainly focused on labor–intensive industries that had been constantly suppressed under traditional development strategy. Because the products of these industries were in short supply and had high rate of return, these enterprises (especially the town–and–village enterprises) quickly thrived. In 1981–1991, the number of non–state–owned enterprises and their employment increased at an average annual rate of 25.6 per cent and 11.2 per cent respectively. In the same period, their output value increased at an average annual rate of 29.6 per cent, which was three times that of state–owned enterprises. Its proportion in the total value of industrial goods increased rapidly from 7.2 per cent in 1978 to 38.1 per cent in 1993 (NBSC, 1995, p.73). This was regarded by some economists as the most remarkable achievement since the adoption of reform and open–up policy (Sun, 1997).

Because the non–state–owned enterprises were not part of the traditional economic system, they could neither obtain resources from nor sell their product through the planned track. They had to act competitively through the market track, which hardened their budget constraints and made their economic performance dependent on the management of the firm. Because of these, their productivity was higher than the state–owned enterprises (Weitzman and Xu 1994; Sun 1997). Faced with this great competive pressure from non–state–owned enterprises, the state–owned enterprises were granted more autonomy. The government was forced to learn from the non–state–owned enterprises and reform the state–owned enterprises. At the same time, it was also forced to reduce price–distortional administrative measures that were intended to increase the profit of state–owned enterprises (Jefferson and Rawski 1995). These reform measures improved productivity in state–owned enterprises (Li 1997). In this sense, the growth of non–state–owned enterprises contributed to the growth of the market outside the planned–track and gradually pushed the state–owned enterprises to the market. Moreover, because they had to select product and technology according to market prices, which reflected the relative scarcity of production factors, most of the non–state–owned enterprises operated in the labor–intensive industries.[70] This partly corrected the imbalanced economic structure and partly improved the low efficiency in resource allocation (Lin et al., 2003, p.184–196).

---

[70] Take 1986 as an example. the average investment per employee in industrial enterprises was RMB¥ 7,510 (CIESM, 1987, p.3), while that for the town–and–village enterprises was only RMB¥ 1,709 (NBSC, 1987, p.205).

Consequently, the improvement in micro–management pushed forward the reform in resource allocation system, so as to satiate the need to invest newly created resources to labor–intensive industries, which were consistent with Chinese comparative advantages and had higher rates of return. As a result, the proportion of resources allocated through the planned track gradually diminished, while that for the market–track increased. The reform was pushed further from micro–management to the resource allocation system.

Resources allocated outside the planned track were priced by the market; those allocated through the planned track were priced by the government. This gave rise to the emergence of a double–track price system. This system provided state–owned enterprises with marginal incentives through relatively higher market price. At the same time, it provided protection and subsidies for non–viable state–owned enterprises through relatively cheaper resources that were allocated through the planned track. In this way, it was hoped that the state–owned enterprises could continue to help realizing the government goal of 'catching–up with the developed countries'. One advantage of such a double–track system was to avoid large–scale bankruptcy of non–viable enterprises in capital– and/or technological–intensive industries. This helped to maintain the stability of the economy. At the same time, this double–track system provided room for the development of viable enterprises in labor–intensive industries that were consistent with China's comparative advantages. This helped to invigorate the economy.

At the beginning, the prices of the two tracks differed a lot. But as time went by, the difference was gradually reduced and the convergence of the two prices created favorable conditions for the final convergence of the two tracks. In the process, the following factors contributed to the price convergence and the growing market track: government adjusted planned–prices according to the market–price level, the rapid growth of non–state–owned enterprises and the increasing state–owned enterprises' production in excess of state quotas. By 1996, prices of most commodities and services were completely determined by the market (SPCPAB, 1997). The reform in exchange rate followed a similar track: at first, there was only the suppressed official exchange rate to reduce the cost of developing heavy industries; then there was the coexistence of the official rate and the 'internal settlement rate' which was designed to encourage enterprises to export and earn foreign exchanges; then government lowered the official rate gradually and established a foreign exchange swap centre,[71] finally the double–track in the

---

[71] By the end of 1980s, over 80 per cent of the foreign exchanges were swapped in this system. See Sung 1994.

foreign exchange rate was converged to the market track and foreign exchange rate began to have a managed floating system.[72]

The reform in the interest rate was the slowest among all these reforms. Although it has been adjusted several times, it is still controlled by the government instead of the market. This phenomenon not only reflects the need of those nonviable state–owned enterprises in capital–and/or technology–intensive industries, but also reflects the fact the government has not fully abandoned the CAD development strategy. Low interest rate leads to excess demand for capital. After delegation of credit approval authority to local banks, local governments, various government divisions and all enterprises began to compete for the loans for investment, so as to expand production. This then led to excess demand for energy, raw materials, transportation and other infrastructure sectors. A 'bottle–neck' of development was thus formed. At the same time, because demand of credit exceeded the planned supply, money was issued to make up for the balance, which then led to inflation.[73] In order to tackle inflation, the government had to use the administrative measures to strictly control the investment and the size of credit supply. As a result, the central government withdrew some of its delegated authority. Such a retrenchment led to a return to the planned economy. As state control tightened, non–state–owned enterprises were affected more severely than the state–owned enterprises. Even though they enjoyed comparative advantages, they could not acquire key economic resources like credit, energy and raw materials because they were excluded from the planned track. Consequently, economic growth slowed down dramatically. Because the state–owned enterprises were in conflict with China's comparative advantages and lacked viability, their poor economic performance could not generate enough profit, state finance became more and more dependent on the non–state–owned sector which was much more efficient (Lin et al., 2003, p.199). As non–state–owned sector was badly hurt by the retrenchment, the state budget became inadequate. At the same time, the centralization of the delegated authorities was resisted by agents at the

---

[72] Vietnam and Laos adopted a similar dual–track system to reform their price and foreign exchange system. They almost completely relaxed government control in these two areas in 1989 and 1988 respectively. This was considered as evidence for the shock therapy (Sachs and Woo 1997; Popov 1996). However, because Vietnam had not completely abolished its trading barriers, nor had it started privatization, its relaxation of price control in 1989 can only be regarded as partial reform instead of shock therapy.

[73] Through rent–seeking activities, non–state–owned enterprises obtained the credit intended for the state–owned enterprises. Because government wanted to sustain the development of state–owned enterprises, it had to increase the money supply to make up for the credit. This is called 'endogenous inflation'. This is also the cause for all the inflations in China since 1978 (Lin 2003, p.242).

micro–management level. In face of all these problems, the government had to re–delegate authorities again and relax its control over credit and investment. Following the same logic, a new round of economic cycle began. This shows that the economic cycles since the adoption of reform and open–up policy are intrinsically different from those in developed countries. The economic cycles in China originate from the inconsistency between its macro–policy environment and its micro–management and resource allocation system. The immediate cause is government control over the interest rate.[74] Because of this government control over interest rate and other administrative measures left over from the planned economy, rent–seeking activities were rampant and income disparities aggravated.

Since all the distortional measures were intended to service the non–viable state–owned enterprises, in order to eradicate government control over interest rate and other administrative interventions, the viability of state–owned enterprises has to be enhanced.[75] The existence of information asymmetry blurred the distinction between losses due to government policy burdens and the losses due to mis–management. This gave rise to the moral hazard problem that firms would report all losses as incurred by government policy and let government bear all the loss, thus creating a soft–budget–constraint for state–owned enterprises (Lin et al., 1998 and 2001; Lin and Tan, 1999). This further dampened the firm's incentives to improve its management, encouraged opportunist activities, and led to the governance problem. If privatization were implemented before the firms were relieved

---

[74] This is also the source for corruption–related rent–seeking activities. The dual–track price system made the price difference between two tracks a target for rent–seeking activities. From 1987 to 1988, the rent reached RMB¥ 2,000 billion and RMB¥ 3,500 billion respectively, which accounted for 20 per cent–25 per cent of the GNP (Hu, 1989). In 1992, the rent for the difference in interest rates alone reached RMB¥ 2,200 billion (Hu, 1994). Because of these corruption–related rent–seeking activities, state–owned enterprises could not get the low–priced resources from the planned track, which aroused wide–spread social discontent. In 1986 and 1988, the government tried to regain its control over the resource allocation system. The measures severely damaged the development of non–state–owned sectors. For the same reason mentioned above, the government had to abandon such efforts soon after.

[75] The shock therapy considers the rapid privatization as a prerequisite for reform (Sachs and Lipton, 1990; Sachs, 1992), and a prerequisite for the restructure of state–owned enterprises (Blanchard et al., 1991). The empirical studies on the East European countries and the former Soviet Union show that the performance of enterprises does not solely depend on the arrangement of property rights. It also depends on the incentive structure and the market competition. State–owned enterprises can also achieve high efficiency (see Pinto et al.,1993; Sereghyova,1993; Brada et al., 1994 and 1997; Mencinger, 1996; Frydman et al., 1996; Jones, 1997).

from government policy burdens, government subsidies would be embezzled directly with the lack of supervision. It would also encourage firms to seek for more subsidies. Because of their strategic importance and the concern for dramatic increase in unemployment in case of their bankruptcy, the government had to continue its protection and subsidies for these firms. Consequently, government subsidies would increase rather than decrease. After large–scale privatization, government revenue would decrease while its subsidies would increase. This would lead to high government deficit, which would then result in increase in money supply and inflation (McKinnon, 1995). In fact, this was exactly what happened in the former Soviet Union and the East European countries.[76]

Under the traditional planned economic system, the state–owned enterprises lacked viability because they shouldered the responsibilities assigned by the government, that is, to catch up with the developed countries. Before these state–owned enterprises are transformed into viable firms, the implementation of shock therapy[77] and the maintenance of macro–economic stability will be in irreconcilable conflict.[78] The big–bang approach suggests that all price distortions and market interventions should be abolished at once along with a rapid privatization in large–scale; while at the same time, it hopes that social stability could maintained in the process. This approach is doomed to failure.[79] The transformation of nonviable state–owned enterprises

---

[76] After large–scale privatization in Russia, although the direct subsidies decreased, there were still numerous indirect subsidies. Even in Poland, default in tax payment was still as before (World Bank, 1996, p.45). After the privatization of state–owned properties, various government regulations, protection and subsidies were still in practice (see Brada, 1996; Frydman et al., 1996; Lavigne, 1995; Stark, 1996; Sun, 1997). For description on inflation, see World Bank 2002; Lin et al., 2003, p.4–7.

[77] Macro–stability, liberation of price, and rapid and large–scale privatization were considered to be the prerequisite of a successful transition from a planned economy to market economy. See Gomulka, 1989; Lipton and Sachs, 1990; Kahn and Richardson, 1991; Blanchard et al, 1991.

[78] As discussed above, because of the state–owned enterprises are nonviable, privatization and price liberalization will inevitably lead to deterioration in government revenue and high inflation. It is impossible to maintain macro–stability at the same time. Moreover, rapid and large–scale privatization was impractical, because of the capital immobility in heavy industries (Brada and King 1991). The retraining of workers and the establishment of new market system also takes time and resources (Lin, 1989; Murrel and Wang, 1993). The World Bank studies show that privatization usually takes several years to complete; the establishment of legal and financial system takes even longer. Therefore, even the shock therapy is a gradual process (See Lavigne, 1995, Chapter 10; World Bank, 1996 and 2002).

[79] The countries that adopted shock therapy all experienced output decrease, high inflation and deteriorating social conditions (World Bank, 2002). Although the collapse of the Warsaw Treaty Organization exacerbated the decrease in

to viable enterprises is the key in the transition from planned economy to market economy. Its resolution requires that the elimination of their policy burdens (Lin et al., 1998 and 2001). When firms have no policy burdens, it will be unnecessary for the government to maintain low–interest policy loans, favorable taxation treatment and financial subsidies, because it is no longer responsible for the losses of the firms. Then the market determination of interest rate and the commercialization of banks will become feasible (Lin, 2000); and so will the coordination between the macro–policy environment and the micro–management and resource allocation system.

In retrospect, Chinese reform has proceeded gradually through trials and errors along the way, which is best described by a Chinese saying: 'to cross a river by groping the stones'. Because the trinity of the traditional planned economic system originates from the CAD strategy that prioritized heavy industry, although Chinese gradual approach of reform has no well–defined blueprint, its transition process has followed an intrinsic logical process. The reform started from the micro–management system which, under the traditional system, deprived micro–agents of all autonomy and resulted in poor economic performance. Such reforms rapidly improved the economic efficiency and increased economic resources available. In order to encourage the micro–agents to invest resources into traditionally suppressed sectors that followed Chinese comparative advantages, the existence of market allocation system and market price outside the traditional planned economic system was necessary. The introduction of the market system further improved the allocation efficiency. As more and more resources were allocated through the market system, the planned–track price and allocation system finally converged to the market track. Therefore, this gradual approach is logically inherent and irreversible. It also makes it possible to bridge a chasm in two steps.[80] The consequent improvement in the micro–management and the increased new resources benefited most of the population. Without large–scale privatization, Chinese reform avoided the social conflict due to the reallocation of the existing stock of resources. Therefore, it is closer to the Pareto improvement (Lin et al., 2003, p.327). The shock therapy based on neo–classical economics neglected the key issue that the state–owned enterprise lack viability, and thus encountered great difficulties in real

---

production, the shock therapy was still doubtlessly the chief criminal (Brada and King, 1991; Csaki, 1994).

[80] During the transition from planned economic system to comparative–advantage–following market economic system, because the extent and degree of distortion were large and severe, the direct reform of macro–policy environment and the attempt to achieve the goal in one stoke in the Soviet Union and the East European countries were doomed to failure. However, the dual–track system also has to pay the cost of rent–seeking activities (Lin et al., 1996).

practice (Lin, 2005). On the contrary, the gradual approach can successfully address this issue: as managerial discretion and market competition pressure increases, the efficiency of the state–owned enterprises improves. With the maintenance of planned allocation of resources, government can continue its provision of low–price resources to state–owned enterprises, so as to avoid the economic collapse and social turbulence. The rapid development of non–state–owned sector that follows the comparative advantages of the economy gradually reduces the opportunity cost of reforms in the state–owned enterprises. It not only facilitates the reform in state–owned enterprises but also provides further impetus for such a reform. Because of this, even though the gradual reform in China had not been highly regarded at first,[81] it has proved its effectiveness through the practice.[82] Its success has wider implications to other countries as well. Because countries that adopted CAD strategy established the planned economic system following the same logic, they were faced with the same problems like distorted economic structure and poor performance of micro–management (Brada and King, 1991; Newbery, 1993; Sachs and Woo, 1994). This makes Chinese gradual approach to reform a good reference for these countries.[83]

However, although the gradual reform through the dual–track system has created miraculous Chinese economic growth in the past 20 years, its large state–owned enterprises still lack viability in market competition. Because this viability problem has not been completely resolved, the reforms in macro–policy environment, especially those on interest rate, are still lagging

---

[81] The gradual reform in China was believed to be intrinsically flawed, while the shock therapy was considered to be theoretically perfect and practically feasible (Sachs, 1993).

[82] The success convinced many economists that Chinese gradual reform is better than the shock therapy (see Singh 1991; Murrell, 1991 and 1992; Chen et al, 1992; Harrold, 1992; McMillan and Naughton, 1992; Perkins, 1992; McKinnon, 1994; Rana, 1995; Rawski, 1995; Jefferson and Rawski, 1995). If the cost of institutional changes and path dependence are considered, the gradual approach of Chinese reform is superior to the shock therapy both theoretically and empirically (Wei, 1993).

[83] Some economists attributed Chinese success in reform to its particular initial conditions: such as the huge agricultural population, the relatively small amount of subsidies, the relatively scattered economic system, large amount of overseas Chinese and so on (see Woo, 1993; Balcerowicz, 1994; Qian and Xu, 1993; Sachs and Woo, 1994 and 1997). Some economists regarded Chinese success in economic transition as a challenge to traditional economic theory (see Chow, 1997; Perkins, 2002). It is true that these particular conditions have contributed to the Chinese success, and every country should fully consider and utilize its particular conditions before and during its reform. However, the similarities in economic systems and difficulties make Chinese reform an important reference for other transitional economies.

behind. The conflict between this macro–policy environment and the micro–management and resource allocation system is still a major source of various economic and social problems such as economic fluctuation and rent–seeking activities. Therefore, in order to completely transform the nonviable state–owned enterprises into viable enterprises, the Chinese government has to completely abandon it CAD strategy that prioritizes the heavy industry. Only in this way, will China be able to maintain its growth through the rapid development of sectors that are consistent with its comparative advantages. And only in this way, will China be able to carry out the gradual reform according to its own logic and accomplish its historic transition from planned economy to market economy.

3.4   SUMMARY AND FUTURE PROSPECTS FOR THE CHINESE ECONOMY

In this chapter, I have provided a brief overview of China's economic performance since the Sung dynasty. The experience in the past millennium shows that continuous upgrade of technology is the key to a sustainable long–term economic growth. China's outstanding performance over the West in the pre–modern times was due to the advantages of large population in the era of experience–based technology inventions. The scientific revolution in the fifteenth century made it possible for the West to replace the experience–based technology inventions with a science–cum–experiment based inventions and ignited the industrial revolution in the eighteenth century. The incentive system embedded in the civil service examination system in the pre–modern times made Chinese talents focusing on Confucian classics, prevented them from accumulating human capital in other areas and thus deprived China the opportunity of indigenous scientific and industrial revolutions. Because of these, after the industrial revolution when the speed of technological upgrade was accelerated, China was left behind by the West.

In the modern times before 1978, as a less–developed economy, China could have utilized such advantages in its technological innovations if it had followed the comparative advantages in its industrial and technological selections. According to this comparative–advantage–following strategy, China would have learned the mature technologies from the developed countries, which could have enabled China to upgrade its technology at a lower cost and at a lower risk. However, like many other socialist and developing countries, after the World War II, China adopted a heavy–industry–oriented development strategy which defied China's comparative advantages. Because firms in these prioritized sectors were inconsistent with the comparative advantages of the economy, they were non–viable and had to rely on government subsidies, protections and other distortional and interventional measures. With this strategy, China was able to establish its own modern heavy industries. However, this was only achieved at the cost of economic inefficiency and the stagnant low living standards of its people.

In 1979, China started its gradual transition from planned to market economy through a dual–track system. This approach led to a miraculous economic growth in the past 27 years. Since the per capita income in China was only US$ 1,730 in 2005, there is still a large gap between China and the developed countries. Will China be able to maintain a dynamic growth in the coming decades? This is an important question not only for its own people but for the people of other countries as well. In 2005, its trade dependent ratio (that is, the export and import as a percentage of GDP) reached 64.1 per cent. If China is able to maintain its growth, other countries will also benefit, due to the openness of Chinese economy and its large size.

If it is able to complete its transition to a market economy and continue to tap into the growth potential of 'the advantage of backwardness', it is very likely that China will maintain a dynamic GDP growth rate for several more decades. As argued, continuous technological innovation is the most important determinant of long–term economic growth. As a developing country, China's technological level lags far behind that of developed countries. Therefore, it can adapt technological know–how's from advanced countries at a lower cost and acquire the technological innovations necessary for its economic development. Because Japan and the four East Asian Tigers had effectively exploited their advantage of backwardness in technology after World War II, they were able to achieve the dynamic growth for about 40 years.

From all major indicators, the stage of China's development today is very similar to that of Japan in the early 1960s.[84] China should have as large a growth potential as that of Japan in the early 1960s. If China realizes this potential, it will become the largest economy in the world in the early 21st century as predicted by Maddison in his preface to the Chinese edition of *the World Economy: A Millennial Perspective*. China will be the first major civilization to go from the zenith to nadir and then recover from it.

However, in order to bring this potential into full play, China needs to complete its transition from a planned economy to a market economy. China should also follow a right development strategy that promotes industrial development according to China's comparative advantages (Lin, 2003). At

---

[84] The life expectancy in China was 72 for female and 68 for male in 1998; while it was 72.9 for female and 67.7 for male in Japan in 1965. The infant mortality rate was 31 per thousand births in China in 1999 and 30.7 per thousand in Japan in 1960. The primary sector's share in GDP was 15.9 per cent in China in 2000 and it was 16.7 per cent in Japan in 1969 (Kwan, 2002).

the same time, China also needs to integrate itself into the world economy so as to facilitate the borrowing of technology. China's entry into WTO in 2001 is a commitment to such a transition, strategy and integration.

REFERENCES

Amsden, A.H (1989), *Asia's Next Giant: South Korea and Late Industrialization*, New York: Oxford University Press.

Balazs, S. (1931), Beitrage zur Wirtschaftsgeschichte der T'ang–Zeit (618–906), *Mitteilungen des Seminars fur Orientalische Sprachen zu Berlin*: Jahrgang xxxiv, Berlin: Gedruckt in der Reichsdruckerei.

Balcerowicz, L. (1994), 'Common Fallacies in the Debate on the Transition to a Market Economy', *Economic Policy*, **9** (19–supplement), 16–50.

Blanchard, O., R. Dornbusch, P. Krugman, R. Layard and L. Summers (1991), *Reform in Eastern Europe*, Cambridge, MA: MIT Press.

Boulding, K. (1976), 'The Great Laws of Change' in Anthony M. Tang, Fred M. Wsetfield and James S. Worley (eds), *Evolution, Welfare and Time in Economics*. Lexington: S.C. Heath Lexington Books.

Brada, J.C. (1996), 'Privatization Is Transition, Or Is It?', *Journal of Economic Perspectives*, **10** (2), 67–86.

Brada, J.C. and A.E. King (1991), 'Sequencing Measures for the Transformation of Socialist Economies to Capitalism: Is There a J–Curve for Economic Reform?' *Research Papers Series, No. 13*, Washington, D.C.: Socialist Economies Reform Unit, World Bank.

Brada, J.C., A.E. King. and C.Y. Ma (1997), 'Industrial Economics of the Transition: Determinants of Enterprise Efficiency in Czechoslovakia and Hungary'. *Oxford Economic Papers*, **49**, 104–27.

Brada, J.C., I. Singh, and A. Torok (1994), 'Firms Afloat and Firms Adrift: Hungarian Industry and the Economic Transition Series', *The Microeconomics of Transition Economies*, Vol. 1, Armonk, New York: M.E. Sharpe.

Buck, J.L. (1964), *Land Utilization in China: a study of 16,786 farms in 168 localities, and 38,256 farm families in twenty–two provinces in China, 1929–1933*. New York: Paragon Book Reprint Corp., First edition published by the University of Nanking, 1937.

Cameron, R.E. and L.P. Neil (1989), *A Concise Economic History of the World: from Paleolithic Times to the Present*, New York: Oxford University Press.

Chaffee, J.W. (1985), *The Thorny Gate of Learning in Sung China: Social History of Examination*, Cambridge: Cambridge University Press.

Chao, K. (1986), *Man and Land in Chinese History: An Economic Analysis*, Stanford: Stanford University Press.

Chen, K., G. Jefferson and I.J. Singh (1992), 'Lessons from China's Economic Reform', *Journal of Comparative Economics*, **16** (2), 201–25.

Chen, K., H. Wang, Y. Zheng, G. Jefferson, and T. Rawski (1988), 'Productivity Change in Chinese Industry: 1953–1985', *Journal of Comparative Economics*, **12** (4), 570–591.

Chenery, H.B. and M. Syrquin (1988), *Patterns of Development, 1950–1970*, Beijing: Economic Science Press.

Chow, G.C. (1997), 'Challenges of China's Economic System for Economic Theory', *American Economic Review*, **87** (2), 321–7.

Cipolla, C.M. (1993), *Before the Industrial Revolution: European Society and Economy, 1000–1700*, Third edition, London: Routledge.

CPC Central Committee, Documentation and Research Office (1955), *Documents of the Second Session of the First National People's Congress of the PRC*, Beijing: People's Press.

Csaki, C. (1994), 'Where is Agriculture Heading in Central and Eastern Europe? Emerging Markets and New Role for the Government' *Presidential Address to the XXII International Congress of Agricultural Economists*, Harare, Zimbabwe.

Dollar, D. (1990), 'Economic Reforms and Allocation Efficiency in China's State–Owned Industry', *Economic Development and Cultural Change*, **39** (1), 89–105.

Domar, E.D. (1983), 'The Growth Model of the Soviet', in *Essays on the Theory of Economic Growth*, Chapter 9, Beijing: Commercial Press.

Eberhard, W. (1956), 'Data on the Structure of the Chinese City in the Pre–Industrial Period', *Economic Development and Cultural Change*, **4**, 253–268.

Elvin, M. (1973), *The Pattern of the Chinese Past*, Stanford: Stanford University Press.

Fan, S. (1991), 'Effects of Technological Change and Institutional Reform on Production Growth in Chinese Agriculture', *American Journal of Agricultural Economics*, **73** (2), 265–75.

Feuerwerker, A. (1990), 'Chinese Economic History in Comparative Perspective', in Paul S. Rop (ed). *Heritage of China: Contemporary Perspectives on Chinese Civilization*, Berkeley: California University Press.

Frydman, R., C.W. Gary, and A. Rapaczynski (eds.) (1996), *Corporate Governance in Central Europe and Russia. Vol. 2: Insiders and the State,* Budapest: Central European University Press.

Gernet, J. (1982), *A History of Chinese Civilization*, New York: Cambridge University Press.

Goldsmith, R.W. (1984), 'An Estimate of the Size and Structure of the National Product of the Roman Empire', *Review of Income and Wealth*, **30** (3), 263–88.

Gomulka, S. (1989), 'Shock Needed for Polish Economy'. *Guardian*, **19**, 5.

Gordon, R. and W. Li (1991), 'Chinese Enterprise Behaviour Under the Reforms', *American Economic Review: Papers and Proceedings*, **81** (2), 202–06.

Griffin, K. (1992), *The Alternative Strategies for Economic Development*, Beijing: Economic Science Press.

Groves, T., Y. Hong, J. McMillan, and B. Naughton (1994), 'Autonomy and Incentives in Chinese State Enterprises', *Quarterly Journal of Economics*, **109** (1), 183–209.

Harrold, P. (1992), 'China's Reform Experience to Date', *World Bank Discussion Paper, 180*, Washington D.C.: the World Bank.

Hartwell, R.M. (1962), 'A Revolution in the Chinese Iron and Coal Industries During the Northern Sung, 960–1126 AD', *Journal of Asian Studies*, **21**, 153–162.

Hartwell, R.M. (1966), 'Markets, Technology and the Structure of Enterprise in the Development of the Eleventh Century Chinese Iron and Steel Industry', *Journal of Economic History*, **1**, 29–58.

Hartwell, R.M. (1967), 'A Cycle of Economic Change in Imperial China: Coal and Iron in Northern China, 750–1350', *Journal of the Economic and Social History of the Orient*, **10** (1), 102–159.

Hicks, J.R. (1932), *The Theory of Wages*, London: Macmillan.

Ho, P.–ti. (1962), *The Ladder of Success in Imperial China: Aspects of Social Mobility, 1368–1911*, New York: Columbia University Press.

Ho, P.–ti. (1969), *Huangtu yu zhongguo nongye de qiyuan* (Loessand the origin of Chinese Agriculture), Hong Kong: Chinese University Press.

Hoffman, W. (1958), *Growth of Industrial Economics*, Manchester: Manchester University Press.

Hu, H. (1989), 'Three Measures for a Clean Government', *Corruption: Trading of Power for Money*, Beijing: China Outlook Press, 36–43

Hu, S. (1994), '1994: Reforms Have No Romantic Melody', *Gaige* (Reform), No. 1.

Huang, J. and Rozelle, S. (1996), 'Technological Change: The Re–Discovery of the Engine of Productivity Growth in China's Rural Economy', *Journal of Development Economics*, **49** (2), 337–69.

James, L. (ed.)(1960), *The Chinese Classics: with a Translation, Critical and Exegetical Notes, Prolegomena, and Copious Indexes*, vol. 2, The Works of Mencius, Hong Kong: Hong Kong University Press.

James, W.E., S. Naya and G.M. Meier (1987), *Asian Development: Economic Success and Policy Lessons*, San Francisco: ICS Press.

Jefferson, G., and T. Rawski (1995), 'How Industrial Reform Worked in China: The Role of Innovation, Competition, and Property Rights', *Proceedings of the World Bank Annual Conference on Development Economics 1994*, Washington, D.C.: World Bank, 129–56.

Jefferson, G., T. Rawski and Y. Zheng (1992), 'Growth, Efficiency and Convergence in China's State and Collective Industry', *Economic Development and Cultural Change*, **40** (2), 239–66.

Jefferson, G., J.X. Zhao and M. Lu (1995), *Reforming Property Rights in Chinese Industry*, Mimeographed, Waltham, MA: Department of Economics, Brandeis University.

Jin Y. (1987), 'An Explanation of the East Asian Economic Development from a Cultural Perspective', *Information Newspaper Finance and Economic Monthly*, No. 11.

Johnson, C.A. (1982), *MITI and the Japanese Miracle: the Growth of Industrial Policy, 1925–1975*, Stanford, Calif.: Stanford University Press.

Jones, D.C. (1997), 'The Determinants of Economic Performance in Transitional Economies: The Role of Ownership, Incentives and Restructuring', *Research for Action 39*, UNU/WIDER.

Jones, E.L. (1988), *Growth Recurring: Economic Change in World History*, New York: Oxford University Press.

Jones, E.L. (2003), *The European Miracle: Environments, Economies, and Geopolitics in the History of Europe and Asia*, Third edition, New York: Cambridge University Press.

Jones, H.G. (1976), *An Introduction to Modern Theories of Economic Growth*, New York: McGraw–Hill.

Kahn, A.R., T.J. Richardson (eds) (1991), *What Is To Be Done: Proposals for the Soviet Transition to the Market*, New Haven: Yale University Press.

Kornai, J. (1986), *Shortage Economics*, Vol. 1, Beijing: Economic Science Press.

Krueger, A.O. (1992), *Economic Policy Reform in Developing Countries*, Oxford: Basil Blackwell.

Kuznets, S. (1966), *Modern Economic Growth: Rate Structure, and Spread*, New Haven: Yale University Press.

Kwan, C.H. (2002), 'Overcoming Japan's China Syndrome', paper presented at 'Asian Economic Integration: Current Status and Future Prospects' organized by

Research Institute of Economy, Trade & Industry of Japan at Tokyo on April 22–3.

Lavigne, M. (1995), *The Economics of Transition: From Socialist Economy to Market Economy*, New York: St. Martin Press.

Li, J. and Y. Zheng (ed.) (1989), *Jishujinbu yu Chanye Jiegou Xuanze* (Technological Progress and the Choice of Industrial Structure), Beijing: Science Press.

Li, W. (1997), 'The Impact of Economic Reform on the Performance of Chinese State Enterprises, 1980–89'. *Journal of Political Economy*, **105** (5), 1080–1106.

Li, Y., (1983), *Zhongguo Gongye Bumen Jiegou* (The Structure of Chinese Industry), Beijing: China People's University Press.

Lin, J.Y. (1988), 'The Household Responsibility System in China's Agricultural Reform: A Theoretical and Empirical Study', *Economic Development and Cultural Change*, **36** (3), S199–S224.

Lin, J.Y. (1989), 'An Economic Theory of Institutional Change: Induced and Imposed Change', *Cato Journal*, **9** (1), 1–33.

Lin, J.Y. (1990), 'Collectivization and China's Agricultural Crisis in 1959–1961', *Journal of Political Economy*, **98**, 1228–1252.

Lin, J.Y. (1992), Justin Yifu. 'Rural Reforms and Agricultural Growth in China', *American Economic Review*, **82** (1) 34–51.

Lin, J.Y. (1995), 'The Needham Puzzle: Why the Industrial Revolution did not Originate in China', *Economic Development and Cultural Change*, **43**(2), 269–92.

Lin, J.Y. (2000), 'What is the Direction of China's Financial Reform?', in Hai, W. and F. Lu (eds), *China· Economic Transition and Economic Policy*, Beijing: Peking University Press.

Lin, J.Y. (2003), 'Development Strategy, Viability and Economic Convergence', Economic Development and Cultural Change, **53** (2), p. 277–308.

Lin, J.Y. (2004), 'Lessons of China's Transition from a Planned Economy to a Market Economy', *Distinguished Lecture Series, No.16*, Warsaw: Leon Kozminski Academy of Entrepreneurship and Management.

Lin, J.Y. (2005), 'Viability. Economic Transition and Reflection on Neoclassical Economics', *Kyklos*, **58** (2), 239–64.

Lin, J.Y., F. Cai and Z. Li (1996), 'The Lessons of China's Transition to a Market Economy', *Cato Journal*, **16** (2), 201–31.

Lin, J.Y., F. Cai and Z. Li (2003), *The China Miracle: Development Strategy and Economic Reform*, Revised Edition, Hong Kong: The Chinese University Press.

Lin, J.Y., F. Cai and Z. Li (1998), 'Competition, Policy Burdens, and the State–owned Enterprise Reform', *American Economic Review: Papers and Proceedings*, **88** (2), 422–7.

Lin, J.Y., F. Cai and Z. Li (2001), *State–owned Enterprise Reform in China*, Hong Kong: the Chinese University Press.

Lin, J.Y. and G. Tan (1999). 'Policy Burdens, Accountability, and the Soft Budget Constraint', *American Economic Review: Papers and Proceedings*, **89** (2) (May), 426–31.

Lipton, D. and J. Sachs (1990), 'Privatization in Eastern Europe: The Case of Poland', *Brookings Papers on Economic Activities*, **2**, 293–341.

Liu, H.–feng and B. Li (2004), *Zhongguo Keju Shi* (The History of Chinese Civil Service Examinations), Shanghai: Oriental Press Center.

Luo, H. (1985), *Economic Changes in Rural China*, Beijing: New World Press.

Maddison, A. (1998), *Chinese Economic Performance in the Long Run*, Paris: OECD.

Maddison, A. (1995), *Monitoring the World Economy, 1820–1992*, Paris: OECD.

Maddison, A. (2001), *The World Economy: A Millennial Perspective*, Paris: OECD.

Malinowski, B.K. (2002), *The scientific theory of culture*, Translated by Fei, H.–tung, Beijing: Huaxia Press.

Mathias, P. (1972), 'Who Unbound Prometheus? Science and Technical Change, 1600–1800', in Musson, A.E. (ed.), *Science, Technology and Economic Growth in the Eleventh Century*, London: Methuent.

McKinnon, R.I. (1994), 'Gradual versus Rapid Liberalization in Socialist Economies: Financial Policies and Macroeconomic Stability in China and Russia Compared', *Proceedings of the World Bank Annual Conference on Developing Economics 1993*, 63–94, Washington D.C.: World Bank.

McKinnon, R.I. (1995), 'Taxation, Money and Credit in the Transition from Central Planning', in Rana, P.B. and N. Hamid (eds), *From Centrally Planned to Market Economies: The Asian Approach*, Vol. 1, 35–72, Hong Kong: Oxford University Press.

McMillan, J. and B. Naughton (1992), 'How to Reform A Planned Economy: Lessons from China', *Oxford Review of Economic Policy*, **8** (1), 130–143.

McMillan, J., J. Whalley and L. Zhu (1989), 'The Impact of China's Economic Reforms on Agricultural Productivity Growth', *Journal of Political Economy*, **97** (4), 781–807.

Mencinger, J. (1996), 'Privatization Experiences in Slovenia', *Annals of Public and Cooperative Economics*, **67** (3), 415–428.

Miyazaki, I. (1976), *China's Examination Hell: The Civil Service Examination of Imperial China*, New York: Weatherhill.

Monter, W. (1985), 'Forward', in Qian, W.–yuan (ed.), *The Great Inertia: Scientific Stagnation in Traditional China*, London: Croom Helm.

Murrell, P. and Y. Wang (1993), 'When Privatization Should Be Delayed: The Effect of Communist Legacies on Organizational and Institutional Reforms', *Journal of Comparative Economics*, **17** (2), 385–406.

Murrell, P. (1991), 'Can Neoclassical Economics underpin the Reform of Centrally Planned Economies?', *Journal of Economic Perspectives*, **5** (4), 59–76.

Murrell, P. (1992), 'Evolutionary and Radical Approaches to Economic Reform', *Economic Planning*, **25**, 79–95.

Musson, A.E. (ed.) (1972), *Science, Technology and Economic Growth in the Eighth Century*, London: Methuen.

National Bureau of Statistics of China (1987), *China Industrial Economy Statistical Material 1987*, Beijing: China Statistics Press.

National Bureau of Statistics of China (1988), Urban Social and Economic Survey Team. *Zhongguo wujia tongji nianjian*, 1988 (China Price Statistical Yearbook, 1988), Beijing: China Statistical Press.

National Bureau of Statistics of China (1992), *China Statistical Yearbook, 1992*, Beijing: China Statistics Press.

National Bureau of Statistics of China (1995), *Zhongguo Tongji Zhaiyao, 1995* (A Statistical Survey of China, 1995), Beijing: China Statistics Press.

National Bureau of Statistics of China (2006), 'The International Comparison of China's Economic and Social Development in the Tenth Five–Year Plan Period', *Retrospective Reports Series of China's Economic and Social Development in the Tenth Five–Year Plan Period*, Beijing: China Statistics Press.

Needham, J. (1954), *Science and Civilization in China*, Vol. 1, Cambridge: Cambridge University Press.

Needham, J. (1969), *The Grand Titration: Science and Society in East and West*, London: George Allen & Unwin.

Needham, J. (1981), *Science in Traditional China: A Comparative Perspective*, Cambridge, MA: Harvard University Press.

Needham, J. (1986), 'Introduction' in Robert K.G. Temple, *China Land of Discovery and Invention*, Wellingborough: Patrick–Stephens.

Newbery D.M. (1993), 'Transformation in Mature versus Emerging Economies: Why has Hungary Been Less Successful than China?', Paper presented to the International Symposium on the 'Theoretical and Practical Issues of the Transition towards the Market Economy in China' (Hainan, China: China Institute of Economic Reform and Development, 1–3 July.

Ohlin, B. (1968), *Interregional and International Trade*, Cambridge, MA: Harvard University Press.

Perkins, D.H. (1966), *Market Control and Planning in Communist China*, Cambridge, MA: Harvard University Press.

Perkins, D.H. (1969), *Agricultural development in China 1368–1968*, Chicago: Aldine Publications.

Perkins, D.H. (1988), 'Reforming China's Economic System', *Journal of Economic Literature*, **26**, (2), 601–45.

Perkins, D.H. (1992), '*China's 'Gradual' Approach to Market Reforms*', Paper presented as a conference on 'Comparative Experiences of Economic Reforms and Post–Socialist Transformation', El Escorial, Spain, July 6–8.

Perkins, D.H. (2002), 'The Challenge China's Economy Poses for Chinese Economists', *China Economic Review*, **13**, 412–8.

Perkins, D.H. and Y. Shahid (1984), *Rural Development in China* (A World Bank Publication), Baltimore: The Johns Hopkins University Press.

Pingali, P. and V.–tong. Xuan (1992), 'Vietnam: De–Collectivization and Rice Productivity Growth', *Economic Development and Cultural Change*, **40** (4), 697–718.

Pinto, B., M. Belka and S. Krajewski (1993), *Transforming State Enterprises in Poland: Microeconomic Evidence on Adjustment*, Washington, D.C.: Brookings Papers on Economic Activity, No. 1.

Popov, Vladimir (1996), 'Hard Facts and Fancy Theories: A Fresh Look at the Transition Debate', *Wider Angle*, No. 2/96 1–3.

Qian, M.–wei. (2004), *Guojia, Keju yu Shehui* (Nation, the Civil Service Examinations and Society), Beijing: Beijing Library Press.

Qian, Y. and C. Xu (1993), 'Why China's Economic Reforms Differ: The M–Form Hierarchy and Entry/Expansion of the Non–state Sector', *The Economics of Transition*, **1** (2), 135–70.

Qian, W.–yuan (1985), *The Great Inertia: Scientific Stagnation in Traditional China*, London: Croom Helm.

Rana, P.B. (1995), 'Introduction: The Asian Approach to Reforming Transitional Economies', in Rana, P.B. and N. Hamid (eds), *From Centrally Planned to Market Economies: The Asian Approach*, Vol. 1, 1–33, Hong Kong: Oxford University Press.

Rawski, T. G. (1995), 'Implications of China's Reform Experience', *China Quarterly*, 144, 1150–1173.

Riskin, C. (1975), 'Surplus and Stagnation in Modern China', in Perkins D.H. (ed.), *China's Modern Economy in Historical Perspective*, Stanford: Stanford University Press.

Rostow, W.W. (1960), *The Stages of Economic Growth*, Cambridge: Cambridge University Press.

Sachs, J.D. (1992), 'Privatization in Russia: Some Lessons from Eastern Europe', *American Economic Review*, **82** (2) 43–8.

Sachs, J.D. (1993), *Poland's Jump to the Market Economy*, Cambridge, M.A.: MIT Press.

Sachs, J.D. and D. Lipton (1990), 'Poland's Economic Reform', *Foreign Affairs*, **69** (3), 47–66.

Sachs, J.D. and W.T. Woo (1994), 'Structural Factors in the Economic Reforms of China, Eastern Europe and the Former Soviet Union', *Economic Policy*, **18**, 101–45.

Sachs, J.D., and W.T. Woo (1997), 'Understanding China's Economic Performance', *Manuscript*.

Schultz, T.W. (1964), *Transforming Traditional Agriculture*, New Haven: Yale University.

Sereghyova, J. (1993), *Entrepreneurship in Central East Europe*, Heidelberg: Hpysica Verlag.

Shen, D.–miao, S.–wei Du. (2006), Jin–shi, Wei–ke Renwu yu Rencai (Jin–shi and Its Top Elites vs. Other Specialists), *Keju Bai Nian* (A Century After the End of Civil Service Examinations), Beijing: Tong Xin Press.

Sheng, B. and L. Feng (ed.) (1991), *Census Report on China*, Shenyang: Liaonin People's Press.

Shiba, Y. (1970), *Commerce and Society in Sung China*, Ann Arbor: University of Michigan, Center for Chinese Studies.

Simon, J.L. (1986), '*Theory of population and economic growth*', New York: Basil Blackwell.

Singh, I.J. (1991), 'China and Central and Eastern Europe: Is There a Professional Schizophrenia on Socialist Reform', *Research Paper Series, No. 17*, Washington D.C.: Socialist Economies Reform Unit, World Bank.

Stark, D. (1996), 'Networks of Assets, Chains of Debt: Recombinant Property in Hungary' in Frydman, R., C.W. Gary and A. Rapaczynski (eds), *Corporate Governance in Central Europe and Russia. Vol.2: Insiders and the State*, Budapest: Central European University Press.

State Planning Commission, Price Administration Bureau (1997), 'The Weights and Changes of Three Patterns of Prices', *Price in China*, **12**, 31–34.

Sun, L. (1997), Emergence of Unorthodox Ownership and Governance Structure in East Asia: An Alternative Transition Path, *Research for Action*, **38**, Helsinki: UNU/WIDER.

Sung, Y.-H. (1966), *T'ien–Kung K'ai–Wu* (Chinese Technology in the Seventeenth Century), published in Chinese in 1637, translated by Zen Sun, E–tu and S.–C. Sun, University Park, PA.: the Pennsylvania State University Press.

Sung, Y.–W. (1994), 'An Appraisal of China's Foreign Trade Policy, 1950–1992', in Srinivasan, T.N. (ed.), *The Comparative Experience of Agricultural and Trade Reforms in China and India*, San Francisco: International ICS Press, 109–53.

Tang, Anthony (1979), 'China's Agricultural Legacy', *Economic Development and Cultural Change*, **28** (1), 1–22.

Temple, R.K.G. (1986), *China land of discovery and invention*, London: Multimedia.

United Nations Industrial Development Organization (1980), *Basics and Trends of Industrialization in World Countries and Regions*, Beijing: China Foreign Transition Publishing Co.

Wade, R. (1990), *Governing the Market: Economic Theory and the Role of Government in East Asian Industrialization*, Princeton, N.J.: Princeton University Press.

Wei, S. (1993), 'Gradualism Versus Big Bang: Speed and Sustainability of Reform', *Working Paper Series, R93–2*, Cambridge, MA: John F. Kennedy School of Government, Harvard University, Faculty Research.

Weber, M. (1968), *The Religion of China: Confucianism and Daoism,* Translated from the German and Edited by Hans H. Gerth with an Introduction by C.K. Yang (paperback edition; New York and London: Free Press).

Weber, M. (1997), 'Confucian Politics in China and the Sprout of Capitalism in China: Cities and Industrial Associations', Collected Works of Max Weber: The Historical Steps of Civilizations, Shanghai: Shanghai Sanlian Bookstore.

Weitzman, M.L., and C. Xu (1994), 'Chinese Township–Village Enterprises as Vaguely Defined Cooperatives', *Journal of Comparative Economics*, **18** (2), 124–45.

Wen, G.J. (1993), 'Total Factor Productivity Change in China's Farming Sector: 1952–1989', *Economic Development and Cultural Change*, **42** (1), 1–41.

Woo, W.T. (1993), 'The Art of Reforming Centrally–Planned Economies: Comparing China, Poland and Russia', Paper presented at *the Conference of the Tradition of Centrally–Planned Economies in Pacific Asia.* San Francisco: Asia Foundation in San Francisco, May 7–8.

World Bank (1985a), *China: Economic Structure in International Perspective, Annex to China: Long Term Issues and Options*, Washington, D.C.: the World Bank.

World Bank (1985b), *China: Long Term Issues and Options*, Oxford: Oxford University Press, published for the World Bank.

World Bank (1992), *World Tables (1992)*, Baltimore: Johns Hopkins University Press.

World Bank (1993), *The East Asian Miracle: Economic Growth and Public Policy*, New York: Oxford University Press.

World Bank (1996), *World Development Report, 1996: From Plan to Market*, New York: Oxford University Press.

World Bank (2002), *Transition: the First Ten Years, Analysis and Lessons for Eastern Europe and the Former Soviet Union*, Washington D.C.: the World Bank.

Wu, J. and Z. Zhang (eds) (1993), *Zhongguo Jinji Jianshe Baikequanshu* (The Encyclopedia of China's Economic Construction), Beijing: Beijing Industrial University Press.

Xiao, G. (ed.) (2004), *Zhonghua Renmin Gongheguo Jinji Shi* (The Economic History of the PRC), Beijing: Huawen Press.

Young, A.N. (1971), *China's Nation–building Effort, 1927–1937: The Financial and Economic Record*, Stanford, Calif.: Hoover Institution Press.

Zhang, Z. (1991), *Zhongguo Shenshi* (The Chinese Gentlemen), Shanghai: Press of Shanghai Academy of Social Sciences.

4.   An Indian Miracle?[1]

Deepak Lal

4.1   INTRODUCTION

In explaining the acceleration in Indian growth, and to judge if an Indian economic miracle is on its way, it is first necessary to establish when this acceleration began, as this is still subject to controversy. Second it is necessary to identify the sources of this acceleration and to see to what extent these are the results of policy. Third, to provide some reading of the tea leaves until 2030, it is necessary to outline the current constraints on growth. But before that, the current change in Indian economic fortunes needs to be put into historical perspective. This is done in the first part of this article, followed by the next three parts, which deal with the other three broad themes outlined above. As this article is in honor of Angus Maddison, I rely wherever possible on the growth accounting method that he has made so much his own.

4.2   REPRESSION, CRISIS AND REFORM

Like many other developing countries, India at its independence in 1947 followed an inward-looking heavy industry biased industrialization strategy. This was in part a reaction to the laissez faire and free trade policies followed by the British Raj in the nineteenth century, which were erroneously thought to have led to India's continuing stagnation. Though contemporary research has questioned the validity of this nationalist and often Marxist perspective, it still colors the minds of Indian elites. Like elites in many other developing

---

[1]   This chapter was originally published in *Cato Journal*, Vol. 28, No. 1 (Winter 2008). Copyright © Cato Institute. This chapter was written while the author was a Distinguished Visiting Fellow at the National Council of Applied Economic Research in New Delhi, and presented at a seminar in honor of Angus Maddison at the University of Queensland in December 2006. It is based in part on Lal (2005).

countries, they have been haunted by their helplessness against the Western assault in the Age of Imperialism. They have sought (like the Chinese) a middle way between the modernity promised by Western globalizing capitalism and their own ancient traditions.

Unlike the Japanese, who saw that they could modernize while keeping their traditions, there were two alternative Indian responses. The first represented by Gandhi was to hold on to tradition, and to reject modernity. The second by Nehru was to reconcile modernity with tradition by adopting a form of Fabian socialism. This development model represented a compromise between an Enlightenment strand promoting modernization and a Romantic revolt against the Enlightenment, represented by the younger Marx and English socialists like William Morris (see Lal, 2006c).

At Independence in 1947, with Gandhi dead soon thereafter at the hands of an assassin, it was Nehru's ideas that determined India's economic policies. They entailed massive dirigiste interventions in the form of centralized planning and a draconian set of economic controls on foreign trade, capital flows, and prices. They, however, yielded a higher growth rate than that experienced under the Raj (see Table 4.1). This acceleration of growth was based on three factors.

The first was a rise in public social overhead investment, particularly on irrigation, and from the late 1960s on R & D in agriculture. The British Raj had been hamstrung in raising public investment as it was always wary of a nationalist revolt that might be provoked by any rise in taxes for its finance. With no such constraint faced by independent India, public investment, which had averaged about 2.2 per cent in the interwar period, rose to nearly 7 per cent of GDP by 1960–61.

The second was a rise in the rate of savings and capital formation in the economy compared with the century of alien rule. Gross domestic savings which were about 8 per cent of GDP at Independence rose to 11.6 per cent by 1960–61, and by 1999–2000 were 22.3 per cent of GDP.

The third was the rise in population from 1921 induced by a declining death rate, which led to a rising labor force in agriculture. It had grown by 12.6 per cent between 1901 and 1940, but rose by 25.4 per cent between 1950 and 1970 (Lal, 2005, Table 7.4). This growth spurt, on Boserupian lines, (Boserup, 1965; Lal, 2005, 2006a) led to an intensification of agriculture with an increase both in labor and capital inputs per unit of land, and a rise in the annual growth rate in agriculture from 0.44 per cent between 1900 and 1947 to 3.3 per cent between 1950 and 1965. The elasticity of agricultural output with respect to rural labor remained constant at about 2.5 in both the pre-Independence period (1900–40) and the post-Independence period (1950–70), while that of capital to labor rose from about 1 to 2.54, as predicted by the Boserup model (Lal, 2005, Table 7.4).

Table 4.1 Sources of real GDP growth: India – 1990–97/98

Annual Rates of Growth	Undivided India 1900–01 to 1946-47			India 1950–51 to 1997–98		
	Agriculture	Non-agriculture	Total	Agriculture	Non-agriculture	Total
GDP	0.44	1.69	0.92	2.6	5.1	4
Persons employed	0.4	0.42	0.41	1.5	2.1	1.7
Capital stock including land	0.45	3.02	1.13	2.5	4.5	4
Combined factor inputs	0.41	1.12	0.56	1.69	2.74	2.22
Increase in output per unit of input	0.03	0.57	0.36	0.91	2.36	1.78

Source: Sivasubramonian (2004, Tables 7.21 and 9.34).

The economic repression under the Nehruvian settlement, however, had led by the mid-1960s to a 'quiet crisis' in India (Lewis, 1962), with the Hindu rate of growth of 3.5 per cent and population growing at 2.2 per cent until the early 1980s, yielding meager annual rises in per capita income of just over 1.3 per cent. This performance failed to make any marked dent on India's ancient poverty.

The first signs of crisis appeared in agriculture, as the Boserupian process, with an unchanged agricultural technology, soon faced diminishing returns. The food crisis of the 1960s forced the government to reverse its previous neglect of agriculture, based on the faulty prescriptions of the Arthur Lewis model that the route to growth in a labor surplus economy was through massive industrialization, with agriculture being left alone until the surplus labor had been worked off. India then adopted the new technology embodied in high-yielding seeds and large inputs of fertilizers and water that led to the Green Revolution. The average annual agricultural growth rate had slowed to only 1.8 per cent from 1960 to 1973. The Green Revolution of the 1970s, which was by and large a wheat revolution, raised the growth rate of agriculture to about 2.9 per cent from 1973 to 1999. Thereafter, it has slowed as the area under high-yielding varieties has reached its limits, with the potential irrigable area having been utilized with diminishing returns setting in on the new Green Revolution technology.

Industrial growth, which had been 6.8 per cent between 1950 and 1965 slowed to 4.3 per cent between 1976 and 1980, as the limits of import substitution were reached. There was a foreign exchange crisis in the mid 1960s that led Indian economists to question the dirigiste, inward-looking path India had taken. This reaction was strengthened by the neoclassical resurgence in the 1970s, which questioned the intellectual basis of post-war development economics (Lal, 1985; Little, 1982). But it was the switch made by Deng Xiaoping from the plan to the market in China, in 1978, that probably most concentrated Indian minds.

With its tradition of Gladstonian public finance, India had avoided the chronic macroeconomic imbalances associated with dirigisme. However, the creation of a rent seeking society, and the microeconomic distortions introduced by public policy in the planning era, gradually led to a fiscal crisis (Lal, 1987).

The first sign was the growth of the underground economy, variously estimated to be 18 to 45 per cent of GDP. Second, government revenue, which had risen from about 11 per cent of GDP in 1960 to about 20 per cent in 1986, stagnated thereafter. Public expenditure rose from about 19 per cent of GDP in 1960 to more than 32 per cent by 1986. Thus, the public sector borrowing requirement (PSBR) rose from about 8 per cent of GDP in the 1960s and 1970s to more than 11.5 per cent in 1990, the year preceding the crisis and reform (Lal, 2005, Table 12.1). Third, the growing fiscal crisis was met by internal and external borrowing and, finally, by levying the inflation tax. Inflation, which had hovered around 4–5 per cent except for years of drought, rose steadily from 1988 to reach a peak of nearly 14 per cent in 1991, a year with a bumper harvest. The internal public debt rose from 42 per cent of GDP in the early 1980s to nearly 58 per cent in 1991, as the government tried to meet its fiscal bind through promoting large inflows of short-term capital from the Indian diaspora after 1985 (Lal, 2005, Table 12.1b). When they took fright at the deteriorating fiscal and inflation position and moved their money out of India, a Latin American style crisis was triggered.

In the dash for growth, a halfhearted liberalization effort began with Rajiv Gandhi's election, after his mother's assassination in 1984. It raised the growth rate, but this liberalizing impetus soon petered out, as his government was caught in a web of corruption charges. The dash for growth did generate an unsustainable boom, with GDP growing at 7 per cent in 1989. A weak coalition came to power in 1989 and was unable to deal with the impending crisis. When it collapsed and a minority Congress government with Dr. Manmohan Singh as the finance minister came to power in 1991, the country was essentially bankrupt, with foreign exchange reserves barely sufficient to finance 10 days of imports, galloping inflation (by Indian standards) of 14 per cent, a Public Sector Borrowing of nearly 12 per cent, and an impending growth collapse.

The new finance minister began the reversal of nearly a century's creeping and under Mrs. Gandhi, galloping dirigisme. The PSBR was squeezed by about 2 per cent of GDP with little pain. The Permit Raj began to be dismantled with the virtual ending of industrial licensing, and with the removal of import controls (except on consumer goods, which were only removed in 2001 when they were declared illegal by the World Trade Organization). The import-weighted tariff was cut from an average of 87 per cent in 1991 to 27 per cent in 1996. The rupee was devalued initially by about 20 per cent. Direct foreign investment was once again welcomed, though it was still controlled and restricted to 51 per cent foreign ownership.

Even these partial reforms lifted the growth rate, exports, foreign reserves, and inflows of foreign capital. The savings and investment rates rose and the incremental capital-output ratio fell from a pre-reform average of 4.5 to 3.8 in the post-reform period, as the reforms increased economic efficiency. Poverty rates, after rising during the short period of stabilization, came down substantially.

With the quick success of the stabilization measures and the boost to growth from the partial liberalization, the element of crisis that had led to the reforms disappeared. Thereafter, there has been piecemeal reform by successive coalitions of varying political hue. The most notable being those in fiscal policy and the easing of financial repression (created by Mrs. Gandhi's 1970s nationalization of banks) through financial reform. The coalition led by the BJP also notably began the process of privatizing the inefficient public sector. But this process has stalled with the veto imposed by the Congress Party's communist coalition partners. They also prevented the dismantling of the labor laws imposed by the British Raj in the late nineteenth century (at the behest of protectionist Lancashire textile manufacturers), which raised the price of using Indian's most abundant resource for industrialization and led to a century of a growing capital-intensive bias in Indian industry.

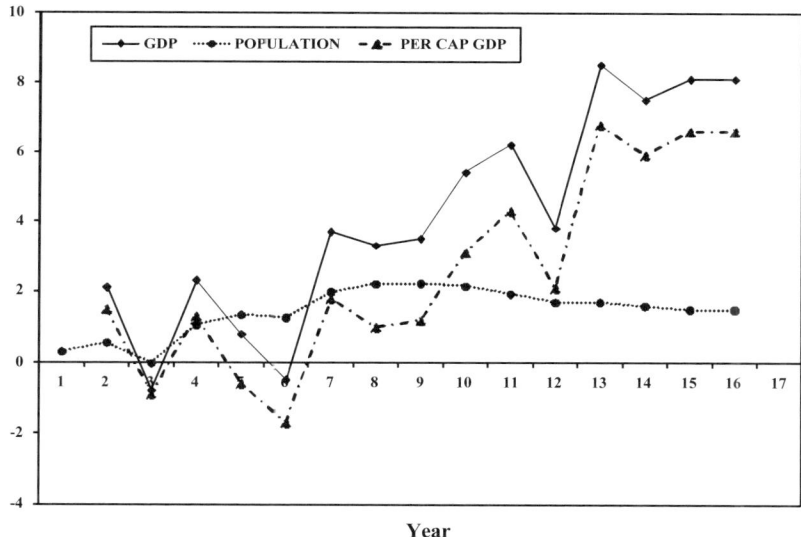

Sources: Lal (2005); Government of India (2006), *Economic Survey 2005–06*; World Bank (2007).

Figure 4.1   Annual Growth Rates in India, 1901–2006

Figure 4.1 shows the growth rates of GDP, population, and per capita GDP for the twentieth century. It shows the rise in the GDP and per capita growth rates from 1951 until the 1960s, compared with the pre-Independence period. One can also see the stagnation in the 1960s and 1970s, with the trend rate of growth until the early 1980s being a meager 3.5 per cent a year dubbed by Raj Krishna as the 'Hindu rate of growth'. In the 1980s, with partial economic liberalization under Rajiv Gandhi and with the abandonment of many aspects of the Permit Raj and industrial planning, growth accelerated to 5.6 per cent, and from 1991 to 2000, growth increased to 6.6 per cent a year (Lal, 2005, Table 11.1b). Since that time, there was a further acceleration of economic growth to nearly 9 per cent per year from 2003 to 2007.

4.3   WHEN DID INDIA'S GROWTH ACCELERATION BEGIN?

From the earlier account of the partial liberalization in the 1980s, it would appear that there was some acceleration in the growth rate in the 1980s. But the dash for growth, which raised growth rates just before the 1991 crisis, was not sustainable. It was the much fuller liberalization in 1991 that put India on a higher-growth path. So the 1990s should really be taken as the period when India's growth acceleration began.

Rodrik (2002) and De Long (2002), using the official time series of Indian GDP, have contested this view. They argue that the acceleration in Indian growth began in the 1980s before the Manmohan Singh–Narasimha Rao reforms, when it was 5.6 per cent per year and was not much higher after the reforms. Hence, the liberalization of trade and industrial policies of the 1990s cannot be taken to have made any significant difference to growth in India. Panagriya (2005) and Srinivasan (2003) have countered this view. They argue that partial liberalization during the mid-1980s had favorable efficiency effects but that the resulting rise in the growth rate was fragile. Moreover, if the exceptionally high growth rate of 7.6 per cent in 1988–89, due to the unsustainable foreign borrowing, is removed from the GDP series, the average growth rate in the 1980s would be significantly lower than in the 1990s (Panagriya, 2005, p.174). Finally, Wallack, (2003) has identified structural breaks in the Indian GDP series. She finds a statistically significant (at the 10 per cent level) breakpoint in 1980. But when the exercise is carried out on the GNP series, the statistically significant breakpoint is 1987.

One basic problem with these diagnoses based on the GDP and GNP time series is that they do not take account of the underlying fragility of the data from which they derive strong inferences using either national time series, or much worse from cross-country regressions.[2] In an important paper, Bosworth, Collins, and Virmani (2006; hereafter BCV) rightly note the extreme fragility of the annual time series data. For as most of India's output and employment is in the unorganized sector, the only reliable estimates on

---

[2]   For discussion of these weaknesses of the cross-country, cross-section studies that have recently proliferated, see Srinivasan and Bhagwati (2001).

them is for the dates on which there are data from the quinquennial surveys of households and small enterprises. The annual estimates between the surveys are largely based on interpolations or extrapolations of the underlying source data. Sivasubramonian (2004) provides the only reliable and comprehensive analysis of the national income data until 2000. BCV have relied on an extension of his data, including recent revisions of the national accounts to derive quinquennial growth accounts for India from 1960 to 2005. They have also derived additional growth accounts for the subsectors, agriculture, industry, manufacturing, and services, and have included estimates of the contributions of the improvement in the quality of the labor force through education. Their estimates are presented in Table 4.2 for the aggregate economy and Table 4.3 for the major subsectors.[3] From Table 4.2, BCV (2006, p.17) conclude,

> Growth in output per worker strengthened from 1.8 per cent in 1973–83 to 2.9 per cent in 1983–93 and 5.8 per cent in 1993–99. These figures seem to imply a sustained improvement in the underlying trend. However, they do not allow us to pin down the precise timing of the growth acceleration. Growth did slow over the 1999–04 period, but this appears largely due to a severe agricultural drought in 2002–03. Moreover, preliminary data for 2005–06 suggest a strong 8.4 per cent annual growth rate, and a three-year average about 8 per cent.

As the growth rate in both 2005–06 and 2006–07 have now been officially estimated to be over 9 per cent per year, this record would yield an average annual growth rate of 8.6 per cent in the four years following the drought of 2002–03.

---

[3] For an alternative growth accounting based on the traditional contribution of capital, labor and technical progress derived from the official time series, see Singh and Bery (2005).

Table 4.2 Source of economic growth, major sectors, 1960–2005 (annual percentage rate of change)

Period	Output	Employment	Output per worker	Contributions of			
				Physical capital	Land	Education	Total factor productivity
1960–04	4.7	2.0	2.6	1.2	-0.1	0.3	1.2
1960–80	3.4	2.2	1.3	1.0	-0.2	0.2	0.2
1980–04	5.8	1.9	3.8	1.4	0.0	0.4	2.0
1960–73	3.3	2.0	1.3	1.1	-0.2	0.1	0.2
1973–83	4.2	2.4	1.8	0.9	-0.2	0.3	0.6
1983–93	5.0	2.1	2.9	0.9	-0.1	0.3	1.7
1993–99	7.0	1.2	5.8	2.4	-0.1	0.4	2.8
1999–04	6.0	2.4	3.6	1.2	0.1	0.4	2.0

Source: Bosworth, Collins, and Virmani (2006).

Table 4.3 *Source of economic growth, major sectors, 1960–2005 (annual percentage rate of change)*

Period	Output	Employment	Output per worker	Physical capital	Land	Education	Total factor productivity
				Contributions of			
			Agriculture				
1960–04	2.4	1.4	1.0	0.4	-0.1	0.2	0.6
1960–80	1.9	1.8	0.1	0.2	-0.2	0.1	-0.1
1980–04	2.8	1.0	1.8	0.5	-0.1	0.3	1.1
1960–73	1.8	1.9	-0.1	0.2	-0.2	0.1	-0.2
1973–83	2.9	1.7	1.2	0.3	-0.2	0.2	0.9
1983–93	2.9	1.4	1.5	0.2	-0.1	0.2	1.2
1993–99	2.6	0.2	2.4	0.7	0.1	0.3	1.3
1999–04	1.8	1.0	0.8	0.9	-0.2	0.4	-0.1
			Industry (inclusive of manufacturing)				
1960–04	5.6	3.3	2.3	1.6		0.3	0.3
1960–80	4.7	3.1	1.6	1.8		0.3	-0.4
1980–04	6.4	3.5	2.9	1.6	0.3	1.0	1.0
1960–73	4.7	2.3	2.4	2.3	0.2	-0.1	-0.1
1973–83	5.2	4.5	0.7	1.1	0.3	-0.8	-0.8
1960–73	4.7	2.3	2.4	2.3		0.2	-0.1

Table 4.3 (Continued)

Period	Output	Employment	Output per worker	Contributions of			
				Physical capital	Land	Education	Total factor productivity
1973–83	5.2	4.5	0.7	1.1		0.3	-0.8
1983–93	6.0	2.9	3.1	1.3		0.3	1.4
1993–99	6.9	2.4	4.5	3.0		0.5	1.0
1999–04	6.4	5.5	0.9	-0.1		0.2	0.9
Manufacturing							
1960–04	5.7	2.6	3.1	1.8		0.3	0.9
1960–80	4.6	2.7	2.0	1.5		0.3	0.2
1980–04	6.6	2.6	4.0	2.1		0.4	1.5
1960–73	4.9	1.5	3.4	2.1		0.2	1.1
1973–83	5.3	4.3	1.0	1.0		0.4	-0.3
1983–93	6.0	2.1	3.9	1.3		0.4	2.1
1993–99	7.2	1.7	5.5	4.6		0.6	0.3
1999–04	6.4	4.4	2.0	0.4		0.3	1.4

Table 4.3   (Continued)

Period	Output	Employment	Output per worker	Contributions of				Total factor productivity
				Physical capital	Land	Education		
			Services					
1960–04	6.3	3.2	3.1	0.9	0.4			1.7
1960–80	4.9	2.8	2.0	1.1	0.5			0.4
1980–04	7.6	3.6	4.0	0.7	0.4			2.9
1960–73	4.7	1.9	2.8	1.8	0.4	0.5		0.5
1973–83	5.3	4.2	1.0	0.0	0.5	0.5		0.5
1983–93	6.5	3.8	2.7	0.3	0.4	2.0		2.0
1993–99	10.2	3.1	7.0	1.5	0.5	4.9		4.9
1999–04	7.8	3.5	4.4	0.9	0.4	3.1		3.1

Source: Bosworth, Collins, and Virmani (2006).

4.3.1   Sources of Growth Acceleration

Both the BCV and Singh–Bery growth accounts for the economy as a whole show that the acceleration in growth from the mid 1980s was due less to an increase in factor inputs than to an increase in total factor productivity (TFP), unlike the period until 1983, when most of the growth was due to increased factor inputs. However, improvements in the quality of the labor force from education have contributed modestly to growth performance.

The increase in TFP shows the effects of improved efficiency that followed the movements from the plan to the market and the gradual easing of the economic repression of the Indian economy. Those efficiency gains from economic liberalization, which have become most marked since the 1991 Manmohan Singh reforms, are brought out in the reallocation effects BCV have estimated from their growth accounts (shown in Table 4.4).[4] Usually, these reallocation effects are due to shifts in employment from low productivity uses in agriculture to higher productivity uses in industry. But in India while the share of agriculture in total output has declined, it has only decreased marginally as a share of employment.

Table 4.4   Growth in output per worker (Annual percentage rate of change)

Period	Total economy (1)	Weighted sectoral growth (2)	Reallocation effects (1) - (2)
1960–80	1.3	0.9	0.4
1980–04	3.8	2.8	1.0
1960–73	1.3	1.1	0.2
1973–83	1.8	1.0	0.8
1983–93	2.9	2.3	0.6
1993–99	5.8	4.8	1.0
1999–04	3.6	2.4	1.2

Source: Bosworth, Collins, and Virmani (2006).

To determine the sources of these reallocation gains we need to look at the sectoral growth accounts in Table 4.3. Those for agriculture confirm the effects of the Green Revolution that took off in 1973 and strengthened in the 1980s. It raised the TFP rate in agriculture until 1999. Thereafter, as it

---

[4] These have been derived from Tables 4.1 and 4.2, which give the total and sector growth in output per worker and the sectoral shares to give the figures in column (2) of Table 4.3. The reallocation effects are then given by the difference between the first two columns.

reached its limits with virtually the whole irrigable area being irrigated, these TFP gains have disappeared, with growth being dependent on increasing factor inputs (as in the pre-Green Revolution Boserupian phase) subject to diminishing returns. The seemingly surprising growth in agricultural employment in the Green Revolution period (1973–99) is due to its labor intensive nature. With this process having reached its limits, the prospects for further increases in agricultural employment are not bright.

For industry as a whole, there was an acceleration of TFP in the 'reform by stealth' period from 1983, which remained constant in the first post-reform period, fell during the investment slump after 1999, and should have recovered in the last four years of 8.6 per cent growth. In the two, pre-1991 and immediate post-reform 1993 periods, there was little industrial employment growth, though this changed with a rise in the industrial employment growth rate to over 5 per cent since 1999. Much of industrial growth was due to capital deepening. The trends for the manufacturing subsector are similar. The low labor absorption by industry, and its continuing capital intensity, reflects both the failure of India to rescind its nineteenth century labor laws, which raise the relative price of its most abundant factor, as well as the reservations for the relatively labor intensive small-scale sector, which prevents their expansion to garner both economies of scale and increase unskilled labor employment. In contrast, China's post-reform growth was based on a massive expansion of its private sector originating from the township and village enterprises established after Deng Xiaoping began to liberalize the economy in 1978. Whether the recent introduction of Special Economic Zones (SEZs) to overcome these constraints will allow India to use its abundant factor of production, low-skilled labor, efficiently in its future industrialization remains to be seen.

The rise in the growth of industrial employment from 1999 to 2004 and the acceleration of industrial growth from 6.4 per cent to 8.4, and to 10.8 per cent in 2006–07, suggests that the economic effects of the ending of the Permit Raj in 1991 and India's growing integration with the world economy are now at last bearing fruit. This enhanced performance is consistent with the experience of supply-side reforms in other countries. For example, Thatcher's reforms of the 1980s did not begin to bear fruit until the mid-1990s. India's recent trends augur well for the future growth of the industrial sector.

The most surprising feature of the sectoral Indian growth accounts (Table 4.3) is that services have been the main growth agent since the 1980s, growing faster than both industry and manufacturing, while having comparable rates of growth in employment. The major source of the surge in services growth is due to TFP growth rates of about 3 per cent per year. Also there is a large improvement in the quality of the labor force as compared with the other sectors. BCV argue that as the modern services sector including the burgeoning IT and communications sectors, only contributed less than 4 per cent to total services' growth, of 7.8 per cent between 1993 and 2004, the data imply that the bulk of TFP growth in services is accounted by traditional services. But this goes against all international experience. BCV's hypothesis is that the prices of services in the Indian national accounts are being underestimated, leading to an overestimate of their real rate of growth.

Summing up, agricultural growth based on the Green Revolution has been a major source of India's acceleration of growth from its pre-Independence levels. Agriculture has also absorbed much of the increase in the labor force, even as its share in output has shrunk. But it is now reaching its limits, with diminishing returns setting in on the 'new' agricultural production function. Industrial and manufacturing growth rates have risen, most markedly in the last four years. But industrial employment growth has been anemic. Increased factor inputs, rather than dramatic increases in TFP, account for most of the growth in the industrial and manufacturing sectors. The fastest growth rate has been in services, which accounts for a large part of the recent growth acceleration. This has been due to both increased factor inputs and high rates of TFP growth, which is not confined merely to the modern services of business, finance, and communications but has also occurred in the traditional services. This is an internationally atypical pattern of growth. But, statistical problems in underestimating the price of services and, hence, an exaggeration of the real growth rate of the sector may explain this anomaly.

4.4   OUTLOOK TO 2030

In examining the outlook to 2030, it is useful to identify the constraints on Indian growth that were widely held to be responsible for the derisory Hindu rate of growth until 1980. These were a shortage of savings and foreign exchange.

The inward-looking heavy industry biased industrialization strategy, rationalized in the Mahalanobis model, was based on a development path that could break the foreign exchange bottleneck purportedly facing India. Meanwhile, a large public sector in the 'commanding heights' of the economy was expected to generate profits to bolster the economy's savings rate. As was made clear by many observers, including the present author, the foreign exchange bottleneck became a self-fulfilling prophecy because of the dirigiste trade and exchange rate polices India followed with their heavy indirect tax on exports. When these policies began to change in the 1980s, and more fully after the 1991 reforms, India's exports went from 0.1 per cent of world exports in 2001 to 1 per cent today. In 2006–07, exports grew by more than 30 per cent (Economic Survey, 2005–06, Table 6.4; Economic Survey, 2006–07, 113).

India's share of world trade (one sixth) is tiny when compared with China, which became the world's third largest trading country in 2003, when its foreign trade increased by over $200 billion – twice the level of India's total trade in 2002. However, in 2005 and 2006, India's export growth rate surpassed China's.

India's poor export performance compared with China is because protection has declined substantially in the post-reform period, but is still high, unlike China, which has carried out one of the largest unilateral liberalizations of trade since Britain's repeal of the Corn Laws. Further trade liberalization will allow growing efficiency gains to the Indian economy, boosting its growth rate. Yet, even the limited trade liberalization together with the maintenance of an undervalued exchange rate has led to burgeoning foreign exchange reserves, which in 2005–06 stood at $134 billion or 19 per cent of Indian GDP, and have risen further to over $200 billion in 2007. So, limited foreign exchange is no longer a constraint on Indian growth.

India's gross domestic savings have increased from about 15 per cent in 1960–79 to 32.4 per cent in 2005–06. The bulk of this increase is due to a substantial rise in the household savings rate from 10.4 per cent in 1960–79 to 22.3 per cent of GDP in 2005–06. The private corporate sector's savings rate has risen from 1.5 per cent in 1960–79 to 8.1 per cent in 2005–06. The public-sector savings rate reached a peak in 1980–84 of 3.7 per cent and became negative in 1990–91, largely due to rising fiscal deficits of the state and central governments. There has been a turnaround since 2003–04, with the public-sector savings rate being 2 per cent in 2005–06. This improved public-sector savings performance is largely due to a reduction of both the centre and state fiscal deficits, due to rising tax revenues with growing output, as well as a simplification and reduction of marginal central direct tax rates and the adoption of a value-added tax instead of sales taxes by many states that have improved tax compliance. The latest (12th) Finance Commission's recommendation of tying debt relief to the state enactment of fiscal reform and budget management acts, which mandate the reduction of their revenue deficits, has also brought down their budget deficits. However, the period of public dissavings was also caused by the growing losses in public-sector industries, whose privatization has stalled because of the veto exercised by the communist coalition partners of the current government. If they are privatized, as they should be, it will further reduce the public sector's draft on domestic savings.

As India has just begun its demographic transition, it can be expected to have a private savings bonanza until the population stabilizes by 2045, when the United Nations estimates it will be 1.6 billion, and thereafter begins to age. The proportion of the population in the 15–64 working age group is expected to increase from 62.9 per cent in 2006 to 68.1 per cent in 2026. With the total fertility rate reaching the replacement rate of 2.1 by 2010, total population will continue to increase until 2045. During these three decades of the demographic transition India's savings rate should rise. Private savings rates could well rise to over 30 per cent by 2030. If the public sector does not dissave and corporate savings remain at the current level of 8 per cent, India's gross domestic savings rate could well be 38–40 per cent over the next two decades. So, clearly India does not face any savings constraint in the near future.

Foreign capital inflows into India before the 1991 economic reforms were mainly in the form of foreign direct investment (FDI), and only 0.2 per cent of GDP on average until 1992–93. Since the reforms they increased to 1.6 per cent of GDP in 1996–97 and about 2 per cent of GDP since 2003 (Government of India, 2006, *Economic Survey 2006–07*: p. 127). In the years since 2003, most of the foreign investment in India has been portfolio rather than direct investment, in the form of foreign institutional investment (FII). Thus, in 2004–05, of the total of $12 billion of foreign inflows, FDI flows were only 3.2 billion the rest being FII. Bhalla (2006) has estimated that because China's inflows are mainly in the form of FDI, reflecting the limited financial reforms it has undertaken, the share of both FDI and FII in GDP in the two countries since 2003–04 have been about the same at 3–5 per cent of GDP (as China has a higher GDP than India's).

Gross domestic investment has risen to 31.5 per cent of GDP in 2004–05 and 33.8 per cent in 2005–06. If the domestic savings rate increases to 35 per cent and the foreign savings rate to 5 per cent, gross domestic investment could increase to 40 per cent. Singh and Bery (2005) estimate that the ICOR (gross capital formation as a percentage of GDP), has been stable at about 4 since 1995. This would then yield a 10 per cent growth rate in the foreseeable future,[5] even without any further reforms.

Bhalla (2006) reaches a similar conclusion using a simplified growth accounting framework. The annual growth rate between 1993 and 2000 was about 6 per cent, with an investment rate of about 24 per cent of GDP. If the investment rate rises to 40 per cent, the growth contribution of the extra 15

---

[5] Bhalla (2006) maintains 'that projections based on econometric analysis of investment spending, non-food credit, bank credit to industry, real interest rates etc., give a minimum estimate of investment spending as a share of GDP of 41 per cent in 2006–07'. If this is correct it would yield a growth rate of 10 per cent in 2006–07. Given the two-year lag in getting firm official national income statistics, we will have to wait and see if this is true.

per cent in the share of investment will lead to a growth contribution of 2.3 per cent per year, as each extra percentage point increase in investment leads to a 0.15 per cent increase in the GDP growth rate. Adding 1.3 per cent per year due to labor force and increases in TFP yields a trend growth rate of 9.6 per cent per year.

From the partial quantitative evidence that is available for the two years since 2004–05 (as the capital formation, and savings data is produced with a two-year lag) there does appear to have been a structural break in the performance of the Indian economy since 2003–04. In fact, many Indian economic observers have been puzzled by this more recent growth acceleration as the reform process is by and large stalled, because of the veto imposed by the communist coalition partners of the government to rescind the colonial labor laws, to allow foreign investment into many sectors, and the refusal to privatize the remaining dysfunctional public sector industries. The major reforms have been in the financial sector where India has now largely reversed the financial repression of the planned era, and is able to efficiently mediate savings and investments through its banks and stock markets. This is in stark contrast with the continuing financial repression in China.

The main factor (apart from the jump in the investment rate from about 25 per cent until 2002–03 to nearly 34 per cent in 2005–06) in the most recent growth acceleration without further reforms is more likely to be due to the lagged adjustments in private producers' expectations (particularly in the industrial sector) to the ending of the automatic protection they had previously obtained from both foreign and domestic competition through the industrial licensing and import control systems.

With the liberalization of these controls, industrial producers would have been left with redundant and unprofitable production lines. They would have to retool and create fresh capacity to meet the demand generated by the new open economy price structure. This takes time. I surmise that by 2003 these adjustments had been made and Indian industry was able to grow more efficiently, with the manufacturing sector growing at the rate of 9.2 per cent in 2004–05, 9.1 per cent in 2005–06, and 11.5 per cent in 2006–07 (Government of India, 2006, *Economic Survey, 2006–07*: p.136).

One example of this changed industrial mind-set and its likely future contribution to Indian growth is provided by the relatively labor intensive automobile components industry. The Indian automobile industry until the 1991 reforms was a byword for inefficient production behind high protective barriers. With the reforms and delicensing of car production, India has become a major producer of a whole series of domestically produced cars and auto components, whose output has grown from $4.47 billion on 2001–02 to $10 billion in 2005–06, with most major automobile manufacturers outsourcing their component manufacture to India. Since 2002, exports of auto components have been growing at over 30 per cent per year (NCAER, 2006).

The recent rush of India's big business houses to go global by purchasing foreign companies (of which Tata Steel's acquisition of Corus is an example) also demonstrates industry's newfound confidence in taking on the world. This global thrust by private Indian entrepreneurs is different from the state-led one being organized by China to convert some of its state and state-fronted large enterprises into global champions (see Lal, 2006b). The Indian corporate sector is also beginning to extend its reach into the rural sector by organizing contract farming as part of a seamless supply chain from the farm to local urban supermarkets. This is going to lead to the next stage of agricultural development (the Green Revolution having reaching its limits) with the move to more high-valued crops like fruits and vegetables. The Indian corporate sector, envisaging a supply chain from the farm to the towns and then to export markets, is also increasingly investing in the infrastructure that will be required (see Witsoe, 2006). But the recent political backlash against the growth of retail supermarkets, which it is feared will kill the traditional 'mom and pop' stores that have dominated retail trade in India, may delay these developments.

As Bhalla (2006) shows, India's current infrastructure development lags China's by 10 years, and its existing infrastructure closely parallels that of China in 1995. So India's infrastructure is likely to expand with its accelerated growth rate. But, increasingly, unlike China it will be privately provided. This reflects another emerging trend. Despite protestations to the contrary, the Indian state has by and large failed to aid economic development. This is because of the inevitable degeneration of its politics to populist pressures and the ensuing degradation of economic policymaking by blatant rent seeking. Under the Nehruvian settlement, despite large increases in public investment, the Indian state abysmally failed to efficiently provide the requisite quality and quantity of non-traded goods like power, transport, clean water, and sanitation as well as the merit goods of health and education. Since the 1991 reforms and the ensuing acceleration of per capita income, many of the old avenues for rent seeking have been closed. With the fiscal burden of large, unjustified public subsidies to power and irrigation continuing and with the limits of overt taxation having been reached, the government remains in a fiscal bind and has had to rely on public-private partnerships (PPPs) for the provision of these non-traded goods. Though this new organizational form (along with the creation of the SEZs on the Chinese model) provides a new avenue for rent-seeking, the PPPs are likely to provide a more efficient alternative than the previous state monopoly in providing these non-traded goods.

Finally, and perhaps most important of all, by greatly diminishing the area in which the dead hand of the state now operates, the 1991 reforms have created much more space for private agents to act. Unlike China, India has had a flourishing civil society for over 100 years (some would say for millennia). It is increasingly taking over in areas where the state has failed to provide the necessary services. A few examples will suffice.

With the failure of the state to live up to its constitutional obligation to provide primary education for all the people, despite large public expenditures, even the poorest are now sending their children to private schools. Moreover, most Indians, including the poorest, rely on private provision for their health because of the inefficiencies and low quality in public provision.

In agriculture, the failures of state provision and the corrupt state-controlled allocation of irrigation water have led to an explosion of private provision through tube wells that exploit the giant aquifer below the Indo–Gangetic northern plain. This has created a massive problem of 'the commons', as the unregulated growth in ground water irrigation leads to exploitation of the sub-continental aquifer (see Shah, 2006; Johl, 2006 and Vaidyanathan, 2006). The government has at last woken up to this problem.

The failure of the state to provide a reliable power supply has led to the development of an informal parallel grid in many urban areas. Shop owners have set up collective kerosene or diesel generators, each of which provides lighting to 50 to 100 shopkeepers and vendors in a neighborhood or marketplace. The fee charged is based on the number of light bulbs connected during a certain number of hours each evening. Though the cost per unit is much higher than it would be if provided by the public grid, given the latter's failures, shopkeepers can decide if the benefit of attracting customers in the evening shopping hours outweigh the higher costs.

Another example is provided by the private cable television operators, who by 1990 had connected 30 million urban households to cable TV through their local satellite dishes. These were more than the telephone connections the public sector companies had managed to install in the previous 50 years.[6]

Finally, the granting of private licenses to mobile phone companies in the 1990s has created a virtual telecommunications revolution that has reached even remote villages. This is in stark contrast to the old regime monopolized by state telephone companies, which are now gradually going to the wall.

The greatest prize offered by economic liberalization is in the changed perceptions of the young. One of the baleful effects of the Nehruvian

---

[6] See Mitra (2006) for these and other examples of private provision replacing public for many quasi-public goods.

settlement was that the economic policies supported by the English speaking castes damaged the prospects of their progeny, except for those agile enough to become rent seekers. They, as well as others among the political classes, then sought and succeeded in placing their progeny in jobs abroad, thereby demonstrating by their private actions the bankruptcy of the public policies they supported. From international experience, I have come to see the ability of a country to retain its 'best and brightest' as an important sign that it is on the road to economic prosperity. With economic liberalization the perceptions of the young about the possibilities of a fruitful life in India have changed. There is a vitality and élan among the 'best and the brightest' in India, with a growing belief that even when based in their homeland, the world is now their oyster. But this optimism could change with the current government's desire to extend caste-based reservations of places in government-aided educational institutions and public employment, hitherto confined to the scheduled castes and tribes to the more numerous Other Backward Castes (OBCs). These would amount to 50 per cent of the available places. It is even proposed to extend these reservations to employees in the private sector.

If all these proposals of basing economic outcomes on birth not merit are enacted, we can say goodbye to a knowledge-based 'Incredible India' being touted by politicians. It would be a reenactment on an Indian canvas and Indian characteristics based on caste of the Chinese Cultural Revolution, which had implemented class-based reservations for employment and education and in the process lost a whole generation of well-educated youth. Deng reversed this policy and oversaw the creation of a highly educated, technocratic class of meritocratic mandarins, and increasingly a meritocratic society.

India's past policy of reservations has already seriously affected governance, by damaging the functioning of the public sector (Shourie, 2006). Moreover, as the eminent Indian sociologist, the late M.N. Srinivas (1996) noted, existing reservations led the 'forward' castes to evolve a strategy for survival – namely, emigration. It would be retrograde and greatly damage India's economic future, if the current rush to reservations were to lead India's 'best and brightest' to once again look abroad for their future. As many Indian observers have noted, the way to deal with the problems faced by the economically and socially disadvantaged is not through reservations in higher education and employment, but to provide them the means to compete in a meritocratic society. This above all means access to primary and secondary schools. The Indian state's abysmal failure to provide the merit goods of education and health to its populace has increasingly led even the poorest to rely on private provision. Ideally what India needs is a program of state-funded vouchers so the disadvantaged could finance their use of private-sector services. Whether the dysfunctional Indian state can implement this efficiently remains doubtful. But, perhaps NGOs could be usefully used to distribute the vouchers to their intended beneficiaries.

Despite these prospective woes and the ever present danger that a dysfunctional political system might still shoot the economy in the foot, I believe that given the space available since the 1991 liberalization for private action, combined with the flexibility private agents in civil society have shown in getting around state failure, issues of governance are now less likely to damage India's economic future. Thus, it might not be too rash to predict that India will be able to grow at about 10 per cent per year, which with population growing at 1.5–1 per cent would lead to a per capita income growth of about 8.5–9 per cent per year for the next two decades. India will be the fourth economic miracle I have witnessed in my lifetime – Japan in the early 1960s, Korea in the early 1970s, China in the 1990s, and now India.

REFERENCES

Bosworth, B., S.M. Collins and A. Virmani (2006), *Sources of Growth in the Indian Economy*, India Policy Forum 2006–07, ER and the Brookings Institution, New Delhi: Sage.

Boserup, E. (1965), *The Conditions of Agricultural Growth*, London: Allen and Unwin.

Bhalla, S. (2006), 'Second among Equals: The Middle Class Kingdoms of India and China', Mimeographed.

Delong, J.B. (2002), *India since Independence: An Analytic Growth Narrative*, Available at http//:ksghome.harvard.edu/drodrik/growth volume/Delong-India.pdf.

Government of India (2006), *Economic Survey 2005–06*, New Delhi: Economic Division, Ministry of Finance.

Government of India (2007), *Economic Survey 2006–07*, New Delhi: Economic Division, Ministry of Finance.

Johl, S.S. (2006), 'Environment in Degradation and Its Correctives in the Agricultural Sector', ICRIER's Silver Jubilee Conference, ICRIER, New Delhi.

Lal, D. (1985), *The Poverty of Development Economics*, Cambridge, Mass.: Harvard University Press.

Lal, D. (1987), 'The Political Economy of Economic Liberalization', *World Bank Economic Review*, **1** (2), 273–99.

Lal, D. (2005), *The Hindu Equilibrium: India c.1500 B.C–2000 A.D.* (Revised and abridged ed.), Oxford: Oxford University Press.

Lal, D. (2006a), 'India: Population Change and Its Consequences', *Population and Development Review*, **32** (supp.), 121–58.

Lal, D. (2006b), 'A Proposal to Privatize Chinese Enterprises and End Financial Repression', *Cato Journal*, **26** (2), 275–86.

Lal, D. (2006c), *Reviving the Invisible Hand: The Case for Classical Liberalism in the 21st Century*, Princeton, N.J.: Princeton University Press.

Lewis, J.P. (1962), *Quiet Crisis in India*, Washington: Brookings Institution.

Little, I.M.D. (1982), *Economic Development: Theory, Policies and International Relations*, New York: Basic Books.

Mitra, B. (2006), *Grassroots Capitalism Thrives in India*, in M.A. Miles, K.M. Holmes and M.A. O'Grady (eds), *Index of Economic Freedom*, chap. 3, Washington: Heritage Foundation and Wall Street Journal.

NCAER (2006), *Quarterly Review of the Economy*, New Delhi: NCAER (November).

Panagriya, A. (2005), 'India in the 1980s and the 1990s: A Triumph of Reforms', in W. Tseng and D. Cowen (eds), *India's and China's Recent Experience with Reform and Growth*, Basingstoke, UK: Palgrave Macmillan.

Rodrik, D. (2002), *Institutions, Integration and Geography: In Search of the Determinants of Economic Growth*, Available at http://ksghome.harvard.edu/~drodrik/growthintro.pdf.

Shah, T. (2006), 'India's Irrigation Economy: In the Throes of a Transition', Paper presented at ICRIER Silver Jubilee Celebrations, ICRIER, New Delhi.

Shourie, A. (2006), *Falling Over Backwards: An Essay on Reservations and Judicial Populism*, New Delhi: ASA Publication.

Singh, K., and S. Bery (2005), 'India's Growth Experience', In W. Tseng and D. Cowen (eds.), *India and China's Recent Experience with Reform and Growth*, Basingstoke, UK: Palgrave Macmillan.

Sivasubramonian, S. (2004), *The National Income of India in the Twentieth Century*, New Delhi: Oxford University Press.

Srinivas, M.N. (1996), *Village, Caste, Gender and Method*, New Delhi: Oxford University Press.

Srinivasan, T.N. (2003), *Indian Economic Reforms: A Stocktaking*, Stanford Center for International Development, *Working Paper* No. **190**.

Srinivasan, T.N. and J. Bhagwati, (2001), 'Outward-Orientation and Development: Are the Revisionists Right?', in D. Lal and R. Snape (eds), *Trade, Development and Political Economy: Essays in Honour of Anne O. Krueger*, Basingstoke, UK: Palgrave Macmillan.

Vaidyanathan, A. (2006), *Agrarian Crisis: Nature, Causes and Remedies*, The Hindu (8 November).

Wallack, J.S. (2003), 'Structural Breaks in Indian Macroeconmic Data', *Economic and Political Weekly* (11 October), 4312–4315.

Witsoe, J. (2006), *India's Second Green Revolution? The Sociopolitical Implications of Corporate-led Agricultural Growth*, Philadelphia: Center for Advanced Studies of India, University of Pennsylvania.

World Bank (2007), *World Development Report*, Washington, DC.

5. Analysis of Russian Performance since 1990 and Future Outlook[1]

Stanislav Menshikov

5.1 OVERVIEW

This chapter reviews the anatomy of Russia's economic performance 1991–2005 decomposing GDP statistical data into principal utilization components. It accounts for the long depression of 1991–1998 and the subsequent economic expansion of 1999–2005. Dependency on fuel and metals exports is traced to the practical disappearance of government defence expenditure and sharp decline in capital investment. The deceleration inertia in the economy is explained by the persistent narrowness of the domestic market caused by the combination of low wages and the skewed distribution of gross profit. The average annual growth rate is decomposed into principal production factors. This analysis is used as a basis for determining future growth for 2004–2015 and subsequently for 2016–2030. Projected growth in Russia's GDP is compared with projected data for 14 other nations and world GDP. In this projection Russia moves from its current tenth place in the world to fifth place in 2030 after China, USA, India, and Japan.

5.2 PERFORMANCE IN 1991–2005

From the standpoint of Russian economic dynamics, two periods may be clearly distinguished: (i) the overall decline of production in 1992–1998, with a short pause in the stagnation year of 1997; and (ii) the overall growth of production, starting in 1999.

---

[1] This chapter is based on a paper presented at the Workshop on World Economic Performance: Past, Present, and Future, University of Groningen, the Netherlands, October 27, 2006, on the Occasion of Angus Maddison's 80th Birthday; and Section 5.6 written in August, 2009.

The specific features of these two periods are evident from the data presented in Table 5.1.

Table 5.1   Russian GDP by utilisation, 1991–2005

Year	GDP		Personal consumption		State consumption		Gross fixed capital investment	
	1	2	1	2	1	2	1	2
1992	85.5	-14.5	69.6	-30.4	72.3	-27.7	88.7	-11.3
1993	78.1	-8.7	70.4	+1.2	67.7	-6.4	65.8	-25.8
1994	68.1	-12.7	71.3	+1.2	65.7	-2.9	48.7	-26.0
1995	65.3	-4.1	69.3	2.8	66.4	+1.1	45.0	-7.5
1996	60.9	-6.7	66.0	-4.7	66.9	+0.8	36.4	-19.3
1997	61.5	+0.9	69.6	5.4	65.3	-2.4	34.3	-5.7
1998	58.9	-4.3	67.9	-2.4	65.7	+0.6	30.9	-9.8
1999	61.3	+4.7	65.6	-3.4	66.1	+3.0	32.4	+4.7
2000	67.0	+8.7	71.4	+8.9	67.2	+1.6	37.4	+15.5
2001	70.1	+4.9	77.7	+8.7	66.6	-0.9	41.7	+11.4
2002	73.4	+4.7	84.3	+8.5	68.3	+2.6	42.9	+2.8
2003	78.7	+7.3	90.6	+7.5	69.8	+2.2	48.4	+12.8
2004	84.4	+7.2	100.8	+11.3	71.4	+2.3	53.6	+10.8
2005	89.8	+6.4	112.0	+11.1	72.8	+1.8	59.2	+10.5

Notes: 1: Index (1991 = 100); 2: Year–on–year growth (+) or decrease (-), %

Source: Russian Statistical Yearbook for relevant years.

5.2.1   The Crisis and Stagnation of 1992–1998

The cumulative collapse of GDP during the seven years of the first period was 41.1 per cent, or 7 per cent annually on average. The greatest rates of decline were experienced in the initial reform period (1992–1994), after which the rate of shrinkage became comparatively moderate. The composition of the collapse varied from year to year. In 1992, for example, every single domestic component of GDP fell sharply: personal consumption by 30 per cent, government consumption by 28 per cent and the accumulation of fixed capital by 11 per cent. The domestic market essentially collapsed, and it was only the forty-fold increase of net exports (achieved through the contraction of imports) that held the officially reported total decline of GDP in 1992 to 14.5 per cent. In reality, domestic demand shrank by 22.5 per cent, with the greatest part (almost 60 per cent) of the contraction being accounted for by personal consumption, more than a fifth (22 per cent) by government consumption, and another fifth (19.5 per cent) by fixed capital investment.

Thus the main factor in the acute crisis experienced by the economy was shock therapy, in the form of the instantaneous decontrol, without proper preparation, of the vast majority of prices, especially the prices of consumer goods and services. In the resultant inflationary spiral, personal incomes lagged behind the rising prices. In a single year, the real disposable income of the population fell by 47.4 per cent. Inflation also devalued enterprises' working capital, to the extent that the enterprises were forced to make drastic cutbacks in production and investment in fixed capital. But the scale of collapse of capital investment during that first year, large as it was, still lagged behind the rate of decline of personal consumption. Some capital construction or new equipment programs continued by the force of inertia, carried forward from previous years.

Unlike these spontaneous processes, the reduction of state consumption was slashed by the government deliberately and with forethought. Yegor Gaidar, the acting prime minister in that initial period, relates in his memoirs how, in November 1991, he convened the executive board of Gosplan, the state planning authority, and ordered steep reductions in weapons and military equipment production targets. In 1992 alone, real defense spending shrank by 46 per cent, while the output of military equipment and weapons fell by 50.5 per cent. On a macroeconomic scale, this was equivalent to a 20 per cent contraction of aggregate domestic demand. But the actual destructive impact was at least twice as great, since the collapse of defense production was followed by a steep reduction of demand for the output of related sectors of the economy.

The crisis shock of 1992 resulted practically entirely from the economic and financial policies of the Gaidar government. Had it not been for the inflationary take-off of prices, caused by those policies, and the administrative reduction of defense spending, the decline of production would have been much less. For all practical purposes, it was predominantly a government created crisis.

In this section we concentrate on an analysis of each component of the GDP decline, without going into the accompanying institutional changes, which played a destructive role of their own. By institutional changes, we mean the collapse of the previous system of central planning and distribution of output, the liquidation of centralized planning and financing of capital investment, the destruction of Russia's economic ties with the former Union republics, the destruction of cooperation in the framework of the Comecon, etc. All of these processes played an enormous role, but our objective in this section is to present a quantitative estimate of the composition of the shrinkage of the final product. Let us sum up our analysis of the components of GDP for the entire 1991–1998 period (see Table 5.2).

Table 5.2   Anatomy of GDP shrinkage, 1991–1998

	1991	1998	1991–98	% change
	Change as % of 1991 GDP			
GDP	100.0	58.9	- 41.1	100
Personal consumption	41.4	32.2	- 9.2	22.4
State consumption	26.9	11.0	- 15.9	38.7
Gross fixed capital investment	23.8	10.0	- 13.8	33.6
Net export of goods and services	0.3	4.2	+ 3.9	-9.5

Source: Russian Statistical Yearbook for relevant years.

The predominant factors in decline and stagnation in this period as a whole were state consumption, which accounts for nearly 40 per cent of the absolute shrinkage of GDP, gross fixed invested (another third) and household consumption, which accounts for 22 per cent. The only positive factor was an increase in net exports of goods and services, which, however, at the time was comparatively small (+ 10 per cent).

The differences in the dynamics of these various components are of fundamental importance. Both personal and government consumption plunged practically right away, in 1992–1993, after which time they remained depressed at a low level. The decline of fixed investment, however, continued throughout the entire period, making continued overall crisis, and then stagnation, inevitable, despite the stabilization of personal and government consumption.

Since total final consumption remained essentially unchanged after 1994, the subsequent significant and persistent decline of capital investment cannot be explained solely by the contraction of domestic market demand. To some extent, the decline in investment became an independent and autonomous factor in the overall decline.

Several additional observations are in order at this point. The overall level of consumer demand remained very low during these years and would not have inspired new investment. Moreover, the share of imports in domestic sales was steadily rising, which set the stage for a further reduction of domestic consumer goods production. This was reflected both in the stagnating level of heavy industry output, which consisted chiefly of products for intermediate consumption. Output continued to decline in the overwhelming majority of industrial sectors, especially machine-building, light industry, and even the food industry. In 1996–1997 productive capacity utilization in industry stood at only 54 per cent of the level considered normal by the enterprises.[2] Not even large companies were in any position to undertake new investment.

Payments within the economy became increasingly disrupted during these same years. In 1998 the average share of barter in industrial companies' sales (not counting other forms of non-monetary settling of accounts, such as promissory notes) rose to 51 per cent, as against 42 per cent in 1997, 35 per cent in 1996 and 22 per cent in 1995.[3] Under these conditions the prospects for new capital investment in the economy appeared unfavourable. Total capital investment was below even the level necessary for replacement of fixed assets retired due to obsolescence.

5.2.2   A Period of Growth (after 1999)

At the height of the 1998 crisis, few people expected that the economy would be able to turn around quickly and resume even moderate growth. But that is what happened. In the next few years (1999–2005) real GDP grew by 52.5 per cent (an annual average of 6.2 per cent). And though national output in 2005 remained a full 10 per cent lower than the pre-reform level, it presented a decisive contrast to the preceding period.

Two main factors are usually mentioned in analyses of this turnaround:

1.   The nearly 85 per cent devaluation of the ruble, which made a significant portion of domestic products price-competitive with imports and produced a strong import-substitution effect; and,
2.   The sharp increase of prices of exported oil and natural gas, which significantly increased the resources available for economic growth.

The first hypothesis is largely substantiated. In fact, imports did begin a steep decline in 1998, both due to falling demand as a result of financial paralysis and a sharp increase of import prices. The result was a reduction of imports by 20 per cent that year. But the steepest decline occurred in 1999, when imports were 45 per cent lower than in 1997, and 32 per cent below the 1998 level (Table 5.3).

Imports made a gradual comeback in subsequent years, but the 1997 pre-crisis year level was surpassed only six years later, in 2003. By that time, import-substitution had been used up as a growth factor.

---

[2] For further analysis of recent Russian economic trends see Menshikov (2003, 2005, and 2007).

[3] For more details see Menshikov (2007).

World Economic Performance

Table 5.3   Imports, 1997–2003

Year	Billions of dollars	1997=100
1997	72	100
1998	58	80.6
1999	39.5	54.9
2000	44.9	62.4
2001	53.8	74.7
2002	60.9	84.5
2003	75.4	104.7

Source: Russian Statistical Yearbook for relevant years.

Oil and natural gas export prices were able to spur nominal GDP, but they made only an indirect impact on real GDP growth. Rising prices led to increased oil and gas production. But the industry represented only 13 per cent of total industrial output, and 6.5 per cent of value added in the economy as a whole. Consequently this sector directly accounted for only 3.2 out of the 52.5 per cent increase of GDP in 1998–2005.

An indirect additional impact of higher oil and gas export prices on real GDP growth is also observable: (1) through the use of this sector's gross profits to finance capital investment in the fuels industry, as well as other sectors; (2) through the redistribution of these profits via the tax mechanism into growing government expenditure; (3) through the oil and gas sector's increased intermediate consumption and higher spending on labor compensation; and (4) through increased banking sector assets due to a substantial petrodollar influx. Continuing our analysis of the components of GDP growth, will help sort out this issue and its significance for overall economic growth. The results are shown in Table 5.4.

According to our calculations domestic demand accounted for 74.4 per cent of total GDP growth, while 25.6 per cent was attributable to net external demand (real growth of exports plus the import-substitution effect). Nearly one-third of the increased demand was accounted for by personal consumption, 20 per cent by capital investment, while increasing government expenditure contributed only 12 per cent – half net exports.

The results shown here are important in several respects. As noted above, personal consumption fell sharply in 1999, before rebounding in the years that followed. On the whole, the relative weight of household consumption increased significantly, becoming the largest growth factor and replacing capital investment in its initial role as the major demand factor. Steady economic growth at fairly high rates is impossible, without capital investment growth in the lead. In fact, it grew at rates that were higher on the average than growth in GDP. However, its role was less significant than that of net exports.

Table 5.4   The anatomy of growth, 1991–2005 (percentage of 1991 GDP)

	1991	1998	1998–1991*	2005	2005–1998	% of change	2005–1991
GDP	100	58.9	- 41.1	89.8	30.9	100	- 10.2
Personal consumption	41.4	32.2	- 9.2	42.2	10.0	32.4	+ 0.8
State consumption	25.9	11.0	- 15.9	14,8	3,8	12.3	-12.1
Gross fixed capital investment	23.8	10.0	- 13.8	16.3	6.3	20.4	-7.5
Net exports of goods and services	(.3	4.2	+ 3.9	12.1	7.9	25.6	+ 11.8

Note: * as a % of 1991 GDP

Source: Russian Statistical Yearbook for relevant years.

Also indicative are changes in the composition of Russia's GDP in the whole period between 1991 and 2005 (see last column of Table 5.4). The largest change is the fall in government consumption (12.1 per cent of pre-reform GDP) and capital investment (7.5 per cent). The reduction in these two items effectively took out a full 20 per cent of pre-reform GDP, only slightly more than a half of that gap was compensated by net exports (12 per cent).

When capital investment growth resumed in 1999–2002, at the good clip of 5 per cent in 1999, 17 per cent in 2000 and 7 per cent in 2001, the question immediately arose of the extent to which it would get the economy and industry as a whole moving. Table 5.5 summarizes the results of calculations designed to show the distribution of capital investment growth by sector.

In 1999–2003 practically the entire real growth of capital investment went to the oil and natural gas industries, ferrous and non-ferrous metallurgy, and communications. Machine-building received only 8 per cent of the increase. In other sectors of industry, capital investment growth in this period was very low. In the critical electric power industry, real investment even fell.

The limited range of sectors receiving capital investment was due to the great difference in profitability levels between the main export sectors, and those producing primarily for the domestic market. Because of super profits in the oil and gas industries, as well as steel and non-ferrous metals, due to favourable external economic conditions, significant investment growth became possible in those sectors. Machine-building experienced some indirect benefit because of orders from export-oriented industries. In most other sectors, however, the temporary restoration of competitiveness through the devaluation of the ruble did not create sufficient incentives for the renovation of fixed assets. Growth in output in these sectors was achieved almost exclusively by making use of idle capacity. The food industry was a partial exception, and only for a short period of time.

Table 5.5　　Distribution of capital investment growth by sector (1999–2003)

	2003/1999
Real growth (%)	50.0
Including (% of total growth)	
Industry	86.4
Fuels	44.1
Steel	13.2
Non-ferrous metallurgy	13.6
Machine-building	8.2
Food industry	2.3
Other industries	5.1
Electric power	-22.2
Transport	-2.7
Communication	18.2
All other sectors	-4.6

Source:　　Our calculations based on Russian Statistical Yearbook for relevant years.

This uneven development resulted in a situation, where, even in years of significantly increased total capital investment, the greater part of the economy's potential to finance capital investment went unrealized. The surplus profit received in the export sectors due to natural and export rent continued to go abroad, rather than being used in capital-deficit sectors.

Thus a dilemma arose: without elimination of that structural imbalance between the rates of profit in these two most important areas of the economy, there would be no renovation of fixed assets. Therefore modernization of the economy as a whole would be blocked, as would the creation of preconditions for rapid economic growth to develop on its own.

To summarise, the basic problem of the Russian economy in the 1990s and early 2000s was that it had lost most of government military and civilian demand that had driven the economy in Soviet times and thus created a large vacuum that had to be filled by other means. This led to two parallel consequences: (i) a sharp decline in aggregate domestic demand via the multiplier mechanism; and (ii) excess supply of capital and intermediate goods that formerly were used by the military-industrial complex but would now have to be largely sold abroad due to the narrowness of the domestic market and high world prices for metals and fuels. This led to the large dependence of economic growth on net exports, which is another way of saying that in its current structure Russia is doomed to producing much more than it can use domestically. A less dramatic way of putting it is that Russia's current growth pattern is export led.

This particular type of growth can only be sustained by a continuous net capital outflow and/or by accumulating excess unused money capital and/or foreign currency reserves. This is exactly what was happening in Russia. By mid 2006, it had accumulated $265 billion of foreign currency reserves and another $59 billion in the federal Stabilisation Fund. In addition, private Russian capital invested abroad over the years is estimated at about $200 billion, bringing the total of domestic underinvestment to $524 billion, or about equal to Russia's annual GDP calculated at the official exchange rate and about half its GDP in PPP dollars.

The outstanding feature of this kind of growth is that financial resources available are far in excess of actual domestic capital investment. Were these funds used for investment inside the country, economic growth could be substantially accelerated.

From another perspective, the situation is somewhat similar to the famous Keynesian $S>I$ formula, where S stands for national savings and I for gross capital investment. In Keynes's analysis, excess national savings occurred in the recession phase of the business cycle, whereas in the Russian case underinvestment came at the recovery stage after a prolonged and deep depression.

5.3 INERTIA MECHANISM OF RUSSIA'S GROWTH DYNAMICS

The type of growth described above is unstable for various reasons. One is the so called "Dutch disease" that infects an economy with a constant balance of payments surplus on current account (external balance on current account is roughly equal to net exports in national accounts statistics). This surplus tends to drive up the country's exchange rate, making its products less competitive in world markets and thus slowing down overall growth. In Russia's case, the ruble/dollar exchange rate hit a high of 31.9 in September 2002 after which it fell to 26.7 by late August 2006. Within four years the ruble had revalued against the dollar by 19.5 per cent. Every billion dollars earned on oil exports in 2002 is equivalent to only 836 millions today. This loss is only relative, rather than absolute due to the drastic rise in export dollar prices. On items where export prices did not rise (e.g. in manufactured goods) the loss to Russian exporters in ruble terms was 16.4 per cent.

Because oil and natural gas account for more than a half of Russia's exports in value terms and because their price sky-rocketed in the early 2000s, the deceleration effect inherent in the export led growth of 1990–2006 has not shown fully, except for the last two years, i.e. 2005–2006. If world-wide prices of fuels simply stay at their current peak levels, Russia's overall growth rate will be somewhat reduced. That is, assuming that the current structure of GDP remains unchanged. However, this present structure reflects two main imbalances that may be overcome through changes in economic policy:

1.   the bias in favor of gross profit at the expense of inadequate labor compensation, leading to an extremely narrow domestic market; and
2.   the bias in favor of the export sectors, sustained by excessively high profitability there.

These two biases underlie the inertia mechanism of the Russian economy that does not permit it to fully utilize its potential for sustained fast growth.

The picture presented in the preceding section, is of a self-perpetuating system, which moves in on its own characteristic trajectory and is extremely difficult to change.

The principal institutional characteristics of the system are these:

- monopolistic practices prevail over competitive ones;
- oligarchic financial groups have a dominant role, while banking is relatively underdeveloped;
- the oligarchy is closely intertwined with the government, which does very little by way of economic regulation;
- the share of gross profit in national income is excessively high; and
- the shadow economy is inordinately large, as is the amount of the national product swallowed by corruption and organized crime.

The prevalence of monopoly – or of oligopoly, to put it more precisely – causes companies to orient, typically, towards obtaining profit more by maximizing profit margins, than by increasing the volume of output and sales. This pattern of behaviour set in during the first few capitalist years, when output was either declining or stagnating, while price inflation continued. Since it made no sense to increase output under such conditions, the only available rational tactic was to maximize short-term profit by playing on the price spreads. In practically no cases during those first years did a company attempt to beat its competitors by lowering prices. On the contrary, every pretext and opportunity to raise prices was seized upon, even in cases where there would seem to have been a possibility of increasing sales at the expense of competitors. This may not always have held true for small business operators, who regularly practiced competitive pricing, but it was the case for the major concerns and even for medium-sized enterprises, which dominated local markets and preferred non-economic means – often involving the use of force – to eliminate their rivals.

The overall competitiveness of Russian producers on the domestic market rose after the financial crisis of 1998, thanks to the steep devaluation of the ruble. This created an opportunity to get ahead of imported goods sellers. For the first time, profit could be increased on the basis of a company's volume of production and sales, rather than only through high profit margins. Even in this new, more favorable situation, however, production was geared up at a pace calculated not to reduce profitability. Of course the result was a faster rate of increase of domestic prices than was justified by market conditions, leading to a fairly rapid loss of the competitive advantages provided by devaluation.

In modern economies, the domination of oligopoly and the lack of competition in pricing often function to stimulate companies to improve product quality and develop new products and market niches, which bring them super-profits, even if only temporarily. This type of behaviour did not materialize in Russia, which instead set out to prove Lenin's dictum, that monopolies cause decay and act as a brake on technological progress, including product differentiation.

Most Russian companies, even large ones with ample resources, simply do not have any well developed long-term strategies preferring instead short-and medium term profit maximisation schemes. In well over a decade of its existence, Russian capitalism has so far built precious few new production plants, contenting itself with use of existing capacities and exploiting natural resource deposits that were explored and essentially developed in Soviet times. Even in a super profit-laden sector like oil and gas, new construction has largely been restricted to building pipelines to the relevant export markets and this has been done by the government at public expense.

Let us return briefly to the question of the economy's tilt towards the fuel and raw materials sectors. As we have explained, what underlies this phenomenon is the uneven distribution of gross profit (surplus value), which is a self-feeding process that will not sort itself out automatically (see Table 5.6). In a well-functioning competitive market system, no sector's profitability (rate of profit) should deviate greatly from the average rate of profit in the economy as a whole. If some industry does have a higher-than-average rate of profit, capital will be attracted there from other sectors, until the profitability of the various sectors evens out. But this leveling will not occur, in the face of economic or natural barriers. In the case of oil and non-ferrous metals in Russia, there are both types of barriers. The oil fields have been seized by a small group of companies, which used their natural and geographical delimitation to shut out new competitors. Conversely the profitability gap blocks capital formed in the fuels and raw materials industries from being invested in other sectors, where the rate of profit is much lower. Thus we have a trap – one of the two vicious circles referred to earlier.

Broadly speaking, the failure to solve this problem is retarding the country's economic growth. GDP growth depends on the rate of growth of its components in each industry. If half of Russia's capital investment, or more, continues to go into the fuel and raw materials sector, that sector will determine the overall GDP growth rate. Since those industries are oriented towards export, their growth rates will be tied to the growth of demand abroad – i.e. to average world economic growth rates. In that case, Russia can forget about faster overall growth and catching up with industrially developed nations in terms of GDP and living standards.

Table 5.6   Profit margins in various branches of industry (profit/sales, %)

	1999	2000	2001	2003
Industry average	25.5	24.7	18.5	13.5
Oil	57.9	66.7	46.5	20.7
Natural gas	22.6	30.0	17.4	20.5
Steel	28.2	25.6	12.5	21.8
Non-Ferrous metals	57.4	51.6	34.4	33.8
electric power	13.7	13.5	15.7	10.1
Machine-building and metal-working	17.4	14.1	13.6	8.7
Chemical and petrochemical	22.3	17.0	11.5	9.0
Wood and paper	23.9	16.5	11.5	7.0
Construction materials	8.6	9.0	9.8	9.5
Light	9.5	7.2	5.4	1.7
Food	13.0	10.1	11.5	8.5

Source: Russian Statistical Yearbook.

Fast growth rates of GDP can be achieved only if the manufacturing industries grow rapidly and that is determined by the potential capacity of the domestic market, which is by no means limited to average world economic growth rates. But the only way for manufacturing, and the economy as a whole, to maintain higher rates is by redistributing capital created in the rent-producing industries, to other sectors. Such a redistribution will only happen with active government intervention.

Only recently has the government tried to directly support two important sectors of manufacturing – aircraft and automobiles. It is consolidating the aircraft building industry into a single holding company under its majority control and has also bought indirect control over the largest car company, AVTOVAZ, with plans to substantially increase its production capacity. Both projects involve heavy capital investment, in part from government funds.

Oligarchic domination of the economy has resulted in a persistently high share of gross profit in national income. The share of labor income is correspondingly too low. Quite apart from the structural bias in favor of the fuel and raw materials sector, this produces the persistent problem of a narrow domestic market that is too small to fully accommodate capital generated in the country. Even if the raw materials tilt were to be eliminated, the existing disproportionately high ratio of gross profit to labor income would make it impossible to realize its potential for maintaining faster overall economic growth.

The share of gross profit in GDP has been around 40 per cent in recent years, while labor income's share (after deducting net indirect taxes) stands at only 44 per cent. Accordingly the share of personal consumption in GDP barely reaches the 50 per cent level. Combining it with gross capital investment's average share (17 per cent of GDP), only 66 per cent of GDP is utilized in the economy as the result of aggregate private demand. In other words, Russia's produced output can be fully sold only if government purchases and net exports together amount to 34 per cent of the total national product. Since half of that portion is consumed by government purchases (17 per cent), another 17 per cent of what Russia produces has to go to net exports, i.e. has to be exported in excess of imports. This is possible only in the extreme situation that an unnaturally large portion of the national product is being sold abroad instead of being used domestically to support faster economic growth.

It would be unrealistic to count on this situation to last for long. A more rational approach would be gradually, but steadily, to increase the share of labor income, and hence of personal consumption, in GDP. In other words, such an approach would expand the domestic market for Russian manufactured goods and thus ensure faster growth of the whole economy.

We can better visualize the problem by comparing the Russian indicators cited here with the long-term proportions in the U.S. economy (see Table 5.7). In the USA, with more normal relative shares of labor income, the total share of personal consumption and gross capital investment in GDP is as high as 85.5 per cent compared to only 66 per cent in Russia. Since government purchases account for 18 per cent, practically all of U.S. national output (in value terms) is sold inside the country, while the relatively small share of exported goods and services is more than compensated by imports.

Table 5.7   Comparison of dynamic proportions of the Russian and U.S.
economies (share in GDP, %, 1998–2005)

	Russia	USA
Gross profit	38.9	35.4
Labour income	44.3	57.7
Personal consumption	49.1	69.3
Gross capital investment	17.0	16.2
Personal consumption and capital investment	66.1	85.5
Government purchases	16.8	18.3
Net exports	17.0	-3.3

Sources: Russian Statistical Yearbook and Statistical Abstract of the U.S

Increasing the share of labor income would help relieve the Russian economy of its excessive dependence on external markets and create a solid foundation for sustained economic growth, oriented mainly towards the domestic market. A similar comparison with China is also relevant.

Table 5.8   China's GDP utilisation structure (2003, per cent of total)

Personal consumption	44
Government consumption	13
Gross capital investment	42
Personal consumption and capital investment	86
Net exports	0 1
GDP	100

Source: World Development Report 2005, Selected Indicators, World Bank, 2005.

As shown in Table 5.8, China is similar to Russia in that its share of personal consumption in GDP is very low. However, together with capital investment, the two items account for 86 per cent of GDP, much larger than in Russia (66.1 per cent) and nearly as much as in the USA. This means that, while China's dependence on exports is substantial, it is able to utilize practically its entire GDP inside the country, including large imports. Its domestic market is therefore relatively wide and its net exports relatively small. The big difference is the much larger share of capital investment (42 per cent in China, 17 per cent in Russia) which makes its faster growth possible.

5.4 FACTORS OF GROWTH: PAST AND FUTURE

Future Russian growth depends on production factors as much as it does on aggregate demand. These are summarized in Table 5.9. These estimates show the very small contribution of growth in stock of fixed capital, which indeed, expanded during this period at the annual rate of only 0.7 per cent. On the other hand labour contributed 2.4 per cent due to falling unemployment and despite declining population figures. Together, capital and labour accounted for only 3.09 per cent, slightly more than 40 per cent of actual GDP growth.

Table 5.9   Factors of growth

	2005/1998	2015/2003	2030/2015
1	2	3	4
Capital	0.69	1.50	2.00
Labour	2.40	2.00	1.00
K + L	3.09	3.50	3.00
Capacity	1.69	0.50	0.00
TFP	2.37	3.00	2.50
GDP	7.15	7.00	5.50

Sources: Russian National Accounts and Russian Statistical Yearbook, 2005.

Another important factor was unused capacity, which in 1998, at the start of the period amounted to 40 per cent, but by 2005 was reduced to 13 per cent. Additional capital brought in that way added 1.69 per cent of annual growth to the economy, or nearly a quarter of the total. The remainder, 2.37 per cent in annual growth has to be accounted for by total factor productivity (TFP). This is relatively high considering the slow technological progress in the country, but can be partly explained by recovery in organization and management techniques from the troughs of the long depression of the 1990s.

In projecting future growth we divide our forecast into two periods – the immediate future, 2006–2015, which is to a large extent, a modified continuation of recent trends, and the more distant future, 2016–2030, where we are on less solid ground.

The principal features of the immediate future up to 2015 can be seen comparing columns 2 and 3 of Table 5.9. One certain change is the contribution of labour from 2.4 to no more than 2, probably 1.5 per cent. There will be only modest improvements in the demographic situation, so that the labour market will have to rely heavily on cutting unemployment and immigration.

Also, underutilized capacity will be exhausted as an imported factor of growth, its contribution falling to an annual 0.5 per cent. These losses would amount to a total of 1.7–2.2 per cent of annual growth, i.e. to a deceleration from 7.15 to 5–5.5 per cent if not compensated for by other factors.

However, current trends also show improvement in private and government capital investment that could easily increase the annual growth contribution of capital 0.8 and of TFP by another 0.7 per cent. If these compensatory changes materialize and are not sabotaged by unfavourable aggregate demand developments, the average annual growth rate of GDP may well amount to 7 per cent.

For the more distant future (see column 4 of Table 5.9) we foresee more change, both negative and positive. A further slowing down of labour to at most 1 per cent and the complete disappearance of reserve capacity by a total of 1.5 percentage points of annual growth will probably only be partly compensated by capital growth while some further slowdown in total factor productivity. This would result in an average annual GDP growth rate of only 5.5 per cent in 2016–2030.

In the international context, if compared to the high income countries this is not bad, at all.

5.5   FUTURE GROWTH: AN INTERNATIONAL COMPARISON

Projecting Russia's future growth rates also makes it possible to estimate long-term changes in its position in the world economy. Because Russia is expected to grow faster than the world economy, it should be able by 2030 to substantially increase its share in world GDP. Also, because it is expected to grow faster than leading industrialized nations, it should at some point in the future become the largest European country in GDP, overtaking Germany, France, UK and Italy. At least, that is what some experts have been recently forecasting. At the same time, Russian growth will most probably be slower than China's and, possibly, slower than India's. If these expectations are borne out by facts, Russia might continue to lag behind these two Asian nations in terms of GDP while making progress vis-à-vis the current European economic leaders.

To verify these forecasts, we had to make our own projection of world GDP and its principal country components. The starting point in this exercise is determining country shares for the base period (2003). This looks easy since all relevant country GDP data are available. Problems start when one has to choose which common denominator to use in converting country data – current exchange rates, purchasing power parities (PPP) etc. The results of these alternative calculations in some cases are so different that doubts arise as to whether any reflect the true proportions at all. Table 5.10 reflects these differences for 15 leading countries that accounted for approximately 80 per cent of world GDP.

Table 5.10   Percent shares of world GDP, 2003

Country	Percent shares of world GDP			
	Exchange rate	PPP	Arithmetic mean	Geometric mean
Brazil	1.4	2.6	2.0	1.91
China	3.9	12.5	8.2	6.98
Canada	2.3	1.8	2.1	2.03
France	4.8	3.2	4.0	3.92
Germany	6.6	4.4	5.5	5.39
India	1.6	6.0	3.8	3.10
Italy	4.0	3.0	3.5	3.46
Japan	11.9	7.1	9.5	9.19
Korea. Rep	1.7	1.7	1.7	1.7
Mexico	1.7	1.8	1.8	1.75
Netherlands	1.4	0.9	1.2	1.12
Russia	1.2	2.5	1.9	1.73
Spain	2.3	1.8	2.0	2.03
United Kingdom	4.9	3.2	4.0	3.96
United States	29.9	21.3	25.6	25.24
World	100	100	100	100

Notes: Arithmetic mean (column 4); and geometric mean (column 5) are computed using exchange rate (column 2) and purchasing power parity(column 3).

Source: World Development Report Statistical Annex, 2005.

For instance, the difference between estimates for China is more than threefold (3.9 and 12.5), for India nearly fourfold (1.6 and 6.0), and for Russia more than twofold (1.2 and 2.5). When projected into the distant future, such estimates can produce unreliable results. In such cases, one possible solution is to use averages between the divergent estimates. For Russia we take the largest available estimate – 2.5 because we feel that all alternative estimates are too small to be true.

The next step in our world GDP projection is to determine average annual country growth rates for the two forthcoming periods 2003–2015 and 2015–2030. These are presented in Table 5.11.

*Table 5.11   Actual and projected country and world GDP annual growth
rates, 2003–2030 (geometric averages. %)*

Country	1990–2003	2003–2015	2015–2030
Brazil	2.0	3.0	3.0
China	8.2	8.0	6.5
Canada	3.2	3.0	1.0
France	1.9	1.5	1.0
Germany	1.5	1.5	1.0
India	5.8	6.0	5.0
Italy	1.6	1.5	1.0
Japan	1.3	1.5	1.0
S. Korea	5.5	5.0	3.0
Mexico	3.0	3.0	3.0
Netherlands	2.7	2.0	1.0
Russia	-1.8	7.0	5.5
Spain	2.8	2.0	1.0
UK	2.6	2.0	1.0
USA	3.2	2.5	1.0
Rest	2.9	3.0	3.0
World	2.6	3.2	3.0

Sources: Base period – World Development Report; Projections – our estimates.

In projecting future growth rates we followed a few assumptions:

- In the case of industrially developed countries growth would slow down in 2003–2015 and further decelerate in 2015–2030 compared with past growth in 1990–2003. The reason for this assumption is that growth in the 1990s was exceptionally high due to the intensive introduction of information technologies, and that these very favourable conditions will not be repeated in the future. In 2015–2030 an additional factor will lead to a further deceleration, namely strong competition in most industrial products, including high-tech from China. India and other newly industrialized countries.
- Most newly industrialized countries will grow at rates that are higher than in the past. China will continue its exceptionally fast growth at 8 per cent until 2015 before somewhat slowing down to 6.5 per cent in the later period. India will maintain growth at 6 per cent slowing down later to 5 per cent. Mainly due to fast growth in this group of

nations, total world growth will continue around 3 per cent per annum despite low growth rates in the high income nations.

- Over the projected quarter of a century substantial changes are projected in country shares (see Table 5.12). Russia's share is expected to reach 5.5 per cent of the world total. A more than twofold increase compared with 2003. Its GDP will exceed gross product of all major European nations and will be about equal to that of Japan though still far behind USA (only a third of its level).

Table 5.12   Actual and projected shares in World GDP (%)

Country	2003	2015	2030
Brazil	2.6	1.94	1.95
China	9.5	14.04	23.32
Canada	2.1	3.10	2.31
France	4.9	3.99	2.99
Germany	5.5	4.48	3.35
India	3.8	5.21	6.99
Italy	3.5	2.84	2.13
Japan	9.5	7.74	5.80
S. Korea	1.7	2.07	2.07
Mexico	1.8	1.75	1.76
Netherlands	1.2	1.036	0.78
Russia	2.5	3.83	5.52
Spain	2.0	1.73	1.29
UK	4.0	3.45	2.59
USA	25.1	23.00	17.24
Rest	20.3	19.72	19.84
Sum of 15	79.7	80.28	80.16
World	100	100	100

Source: Our calculations based on Tables 5.10 and 5.11.

But despite its progress, Russia will stay in the backyard of the most spectacular shifts in global economic power. That is, the expected emergence of China as the largest economy in the world overcoming US may/or will occur somewhere around 2024. Approximately at the same time, India will overcome Japan as the third largest economy after China and USA, as Russia will stay fifth (see Table 5.13).

Table 5.13   Country rating in GDP race

Place	2003	2015	2030
1	US	US	China
2	Japan	China	US
3	China	Japan	India
4	Germany	India	Japan
5	France	Germany	Russia
6	UK	France	Germany
7	India	Russia	France
8	Italy	Canada	Canada
9	Brazil	Italy	Italy
10	Russia	Brazil	Brazil

Note: Russia's rating in 2030 will not change even if the much different projection made public by the Russian Ministry of Finance in late August 2006 holds true. The Ministry projects an average annual GDP growth rate of only 5 per cent for the whole period compared with 6.2 per cent in our projection. That leads to a share of 4.09 per cent in world GDP which is smaller than 5.52 in our projection, but is still larger than that of all other European nations.

We did not attempt to make projections of world trade and changing country shares in that sphere. That would be a useful next step in this exercise. However, even at this stage, two preliminary observations could be made as to Russia's involvement in the world economy.

1. Maintaining fast GDP growth rates would need a substantial increase in Russia's domestic capital investment, particularly in automotive, aircraft and high-tech manufacturing but also in modernizing and developing the country's economic infrastructure. There would be a smaller share of net exports in GDP and a faster growth of imports than exports. Exports of fuels and metals would encounter increased natural supply constraints, and a larger share of high-tech products in exports might be expected. Russia would also become a much wider market for imported capital and consumer goods.

2. However, the external surplus in goods and services would only be reduced step by step allowing Russia to continue and even increase its role as a capital exporter. Its foreign direct investments are currently on the rise and might increase even more rapidly in the near future. So far, this trend is particularly evident in fuels and metals where more Russian corporations are becoming transnational. But there are already signs that this new Russian expansion might spread into manufacturing.

In the near and more distant future Russia will become a much more active player in global trade and investment.

5.6 REVISED FORECASTS OF RUSSIAN GROWTH AFTER THE GLOBAL FINANCIAL CRISIS

This Chapter was written before the recent global financial crisis and for obvious reasons could not touch upon the effects of the economic and financial crisis that started in the U.S. in December 2007. In this section we present a few thoughts on changes up to mid 2009.

The crisis did not reach Russia until September 2008, and for quite a few months the Russian government believed that it could avoid the crisis – remaining, in the words of one of its cabinet ministers, as an island of stability.

This claim, however, did not come true. In fact, the downturn in Russia was quite deep reaching by mid-2009 an annual 10 per cent in GDP and 15 per cent in industrial production.

Underlying the Russian crisis was a strong dependence on the world economy that had built up during the long upturn of the 2000s. Russia had become a major supplier of petrochemicals and metals to the world market and its growth by the mid-2000s was largely export driven. After the world crisis started, international trade contracted and Russian revenue from exports shrank eventually causing a fall in GDP.

The fall in exports was uneven. In metals the shrinkage was both in volume and value while in oil predominantly in value. Oil prices first exploded in the first phase of the crisis, from around 100 dollars per barrel in January 2008 to 147 dollars in early July, falling thereafter precipitously to 45 dollars in September. It should be noted that in the course of the long economic upturn oil exports had become a major source of currency earnings. After 2005, they also turned into a major source of Russian government income. Not only was the tax rate on oil production tied to its export price so that the rate automatically increased when the price went up. An exports duty was introduced which also rose as the price increased. At the extreme, the duty was as high as half of the price. In addition, part of oil export earnings was transferred to a special government Stabilisation Fund to be used as a reserve in the future.

The idea of these measures was to create a defence shield against a possible external shock, most probably a sharp drop in oil price. By the end of 2007, Russia had accumulated an official currency reserve of around 600 billion dollars, third in size after China and Japan, Also, two government funds in rubles and foreign currencies, the Reserve Fund and National

Welfare Fund, formerly the combined Stabilisation Fund, contained the equivalent of another 240 billion dollars. These monies were thought to be adequate to take care of all emergencies for two or three years.

The country was thus prepared for one emergency but not for others. Russia had also become highly dependent on foreign capital. In the mid 2000s it was enjoying a stock market boom but most of the short-term speculative capital involved was foreign, largely US or European. Neither had Russia created a domestic market of long-term capital and had to rely for it on outside sources. By the end of 2007, Russian corporations were in debt to foreign lenders to a total of some 400 billion dollars, a fourth of that sum due for repayment in 2009. Both these dependencies combined proved to be close to catastrophic when the crisis struck.

When the U.S. financial crisis developed, it led with a time lag to a crash in the Russian stock market. Shares fell by more than 75 per cent. Because large blocks of shares had been used as collateral for corporate loans from abroad, Western lenders were quick to call their margins. Russian big companies and their majority owners, some of them the infamous oligarchs, found themselves suddenly on the brink of insolvency. Clamouring for help, some of them managed to get dollar loans which the government paid from the official currency reserve. In only 4 months from September 2008 to January 2009, the country lost through capital flight a good third of its currency defense shield, i.e. 200 out of 600 billion dollars. At this rate, the country would be left without a currency reserve by the end of the same year.

The government managed to stop this haemorrhage, but in the course, the banking system was largely demoralized and the production sphere was left without a normal flow of money and credit. The negative effect on GDP was unexpectedly heavy. In addition to a steep fall in exports, capital investment decreased by 20 per cent. As a general rule, both business and consumers cut expenditure preferring hard cash to any kind of spending. There was a fall of 50 per cent and more in the output of cars, housing construction and consumer durables.

To fight the crisis the government first used financial subsidies to banks but with no effect since the latter converted ruble subsidies into dollars rather than provide credits to the real sector. Later, when a more comprehensive anti-crisis program was being considered, fiscal stimuli to bolster aggregate demand were excluded because of a large budget deficit. 8.6 per cent of GDP in 2009 and a projected 7.5 per cent in 2010. The deficit was financed from the Reserve Fund which could no longer be used for fiscal stimulus.

In early 2007, just before the crisis hit Russia, the new president Dmitri Medvedev and prime minister Vladimir Putin announced a long-term program of capital investment to modernize industrial stock of equipment and the economic infrastructure from 2008 to 2020. Due to newly emerged budget problems this program that could have been used as an anti-crisis measure, had to be largely postponed.

For all these reasons the crisis was not only deep, but the post-crisis recovery was expected to be very slow and long. Its length largely depended on the developments in the world economy affecting Russian export markets, particularly the price of oil, but also on how fast the country would be able to overcome its budget deficit.

According to official projections GDP was expected to grow by 1 per cent in 2010, 2.5 per cent in 2011, and 3.5 per cent in 2012. That is much slower than the previous average growth rate. The pre-crisis peak will be regained only in 2012, a full four years after the crisis began.

Assuming the long-term growth rates projected in this chapter hold, Russia would reach the levels forecasted a few years after 2030 rather than a couple of years before. But is it reasonable to expect changes in the long-term growth rates as a result of the crisis?

Let us recall that our growth rate projections are based on two sets of assumptions about GDP structure – by production factor input and by use. We started our calculations by separating average annual growth of GDP in 1998–2005 by the contribution of capital, labour and total factor productivity (TFP). Thus labour accounted for 2.0 out of 7.15 per cent annual growth, capital – 2.38 per cent (including new additions and unused old capacity), while TFP added another 2.37 per cent. Our next step was to calculate growth rates and their components for 2006–2015. These, shown in Table 5.9 of the chapter, are no longer valid due to the crisis. They have to be substituted by other, newly calculated figures and for a new period, 2013–2020. As shown in Table 5.14, these are now 1.5 per cent for labour, 2.0 per cent for capital, and 2.5 per cent for TFP, and a total growth rate of 6.0 per cent for GDP. In the final forecast period, the growth rates are 0.5 for labour, 2.5 for capital, 2.5 for TFP and 5.5 per cent for GDP.

Table 5.14   Russian growth revised (per cent per factor)

Factors	1998–2005	2013–2020	2021–2030
Labour	2.0	1.5	0.5
Capital	0.69	2.0	2.5
Labour+capital	2.69	3.5	3.0
Unused capacity	1.69		
Total factor productivity	2.37	2.5	2.5
GDP	7.15	6.0	5.5

Source: Our estimates.

Notice that the share of labour in the base period was high due to stock of unemployment left over from the long transformation crisis of the 1990s. Labour was also high in the first forecast period for three reasons: (i) A large stock of unemployment after the current crisis; (ii) Turnaround to growth in Russian demographic trends and (iii) Large labour migration from former Soviet republics. We further assume that in the final period these factors will lose much of their importance.

New capital was not widely used in the base period due to abundance of old unused capacity. We assume that in both forecast periods, growth in capital is accelerated due to the increase in the share of new capital investment to around 25 per cent of GDP as compared to below 20 per cent in the 2000s. This should be the logical consequence of the long-term government economic modernization program which is expected to restart after the current crisis is over. Modernization of industry and infrastructure should also result in high total factor productivity. Overall efficiency is also expected to rise as a result of industry diversification and expansion of manufacturing rather than the primary sector. However, the country would probably continue to use petrodollar and other exports earnings as a source of building up reserve against possible new external shocks.

5.7   CONCLUDING REMARKS

One important lesson to be learned from the recent global financial crisis is that forecasts of long-term economic growth have to account for future recessions. These, at least in the U.S., occur, as a rule, every 8–10 years and are often duplicated in other industrially developed countries. While long and deep recessions like the current one are rare, shallower recessions are a regular feature of the market economy and should not be forgotten in the forecast. In practical terms, every moderate recession reduces the preceding 7 to 10 year average growth rate by about 1 per cent. Assuming that Russia would follow a world recession with one of its own, its growth rates in the two projected periods should be corrected downward by 0.5–1.0 per cent.

The reader will notice that the revised growth rates are not substantially different from those shown in the chapter. Therefore the picture drawn there of Russia and its place in the world economy around the year 2030 is generally confirmed with minor modifications. Let us not forget though that this projection is based on a best case scenario which assumes, among other things, success of current plans of modernizing the economies as well as a favourable development of the global economy. These conditions are not automatically guaranteed.

REFERENCES

Menshikov, S. (2003), 'Structural Problems and Solutioms in the Russian Economy' paper presented at the international seminar on 'Development and Democracy', Moscow, (http://www.fatcenter.ru/smenshikov).

Menshikov, S. (2005), 'The Anatomy of Russian Capitalism', *Challenge Magazine*

Menshikov, S. (2007), *Anctomy of Russian Capitalism*, Washington D.C.: EIR Press.

Russian National Accounts Statistics, Federal Service of State Statistics, http://www.gks.ru/bd–1.asp.

Russian Statistical Yearbook, 2000–2005, Goskomstat, Moscow.

Statistical Abstract of the United States, various years, United States Census Bureau, Washington D.C.

World Bank (2005), *Wor'd Development Report 2005, Selected Indicators*, World Bank, Washington, D.C.

6. Japan's Alternating Phases of Growth and Future Outlook[1]

Kyoji Fukao and Osamu Saito

6.1 INTRODUCTION

Japan's economic history since the Meiji Restoration of 1868 is characterised by alternating phases of less conspicuous growth performance in pre-war times, phenomenal growth of the 1955–73 period, and marked deceleration thereafter. The first two phases are the period of industrialisation and the third was that of rapid de-industrialisation and a rise of the service economy. This chapter reviews issues and evidence concerning her growth performance in the century-long period of industrialisation, and places the recent decades of slowdown and the prospect for the future in the long-term historical context. The issues to be examined may be grouped under the following headings: the Gerschenkronian effects (which include not only the transplanting of the factory and other western systems in early stages but also technology transfer through FDI and licensing in later periods); changing international environments (in both commodity and capital markets, which in turn were influenced by changing global power balances); the role of industrial and economic policies, investment in infrastructure and human capital; and the distinct mode of skill formation.

The chapter identifies a set of factors that contributed to enhancing productivity of the manufacturing sector in the industrialisation period (placing greater emphasis on saving ratios, human capital investment and a distinct mode of skill formation within the firm, than on government policies). Then it turns to the new phase of de-industrialisation and the rise of a service economy from 1973 on, asking if a new regime of productivity growth has emerged in the rapidly expanding service economy.

---

[1] This chapter is based on a paper presented at the Asia–Pacific Seminar on *World Economic Performance: Past, Present and Future*, to mark the occasion of Angus Maddison's 80th birthday, at the University of Queensland, Brisbane, 5–6 December 2006.

6.2 GERSCHENKRONIAN SITUATIONS

When Japan opened the country in 1859, she found herself in a typical Gerschenkronian situation. Compared with the West, Japan was materially and institutionally 'backward'. Meiji statesmen, government officials and intellectuals, who saw Britain and other Western countries at first hand, realised that their country was lagging behind the West where unprecedented progress had been made since the industrial revolution. In the words of a contemporary who was on a mission to the USA and European countries in the early 1870s,

> 'It is since 1800 that Europe has attained its present wealth; and it is *only* in the last forty years that it has achieved the truly remarkable level of prosperity we now see' (Kume, 2002; p. 57).

This remark is interesting because the author, having gauged the degree of his country's backwardness, thought that Japan would be able to close the forty years' gap. Judging from this and other contemporary writings, what Meiji leaders saw was 'iron and coal' being the material base of the wealth of the West. It implies that the lack of the factory system and its energy base in the manufacturing sector was the real cause of Japanese backwardness, and the view was shared by many contemporaries, ranging from statesmen like Toshimichi Okubo, who was a vice ambassador of the Iwakura mission, to liberal-minded intellectuals such as Yukichi Fukuzawa, the prominent Meiji enlightenment leader. As Alexander Gerschenkron argued, such components of the West's material culture are *transferable*. This often led to emphasis on state-led import substitution and on heavy rather than light industry as the policy target industry, and such efforts may well have resulted in a sudden but unstable 'big spurt' (Gerschenkron, 1962).[2] Thus, the conventional wisdom was that the more backward, the larger the role of the state and the higher the rate of initial growth. Japan has often been regarded as a typical case in which the state played a substantial role in promoting successful industrialisation.

---

[2] The idea of 'big spurt' is also shared by Rostow (1960), although Gerschenkron was critical of Rostow's stage theoretic approach. See Gerschenkron (1962).

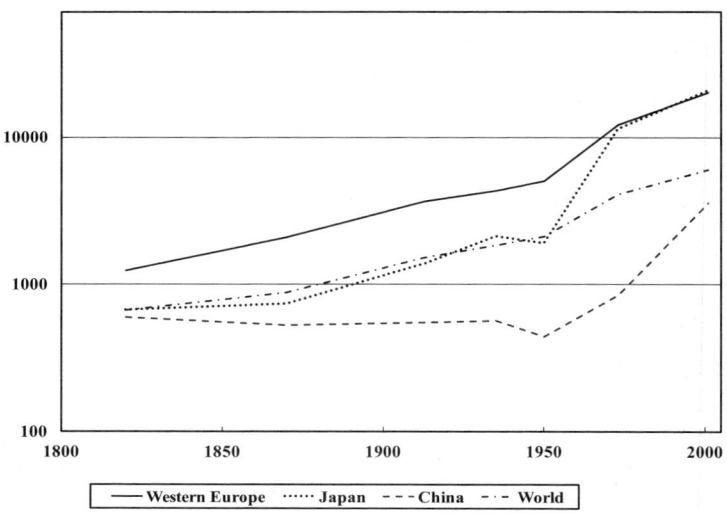

Source: Maddison (2003), Tables 1C, 5C and 8C, pp. 441, 560 and 642.

*Figure 6.1   Japan's GDP per capita in the global context, 1820–2001 (1990
             international dollars)*

Let us first look at Japan's actual performance in the nineteenth and early
twentieth centuries, by placing it in global perspective. If we chart Angus
Maddison's per-capita GDP estimates for Japan, together with those for
China, Western Europe and the world in one diagram (Figure 6.1),[3] it is
evident that Japan's growth performance was not particularly spectacular
until 1950. In the period between the Meiji Restoration and 1950, the level
was well below the west European curve although the rate of growth was
somewhat higher than that for Europe and the world average. It was in the
very short period of the third quarter of the twentieth century, the era of 'high
economic growth', when Japan changed the position from the world average
to the advanced countries' group. This implies, on the one hand, that Japan
did not fail to keep up with the others, which should be contrasted with
trouble-ridden China of the late imperial and republican period. It should also

---

[3] Maddison chose 1820, 1870, 1913, 1950, 1973 and 2001 for the benchmark years;
     here 1935 is added in order to see how the individual players' positions changed
     during the interwar period. The 1935 figures for western Europe, China and Japan
     are from his regional tables (pp.441 and 560), while that for the world is
     interpolated from the 1913 and 1950 benchmark estimates (Maddison, 2003).

be noted, on the other hand, that Japan was never a high performer during the pre-war period-nothing but one of the average countries of the world. Kazushi Ohkawa once characterised the pattern of Japanese economic growth as 'trend acceleration' (Ohkawa and Rosovsky, 1973; Ohkawa and Shinohara, 1979: Chapter 1). He felt that Japan's growth did not begin with a big spurt as Gerschenkron predicted. What he and his associates found instead was that the estimated rate of economic growth had increased since the end of the nineteenth century. It is true that the slope of the trend line was gentler in the period before the First World War, when the growth process was steady and balanced, than in the inter-war period, during which the process became uneven and unbalanced (Nakamura, 1983). Also true is, as Arthur Lewis pointed out as early as 1949, that the impact of the Great Depression on the Japanese economy in the 1930s was less severe with a swifter recovery than in the advanced countries of the West (Lewis, 1949). However, we all know what followed in the late 1930s and the early 1940s. If comparison is made, as in Figure 6.1, in terms of the relative distance from the top group of the world, then it may probably be more appropriate to say that Japan's catch-up did not take place until 1950. In Japan, a 'big spurt' came as late as the 1950s and 1960s.[4]

Turning to the 'role of the state' question, there are several reasons to believe that the direct role of the government was not great until the late 1930s. First, despite the early Meiji government's well-known emphasis on state-financed Westernisation projects, a close look at what the Meiji state actually did reveal that the proportion of government money spent on industrial promotion in the form of model factories was relatively small, and that most of the funds mobilised in the early Meiji years went to infrastructure building, i.e. railways. Second, even this policy of industrial promotion was abandoned as early as the late 1870s in favour of export promotion. As is well known, the export commodities - raw silk and tea - came from the traditional cottage-industry sector. Third, all the government-run model factories were sold off later to private firms, and the first industrial take-off in the 1890s was due completely to private initiatives. Fourth, although the late Meiji government launched a state-owned iron and steel company, the share of government investment in fixed capital formation and the proportion of government expenditure to GDP were never high as far as the period before 1930 is concerned (see Tables 6.1 and 6.2).

---

[4] Still, one may argue that if the country had not waged the 15 years' war then the whole catch-up process could have been much less abrupt. Not surprisingly, however, this hypothesis remains controversial.

Table 6.1   Capital formation ratios in the private and state sectors, 1888–
1938 (percentage of real GNE)

Year	Percentage of GNE		
	Overall	Private	State
1888	9.2	7.6	1.6
1900	11.7	7.7	4.0
1910	15.1	9.7	5.4
1920	19.3	13.1	6.2
1930	17.0	9.1	7.9
1938	26.2	14.5	11.7

Source: Minami (1986), pp. 174–75.

Table 6.2   Government expenditure as a percentage of GNE/GDP: Japan
and UK

Japan		UK	
Year	%	Period	%
1888	12	1861–1880	7
1900	17	1881–1900	9
1910	22	1901–1920	19
1920	18	1921–1938	15
1930	26		
1938	37		

Note: Japanese figures are percentages of GNE while British figures are those of GDP.

Source: Minami (1986) pp. 333 and 337.

A recent synthesis is that the modern Japanese economy in the period up to the 1930s was in a more or less non-interventionist regime (Okazaki and Okuno-Fujiwara, 1999; Teranishi, 2005). Thus, direct intervention by the government was very much limited in the process of industrialisation, with the notable exception of 1938–45, in which the state geared economic management to a command economy model. All this of course does not necessarily mean that the state did not want to get involved in the business of promoting industry. Rather, despite the Meiji statesmen's firm belief in the slogan, 'rich nation, strong army', i.e. that the nation's development should be guided by government, the menu of means of intervention was limited for the government. The trade treaties with the Western superpowers signed at the time of the opening of the nation did not allow the government to raise customs, and the balance of trade under that trade regime was generally unfavourable. On the other hand, government staff did not have expertise to run factories and companies; nor did they have enough revenue to subsidise all the strategic industries. Some verbal intervention was made in the areas of maritime shipping and shipbuilding, which, one may argue, foresaw industrial policy of the post-war period. The role of the government was most prominent in the areas of science and technology transfer from overseas. Although they were gradually replaced by newly educated Japanese, many science professors and engineers were invited from abroad and employed by the government at extremely high salaries in the early Meiji period. In 1889, however, Japan started to permit inward FDI in return for a revision of the commerce treaty and admission to the Paris Convention Treaty for the Protection of Industrial Property in the same year. Since then, inward FDI and licensing agreements, in addition to reverse engineering and imports of advanced capital goods, became more important as a channel of technology transfer (Goto and Odagiri, 1996). Otherwise, it was only the military sector that the state always cared for. The state-owned Yawata Steel came into existence because of its strategic importance for defence, but it was not until the 1930s when the war against China was launched that a new military-fiscal state replaced the non-interventionist regime of economic management: as tables 1 and 2 show, the proportion of the government's capital formation increased from 6 per cent in 1920 to 12 per cent in 1938 and that of government expenditure to GDP from 18 per cent to 37 per cent.

In infrastructure and education, the government played a larger role. As noted above, early Meiji effort to introduce railways was financed by the government but the further development in the construction of rail networks was made under a dual system of state and private initiatives. While the share of capital formation by railways was higher in earlier periods, total operational mileage increased four-fold between 1900 and 1940 (although the balance between the public and private sectors alternated from period to period) (Minami, 1986, pp. 115–122).

In postal service too, the whole system was transplanted from the West, and remained in the public sector until very recently. However, the Meiji government allowed local notables to run village post offices on their own premises as if the office business were a family business. This mobilisation of de facto private resources enabled the postal network to spread far and wide in fairly early stages of its development. In other areas of transport and communication, the role of the central government is found in allocating subsidies to local government bodies. In road building, for example, much of the actual financial cost was shouldered by local governments. Subsidies became a means of leading local people to accept a national plan, and 'pork barrel' politics adopted by political parties intensified this tendency.

Education is said to have been one of the areas in which the pre-war government was committed to invest. Compulsory education was introduced as early as 1886; the years required was extended from four to six in 1907, but the overall rate of enrolment reached 98 per cent by 1910. Over the period up to 1920, the proportion of students in primary, secondary and higher education to the total population rose to 19 per cent, which meant that although still behind the USA, Japan overtook the record of England and Wales (Minami, 1986, p.19). Two additional points may be made, however. One is that despite this progress in pre-war education, human capital embodied in the workforce increased at a moderate pace since it took several decades for a new better-educated generation to replace the elder, poorly-educated generation. Yoshihisa Godo and Yujiro Hayami have estimated average schooling for the period since 1880, which measures a number of schooling years averaged over all the age groups of the working population in a given year (Godo and Hayami, 2002). According to their estimates (see Figure 6.2), average schooling was only 1.9 years for men and 0.6 years for women in 1890. Both male and female years had multiplied by 1940, but the averages did not reach eight years. The other point is that the system of education in both pre-war and post-war periods was not wholly state-financed. There were private schools at all levels but in secondary and higher education especially, much of the progress was made by private initiatives. Just as in the area of infrastructure building, therefore, educational attainment was made in a relatively inexpensive manner.

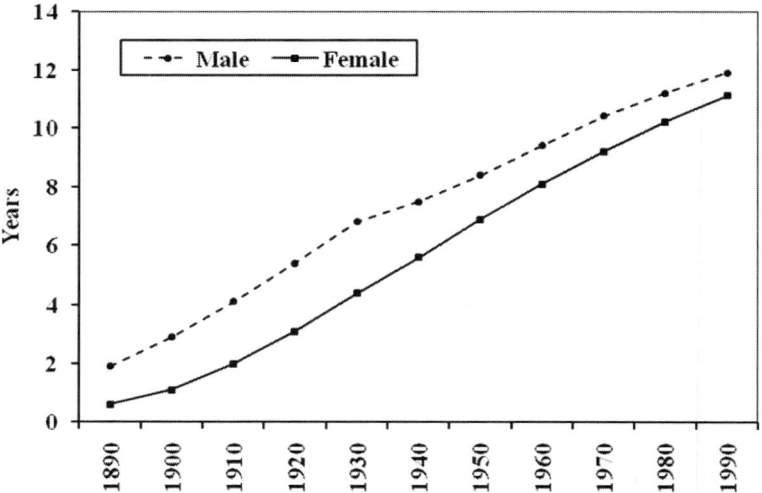

Source: Godo and Hayami (2002), p. 965.

Figure 6.2   Changes in average schooling, 1880–1990

6.3   THE ERA OF HIGH ECONOMIC GROWTH: 1955–73

Japan's fully-fledged drive to industrialisation started in the inter-war period. One favourable factor had been laid out with Japan's adoption of the gold standard in 1897. Since gold had long been stronger than the silver, it changed the trade environment. While it was a blow to export-oriented traditional industries, the import of machinery and other goods to build the modern, heavy and chemical industry became less costly. Then, unexpectedly, the outbreak of the First World War created a trade vacuum in the South and South–East Asian markets. The opportunities were seized by Japanese merchants, shipping agents and producers. The overseas demand was so strong that windfall profits were ploughed back: new firms were set up and further investment made in plant and equipment with license contracts from abroad. Many of such firms went bankrupt when the boom collapsed in 1920; yet a substantial number of new manufacturing enterprises that survived this and subsequent recessions laid the foundation for post-war industrial build-up.

6.3.1   The International Environment and the Domestic Economy

Japan's take-off into fully-fledged industrialisation occurred in an international environment characterised by great instability. The collapse of the *pax Britannica* was followed by the creation of trade blocs and growing exchange rate volatility, leading many countries including Japan to adopt a command economy regime. Having learnt a lesson from this experience, post-war leaders of the West set up an international economic regime aimed at enhancing free international trade and stable exchange rates. Many IMF member countries chose an adjustable-peg currency system until 1973. Except in the case of Article XIV countries, Article VIII of the IMF agreement prohibits member countries from restricting the convertibility of their currencies for current international transactions. Several successful multilateral trade negotiations and the most favoured nation principle of GATT promoted international trade, especially in manufactured products. These international developments contributed to the economic growth of newly industrialising countries such as Japan, poorly endowed with natural resources and hence depending on processing trade.

One defect of the post-war international economic regime was the lack of adequate arrangements for the promotion of international capital flows. For example, the IMF agreement did not prohibit restrictions on capital transactions. The OECD played an important role in the liberalisation of capital controls, but only for member countries. Because of the end of gunboat diplomacy and the difficulty of providing collateral for sovereign debt, borrower countries were tempted to default on their debt. The risk of repudiations, the disappearance of plantations, and capital controls by developed and developing countries substantially reduced international capital flows from the rich to the developing countries after the Second World War. This can be shown by calculating proportions of current account surplus to GDP for the group of developed countries in both pre-and post-war periods: throughout the post-war period the average proportion for the rich group remained well below 1 per cent, while in pre-war years, especially in the period before 1925, the percentage fluctuated between 1 and 3 per cent.[5]

Yet, this defect in the post-war international regime did not act as a constraint on Japan's development, since she never attempted a growth-through-debt policy and strictly regulated direct and indirect international capital flows until the end of the 1970s. Even in the pre-war period, Japan financed capital formation from her own savings: her saving rates in the pre-war period appear to have been modest except in the 1920s (Figure 6.3). Much of the overseas investment by Britain and other advanced countries went to the Americas and the British colonies, such as India and South Africa, not to Japan. And, the graph shows, Japan's current account was generally balanced except in several short deficit periods, such as the period after the Sino–Japanese War of 1894–95 (the current account deficit was financed by reparations), during the Russo–Japanese War of 1904–5, and the period after the Kanto Earthquake of 1923. Figure 6.3 also shows that after the Second World War, Japan's gross saving rate increased considerably. This post-war high saving ratio level, the highest of all developed countries except Luxemburg, must have contributed to her strong economic growth in this period (See Jones and Obstfeld, 2001). According to a growth accounting analysis by Jorgenson and Nomura (2005), out of Japan's aggregate labour productivity growth of 7.58 per cent for the period of 1960–73, 4 per cent was accounted for by capital deepening.

---

[5] 'Developed countries' are defined as those whose per capita GDP in 1990 Geary–Khamis dollars is greater than 50 per cent of the U.S. level. Per capita GDP data are from Maddison (2003); and data on current account surplus from Mitchell (1992, 1993 and 1995) and IMF's, International Financial Statistics. The issue has been explored in full in Fukao (2000).

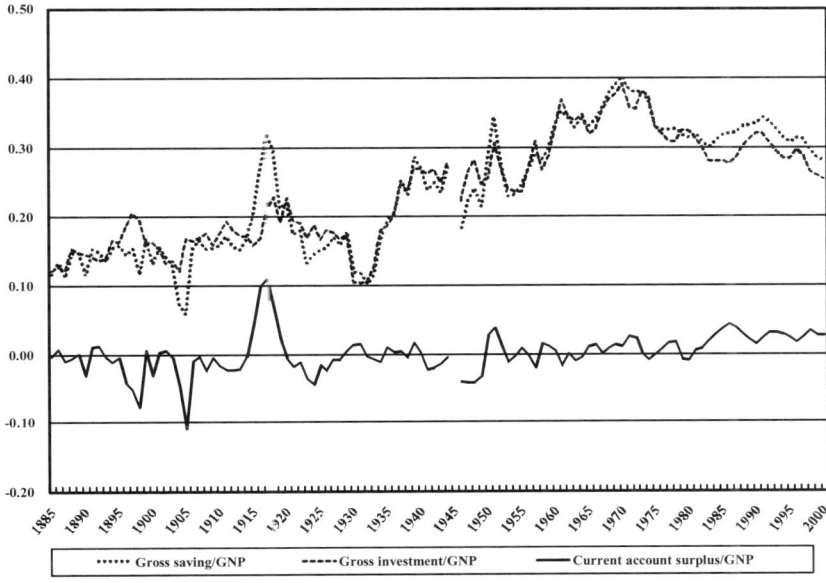

Sources: Data for 1885–1929: Ohkawa et al. (1974), p. 178 and data for 1930–1954: Ohkawa et al. (1974), p.179. Data for 1955–2000 on 1968 SNA basis: Economic and Social Research Institute (2006).

Figure 6.3   *Japan's current account surplus, gross saving rate and gross investment rate: 1885–2000*

The very high saving ratios in the 1950s and 1960s resulted in high capital accumulation, which increased national income, but at the same time made the prices of consumptior goods, especially durable consumer goods such as washing machines, refrigerators, TV sets, and cars, increasingly cheaper. With increasing urbanisation, this virtuous circle enlarged the domestic market, which in turn called for further investment in manufacturing (Yoshikawa, 1995). Thus, the era of high economic growth was accompanied by accelerating industrialisation and saw the country joining the club of developed countries, until the domestic market reached a saturation point and the economy was hit by the oil crisis of 1973–4. However, this did not mark the end of growth through industrialisation. Japan's response to the energy crisis in the subsequent decade was impressive and she was able to outperform most of the developed countries up until the beginning of the 1990s, and the rate of total factor productivity (TFP) growth in the manufacturing sector remained well above the level of 1 per cent per annum.

Much attention has been paid to industrial policy of the government, especially action formulated by the Ministry of International Trade and Industry (MITI) in relation to the phenomenal growth of this period. According to the proponents of this view, it was government ministries who prescribed which industries should be promoted, protected, and phased out, and the prescriptions were dispensed through guidance with a small amount of subsidy (see for example Johnson, 1983). There is some suggestion that the MITI played a certain role in the early stage of the computer industry, and the a disproportionately large amount of subsidies given to coal mining, textiles and other declining industries made their phase-out socially less costly (Beason and Weinstein, 1996). Given the empirical evidence, however, the role of the state in this period seems to have been exaggerated. The principal player of the era of high growth was the manufacturing industries who made large amounts of investment in plants and equipments on their own initiative.

6.3.2   The Japanese System of Employment and Skill Formation

This era also saw the rise of manufacturing firms on the international scene. Toyota, Toshiba, Sony – to name but a few – became internationally known then. All these, as well as other giant but less colourful firms in steel and shipbuilding, made heavy investment in introducing the most advanced packages of technology of the day. This represented a move towards mass production and, at the shop floor level, the installation of conveyor systems which, eventually, led the way to automation. Indeed, the 1950s and 1960s was a period of Americanisation. A number of business missions were sent to the USA. It is interesting to note that missions organised by such bodies as the Japan Productivity Center included even union representatives as members. And the packages imported were not just about technologies but also workplace and other plant management techniques.

However, this drive for mass production did not necessarily result in de-skilling of the workforce. In U.S. manufacturing, historically, all sorts of management practices aimed at mass production, culminated in the Ford system, have tended to take skills away from the shop floor. Whenever a new scheme was introduced, as William Lazonick (1990) notes, steps were taken

'to ensure that new skills would be in the possession of those who were part of the managerial team rather than those who labored for wages on the shop floor' (Lazonick, 1990: p 229).

As a result, engineers and other salaried employees grew over the decades of the twentieth century, while the conveyor system degraded shop-floor workers into 'interchangeable parts'. Japanese manufacturing firms of the

1950s and 1960s were fully aware that the American systems would bring in economies of scale, but at the same time, they did not see workers as 'interchangeable parts'; they did not want the workers to become totally de-skilled.

First of all, a steady increase in human capital formation through the pre-war expansion of primary schooling bore fruit in this post-war period, especially in the era of high economic growth, 1955–70. Compulsory schooling was extended to nine years by a post-war reform. As Figure 6.2 above has indicated, average schooling years of the whole male workforce, reached that level before 1960 and women's during the 1960s. Post-war firms must have benefited a great deal from public investment made by education authorities in the pre-war period.

More significant, however, is the fact that Japanese managers did not follow the American prescription in the area of skill management. As Lazonick puts it, 'Like the British, Japanese managers have left considerable skill on the shop floor' Lazonick (1990, p 23).[6] Japanese firms invested in raising workers' *firm-specific* skills. A case in point is a system developed by Toyota, the car manufacturing giant. The Toyota production system, originated probably from post-war 'Quality Control' movements, gives more importance to factory workers than its pre-war predecessor, the Ford system. It attaches prime importance to work teams, not just as a coordination unit, but also as a monitoring unit for any stoppage in the production line, mechanical breakdowns and any other unusual events at the workplace, and also as a source of workplace improvements and innovations. Workers are encouraged to judge and act as a team beyond what is stated in work manuals. To put it differently, they are encouraged to accumulate firm-specific skills over an extended period, and this attitude towards shop-floor skills is not confined to the auto industry. Indeed, it is commonplace for most manufacturing companies to train workers on the job and to allow them to broaden and enrich their knowledge and skills, mostly firm-specific, by working for the same firm over their work career. Japanese management has thus integrated shop-floor workers into the long-term evolution of the manufacturing industry.[7]

Such workplace practices are closely related to the internal wage structure. A seniority-based wage scheme, adopted by a majority of Japanese firms, reflects the way in which skills are formed in Japanese manufacturing. Under the seniority wage system. the length of service is a crucial, but not the only, factor determining the wage level. For promotion, however, personal

---

[6] In British manufacturing, both skill training and the organisation of labour were practically in the hands of trade unions (Lazonick, 1990, p 23).

[7] For the concept of 'skill' described here, see Koike (1995, especially Chapter 1).

achievement is also important and, since it is likely to be associated with acquired skills over the past years, the system encourages workers to exert themselves to accumulate more and to stay on in the same firm, leading to longer-term employment. It is debatable if the firms of the period in question really made a decision to guarantee life-long employment, but it seems likely that both management and unions preferred stable employment to fluctuating wages (Odaka, 1999). However, *Asia's New Giant*, a Brookings Institution publication of the mid-1970s, went further to proclaim that it was

> 'a completely rational policy in terms of costs and profits for large Japanese employers, and that although workers welcomed the job security that it brought, ... the main reason for its survival has been economic *efficiency*' (Galenson and Odaka, 1976: p.619).

> 'Efficiency' is also guaranteed by the use of temporary employees and subcontracting. And it is these subcontractors who constitute the lower tiers of the so-called dual structure, which has long characterised Japan's industrialisation process since the 1920s. According to *Asia's New Giant*, 'one of their functions is to bear the initial shock of fluctuation in demand, reducing the burden of the employment commitment borne by the major producers' (Galenson and Odaka, 1976: p.621.).

This diagnosis is not incorrect, as many such subcontractors are small in size, much less capital intensive, and hence low in wage rates, with no commitment in life-long employment. What the authors did not see at that time, however, is that it was part of the hierarchically structured relationships between manufacturers/assemblers and suppliers, under which technological knowledge tends to flow from the large to the small and medium. Also important is that they too are skill intensive in a different manner from what large manufacturing firms have been practising. Most of such small and medium-sized enterprises take school leavers as de facto factory apprentices. They too acquire skills on the job, which are more specialised and complementary skills – some firm-specific, some not; and levels of such workers have turned out to be extremely high. This, together with active networking within the industrial cluster (or Marshall's 'industrial district'), has made the small and medium sector a vital component of Japan's whole industrial system.

All this seems to suggest, therefore, that the whole system, formed in the era of industrialisation by integrating the labour-intensive and skill-intensive segments into the capital-intensive and skill-using mode of production, was not just efficient but also conductive to productivity growth in Japanese manufacturing.

6.4 THE ERA OF DECELERATION: 1973–2006

From the mid-1970s on, Japan's economic growth decelerated. The average annual rate of growth in real GDP was 9.3 per cent for 1955–73, 3.8 per cent for 1973–91, and 1.1 per cent for 1991–2005. Various factors caused the deceleration. First, by the early 1970s, the level of TFP in the machinery, chemical and metal industries had almost reached the US level and the technological catch-up process in the manufacturing sector slowed down (Jorgenson et al., 1987). Second, after about 1970, by which the baby boomer generation had entered the workforce, the rate of growth in working-age population declined substantially. In fact, while the 15–64-year-olds grew by an average of 1.7 per cent annually from 1955 to 1973, the growth rate declined to 0.7 per cent from 1973 to 1995; since then, the working-age population has actually been shrinking at an average annual rate of 0.3 per cent.[8] As we have already seen, capital deepening was a factor that accounted for much of Japan's rapid economic growth.

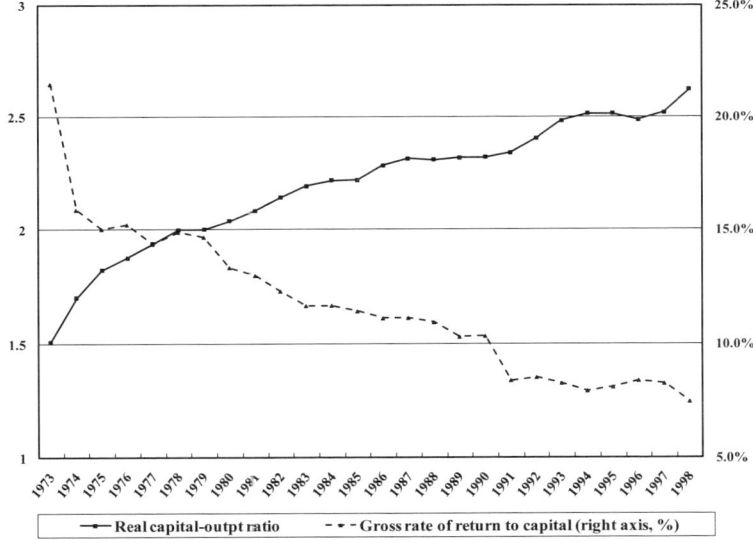

Source: JIP Database (http://www.rieti.go.jp/jp/database/d04.html)

Figure 6.4   Capital deepening and the diminishing rate of return to capital in Japan, 1973–98

---

[8] Calculated from a National Institute of Population and Social Security Research Database.

Usually, the marginal productivity of capital and the rate of return to capital will decline as capital deepening continues, so that, as is well known, countries cannot maintain rapid growth by capital deepening forever. In the Japanese case, however, thanks to her still high saving rates, capital deepening continued even in this era of deceleration. At the same time, it should be noted that she also suffered a serious decline in the rate of return to capital (Figure 6.4) with private sector investment weakened (Figure 6.5).[9] In the case of manufacturing, especially, capital formation became so small that the net real capital stock recorded a decline in the period from 2000 to 2002.[10]

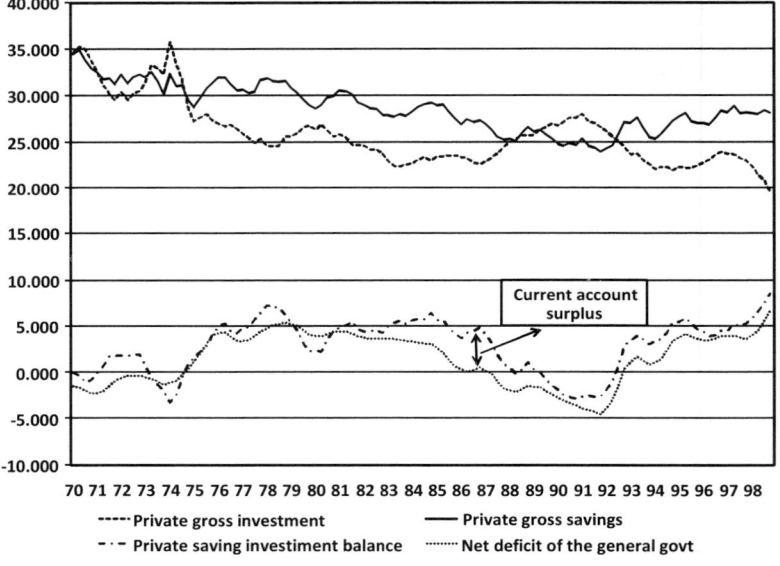

Source: Research and Statistics Division, Bank of Japan (2000)

Figure 6.5   Saving–investment balance of the private sector and general government: 1970–2000 (% of nominal GDP)

---

[9] It is worth reporting here that among OCED countries only Japan and Korea experienced very rapid capital deepening and a swift decline in the rate of return to capital (see Pyo and Nam, 1999).

[10] JIP Database (http://www.rieti.go.jp/jp/database/d04.html).

Table 6.3 Japanese GDP growth and its decomposition, 1970–2002

Real GDP Growth	1970–1975	1975–1980	1980–1985	1985–1990	1990–1995	1995–2000	2000–2006
Real GDP Growth	3.4	5.1	4.3	4.8	1.1	1.0	1.9
Contribution of Labour Service Input Growth	0.5	1.8	1.1	0.9	0.0	-0.2	0.1
Man-hour Growth	-0.4	1.0	0.3	0.5	-0.4	-0.7	-0.5
Labour Quality Growth	0.9	0.8	0.7	0.4	0.5	0.5	0.6
Contribution of Capital Service Input Growth	1.4	1.2	1.9	2.0	1.3	0.9	0.7
Capital Quantity Growth	1.9	1.3	1.5	1.5	1.3	0.7	0.5
Capital Quality Growth	-0.5	-0.1	0.4	0.4	0.0	0.2	0.3
TFP Growth of the Whole Economy	1.5	2.1	1.3	1.9	-0.2	0.4	1.1
Manufacturing	2.2	5.4	4.4	3.1	1.0	1.7	2.3
Non-manufacturing	1.1	0.8	0.0	1.5	-0.6	0.1	0.7

Note: Value-added growth rates are calculated by Laspeyres-type chain-linked index; the figures above therefore do not match those of the government SNA statistics. TFP growth rates of the manufacturing sector and that in the non-manufacturing sector are gross output base. TFP growth rates of the whole economy is value added base. Because of this difference, TFP growth rates of the whole economy are usually higher than weighted average of the TFP growth rates of the two sectors.

Source: Fukao et al. (2006). All the data are from JIP Database (http://www.rieti.go.jp/jp/database/d04.html).

The negative effects of the above-listed factors on Japan's economic growth can be shown by decomposing growth into its components in a growth accounting exercise. Table 6.3 indicates that all three factors contributed to the decline: growth in labour service input (both in man-hours and in labour quality), capital service input, and TFP all slowed down or turned negative. Among the three factors, the decline in capital service input growth is the largest and appears to be the main cause of Japan's deceleration. But it should be remembered that capital accumulation is endogenously determined and the slowdown in labour service input growth and TFP growth reduced the rate of return to capital and brought about a rapid decline in capital accumulation. Table 6.3 also shows that in the 1970s and 1980s, the manufacturing sector enjoyed higher TFP growth than the non-manufacturing sector, but that in the 1990s and early 2000s, TFP growth in the manufacturing sector also stagnated. The swift decline in TFP growth in the manufacturing sector can be partly explained by the idling of capital stock, which was caused by the recession in this period. However, even taking account of the decline in the capacity utilization rate of capital, we obtain a similarly rapid declining trend in TFP growth in the manufacturing sector.

Manufacturing industries are generally more capital intensive than the other sectors, thus enjoying higher TFP growth. Deindustrialization, therefore, will lower a country's rate of TFP growth and of capital deepening, thus decreasing the overall rate of economic growth. Like other developed countries, Japan experienced continuous de-industrialization and an expansion of the service sector.[11] After the 1973–4 oil crisis, in particular, Japan saw deindustrialization accelerate in two stages. The first acceleration occurred immediately after 1973. Before the oil crisis, the proportion of gross value added of the manufacturing sector to GDP stood at 35 per cent or above; from 1973 to 1975 it declined as much as 5 per cent. The second decline took place after the burst of the 'bubble economy' in 1992: in three years' time the share of manufacturing went down by 4 per cent. It further declined to 22 per cent in 2002 (the share in the workforce also declined to reach the level of a little below 20 per cent in the same year).

The second acceleration in de-industrialization seems to have been caused by a decline in domestic demand for investment goods as well as Japan's direct investment abroad. In the 1990s, Japanese firms relocated production to China and the ASEAN countries in order to lower wage and other production costs. In the case of the electrical machinery industry, especially,

---

[11]The following account is based on Economic and Social Research Institute (2006). By 1970, the share of the primary sector in GDP had become well below the 10 per cent mark.

there was a sharp increase in overseas production and a decline in domestic production and net exports in the period 1990–2003. Since it is mainly large productive firms that invested abroad, this relocation led to the closure of many productive establishments in Japan. Between 1990 and 2003, only 44 per cent of all the establishments which had existed in 1990 survived while not many were opened during this period. As a result, the number of establishments declined by 33 per cent. It is important to note that the survival rate is not high even in the case of establishments in the top labour-productivity group in each manufacturing sectors. During the same period only, 47 per cent of establishments survived of all those ranked in the top three deciles in each of the 50 manufacturing sectors at the time of 1990 (Fukao et al., 2006).

In addition to the supply-side factors listed above, there was a demand-side factor that further decelerated Japan's economic growth in the 1980s and 1990s, namely, Japan's excess saving problem. Although private gross investment declined in the 1980s and 1990s, the private gross saving rate remained at a high level (Figure 6.5). This growing saving–investment imbalance created an excess supply of domestic product and kept Japan at a continuous risk of recession. There were three ways in which the excess saving was used. In the early 1980s, Japan used the excess saving for the accumulation of foreign assets. In Figure 6.5, this is reflected in a huge current account surplus. But trade imbalance with the U.S. caused serious trade frictions, which resulted in a realignment of yen–dollar rates after the Plaza Accord of 1985. Frightened by unprecedented yen appreciation and pushed by pressure from the US government, Japan's monetary authority relaxed its monetary policy excessively, thus causing 'bubble' phenomena in the late 1980s economy. In the 'bubble' years, Japan's excess saving was used for fixed capital formation, especially in the real estate sector. As a result of the bubble burst in 1992 brought on by excessively tight monetary policy, Japan was left with a huge unproductive capital stock and mountains of non-performing loans. In order to mitigate deflation, the Japanese government substantially expanded fiscal expenditure. The excess saving was thus used to finance government debt. Although the major uses of the excess saving successively changed during the 1980s and 1990s, Japan always faced the problem of a scarcity of final demand during this period and suffered economic stagnation except during the bubble economy of the late 1980s.

6.5   SECTORAL PRODUCTIVITY DIFFERENTIALS

It is widely recognised that with economic development the centre of gravity in economic activity and employment shits from agriculture to manufacturing, then from manufacturing to tertiary industry. Behind this tendency is the stylised fact that the flow of labour moves from a lower-productivity to a higher-productivity sector. Colin Clark once called this tendency Petty's Law because Sir William Petty observed as early as the late seventeenth century that 'there is much more to be gained by *Manufacture* than *Husbandry*, and by *Merchandise* than *Manufacture*' (Clark, 1951: pp.315–316).[12]

This chapter has shown that the Japanese story of industrialisation fits perfectly with this interpretation of the tendency, as long as the period until the 1970s is concerned. In the early phase of her industrialisation process in which most of the manufacturing methods used were still labour intensive, the gap in average labour productivity between agriculture and manufacturing may well have been small, although it is worth noting that the fact that Meiji Japan was under a strong Gerschenkronian pressure tended to give a false impression that the productivity level of the secondary sector was several times higher than that in the primary sector. Simon Kuznets's classic work on *Economic Growth of Nations* may have given us this sort of impression. According to his statistical tables, the figures for Japan are: in 1872, the share of primary employment was 85 per cent which, according to statistics of 1880, produced 63 per cent of total output, while secondary and tertiary workers, 6 per cent and 9 per cent of the total workforce, produced 16 per cent and 21 per cent of the national product respectively; in 1950, the distribution of employment between the primary, secondary and tertiary sectors became 48 per cent, 27 per cent and 25 per cent while the shares in national product were 26 per cent, 39 per cent and 35 per cent respectively (Kuznets, 1971). For an interpretation from Japanese perspectives, see Chapter 1, Ohkawa and Shinohara (1979). All this seems to suggest that productivity differentials between the primary and the non-primary sector were substantial, and that the differentials narrowed over time. However, this is because the Japanese employment data Kuznets relied on were based entirely on the worker's principal occupation: no allowance was made with respect to his or her subsidiary occupation in the compilation of gainfully occupied population statistics (see Umemura et al., 1988: p.161). By-employment was widespread in Tokugawa and Meiji society where more than 80 per cent of the working-age population were classified as 'farmers'. If this inter-sectoral transfer of labour in the form of by-employment can properly be taken into account, then the level of average labour productivity in the secondary sector will not be different from that in the primary sector

---

[12] The quote is from William Petty, Political Arithmetik, in Hull (1899, vol.1, p.256).

even in the period when the nation was in supposedly Gerschenkronian situations.[13]

As the catch-up process proceeded in the twentieth century, and especially when the real break from the past came in the 1950s, there took place a spectacular rise in labour productivity in the manufacturing sector. In this period of strong growth, unprecedented capital deepening was accompanied by the establishment of a very Japanese mode of skill formation at the shop floor level. All this is reflected in a secular rise in the manufacturing sector's productivity relative to that in the primary sector. In other words, Japan's entire period of industrialisation is consistent with the first proposition of Petty's Law. From 1973 onwards, the industrial sector started to shrink while a service economy expanded. According to the Japan Industry Productivity (JIP) database, TFP growth in the emerging service sector was sluggish.

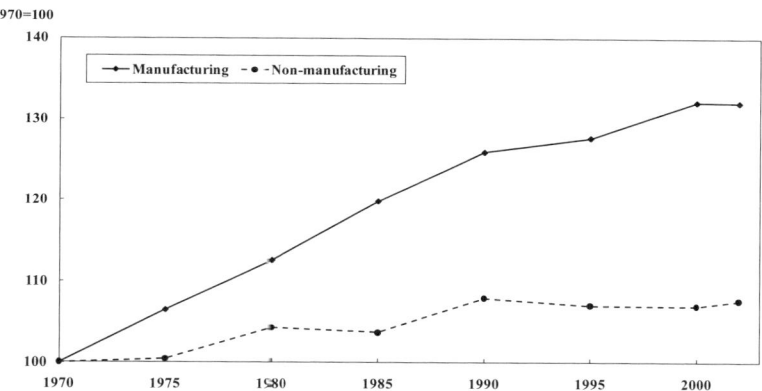

Source: JIP Database, REITI (various years).

Figure 6.6   Total factor productivity growth in manufacturing and non-manufacturing 1970–2002

Figure 6.6 shows that even in this period of de-industrialisation and the rise of the service economy the rate of productivity growth was unmistakably

---

[13] According to a pilot census taken in 1879, in which not just principal but subsidiary occupations were enumerated, 11 per cent of the 194,000 'farmers' had by-employments in industry, who represented a substantially large proportion of the workforce in manufacturing of the day (Tōkei-in, 1882). Based on this and another regional censuses, an attempt has been made to estimate the 'true' size of gainfully occupied population in each sector between 1885 and 1940. See Saito and Settsu (2009).

higher in manufacturing than in the non-manufacturing sector. This is a finding which casts doubt upon the conventional interpretation that structural change is a consequence of changing differentials in productivity and earnings. In the Japanese case, it is likely that the on-going growth of the service economy is not a result of any surge in productivity within the sector. A recent work by M.N. Bailey and Robert Solow on industry-level labour productivity of major developed countries in the 1990s gives us a similarly depressing picture (Bailey and Solow, 2001). According to Table 6.4, the labour productivity levels of Japan's manufacturing industries are high (except in food processing and semi-conductors). In contrast, the levels in non-manufacturing industries such as retail and construction are well below the levels in the US and major EU countries. Given the nature of activities in this sector, the tendency for non-manufacturing's productivity growth to lag behind manufacturing per se may not be particularly surprising, but what the Bailey and Solow paper has revealed is that in Japan the productivity gap between the two sectors is unusually wide .[14]

Thus, what we have seen for the recent move is against Petty's Law, or more precisely, against what Colin Clark has shown with nineteenth-and early twentieth-century international data.[15] The manufacturing-services differential has increased rather than decreased in the recent decades: Japan's commerce and service sector seems to have remained relatively labour intensive. Of course, the sector is diverse and the ways in which value added is created are very different from those in manufacturing. Some of the trades in the sector are skill intensive as well as labour intensive, but even in those skill-oriented areas it seems that there emerged no organisational innovation comparable to the Toyota production system in manufacturing.

---

[14] TFP estimates are also given for several industries in Bailey and Solow (2001). Those estimates are not shown in table 6.4 since they do not alter the general conclusions concerning the relative positions of Japanese manufacturing, services and construction.

[15] See Chapter VII, Clark (1951). One exception the author noted is Britain between 1837 and the 1860s. During that period, the rise in productivity of tertiary industry was swifter than that of manufacturing industry, which he thought, must have been 'due no doubt to the introduction of railway and steamship transport' (p.315).

Table 6.4 International productivity differentials (US=100)

A. Manufacturing

	Auto	Food processing	Steel	Semi-conductors	Computer	Consumer electronics	Beer	Metal-working	Soap and detergent
US	100	100	100	100	100	100	100	100	100
Germany	93[c]	95[b]	100[a]	n.a.	89[a]	62[a]	44[a]	100[a]	88[a]
Japan	145[c]	35[c]	121[e]	43[g]	95[a]	115[a]	69[a]	119[a]	94[a]

B. Services and Construction

	Food Retail	General Merchandise Retail	Total Retail	Telecom	Retail Banking	Airlines[p]	Software	Construction
US	100	100	100	100	100	100	100	100
France	118[h]	n.a.	96[i]	51[h]	100[i]	66[h]	53[i]	80[i]
Germany	n.a.	96[j]	96[i]	51[h]	85[i]	66[h]	65[i]	70[i]
Japan	54[h]	54[i]	n.a.	82[h]	n.a.	n.a.	n.a.	45[k]
Netherlands	n.a.	n.a.	95[i]	n.a.	154[h]	66[h]	59[i]	100[h]
U.K.	89[h]	82[j]	103[i]	49[h]	64[l]	66[h]	n.a.	n.a.
Korea	27[h]	32[m]	n.a.	83[h]	76[n]	100[h]	n.a.	69[h]
Brazil	14[h]	n.a.	n.a.	41[h]	40[o]	47[h]	n.a.	35[h]

Notes: [a]: 1990; [b]: 1992; [c]: 1993–95; [d]: 1994; [e]: 1995; [f]: 1996; [g]: 1991–96, [h]: 1995; [i]: 1994; [j]: 1987; [k]: 1998; [l]: 1989; [m]: 1993; [n]: 1994–95; [o]: 1996; [p]: : Airline productivity for France, Germany, The Netherlands and U.K. is the European average.

Source: M.N. Bailey and R.M. Solow, (2001, pp. 151–172).

6.6   OUTLOOK FOR THE FUTURE

Having had a cursory look at the history of Japan's economic development and recent trends, we are now in a position to speculate on the outlook for Japan's future. Most of the factors which have led to the deceleration of economic growth are likely to continue for a long while. Japan's working age population is expected to shrink at an average annual rate of 0.8 per cent in the next 20 years. As the baby boomers retire, the ageing and shrinking of the population will create social friction and pose an economic burden in the near future. There are no signs that the slowdown in the rise in schooling years will be reversed in the near future. Although Japan experienced a rapid decline in private investment in the last decade, her capital-labour ratio is still at the global top and we can expect no further substantial capital deepening. Many economists expect a continuous decline in the saving rate and a shrinking of the current account surplus, the latter of which will inevitably accelerate deindustrialization. Together with likely consequences of energy constraints and global warming, therefore, it is not surprising that Angus Maddison has recently made his projection of Japan's GDP per capita on the basis of 1.3 per cent per annum between 2003 and 2030, the lowest of all the 20 'biggest' countries (Maddison, 2007: p.345).

There are a couple of positive exceptions in this long list of negative trends. One is that the ageing of Japan's population will rid the economy of the excess saving problem. More important, perhaps, is the other sign which concerns the way in which production skills are utilised, the linchpin of the 'high growth era' regime. Despite the recent fuss about 'new models' of employment practice, the so-called Japanese system will continue to be used by major manufacturing firms such as Toyota and Canon. A telling example is that in recent years a growing number of manufacturing companies started employing a new production system called 'cell production'. This involves a small team of skilled workers (usually two to five) performing multiple production tasks, placing more emphasis on workers' skills rather than line structures and, thus, reversing the previous trend towards automation and conveyor systems (see, for example, Isa and Tsuru, 2002). Although it is premature to predict that this would become *the* new model for Japanese manufacturing in the twenty–first century, the evidence suggests that Japanese manufacturing firms are determined to respond to the prolonged stagnation after the 'bubble' years and to improve manufacturing efficiency by adopting a new model which is indeed a variant of the traditional system centred on human skills.

However, the manufacturing sector's share in the domestic economy has been shrinking so drastically that productivity growth in the non-manufacturing sector will unmistakably be a key for a prosperous future. Yet little is known about how productivity is enhanced in the production of services, be they goods-related or society-related. What is known at this stage is that 'intangible'[16] investment in non-manufacturing suffers by comparison with manufacturing, while on the international front the level of Japan's ICT investment in the non-manufacturing sector is substantially lower than in other countries (Inklaar and Timmer, 2008; Fukao, Miyagawa, Pyo and Rhee, 2009; Fukao, Miyagawa, Mukai, Shinoda and Tonogi, 2009). Unless a new, promising regime of productivity growth emerges in the expanding service sector, Japan's outlook for the early twenty-first century is not very bright.

REFERENCES

Bailey, M.N. and Solow, R.M. (2001), 'International productivity comparison built from the firm level', *Journal of Economic Perspectives*, **15** (3), 151–172.

Bank of Japan (2000) *Major Economic and Financial Data CD-ROM 2000*. Research and Statistics Division, Tokyo: Tokiwa General Service.

Beason, R. and D.E. Weinstein (1996), 'Growth, economies of scale, and targeting in Japan (1955–1990)', *Review of Economics and Statistics*, **78** (2), 286–295.

Clark, C. (1951), '*The Conditions of Economic Progress*', 2nd edn, London: Macmillan, pp 315–316.

Economic and Social Research Institute, Cabinet Office, Government of Japan (2006), *Annual Report on National Accounts 2006*, Tokyo: Cabinet Office.

Fukao, K. (2000), 'Kokusai shihon idō: shihon ha yutakana kuni kara mazushii kuni e nagareruka' [International capital flows: does capital flow from poor to rich countries?], in Shinichi, F., H. Akiyoshi and I. Kazumasa (eds), *Makuro keizai to kinyū sisutemu* (*Macro Economy and Financial Systems*), Tokyo: Tokyo Daigaku Shuppankai.

Fukao, K., S. Hamagata, T. Inui, K. Ito, H. U. Kwon, T. Makino, T. Miyagawa, Y. Nakanishi, and J. Tokui (2006), 'Estimation Procedures and TFP Analysis of the JIP Database 2006 Provisonal Version', paper presented at the Third Meeting of the EU KLEMS Consortium, May 17-9, Valencia.

Fukao, K., T. Miyagawa, M. Mukai, Y. Shinoda, and K. Tonogi (2009), 'Intangible investment in Japan: new estimates and contribution to economic growth', *Review of Income and Wealth*, **55**, 717-736.

Fukao, K., T. Miyagawa, H.K. Pyo and K.H. Rhee (2009), 'Estimates of multifactor productivity, ICT contribtions and resource reallocation effects in Japan and Korea', RIETI Discussion Paper Series, **09–E–021**.

---

[16] 'Intangible' assets may be classified into: (i) computerised information such as custom software, packaged software, in-house software, and databases; (ii) innovative property such as science and engineering R&D, mineral exploitation, copyright and license costs, other product development, design, and research expenses; and (iii) economic competencies such as brand equity, firm-specific human capital, and organisational structure.

Fukao, K., Y.G. Kim and H.U. Kwon (2006), 'Plant Turnover and TFP Dynamics in Japanese Manufacturing', Hi–Stat Discussion Paper Series, **180**, Hitotsubashi University.

Galenson, W. and K. Odaka (1976), 'The Japanese labor market', in Patrick, H. and H. Rosovsky (eds), *Asia's New Giant: How the Japanese Economy Works*, Washington, D.C.: The Brookings Institution.

Gerschenkron, A. (1962), *Economic Backwardness in Historical Perspective*, Cambridge, Mass.: Berknap Press.

Godo, Y. and Y. Hayami (2002), 'Catching up in education in the economic catch–up of Japan with the United States, 1890–1990', *Economic Development and Cultural Change*, **50**, 961–978.

Goto, A. and H. Odagiri (eds), (1996), *Technology and Industrial Development in Japan: Building Capabilities by Learning, Innovation, and Public Policy*, Oxford: Oxford University Press.

Hull, C.H. (ed.) (1899), *The Economic Writings of Sir William Petty*, Cambridge: Cambridge University Press.

Inklaar, R. and M.P. Timmer (2008), 'GGDC Productivity Level Database: international comparisons of output, inputs and productivity at the industry level', paper prepared at the 30th General Conference of the International Association for Research in Income and Wealth, Portoroz, Slovenia, 24–30 August.

Isa, K. and T. Tsuru (2002), 'Cell production and workplace innovation in Japan: toward a new model for Japanese manufacturing?', *Industrial Relations*, **41** (4), 548–578.

Johnson, C. (1983), '*MITI and the Japanese Miracle: The Growth of Industrial Policy 1925–1975*', Stanford: Stanford University Press.

Jones, M.T. and M. Obstfeld (2001), 'Saving, Investment, and Gold: A Reassessment of Historical Current Account Data', in Guillermo A.C., R. Dornbusch and M. Obstfeld (eds), *Money, Capital Mobility, and Trade: Essays in Honor of Robert A. Mundell*, Cambridge: MIT Press.

Jorgenson, D., M. Kuroda and M. Nishimizu (1987), 'Japan–U.S. industry-level productivity comparisons, 1969–1979', *Journal of the Japanese and International Economies*, **1** (1), 1–30.

Jorgenson, D.W. and K. Nomura (2005), 'The Industry Origins of Japanese Economic Growth', *Journal of the Japanese and International Economies*, **19**,482–542.

Koike, K. (1995), 'The Economics of Work in Japan' Tokyo: LTCB International Library Foundation.

Kume, K. (2002) (Compiler), The Iwakura Embassy, 1871–73. A True Account of the Ambassador Extraordinary & Plenipotentiary's Journey of Observation through the United States of America and Europe, Vol.II: Britain, trans. G. Healey Richmond: Curzon Press.

Kuznets, S. (1971), *Economic Growth of Nations: Total Output and Production Structure*, Cambridge, Mass.: Harvard University Press.

Lazonick, W. (1990), *Competitive Advantage on the Shop Floor*, Cambridge, Mass.: Harvard University Press.

Lewis, W.A. (1949), *Economic Survey 1919–1939*, London: Allen and Unwin.

Maddison, A. (2003), *The World Economy: Historical Statistics*, Paris: OECD Development Centre.

Maddison, A. (2007), *Contours of the World Economy, 1–2030 AD. Essays in Macro-Economic History*, Oxford: Oxford University Press.

Matthew, T.J. and M. Obstfe d (2001), 'Saving, investment, and gold: a reassessment of historical current account data', in Calvo G.A., R. Dornbusch and M. Obstfeld, (eds), *Money, Capital Mobility, and Trade: Essays in Honor of Robert Mundell*, Cambridge, MA: MIT Press.

Minami R. (1986), *The Economic Development of Japan: A Quantitative Study*, London: Macmillan.

Mitchell B. (1992), *International Historical Statistics: Europe 1750–1988*, Stockton Press: New York.

Mitchell B. (1993), *International Historical Statistics: The Americas 1750–1988*, Stockton Press: New York.

Mitchell B. (1995), *International Historical Statistics: Africa, Asia & Oceania*, Stockton Press: New York.

Nakamura, T. (1983), *Economic Growth in Prewar Japan*, New Haven, Conn.: Yale University Press.

Odaka, K. (1999), 'Japanese–style" labour relations', in Okazaki, T. and M. Okuno-Fujiwara (eds), *The Japanese Economic System and its Historical Origins*, Oxford: Oxford University Press.

Ohkawa, K., N. Takamatsu, Y. Yamamoto (1974), 'National Income', vol. 1, *Estimates of Long-term Economic Statistics of Japan Since 1868*, in Ohkawa, K., M. Shinohara and M. Umemura, (Eds), Tokyo: Toyo Keizai Shimposha.

Ohkawa, K. and H. Rosovsky (1973), *Japanese Economic Growth: Trend Acceleration in the Twentieth Century*, Stanford: Stanford University Press.

Ohkawa, K. and M. Shinchara (eds.), (1979), *Patterns of Japanese Economic development: A Quantitative Appraisal*, New Haven, Conn.: Yale University Press.

Okazaki, T. and M. Okuno-Fujiwara (1999), 'Japan's present-day economic system and its historical origins', in Okazaki, T. and M. Okuno-Fujiwara (eds), *The Japanese Economic System and its Historical Origins*, Oxford: Oxford University Press.

Pyo, H.K. and K.H. Nam (1999), 'A test of the convergence hypothesis by rates of return to capital: evidence from OECD countries', mimeo., Seoul National University.

RIETI (various years), *Japanese Industrial Productivity (JIP) Database*, Research Institute of Economy, Trade and Industry, Tokyo, Japan: http://www.rieti.go.jp/en/database/index.html

Rostow, W.W. (1960), *The Stages of Economic Growth*, Cambridge: Cambridge University Press.

Saito, O. and T. Settsu (2009), 'Unveiling historical occupational structures and its implications for sectoral labour productivity analysis in Japan's economic growth', paper presented at the Conference of the International Network for the Comparative History of Occupational Structure (INCHOS), held at King's College, Cambridge, 28–30 July.

Teranishi, J. (2005) *Evolution of the Economic System in Japan*, Cheltenham, Glos.: Edward Elgar.

Tōkei-in (1882), Kai no kuni genzai ninbetsu shirabe [Census of Kai province], Tokyo: Tōkei-in.

Umemura, M., K. Akasaka, R. Minami, N. Takamatsu, K. Arai, and S. Itoh (1988), 'Estimates of Long-term Economic Statistics of Japan since 1868, Vol.2: *Manpower*', Tokyo: Toyo Keizai Shimposha.

Yoshikawa, H. (1995), *Macroeconomics and the Japanese Economy*, Oxford: Oxford University Press.

7. Making the International System Work for the Platinum Age[1]

Ross Garnaut

7.1 INTRODUCTION

The most important questions in economics are about why economies grow as fast or slowly as they do, and why some economies grow faster than others. Small differences in economic performance sustained over long periods generate huge differences in the distribution of economic welfare and in economic and, eventually, political power.

These overwhelmingly important questions affecting human economic life are neglected by the deductive methods which dominate modern economics. The deduction of logical conclusions from narrowly specified assumptions provides few insights into the ultimate sources – the institutions and values – of differences in economic growth between countries and over time. These insights come especially from the careful study of economic history. The importance of particular institutions comes to be understood through the association of differences in economic performance with changes and differences in institutional structures. These associations are identified from careful numerical study of economic performance. The starting point is the careful marshalling of data.

In Maddison's words:

'Without measurement, judgements on why some countries got rich, why others are poor, why some catch up and others fall behind, are bound to be fuzzy. Quantification sharpens scholarly discussion and contributes to the dynamics of the research process' (Maddison, 2002, p.1).

---

[1] This chapter is based on a Paper prepared for the Conference to honour the 80th Birthday of Angus Maddison, University of Queensland, 5–6 December 2006 (presented at the Conference by Dr Ligang Song, Director of the China Economy and Business Programme at The Australian National University) and subsequently revised for publication.

To Angus Maddison, and the large numbers of good scholars in many countries who toiled with him in this demanding but in the end productive soil, we are grateful for much careful measurement of economic performance over long periods. This has been the starting point for his own and others' economic histories that have drawn insights about the wellsprings of superior and inferior performance in economic development.

My colleagues and I at the ANU benefited greatly from the regular visits of Angus over many years. This enjoyable personal contact increased our awareness of the vast scope of Angus' curiosity and work and expanded the knowledge that we found in his prodigious published output.

Maddison's work tells us amongst other things how ephemeral is the ordering at any point in time of the relative power and wealth of nations. For example, we are much more sensitive now than before Maddison's work to the overwhelming relative size of the large Asian economies of China and India at the beginning of the modern era. We know much more about how the acceleration of economic growth in various parts of Europe and North America from the late eighteenth and at various times through the nineteenth century, and from Japan after the Meiji restoration in the 1860s, led to huge expansion in their relative roles in the global economy. We understand better the extent of the increases over a relatively short period in economic output and living standards in the economies in which growth accelerated at these times. We know from this work that differentials in economic performance, once established, tend to persist over long periods, with huge cumulative effects. We also know that they can abruptly conclude with war, revolution and less dramatic sources of disorder.

Many of the insights in Maddison's work are brought together in his compelling Millennial Report. This begins with an astounding contrast between two sets of facts. In the first millenium after the life of Jesus Christ, the world's economic output increased hardly at all – by one sixth, all contributed by population growth and none from rising per capita output. By contrast, global output increased 300-fold in the second millennium, which concluded half a decade ago. Over these one thousand years, world population increased 22 times, and average output 13-fold. The expansion in the second millennium occurred overwhelmingly late in the period. In the eight centuries to 1820, 'the advance in per capita income was a slow crawl – the world average rose about 50 percent. Most of the growth went to accommodate a fourfold increase in population'. By contrast, world development has been much more dynamic since 1820. Between then and the end of the millennium, per capita income rose more than eight times, and population more than fivefold (Maddison, 2001, p.17).

7.2   THE BEGINNINGS OF MODERN ECONOMIC GROWTH TO THE GOLDEN AGE

Maddison divides the time of rapid modern economic growth, from the settling down of Europe after the Napoleonic Wars until the present, into five periods. Of these, 1950–1973 was distinctly the strongest for increases in economic activity and living standards. Maddison and others call this the Golden Age. Second best, which we can call the Silver Age, was from 1973 until the end of last century – a period which people who had lived through the Golden Age thought was problematic. In fact, the late twentieth century was an extraordinary period by historical standards. Economic growth was strong by any comparison other than that with the Golden Age. Sustained rapid economic growth spread powerfully from its original locus in the North Atlantic economies, their outliers and Japan, to a large part of Asia.

The third strongest period for rapid economic growth was the long boom from 1870–1913 – roughly between the North American civil war and the first of the great modern European civil wars. This had been the golden age of global economic growth until the second half of the twentieth century demonstrated that even more was possible.

This chapter looks forward by standing on Maddison's shoulders. It draws on some of his insights to sketch the possible shape of the world economy as contemporary tendencies work themselves into history – more powerfully than Maddison has suggested in his published work. It raises issues about the international governance mechanisms that will be necessary to maintain peace and prosperity in the world of the future, in which, at least for a while, four large political entities dominate the global economy.

My starting points are some extrapolations in a paper presented by Maddison as a memorial lecture to Heinz Arndt and published in the November 2006 issue of the *Journal of Asian–Pacific Economic Literature*. The table 5 (Maddison, 2006, p. 33) is reproduced as Table 7.1 and Figure 7.1. Table 7.1 and Figure 7.1 set out the value of economic output in the world's major economies and the world as a whole from 1300 until 2003, and an estimate for 2030.

Back in 1500, India and China – or, rather, two large regions that covered territory later and from time to time largely and today entirely governed as India and China – were of roughly similar economic size, and together represented a bit more than half of global economic output. There had been considerable growth in total economic output in India between 1300 and 1500 during a long period of relative political stability, catching up with a China that was stagnating from the disruption of war, dynastic change and civil disturbance.

Table 7.1 China in the world economy, 1300–2030 AD

Year	China	Japan	India	Western Europe	USA	World	China/World
				Population (million)			
1300	100.0	10.5	88.0	58.4	1.7	360.0	0.28
1500	103.0	15.4	110.0	57.3	2.0	438.1	0.23
1820	381.0	31.0	209.0	133.0	10.0	1,041.8	0.37
1913	437.1	51.7	303.7	261.0	97.6	1,791.1	0.24
1950	546.8	83.8	359.0	304.9	152.3	2,524.3	0.22
1973	881.9	108.7	580.0	358.8	211.9	3,916.5	0.23
2003	1,288.4	127.2	1,049.7	394.6	290.3	6,278.6	0.21
2030	1,458.0	121.0	1,421.0	400.0	364.0	8,175.0	0.18
Year				Per Capita GDP (1990 international $)			
1300	600	475	500	593	400	530	1.13
1500	600	500	550	771	400	566	1.06
1820	600	669	533	1,204	1,257	667	0.90
1913	552	1,387	673	3,458	5,301	1,526	0.36
1950	439	1,921	619	4,579	9,561	2,111	0.21
1973	839	11,434	852	11,416	16,689	4,091	0.21
2003	4,392	21,218	2,160	19,912	29,037	6,432	0.68
2030	14,416	27,758	6,227	30,566	44,574	11,207	1.29

Table 7.1 (Continued)

Year	China	Japan	India	Western Europe	USA	World	China/World
				GDP (billion, 1990 international $)			
1300	60.0	5.0	44.0	34.6	0.7	190.0	0.32
1500	61.8	7.7	60.5	44.2	0.8	248.3	0.25
1820	228.6	20.7	111.4	160.1	12.5	694.6	0.33
1913	241.3	71.7	204.2	902.3	517.4	2,733.3	0.09
1950	239.9	161.0	222.2	1,396.2	1,455.9	5,331.6	0.04
1973	740.0	1,242.9	494.8	4,096.5	3,536.6	16,023.8	0.05
2003	5,659.2	2,699.0	2,267.1	7,857.4	8,430.8	40,384.6	0.14
2030	21,019.0	3,229.0	8,848.0	12,217.0	16,217.0	91,623.0	0.23

Notes: Estimates of GDP levels are adjusted to reflect purchasing power parities in the benchmark year 1990 (see Maddison 1998:149–66). In China the purchasing power of the yuan is much higher than the exchange rate. There is often significant error in comparative economic analysis because ignorance of the pitfalls of exchange rate conversion leads to serious understatement of the level of Chinese GDP. This is true in journalism, political discourse and amongst some economists. Thus newspapers frequently refer to Japan as the world's second largest economy, though its GDP is less than half of the Chinese. It should also be noted that official Chinese statistics exaggerate GDP growth for reasons explained in Maddison (1998), which contains a detailed re–estimation of performance up to 1995. For 1995–2003, I made the same type of downward adjustment to the official estimate of growth in real value added in industry and 'non-productive' services (see Maddison, 2006)

Source: Maddison, 2006.

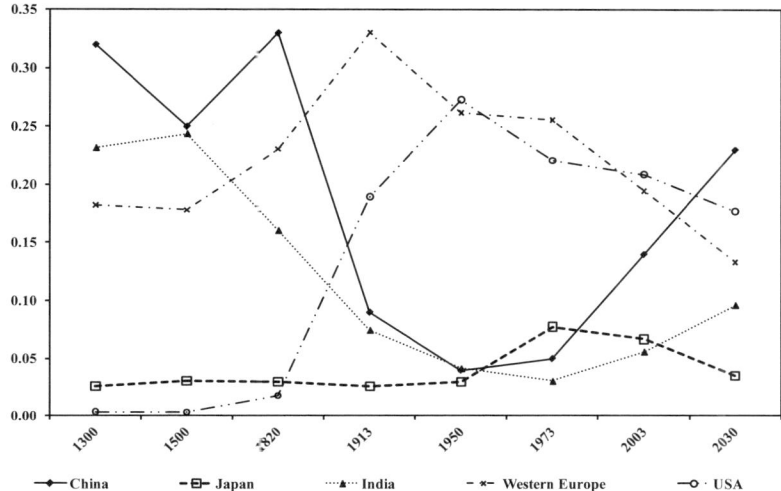

Source: Maddison, 2006, Tab.e 5.

Figure 7.1   China and major countries' share in the world economy, 1300–2030 (%)

After 1500, the dominant trends in the global economy were the restoration of China's earlier relative position over the first one and a half centuries or so of the Qing dynasty, and the acceleration of economic growth in Western Europe – the latter much more powerfully after the Napoleonic wars of the early nineteenth century. In 1820, which in Maddison's Table is the beginning of the modern era of rapid economic growth in the North Atlantic, China accounted for almost a third of global economic output. Europe was responsible for over a quarter. India, through a period of external invasion and disorder, grew reasonably strongly by the standards of earlier times, doubling its size between 1500–1820, but fell back behind both China and Western Europe.

From about 1820, everything changed. The accumulation of conditions that generated an acceleration of productivity growth in Europe began to have powerful effects. The deeper history of these conditions included the establishment for a period under the Mongols of peace across much of Eurasia in the aftermath of conquest. The Mongol hegemony supported the restoration and expansion of trade between China and Europe along the silk route, extending through Persia and into India. The superior technologies of China followed these paths into the European peninsular of Eurasia.

Maddison, Snooks, Jones and, drawing on comparative insights from his intimate knowledge of the long-run economic history of China, Elvin, amongst scholars with whom we at the ANU had the privilege of interacting on campus, have all contributed to our understanding of the European miracle. That phenomenon began its ascent in the middle of the last millennium and accelerated during the nineteenth century. Myriad geographical and institutional characteristics generated effective competition between states for productive people and means of conducting business. Successful political systems expanded, without being so successful – like the Chinese or Moghuls – that they entrenched powerful political entities over such large areas that they were able to stamp out economic and intellectual innovation when they threatened the established political and economic orders.

The acceleration of economic growth spread rapidly from its original heartland in Britain and adjacent areas on the continent gradually through Europe and North America, the latter especially after the American civil war. It spread as well through immigration from Europe to the countries of recent settlement that Maddison calls European outliers, a category that for him includes the United States.

There was one main special case in the nineteenth and early twentieth centuries, of growth outside Europe and its outliers. This was Japan from the 1860s. The case of Japan demonstrated the possibility of sustained economic growth in countries with a recent history of feudal, inward looking political systems. Not any backward, inward-looking political system, but at least those with traditions of an effective overarching state that could maintain order, enforce property rights and establish the range of public goods that in the right circumstances could be the basis of a market economy.

In Japan, the beginnings of institutional development to support a modern economy could be found a couple of centuries before the Meiji restoration in the 1860s. But the big changes came after what was at first a step back into the feudal past, with strong resistance to opening in response to pressure from the North Atlantic. Japan for many centuries had been governed not by the Emperor but by successive hereditary Shoguns, who maintained some nominal respect for the emperor. The Shoguns' power came to be undercut by division within the country about the appropriate response to the intrusion of the industrialising West, manifested dramatically from the 1840s in the foreigners' capacity to impose a substantial opening to international intercourse upon China, for most of thousands of years the East Asian hegemon.

The Court of the Japanese emperor became a centre of resistance to opening to the foreigners. The weakening of the authority of the Shogun by dissatisfaction with the diplomatic response to and partial acquiescence in pressure from America and Europe provided opportunity for that same Court. The renewed authority of the new Emperor made possible a decisive opening to the West in contradiction of the policies upon which the restoration of imperial power had been achieved.

Comprehensive opening to the West, acquiescence in many conditions on foreign trade policy and in foreigners' rights to do business and be resident in Japan under their own laws, and Japan's acceptance or embrace of many productive foreign institutions, set the path for a remarkable period of economic growth. As Maddison notes in his Arndt Lecture, the success of the open policies eventually created conditions under which Japan was able to negotiate an end to the main discriminatory treatment against it. (Some aspects of discriminatory treatment continued to rankle into the period after WW1 and became causally important in Japan's disastrous military course of the1930s.) It also fundamentally unhinged the old, Sino-centric political order, liberating and empowering Japan in its fatal emulation of Western imperialism.

Superior economic growth in Europe, and then the US and Japan, underpinned the phenomenon of imperialism. More advanced economies, with a small minority of global population, came to establish sovereignty with various degrees of effectiveness over a very large part of the population as well as surface of the earth.

There were mixed effects of imperialist pressure on economic performance amongst the colonised people. In China, the colonial wars and the domestic instability associated with reaction to the new foreign presence created civil disturbance on a scale that seriously affected capital accumulation and exchange. From 1820 until 1913, China's total economic output hardly increased at all. The aggregate economic story in India in the early period of intense contact with imperialism was stronger, with output doubling between 1820 and 1913. India had neither the extreme of instability during the period of colonial pressure, nor quite the degree of order of China at the beginning of the period. The first half of the twentieth century in India was unhappy for economic growth.

In what is now the third most populous developing country, Indonesia, there was considerable economic growth between 1820 and 1913, but with a high proportion of it appropriated by the large numbers of resident Dutch (Maddison, Arndt Lecture).

Looking at the Maddison numbers, there was a break in the trajectory of global economic growth and its regional distribution with World War Two. In many respects, the break was as decisive as that at the onset of modern economic growth. The Golden Age was a period of exceptionally strong economic growth in the countries that had already become relatively rich, including those whose past economic achievements had been degraded during World War Two. Growth was most rapid in those countries that were able quickly to recover lost ground. Japan was producing at the level of the immediately pre-war period by the mid 1950s and continued growing strongly until the shocks to the international monetary system and global energy market through 1973 and 1974. By then, Japan had entered the frontiers of average productivity levels and incomes of the then advanced industrial countries.

7.3   EXTENSION OF MODERN ECONOMIC GROWTH TO ASIA IN THE GOLDEN AGE

1950–1973 was a period of strong growth centred in the countries that were or had been rich, but extending to most countries. Global output increased by an average of 4.9 per cent per annum on the Maddison figures. The spill-overs from prosperity in the advanced economies were important in most developing countries. Many newly independent economies, especially those with pre- or non-colonial traditions of an overarching State, received some impetus to growth from independence itself. These include some which were later to experience stagnation or decline.

In China, the Second World War established the conditions for the success of communist revolution. The new Communist Party Government from 1949 quickly restored order over the whole country, for the first time in more than a hundred years. This alone was instrumental in restoring economic growth after a long period of stagnation. Twists and turns in Communist Party policy over the subsequent 29 years led to some periods of disastrously poor performance. The gyrations in policy and performance occurred within a trajectory that on the whole was upwards, but weak compared with Japan and China's East Asian immediate neighbours.

India had experienced some decline in economic output between the onset of World War One and Independence. The new priorities of a national government, concerned for the wider participation of its people in the economic life of the country, brought continuous and reasonably strong economic growth over a long period to India for the first time. The new policies included better and more widespread, although still limited, modern education, easing of constraints on human talent moving to its most productive applications, and removal of discrimination against indigenous investment. Although India's growth was superior to that in any previous extended period, it suffered by comparison with the market economies of East Asia, and to a lesser extent China, and was routinely denigrated inside and outside the country as an inadequate 'Hindu rate of growth'.

The historically distinctive change in the Golden Age was the appearance of the new phenomena of sustained rapid economic growth in many parts of East Asia. It emerged first in Japan as it recovered quickly from the devastation of war. Japan grew so rapidly in the 1960s that its audacious plan to double output in a decade was achieved a couple of years ahead of schedule. More remarkably, the process of sustained rapid internationally-oriented growth was established in both Hong Kong and Taiwan. Those initially poor economies' comparative advantage lay in commodities that used abundant labour intensively. Outward-looking policies allowed this to become the basis for rapid export expansion, as management capacity and capital became available from mainland China after the revolution. Korea's internationally oriented policies and development framework from the early 1960s were built around an objective of rapid growth. Rapid growth continued in each Northeast Asian economy once it was established, until it reached the frontiers of the developed countries in average productivity and incomes, first of all in Japan.

Singapore launched itself on a rapid growth path following the separation from Malaysia in the mid 1960s, and grew more rapidly even than the Northeast Asian developing market economies.

During the Golden Age, growth in Japan, Taiwan, Hong Kong and, in the second half of the period, Singapore and Korea, was stronger for longer than anything that had been previously known in the history of humanity. Sustained economic growth in these economies was essentially catching up with the capital intensity and productivity of the world's advanced economies, within societies that had accepted the primacy of an economic growth objective. The starting point in all cases was the overthrow of priorities and cultural inhibitions associated with old ways of life whenever they were widely recognised as being in clear conflict with the imperatives of economic growth. The challenge from the economically and technologically powerful West in the nineteenth and early twentieth centuries had in many cases generated an initially negative reaction which lasted for varying periods. The ultimate reaction – so far everywhere except North Korea, but may be changing – was one of realisation that maintenance of national sovereignty in any sense demanded economic modernisation, involving opening up to the international economy and absorbing the technological and many aspects of the institutional framework of economies that were already successful. For the smaller countries of East Asia, strategic vulnerability in relation to neighbours was a powerful additional impetus to change in economic strategy.

Sustained rapid economic growth in East Asia was associated with high levels of investment, supported by high and rising levels of savings, including private and public investment in education. It occurred within a range of approaches to utilisation of direct foreign investment and of official intervention in the conditions under which international trade was conducted. The common features were relatively even-handed approaches to export promotion and import substitution, and openness to foreign technology and business ideas, the latter through alternative mechanisms where there were inhibitions on foreign ownership of business.

7.4   SILVER AGE ACCELERATION OF GROWTH IN THE ASIAN HEARTLAND

The second most successful period of global economic growth in the modern era in Maddison's calculation – from 1973 until the end of the twentieth century – contained another important turning point in the locus of global economic activity. It saw the establishment of sustained rapid economic growth, along the lines of the Northeast Asian market economies and Singapore in the Golden Age, in the world's most populous countries and regions – China, India, and less decisively most of Southeast Asia. It will turn out to be a more important point of departure for growth in global economic output than either the period after the Napoleonic wars in Western Europe, or the Golden Age. It laid the foundations for what may turn out to be the strongest period of growth of all – a Platinum Age in the first third of the twenty-first century. Sustained rapid growth was established in major countries which had previously experienced only moderate growth, with the most populous Asian economies joining a process of rapid movement towards the global frontiers of capital intensity and productivity.

The first of the new movers were in Southeast Asia – Thailand and Malaysia from the early to mid 1970s. The most important change came with the new leadership that emerged in China following the death of the founding leader of the communist regime – Mao Zedong. Mao died in 1976 after a long period of inhibited capacity and after the disastrous decade of political instability that was the Cultural Revolution. His death led to two years of indecisive policy as the tiller was contested by various groups within the upper echelons of the Communist Party, with contrasting approaches to economic development strategy. The first main group comprised surviving victims of the Cultural Revolution, who thought that the future of China lay with moving decisively away from Maoism towards a modernising policy. Another was made up of leaders who had been close to Mao during the Cultural Revolution, and who continued to hanker after continuous revolution, autarky, the dominance of the Peoples Communes in the countryside and politically directed state owned corporations in the cities.

The victims of the Cultural Revolution amongst the leaders of the late 1970s, coalescing around Deng Xiaoping, established control of the Central Committee of the Communist Party in December 1978. China embarked on a policy of market-oriented economic reform and opening to the outside world from which it has not looked back.

The new Communist Party leadership had no blueprint for economic reform – no more than the leadership of Taiwan in the 1950s or of Korea through the 1960s, or for that matter of Japan in the 1860s. What Deng and leaders close to him did have was recognition that there would be huge gains from China opening up to foreign economic ideas, technology, ways of approaching business and economic institutions. They recognised the success that widespread use of markets for domestic allocation of resources and exchange of goods and services and opening to the international economy had brought for their neighbours and for their compatriots in Taiwan and Hong Kong. They recognised that allowing a substantial role for markets in domestic allocation of resources had some inevitable consequences for widening dispersion in the distribution of income. They saw acceptance of change as being necessary to maintain long-term stability in China and to maintain China's position relative to the rest of the world including in relation to the Soviet Union, which most in the Chinese leadership had come to see as a threat to China's sovereignty.

The success of East Asian economic reform in lifting the rate of productivity and incomes growth, reinforced over time by the beginnings of China's emulation of the success of other East Asian countries, made it a highly influential model for development in much of the rest of the world. It was the model for which Indonesia reached in the mid-1980s, as a large fall in the oil price came to require new sources of export expansion. It was the natural model to which Vietnam gravitated after the collapse between 1989 and the early 1990s of the Soviet Union and the Comecon trade structures.

The Philippines had been hesitantly groping towards an internationally-orientated growth strategy from time to time from the 1970s. There had been a long detour during the unsuccessful military administration of Marcos. Then under the second President of the democratic restoration, the Philippines took decisive steps towards opening the economy through the mid 1990s, with positive effects on economic growth.

The second decisive economic event of the late twentieth century, after Chinese economic reform and opening to the international economy, was the change of economic strategy in India by degrees from the mid-1980s and decisively from 1991. India, like China, had adopted inward-looking approaches to economic development in the early years of Independence. A large economy like India could have aspirations for self-sufficiency in a wide range of goods and services. This was one source of vulnerability to the appeal of inward-looking policies. The antidote of East Asian developing economies' demonstration of the huge potential benefits from deep integration with the international economy had yet to be developed when independent India's initial development strategy was shaped in the 1950s. The international political developments that led India into the close strategic and economic embrace of the Soviet Union through the 1960s and 1970s reinforced tendencies to adopt autarchic policies. The inward looking ideas about economic policy that had been influential in Britain and to some extent in parts of Western Europe in the immediate postwar years had been absorbed by members of the post-Independence Indian political elite, and survived better than in their original European homes. India's economic and political experience had not been so disastrous as to shake confidence in the old approaches in a decisive way. In this distorted sense, India was at a disadvantage relative to China, where the Cultural Revolution had been an important spur to fundamental change.

Internationally aware Indians, resident abroad and at home, became increasingly concerned at the relative under-performance of their economy as one after another of the East Asian economies did much better. Bhagwati has described one of the origins of Indian reform in 1991 as the disagreeable position of having a superiority complex and an inferior status. In the end, the poor performance relative to China was such a challenge to Indian pride, and also potentially a challenge to Indian sovereignty, that its influence was decisive.

The Indian changes came more gradually than the Chinese, as they must in a democratic polity. Some analysts see clear signs of what was later to come in the Rajiv Ghandi reforms of the mid 1980s. But there is no doubting that the changes in response to difficult macroeconomic circumstances in 1991 were of larger dimension and had more important effects. As in China, and in smaller East Asian economies, as indeed in Japan at an earlier stage in history, the early success of economic reform helped to establish its economic and political credentials. There was always a question in India about whether initially unpopular and counter-intuitive policies of more open trade (not at that stage anything like free trade), more open approaches to investment, and greater utilisation of market mechanisms for allocation of resources, would survive for long. That doubt has been significantly assuaged by the survival of the policy now through two changes in government, the second bringing in as Prime Minister economist Manmohan Singh, who as Finance Minister had played a leading role in the initial reforms in 1991.

One other feature of economic growth in the Golden and Silver Ages is worthy of remark. The period since the Second World War has seen relatively strong growth in smaller countries. By contrast, in ancient times, there were mostly economic advantages in large scale national organisation – or at least of strategic alignment with a large country. A large country was less vulnerable to serious intrusion from neighbours. There was a certain institutional Darwinism in the tendency for states which had mastered the arts of good governance to expand at the expense of others. In the days when free exchange across large distances and between regions with disparate resource endowments required integration within a single political order, the division of labour depended on the extent of the State. For these and other reasons, the conditions for economic growth were more likely to be present in large political communities.

Smaller entities prospered more easily in the Golden and Silver Ages, partly because the more open trade of this era allowed them to achieve economies of scale in many areas of production alongside a relatively small domestic market. They were assisted as well by opportunities for catching up with the capital intensity and technological and institutional quality of more advanced economies by the general conditions of stability and order. They were also helped by the more ready international transmission of ideas about government and economic policy which reduced some of the advantage that had accrued disproportionately to larger entities.

7.5 THE FIRST THIRD OF THE TWENTY-FIRST CENTURY: HARVEST TIME IN POPULOUS ASIA AND THE PLATINUM AGE

How will things look in future? Angus Maddison gives us a start in our thinking with the projections to the year 2030. He notes in the Arndt Lecture that his projections are not the result of some econometric exercise. Rather they seek to incorporate judgements about the momentum of growth and the extent to which this is likely to be retarded, accelerated or maintained in various parts of the world economy. He is cautious on the future growth of China, with his projections embodying a sharp deceleration of the average growth rate from something like 8 per cent in the reform period (Maddison's adjusted data), and 9–10 per cent in the early twenty-first century, to 5 per cent per annum. He is therefore anticipating a major slowdown from the first quarter century of reform.

Maddison's projections for 2030 embody expectations of continued strong growth in India at a rate a bit above China but well below the average so far for the shorter reform period in India, and even below that of the Silver Age. They envisage low growth in Japan (an average of about two thirds of one per cent) – continuing the pattern of the 1990s and early twenty first century. They anticipate slow, positive growth in Western Europe (1.65 per cent). They anticipate somewhat more rapid growth in the US (2.45 per cent) than in other established developed countries because of the more favourable demographics created by much higher rates of immigration. The rest of the world – the other developed outliers; the smaller success stories of Northeast Asia; Southeast and South Asia beyond India; other West Asia and the 'Middle East'; Russia and its old empire in Central Asia and Eastern Europe; Latin America; and Africa – is expected to expand at a touch above the low average rate of the Silver Age (3 per cent compared with 2.8 per cent) and below the Golden Age.

The upshot is a very large change in the distribution of economic activity around the globe by the year 2030. The notable feature of the projections is that China becomes by far the world's largest economy by 2030 – nearly one third larger than the United States – despite the cutting of the average growth rate to half that of recent years. India emerges decisively as the world's fourth largest economy – two thirds the size of Western Europe and approaching three times the size of Japan – despite growth slumping to the average rate of the Silver Age. The Chinese plus Indian share of the global economy rises over the next several decades to something approaching one third by 2030. This is still a long way short of the ratio prior to the modern era. However, there is a considerable partial restoration of the decline in the relative standing of the Chinese and Indian economies through the one and half centuries of accelerated economic growth in Europe. The four largest entities, China, the US, Western Europe, India stand out way ahead of the next echelon, led by Japan. The big four account for nearly two thirds of world economic activity.

The remainder of this chapter does two things. First, it digs a little deeper into Maddison's projections and asks whether it is likely that outcomes along these lines will emerge over the next several decades. Secondly, and at greater length, it explores some implications of this historic shift in the locus of global economic activity for the governance of the international economy and polity. The perception lags in identifying requirements for new institutional arrangements to accommodate new global economic and power realities are long, and the implementation lags after recognition of the need for change even longer. If we are to be ready for a world with a very different distribution of power by 2030, then we need to be thinking through the institutional requirements right now and moving soon towards building the required institutional order.

7.6   HOW GOOD ARE THE MADDISON NUMBERS?

So how good are the numbers in the Maddison histories and projections? Let me jump forward first to my conclusions. It is likely that the Maddison projections will turn out to be below the realities, for the global economy and especially for China. They are probably about right for the developed economies.

With two qualifications, the next several decades, embodying the harvest times of rapid economic growth in the most populous Asian countries, are likely to experience stronger economic growth than the Silver Age, and may take the world into a new Platinum Age in which the average growth rates of the Golden Age are attained or exceeded. One qualification relates to the maintenance of domestic political stability in China and India through the stress of sustained rapid economic growth. The second and more challenging qualification relates to the building of an international institutional order that provides the international public goods for peace and prosperity in a hugely expanded and deeply integrated global economy dominated by four entities.

The strongest growth momentum the world has ever known is now well established in China – with its population more than half as big again as all of the contemporary world's developed countries together. In my assessment of the economic factors – and abstracting for the moment from the possibility of fundamental domestic or external political dislocation – China's growth over the period to 2020 will be similar to that of the three decades of reform so far – faster for a while, and then decelerating as China's labour force ages and falls and as the opportunities for rapid productivity decline as the world's frontiers are approached. Beyond 2020, there is of course a wider range of uncertainty. An alternative view of prospective Chinese and Indian growth, developed within a growth accounting framework, is presented in Garnaut (2008; 2011a and 2011b).

If US growth proceeded at the average rate estimated by Maddison, and Chinese according to mine for the Climate Change Review, the Chinese economy would be more than twice as large as the American by the end of the 2020s. Its per capita output would be about 70 percent of the Western European – a proportion at which opportunities for rapid growth through 'catching up' were diminishing considerably, generating the usual deceleration out of sustained rapid growth at about that time.

There is no necessary or likely economic reason why Chinese growth rates will ease much until the average Chinese labour productivity is closer to the average of the developed economies than it will be through the period to 2020. I will come back to the reasons.

Considerable and accelerating momentum has been achieved in Indian economic growth since 1991. Growth momentum is accelerating, not decelerating, so it would take a major disturbance to push average growth rates 2003–30 back to the levels of the Silver Age. Growth is becoming more securely based politically and economically. A demographic structure that is more favourable than China's for sustaining growth, and the large gap between Chinese and Indian productivity levels that emerged in the 13 years between the dates of commencement of concerted reform in the two countries, and which has widened since, suggest that rapid growth in India will be maintained after China approaches the frontiers of global productivity and slows down. Again excepting fundamental domestic or external political dislocation, India's share of global output will rise strongly after China slows through from the 2020s.

Sustained rapid growth in China and India will keep terms of trade historically high for commodity exporting countries, and create opportunities for others in global markets for labour-intensive manufactures as Chinese labour rapidly becomes more scarce and valuable. It seems unlikely that the economies outside the big four and Japan – the rest of the world in Table 7.1 and Figure 7.1 – will experience an average growth as low as 3 per cent. The more populous Southeast Asian countries, first of all Vietnam, and probably Indonesia as its political leaders learn and apply the art of growth-oriented economic management in a democratic polity, have laid a base for doing much better in the period ahead than through the political transitions and Asian financial crisis of the 1990s. The improved performers now seems likely to include Russia and several of the economies that once formed part of the Soviet Union and its empire in Eastern Europe, after the appalling stagnation and then collapse of the late twentieth century. They may include the more populous economies of Latin America, spurred by historic rises in terms of trade and application of the lessons of sad development experience – but with major questions about continuity of economic strategy.

There are of course qualifications to the expectation of sustained strong economic growth in the currently developing countries. Most significantly, it would be disrupted by increasing pressure from climate change in the absence of effective global mitigation (Garnaut, 2011b), by a breakdown in the international political order, or by domestic political disorder in one or more major countries.

Maddison's projections for Japan seem low, after the evidence that it has worked off the overhang from the investment boom of the late 1980s and beginning of the 1990s that was the source of a decade of stagnation. The estimates for Western Europe and the US seem reasonable, with prospects for doing although better in a buoyant global economy having been diminished by the Great Crash of 2008 (Garnaut and Llewellyn-Smith, 2009).

I have followed with interest and admiration the careful work over more than a decade of Maddison and Harry Wu on China's economic statistics. They have concluded that the established official data, accepted by the international agencies, have underestimated Chinese GDP but modestly overstated the rate of output growth on average over the reform period.

In the early 1990s, with Guonan Ma (Garnaut and Ma, 1993), and later Yiping Huang (Garnaut and Huang, 1994), I sought indirectly to estimate the level of Chinese GDP by reference to per capita consumption of a wide range of foodstuffs and inputs into industrial activity. Ma, Huang and I compared then contemporary Chinese per capita consumption, with that of other East Asian economies, at various times past. Taiwan was our prime comparator. Our conclusion then was that the measures of GDP per capita derived from taking standard national accounts data and converting them to dollars at prevailing exchange rates, underestimated China's GDP relative to other developing economies at times when their announced GDP was similar to China's in the early 1990s, by a factor of about three. The common underestimation for countries at China's level of development and incomes, relative to the advanced economies, was commonly in the vicinity of three. So conventional measures of GDP tended in the early 1990s to underestimate Chinese GDP relative to developed countries by a factor of 9, and PPP estimates by three.

Gradually, in the years since then, we have seen the removal of some of that part of this underestimation that was particular to China, beyond the general tendency for the national accounts data to understate the purchasing power of low income economies. There has been restatement of Chinese national accounts on several occasions, most recently late in 2005. There has been a considerable appreciation of the real effective exchange rate, through inflation in excess of the average of the rest of the world, and since July 2005 the beginnings of what is likely to be sustained and in sum considerable nominal appreciation of the Chinese currency.

I am broadly comfortable with the Maddison and Wu historical estimates, both on levels and on rates of growth of Chinese GDP. I would make two points about the future. First, the sources of modest overestimation of Chinese growth rates in the reform era are less important now than in the late 1990s. Indeed, similarly careful assessment of recent Chinese growth data suggests no grounds for downward adjustment to the strong numbers in the vicinity of 9 and 10 per cent. Second, there is considerable doubt about whether we should expect a deceleration in Chinese growth over the next decade or even over the next several decades. Chinese investment levels are now much higher than the average in the reform period. There is no economic reason why these levels of investment need to fall. Investment shares of GDP in the vicinity of 40–45 per cent are quite sustainable in an economy which is tending to save one half of total incomes (Garnaut and Huang, 2005). Indeed there is room for domestic demand expansion and somewhat higher rates of growth without risking either domestic inflation or external instability so long as other aspects of macroeconomic policy are adjusted accordingly. The crucial adjustment is the faster appreciation of the real exchange rate which is achieved with least risk to economic and political stability through nominal appreciation of the renminbi.

China will reach a turning point in economic development in the years immediately ahead. Previously apparently unlimited supplies of labour will dry up, labour scarcity become the norm and real wages begin to rise rapidly (see Garnaut and Song, 2006, especially Chapters One and Two). This process has already begun in coastal China. There are several reasons why the turning point in economic development has come relatively early in the development process in China, and why the Chinese economy will move through the structural change associated with the turning point relatively quickly. One is the exceptionally rapid rate of growth in total output and demand for labour. The second is the sharp decline in fertility which occurred about the time of the reform policies, which has led to sharply lower rates of total population and now labour force growth. This has now been going on for long enough for the number of new entrants into the labour force each year to be declining absolutely. The third reason for expecting a sharp adjustment in the labour market is that total levels of investment in education have been rising strongly, from reasonably high levels by developing countries standards despite the tragic gap of the Cultural Revolution years. This rising total amount of investment has been focussed on smaller and smaller numbers of Chinese students in the school ages, so that the level of education being made available to each young Chinese is rising sharply. That adds to the market squeeze on unskilled labour in the period ahead and is contributing to rapid increases in real wage rates. This will accelerate China's loss of competitiveness in simple labour intensive manufactures and force transition into technologically more sophisticated and more capital intensive export industries.

As a result, appreciation of the real exchange rate will be achieved through nominal appreciation or domestic inflation. China through these processes will gradually remove the gap between GDP as measured by purchasing power methods and estimated by converting national accounts data into international dollars at prevailing exchange rates – but purchasing power-based estimates of GDP, as applied by Maddison, will not be affected.

There is no necessary reason why this major transition in China will be associated with any slowing of economic growth before the 2020s. Of course, certain conditions must be met if rapid growth is to continue through and beyond the turning point. The most important of these is a high degree of flexibility in domestic resource allocation. This requires acceptance of far-reaching change in the structure of industry as labour-intensive industries decline and technologically more sophisticated industries take their place. China is in a good position to accept changes of this kind. On the whole, they will be supportive of political stability around rapid growth because of the rapid increases in real wages in urban and rural areas with which they will be associated.

Beyond the increased rate of capital intensification of production in China, the second reason for expecting the continuation of high growth is the continuing deepening of integration into the international economy. Chinese import shares of consumption and export shares of production continue to rise at extraordinary rates. China is already the world's third largest export market and, within a few years, will soon occupy a similar status in global import markets. In a few years, it will be the world's largest trading economy. China is by far the largest recipient of direct foreign investment amongst developing countries. These huge direct foreign investment flows with their associated contributions to technological improvement can be expected to continue. These factors and continued reform of the market economy can be expected to lead to high rates of productivity growth for some time, until China is much closer to average productivity levels of the developed countries.

The Chinese authorities have been announcing an objective of reducing the rate of growth now for most of the years of the twenty-first century. They have been supported in this by the international financial institutions and the global investment banks. The basis of this has been a feeling that the investment shares are unsustainably high and that bringing them down will lower growth. However, this view of Chinese growth potential is based on a misjudgement. The current account surplus in the years preceding the great Crash at 7–10 per cent of GDP in such a large economy is not consistent with long-term international acceptance of open trade with China and is inevitably a focus of international protectionist pressures. Currency appreciation alone would not generate an optimal adjustment path. The continuation of at least the current levels of investment and, probably some increase in them, will be a necessary part of the overall adjustment through which China must go in its macroeconomic structure.

The story of Indian growth is currently less familiar to economists in the West. After a long period of growth fluctuating around 4 per cent, the 'Hindu rate of growth', the reforms of the late 1980s and, especially 1991, led to significant and sustained lift in average growth rates. Over recent years, we have seen 7–8 per cent growth rates, in the range that was once familiar only as sustained growth rates in East Asian countries. The economically reputed Prime Minister has announced a medium term objective closer to 10 per cent.

One remarkable feature of recent Indian growth has been that, as in East Asia, the savings rate has risen endogenously with rapid growth in incomes. Having languished in the high teens in earlier years, the Indian savings rate rose to 23 per cent a few years ago, and is 30 per cent in the latest data. This was the rate in Japan at the beginning of the 1960s. Continued high incomes growth saw the savings rate in Japan rise beyond 30 per cent through the 1960s just as continued strong growth over a long period of time led to continued increases in the Korean and Chinese savings rates. Continued incomes growth will see yet higher proportions of income allocated to savings and this will support higher levels of investment in both the private and public sectors without risking macroeconomic instability. This is going to be an important fly wheel for higher growth into the foreseeable future.

The second likely source of an acceleration of Indian economic growth is the recent and short history of reform which means that many of the productivity raising structural changes with which they were associated are still coming through. In a democratic polity, every reform step is contested, but the outcomes have been favourable enough to increase political commitment to going further. The continuation of the current trajectory of reform will lead to continued increases in productivity growth for some time. As a result of this and capital intensification, there is no reason why emerging Indian government hopes and aspirations for sustained growth in the region of 8–10 per cent cannot be achieved. The higher end of this range – and this ambition might not be realised in full – would be well in advance of India's growth rates in the reform era so far. It would be twice the rate presumed in the Maddison projections. It would be in line with average Chinese growth in the reform era.

The bottom line of these assessments is that Maddison's projections for both the relative and absolute Chinese and Indian economies in the year 2030 are likely to be underestimates – and Maddison himself stresses the caution of his China estimates. The realisation of the outlook that I have suggested is most likely would cause global growth rates 2003–2020 to exceed those of the Golden Age, once the two years affected most by the Great Crash are excluded. The extension of sustained rapid growth to the populous Asian countries and their increasing scale would make the early twenty first century a superior Platinum Age.

I have mentioned the qualifications about my suggestion that the Maddison estimates are likely to underestimate growth. As we see from Maddison's work, while growth momentum is commonly maintained over long periods, with sustained rapid 'catch-up' growth easing only when economies enter the range of productivity and average incomes of developed countries, the economic trajectories can be altered fundamentally by international and domestic political events. Failure of domestic political systems to adjust in a timely way to changes in the economic structures could lead to political instability that knocked the growth process off course. I will not now undertake a detailed assessment of the possibilities of domestic political failure. Suffice to say that they are greatest in China, but that even in China, the most likely outcome is continued strong growth at rates in excess of those indicated by Maddison and Wu for the reform period so far.

India is subject to a different range of uncertainties. My own judgement is that the purely domestic political risks to Indian growth are now much less than at the beginning of the reform era and, in fact, small. That judgement depends on a view that the current Congress Party Government will find and implement mechanisms to directly improve the incomes of Indians in rural areas, a large proportion of whom so far have received little benefit from the acceleration of growth and who are influential in the democratic process. Considerable thought and priority is being given to these matters in India today.

The world that is created by the extension of sustained, rapid economic growth to the populous countries of Asia is vastly different in the distribution of power across the international community, and in its demands on international public goods to maintain political stability and prosperity. The Golden Age occurred in a bipolar international order, with the US exercising hegemonic influence and being prepared to accept high leadership costs in maintaining favourable international conditions for economic growth in its (majority) part of the world system. This structure gave way late in the Silver Age to a uni-polar world, in which the idea took root in influential parts of the US that international public goods could be supplied by the exercise of power by one dominant country. Hopes that US hegemonic leadership could maintain a stable international economic and political order have been undermined by the demonstration of the limits of US power in Iraq in particular.

The greatest risks to the world experiencing a Platinum Age are around the challenge to build a suitable institutional framework to accommodate the emerging reality of the world economy being dominated by four great entities, of which the US is no longer the largest. Maddison's work tells us that rebuilding the international framework is a matter of great urgency. The implication of the huge changes is that a failure of timely institutional development could be destructive of both peace and prosperity. My own additional thoughts on prospects for global economic growth do not change this outlook; they just reduce the time in which changes must be made, and increase the costs of failure.

7.7   MANAGING INTERNATIONAL PUBLIC GOODS IN THE PLATINUM AGE

The world of 2030 will be much more deeply integrated in many ways than it is today. The international trade share of output and expenditure will have continued to rise mainly because of continued technological improvement, which is reducing the costs of international transport and communications. Hopefully, there will also be contributions from the liberalisation of trade in many countries, with India having more potential for change than the other major economies.

There will be immense challenges to stability in relations among states in at least five areas. New mechanisms will be needed to deliver international public goods for the maintenance of security in a conventional sense, for promoting development in poor countries and regions so as to reduce the external costs of poverty and State failure, for the avoidance of global environmental failure on a scale that threatens global prosperity, for the redistribution of global savings amongst economies, and for maintenance of an open international trading system.

First, in the security sphere, technological advance, the spread of knowledge across humanity, and rising incomes will have greatly expanded the range, power and availability of weapons of mass destruction.

Second, falling international transport and communications costs and rising incomes will at once have increased concern for international poverty in a prosperous world (because of increased awareness of external poverty and because compassion backed by financial assistance is a superior good), and increased the costs and risks of failures of order and development in parts of the world (through transmission of public health, crime and environmental problems amongst other things).

Third, there will be an increase in the importance of and awareness about the external environmental costs of economic growth that is not modified to take environmental considerations into account.

Fourth, it is likely that, in the absence of fundamental change in consumer behaviour (which is likely to occur only over long periods of time), world savings, and over time probably world wealth, will be concentrated much more than world production and income in the rapidly growing Asian economies. This will pose a challenge to international financial intermediation and to political attitudes to foreign investment in the countries that became rich before others. These words were written for my original essay in honour of Maddison's 80th birthday, and have been underlined by the Great Crash of 2008 (Garnaut and Llewellyn-Smith, 2009).

Finally, in future, as now and in the past, there will be domestic political economy pressures for individual States to raise protectionist barriers, and where these are not resisted effectively, to impose costs on others. In the worst of circumstances, as in the 1930s, this could lead to cumulative protectionist responses, that reduce the gains from trade and threaten sustained rapid growth. This was the reality which lay behind the establishment of the GATT (from 1995, the WTO) in the postwar period.

Last time the world considered comprehensively the need for international institutions to internalise international externalities from the actions of single States was more than half century ago, in the aftermath of the second world war. Out of those discussions emerged the UN system, including the Washington based development (World Bank) and international macro-economic stabilisation (the International Monetary Fund) financial institutions, and the GATT (the latter at first as a compromise, following the failure to establish the WTO originally envisaged by the founders of the post war trading system). These institutions were established when international externalities of State action in the five spheres discussed above were much less important than today. The Nuclear Proliferation Treaty (NPT) came later. The danger of catastrophe from nuclear proliferation is closer than it has ever been.

The links between international development and various threats to national well being has become much clearer and much stronger in the intervening years of deepening integration in the international economy. The biggest of all changes in the perception as well as the reality of international externalities affecting international relations over these past 60 years has been in the environmental area, especially related to climate change. Over these past decades, humanity has been placing increasing stress on the atmospheric commons upon which life depends. As with the exhaustion of other resources which had once been available to humanity in common, the destruction of the atmospheric commons requires a system of property rights that has the effect of internalising to individual economies and ultimately enterprises the external costs of actions that damage the earth's atmosphere in various ways. The Stern Report to the UK Government highlights the growing concern (Stern, 2006), with implications for the international system discussed at length in my Garnaut Climate Change Reviews (Garnaut 2008, Garnaut 2011b). If my own view of the likely growth output for the global economy has merit, the contribution of growth to factors affecting global climate, and so the urgency of corrective measures, is greater than suggested by Stern (Garnaut, 2008).

Let me say a little about each of these five challenges, to demonstrate the difficulty of the task that lies ahead.

7.7.1 International Security

The post war international system embodying the United Nations (UN) was built around the initial military supremacy of the victorious powers of WW2. It gave privileged status to the largest of the allies – US, Britain, France, Soviet Union and China, through their permanent representation with veto power in the UN Security Council. This recognised a simple reality of the early postwar period. These were the strongest States – although the presence of China at the time depended on particular historical circumstances that looked to past and future rather than to present strategic weight – whose support for collective UN action would ensure that that action would not become a cause of global conflict.

The reality of the international distribution of power turned out to be very different from the premise of 1945. Through the 1950s and 1960s it became clear that two superpowers in reality dominated the international system. The operation of the UN had to adjust. In circumstances in which the interests of the two superpowers were in permanent conflict, the UN was hardly ever able to take collective action. International security depended on the maintenance of a balance of power – or of nuclear terror – between the US and the USSR.

This world ended with the collapse of the Soviet Union at the beginning of the 1990s. Without an automatic veto by one superpower of actions proposed by another, there was widely supported UN action against Iraq after the invasion of Kuwait, against the Taliban in Afghanistan after the terrorist attacks on the US in 2001, and in a number of other areas, including in Timor to restore order after the separation from Indonesia in 1999. The failure to take collective action under the auspices of the UN in some other situations was controversial. At least in the most important of these cases to the international system, on the 2003 military action against Iraq, majority US opinion today suggests that there was wisdom in the UN's caution.

Recent developments in Iraq, Afghanistan, Iran and Korea then have shattered US confidence in unilateral military action, before the anticipated shift in the international distribution of economic weight has gone far, and without the rebuilding of faith in collective action.

The postwar security system built around the Security Council and the veto of great powers is, ironically, more suitable to the quadrilateral world that is emerging than to either the bipolar or unipolar worlds of the past half century. None of the great powers will be able to achieve its security interests alone. Collective action by the four overwhelming powers will be able to achieve a great deal.

The 1945 arrangements are not tidily suited for the emerging world. India is not represented in the Security Council. Western Europe is over-represented; but rationalisation is not possible unless the European Union develops an integrated defence structure (see Clunies-Ross (2005) for a rich analytic treatment of future international roles for the European Union). This may happen, but not yet. And its eventual achievement may inhibit a desirable broadening of membership, most importantly to Turkey. Russia is not an economic great power and is unlikely to become one. But the immense military capacity inherited from the Soviet Union will give it a special place for some time, justifying a continuing role in the Security Council.

The NPT is well designed to manage the risk of nuclear proliferation if it has the unambiguous support of the great powers. The problem is that the genie has already escaped, with a number of minor and second rung powers having nuclear weapons and one or more being on the verge of joining them. There was some inevitability in India joining the nuclear club given its emerging status, but the manner of its joining damaged the international control framework.

It will be tempting for the US polity to pretend that nothing has changed; that it can continue to pursue the Neo-conservative dream of permanent military superiority. Any attempt to do so would accelerate the relative economic decline of the US. The US needs early adjustment to a quadrilateral international security framework, while it still has the economic and military capacity disproportionately to shape events. Every action of the US leadership over recent years has been in an opposite direction. It will not be easy for the US political community to adjust to the rapidly changing power realities. A failure to do so would be damaging to global, including US, security.

Technological improvement, rising incomes and the spread of knowledge have greatly reduced entry barriers to the nuclear club. Strong and early support by all of the emerging great powers for reform and enforcement of the NPT would seem to be a condition for avoidance of nuclear catastrophe before the Platinum Age has delivered on its promise.

7.7.2 International Development

International externalities from failures of development and government, and awareness of their importance, have been increasing in recent times. Terrorism, health and the environment have joined traditional economic and social reasons for concern.

The extent to which cooperation across the whole international community is necessary for the correction of these externalities requires analysis. Most development assistance is provided on a bilateral basis, and governed by donors' perceptions of their own interests as shaped by geography and geo-strategy. Most recently, China has become an immense source of bilateral international development assistance, with the geographic dispersion of the assistance strongly influenced by its interests in expanded global supplies of natural resource-based commodities. China and India have become donors through the multilateral organisations – for example, on a modest scale, to the International Agricultural Research Centres from the work of which they have been large beneficiaries.

The principle of subsidiarity is as relevant in this sphere as in many others. Much development assistance can be delivered most effectively by donors who have special knowledge and interest in a recipient country, and this work is best left to them. But multilateral action can be helpful to the debate and transmission of ideas about development, to provide assistance to those which miss out in the geostrategic interest race, and to establish rules to constrain the use of aid for non-development purposes that can generate problems for political stability and the trading system. On the whole, the structure of existing institutions provides a good starting point for this work – although the quality of the work of established institutions leaves much to be desired. The necessary adjustment to the emerging global power realities involves improvement of performance, and induction of the emerging powers into leadership and over time financial support for the multilateral effort, rather than radical institutional change.

7.7.3   International Environmental Externalities

Industrial growth in one country, especially a large economy, imposes external environmental costs on its cross-border and regional neighbours. Within the principle of subsidiarity, these are best managed through bilateral and regional mechanisms. The main external environmental costs of economic growth on a global scale, however, relate to global warming.

It is now widely accepted that the avoidance of risks of hugely damaging costs from global warming will require an international regime for discouraging the emission and encouraging sequestration of greenhouse gases. An international regime in which limited rights to emit greenhouse gases are traded globally is now widely understood to be part of an economically efficient response to the problem. The Kyoto Treaty under UN auspices has expanded practical knowledge in member countries – developing and developed – of the operation of a carbon trading system. The associated expansion of knowledge will allow improvements, as the regime is extended to controls on emissions (and not just participation in trading) in developing countries.

There are two major barriers to the adoption of the necessary constraints on emissions entitlements with opportunities for trade in entitlements. One is acceptance that all major economies must accept constraints on emissions. Major progress on this matter was made in the lead-up to and following the Copenhagen conference of the United Nations framework Convention on Climate Change in December 2009. The second barrier is the inherent difficulty of reaching agreement on a system for allocating initial emissions rights within a global trading system. The Kyoto agreement restricted emissions only of developed countries, as a first step towards universal restrictions. The United States political system is moving only slowly to acceptance of constraints. For developed countries, with high established per capita emissions, it was a relatively easy matter to agree that the initial allocation should be based on established levels of emissions. This would not be an acceptable basis for allocating emissions rights in a regime that placed restrictions on developing countries.

I recall a conversation with leading environmental officials in China in the early 1990s, in which my Chinese interlocuteurs stated that human-induced global warming was a substantial problem that required a global response. They said then that China would accept controls on levels of greenhouse emissions and be ready to join a global system for trading emissions rights, so long as the starting point was equal per capita initial rights. This is not in itself an unreasonable position; but it would provide no basis for agreement with developed countries.

Eventual agreement must be sought somewhere between the 'established levels' and the 'equal per capita' bases for initial allocations. I have supported suggestions for building an international regime around the idea of "contraction and convergence", with rights allocated on the basis of established emissions, with some additional restriction on developed countries and headroom for developing countries. Over a long transition period, there would be a shift towards equal per capita allocations. Such a system would involve large transfers of income to countries whose per capita incomes and emissions remained well below global average levels. It would be important for continued international support for the system that these transfers be embedded into a framework of international cooperation on development that made them productive for development. (These thoughts are presented as they were in the original essay in honour of Maddison, and are expanded in Garnaut, 2008 and 2011b).

The possibility that the period ahead will see growth in the global economy as high as ever before, and from a much higher base, makes the establishment of an effective international regime for greenhouse emissions more urgent than is recognised by the global warming pessimists.

7.7.4   International Financial Intermediation

Exceptionally high and rising savings rates have been a feature of sustained rapid growth in East Asia and now in India. This contrasts with low and falling savings, especially household savings, in the English speaking developed countries. Although investment rates have been exceptionally high in the rich (Japan) and the rapidly growing Asian economies, they have not been high enough to absorb domestic savings. The result has been persistent large current payments surpluses, which have existed alongside persistent deficits in the English speaking countries, first of all the United States.

The largest contemporary imbalances are China's current account surplus and the United States' deficit – each amounting to about 7 per cent of GDP in 2006 and China's surplus reaching 10 per cent in the year leading up to the Crash. While there are potential external costs in the domestic decisions in each country that have contributed to the imbalances, this was not seen as an appropriate subject for multilateral cooperation prior to the Great Crash. Interaction of domestic policy-making with bilateral discussions has seen tensions contained to tolerable levels. The intermediation of global, mostly US–domiciled financial institutions seemed to have been effective, until it unravelled in the Great Crash.

The larger questions for the international community relate to the longer term implications of huge differences in savings rates across countries, accompanied by exceptionally high growth rates in large, high-savings countries. By 2020 on my Platinum Age projections, the real value of per capita savings, and all other things equal the annual increment in per capita wealth, will be higher in China than the United States by a wide margin.

This would be challenging for international economic stability if it became a source of systematic competitive advantage of Asian over Western enterprises in access to and cost of capital, leading to compensating intervention against the activities of foreign enterprises in low-savings countries. Until the Great Crash of 2008, the skills and adaptability of European and especially American financial institutions allowed them to maintain their positions as favoured intermediaries, including with China. In the process, the institutions were losing their national identities, becoming genuinely multinational enterprises. The effective operation of the market seemed to have avoided the need for international cooperation amongst States to internalise external costs of decisions taken in single countries. The Great Crash of 2008 put the regulation of international financial intermediation near the top of the list of requirements for cooperative international action.

7.7.5   The International Trading System

The international public good of the open global trading system may be more difficult to maintain in the future than it was through the Golden and Silver Ages. The gains from maintaining open trade are larger than ever, because technological developments have made finer and finer specialisation possible across a wide range of goods and services. This may not be obvious to observers who simply look at the total scale of contemporary markets and compare it with earlier years. After all, the projected size of the Chinese economy in 2030 in Maddison's projections is larger than that of the world economy at the end of the Golden Age. But it is evident in the changing patterns of international trade.

The global trading system which was established for economies outside the Communist systems after the Second World War was well designed to promote the emergence of the deeply integrated global trading patterns that generated the Golden and Silver Ages. In important sense, that system reached its apogee with the opening up of the Chinese, Vietnamese and recently Russian economies to the international economy and acceptance of their membership of the World Trade Organisation (WTO). But there are awful signs that the system is in decline.

The decline has its origin in a paradox at the heart of the trading system. There is a sense that there are no external costs to domestic trade policy decisions that one State might take in its own national interest. A country damages itself as much or more than others from restricting imports. A country pursuing its own national interest would do the same, thus enhancing the value of the first country's decision to pursue free trade.

The political reality is sometimes different. The difference is encouraged by negotiations between States, whether on a bilateral or multilateral basis, to liberalise trade on a reciprocal basis. Trade negotiations to liberalise trade become the enemy of free trade. It is instructive that the richest period of trade liberalisation in the Western Pacific region, extending from China through Southeast Asia to Australia and New Zealand from the mid-1980s to the Asian financial crisis of 1997–98, involved almost no reciprocal bargaining.

For a range of reasons that I have analysed elsewhere, reciprocity has come to rule trade liberalisation discussion everywhere in the early twenty-first century. Frustration at lack of progress in multilateral trade negotiations has been one factor encouraging the proliferation of preferential trading areas. These have involved little or no net liberalisation, have increased transactions costs with their complex and restrictive rules of origin, and have completed the removal of trade liberalisation discussion from calculation of genuine national interest. There is a danger that extension of this trend into formation of restrictive regional trading blocks could seriously inhibit the globalisation of production that has been at the heart of accelerated economic growth since the middle of the twentieth century.

We need the WTO for its rules on the conduct of trade and its processes for disputes settlement. But the time may have passed when reciprocal negotiations in the WTO, much less bilateral and regional fora, were a useful part of the trade liberalisation process. The relevant international public good in the emerging international trading system is understanding in each country that liberal trade serves its own interest. The role of international organisations in trade liberalisation would be usefully refocussed on providing the knowledge and analysis that makes unilateral trade liberalisation possible.

7.8   CONCLUDING REMARKS

The simple listing and commencement of analysis of the international institutional arrangements that are necessary in the emerging quadrilateral raises serious questions about the international community's capacity to deliver a satisfactory response. In recent years, the world has mostly been heading in the wrong direction (security, the international trading system) or making negligible progress (development assistance and the environment regime). If there is no early change in trajectory on international institutional arrangements, the probability is uncomfortably high that the prospects for a Platinum Age will recede under mushroom or heat clouds, or in a Mad Max world of broken order in unsuccessful developing countries.

Under the clouds or in the Mad Max world, the Maddison projections on global economic output would be optimistic. Some economies would do better than others, and the rapidly expanding new economic powers with the flexibility provided by their stage of development would probably be damaged less than either established developed or poor developing countries. But none would do well. Maddison's work encourages us to think through the big issues before it is too late.

REFERENCES

Clunies-Ross, A. (2005), *Making the World Autonomous: A Global Role for the European Union,* Edinburgh: Dunedin Academic Press.

Garnaut, R. (2008), *The Garnaut Climate Change Review*, Melbourne: Cambridge University Press.

Garnaut, R. (2011a), *Garnaut Climate Change Review Update Paper 3: Global emissions trends*, presented at the Australian Agricultural and Resource Economic Society Annual Conference, Melbourne, 11 February 2011, available online: http://rossgarnaut.com.au/Documents/Garnaut%20Paper%203%20global%20emissions%20trends%20v2.pdf.

Garnaut, R. (2011b), *The Garnaut Review 2011: Australia in the Global Response to Climate Change*, Melbourne: Cambridge University Press.

Garnaut, R. and Y. Huang (1994), 'How Rich is China: More Evidence', Seminar Paper at the Australian National University.

Garnaut, R and Y. Huang (2005), 'The risks of investment-led growth', in Garnaut, R. and L, Song (eds), *The China Boom and its Discontents*, Asia Pacific Press, Canberra, Australia, pp. 1–19.

Garnaut, R. with D. Llewellyn-Smith (2009), *The Great Crash of 2008*, Melbourne: Melbourne University Publishing.

Garnaut, R. and G. Ma (1993), 'How rich is China: evidence from food economy', *Australian Journal of Chinese Affairs*, **30**, 121–48.

Garnaut, R. and L. Song (eds) (2006), *The Turning Point in China's Economic Development*, Canberra: Asia Pacific Press.

Maddison, A. (1998), *Chinese Economic Performance in the Long Run, Organization for Economic Co–Operation and Development*, Paris: OECD.

Maddison, A. (2001), The World Economy: a Millennial Report, Paris: OECD Development Centre.

Maddison, A. (2002), 'Introduction: Measuring Asian Performance', in Maddison, A., D.S. Prasada Rao and W.E. Shepherd (eds), *The Asian Economies in the Twentieth Century'*, Cheltenham UK: Edward Elgar.

Maddison, A. (2006), 'Asia in the world economy 1500-2030 AD', *Asian Pacific Economic Literature*, **20** (2), 1–37.

Stern, N. (2006). *Economic Effects of Climate Change, The Stern Review,* Cambridge University Press, New York, NY 10013-2473 USA http://www.hm-treasury.gov.uk/independent_reviews/stern_review_economics_climate_change/sternreview_index.cfm».

8. Total Factor Productivity and Economic Growth in Indonesia[1]

Pierre van der Eng

8.1 INTRODUCTION

Much of the recent literature on macroeconomic growth in Asia continues to be dominated by discussion of the degree to which Total Factor Productivity (TFP) growth explains the 'Asian economic miracle' of high economic growth. However, Young (1994) argued, on the basis of a four-country study, that the 'miracle' was more the result of the mobilisation of factors of production (labour and capital) than productivity growth, i.e. 'perspiration' rather than 'inspiration', as Krugman (1994) summarised his findings. This incited a series of studies that often used readily available multi-country data sets in order to estimate TFP growth in different parts of the world, on the assumption that the growth accounting residual represents TFP growth.[2]

The multi-country studies that estimated TFP growth all yielded different results. One of the reasons was that authors were forced to make very rough estimates of capital input on the basis of available national accounts data. In the case of Indonesia, close scrutiny of the data reveals inexplicable discrepancies in the original national accounts data produced at the central statistical agency (*Badan Pusat Statistik*, BPS) in Indonesia. Moreover, studies using multi-country data sets take national accounts data for granted. They do not consider revisions in data over time, while their capital stock estimates depend on heroic assumptions on depreciation and lifetime of

---

[1] Previous versions of this chapter were presented at the Seminar on *World Economic Performance: Past, Present and Future*, on the occasion of Angus Maddison's 80th birthday, at the University of Queensland, Brisbane in December 2006, and at a Research Seminar in the ANU Research School of Pacific and Asian Studies in October 2007. I would like to thank Hal Hill, Noriyoshi Oguchi, Peter Warr and Anders Isaksson, as well as participants in the workshop and the seminar, for their comments.

[2] See *e.g.* Chen (1997), Felipe (1999) and Weerasinghe and Fane (2005) for critical summaries of the results of these studies for Asian countries.

different categories of assets. For example, in the case of Indonesia, the estimates of gross fixed capital formation and capital stock deviate significantly from estimates that take close account of the idiosyncrasies in Indonesia's statistical data and the composition of investment and capital stock (Van der Eng, 2009). If this is the case for one country, it is likely to be true for others, which should be a warning to anyone using multi-country data sets, or giving unqualified credence to the results of such studies.

Indonesia's remarkable development experience since the mid-1960s has been the subject of a range of studies (e.g. Hill, 1999). Most of them focused on the key ultimate reasons for Indonesia's development in terms of institutional change and economic policies conducive to economic growth. However, the exact proximate causes underlying the country's high economic growth since the mid-1960s remain unclear. As a major Asian country Indonesia has, of course, been part of the multi-country studies referred to above which almost all found positive TFP growth, albeit to varying degrees. However, there is no reason to regard these studies as conclusive, because they have not explicitly considered the quality and availability of Indonesian statistical data.

The only economy-wide approximation of TFP that took these problems into account is by a former Director of Indonesia's BPS, Hananto Sigit (2004).[3] Notably, he found that TFP growth in Indonesia was significantly negative during 1980–2000 and that economic growth in this period was largely driven by capital accumulation.[4] These findings are in sharp contrast with the results of the multi-country studies referred to above. They also contrast with studies that used data from the annual survey of firms in Indonesia to assess the contribution of TFP to the growth of output in manufacturing industry. These studies revealed positive TFP growth, suggesting that that economic growth in Indonesia was not purely a consequence of resource mobilisation (see below).

In an effort to resolve these inconsistent findings, this chapter follows the approach of Sigit (2004), but enhances it on the basis of new long-term estimates of GDP in 2000 prices (Van der Eng, 2008), new long-term estimates of capital stock in Indonesia in 2000 constant prices (Van der Eng, 2009), new estimates of the share of labour income, new estimates of

---

[3] Osada (1994) also made direct use of data from Indonesia's BPS, but was less concerned about issues of data availability, accuracy and consistency.

[4] Sigit's TFP estimates for Indonesia for 1980–2000 make it a remarkable outlier among the countries covered in Oguchi (2004, p 6–8), such as India (2.1% annual growth of TFP, 41% of output growth explained by TFP growth), Japan (1.8%, 68%), South Korea (1.8%, 25%), Malaysia (1.3%, 20%), Nepal (1.1%, 22%), Singapore (0.8%, 11%), China (1.9%, 25%), Thailand (1.0%, 17%) and Vietnam (3.3%, 51%), except for the Philippines (-0.4%, -15%).

education-adjusted employment, the inclusion of educational attainment, and an extension of the timeframe of analysis to 1971–2008. Unlike the multi-country studies, this chapter is based on statistical data that have been corrected for inconsistencies. The next section outlines the methodology and data we use. This is followed by section 8.3 that estimates key 'proximate'[5] sources of economic growth. It also discusses whether the growth accounting residual can indeed be considered as an indication of TFP. A subsequent section, 8.4, discusses the prominent role of capital stock in Indonesia's growth experience as well as some of the factors that constrained new investment in recent years.

8.2   ESTIMATION OF OUTPUT AND INPUTS

8.2.1   Methodology of TFP Analysis

This chapter uses a simple, direct accounting method to estimate the contribution of TFP to economic growth, based on Oguchi (2004, p.24–29). The model in equation 8.1 indicates that output during a given year is a function of the productive employment of the total stocks of capital and labour.

$$Q_t = A_t \, f(K_t, L_t) \tag{8.1}$$

where Q_t is real output and K_t and L_t are the stock of capital and employment, respectively, in year t and A_t is the efficiency term. Differentiating with respect to time yields equation 8.2

$$\frac{dQ}{dt} = \frac{dA}{dt} f(K_t, L_t) + A_t \frac{\partial f}{\partial K} \frac{dK}{dt} + A_t \frac{\partial f}{\partial L} \frac{dL}{dt} \tag{8.2}$$

Dividing both sides by Q_t yields equation 8.3.

$$\frac{dQ}{dt} / Q_t = \frac{dA}{dt} / A_t + \frac{\partial f}{\partial K} \frac{dK}{dt} / f(K_t, L_t) + \frac{\partial f}{\partial L} \frac{dL}{dt} / f(K_t, L_t) \tag{8.3}$$

---

[5] Maddison (1988) explains the difference between the proximate and ultimate sources of economic growth. Proximate sources are measurable factors such as capital accumulation and technological change, the growth of labour input and human capital, the exploitation of natural resources etc. Ultimate sources are factors that shape the conditions under which proximate factors operate. They include geographic, social and political conditions.

Replacing the marginal productivities by factor prices then gives us equation 8.4.

$$g_t^Q = g_t^{TFP} + (rK_t / Q_t)g_t^K + (wL_t / Q_t)g_t^L = g_t^{TFP} + s_k g_t^K + s_l g_t^L \qquad (8.4)$$

where g_t^Q, g_t^{TFP}, g_t^K and g_t^L are the annual growth rates of output, TFP, capital and employment, respectively, r and w are the per unit service prices of capital and labour, respectively, and s_k and s_l are the shares of income from capital and labour in national income. Assuming constant returns to scale, or perfect elasticity of substitution between capital and labour, yields equation 8.5:

$$s_k + s_l = 1 \text{ or } s_k = 1 - s_l \qquad (8.5)$$

While it is difficult to incorporate a measure of quality change in the stock of capital goods, it is possible to incorporate a measure of quality change in the stock of employment by adjusting it for educational attainment, as equation 8.6 shows.

$$L_t^* = L_t e^{\alpha Y_t} \qquad (8.6)$$

where L_t^* = education-adjusted employment, L_t = number of gainfully employed, α = the elasticity of output for each additional year of education and Y_t = the accumulated number of years of education per person employed. Substituting L_t for L_t^* in equation 8.1 and differentiation with respect to time yields a modified equation 8.4. Inserting equation 8.5 into the modified equation 8.4 yields equation 8.7.

$$g_t^{TFP} = g_t^Q - (1 - s_l)g_t^K - s_l g_t^{L^*} \qquad (8.7)$$

Hence, the key data required to estimate the contribution of TFP to economic growth are annual data on GDP and capital stock in constant prices, education-adjusted employment, and the labour income share in GDP. Since this chapter is concerned with the national economy of Indonesia, it uses nation-wide data.

8.2.2 Output Data

Indonesia's national accounts data have undergone at least six major revisions since the 1950s. These revisions were in part due to the adoption of new estimation procedures, improved estimation, improved coverage, and changes in the base-year for constant price estimates (see Van der Eng, 1999, 2005). Since the 1983 revision, Indonesia's national accounts have been anchored to the quinquennial Input–Output (I–O) Tables. Consequently, the output approach still offers the main substantiation of the national accounts. The last of these revisions was anchored to the 2000 I–O Table. Extrapolation of these data for 2000–10 back in time with existing national accounts data for 1983–2000 and broad indicators of economic activity yields GDP per capita estimates shown in Figure 8.1 (Van der Eng, 1992, 2002, 2008).

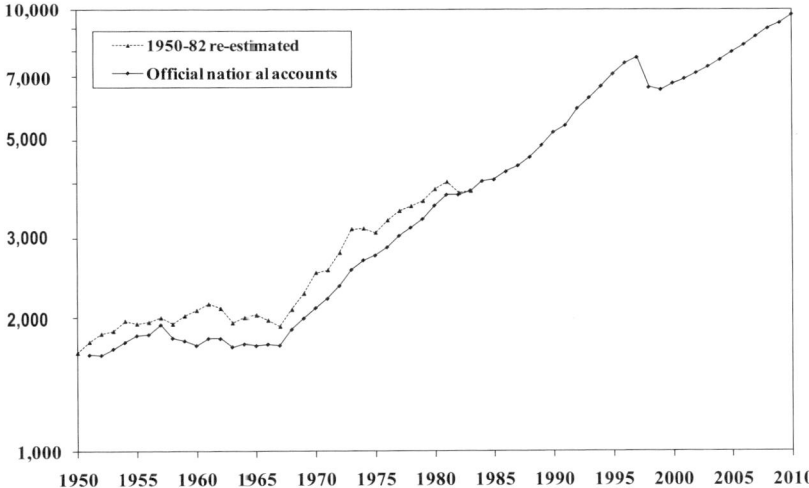

Source: Indonesia's national accounts and Van der Eng (2008), updated to include 2008–10.

Figure 8.1   GDP per capita in Indonesia, 1950–2010 (thousand 2000 Rupiah)

Figure 8.1 confirms that the 1951–82 national accounts data were underestimated. The chart also shows that Indonesia's growth spurt during 1967–97 was momentous. With average population growth at 2.0 per cent per year, average GDP growth was significant at 6.7 per cent per year.

Indonesia's economy contracted drastically in 1998, but growth resumed in 1999. The 1997 level of GDP per capita was regained in 2004.

8.2.3   Capital Stock Data

Closely scrutinised estimates of capital stock in Indonesia are rare. Keuning (1991) offered the first comprehensive estimates for 1975–85. In hindsight, these appear to have been much too high, possibly as a consequence of the methodology used, which relied considerably on extrapolation of short-term disaggregated incremental capital-value added ratios (Van der Eng, 2009).

Estimates of capital stock have recently been made at Bank Indonesia, the country's central bank, based on disaggregation of the growth of investment with quinquennial I–O Tables (Yudanto et al., 2005). These estimates did not take account of all historical information on investment and offered insufficient consideration of key assumptions, particularly the lifetime of different categories of capital goods. This left an opportunity for new capital stock estimates based on applying the perpetual inventory method to 26 categories of productive assets from 1951, with a longest asset life of 40 years (Van der Eng, 2009). Hence, the first 'complete' estimate is for 1990, which was re-estimated back to 1950 for non-residential capital stock on the basis of annual gross fixed investment and assumed depreciation resembling 1991–95 average implicit rates.

Figure 8.2 shows the results of the new estimate of capital stock. It reveals a significant acceleration of growth since 1980 and a slow-down in 1997–98. It also shows that most of the non-residential capital stock consists of structures. Figure 8.3 shows that the capital-output ratio decreased during 1967–80, which suggests that the main sources of high growth during these years were capital-extensive. This is possibly related to the fact that natural resource exploitation, particularly the rapid growth of oil production for export, underlay much of the economic expansion during these years, in combination with greater mobilisation of labour. The ratio increased significantly during 1980–97, which suggests that economic growth during those years was of a more capital-intensive nature and depended, at least partly, on the mobilisation of productive capital. This may have been related to the significant growth of export-oriented manufacturing industry since the early-1980s.

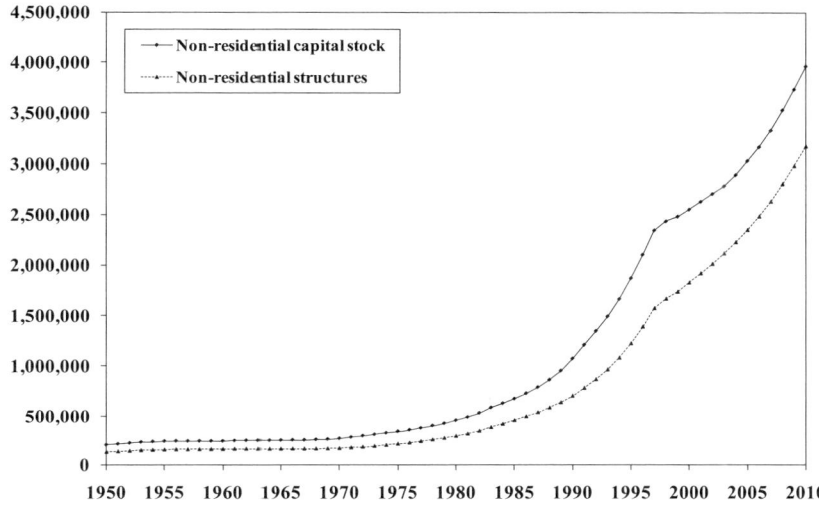

Source: Van der Eng (2009), updated to include 2008–2010.

Figure 8.2 Gross fixed non–residential capital stock in Indonesia, 1950–2010 (billion 2000 Rupiah)

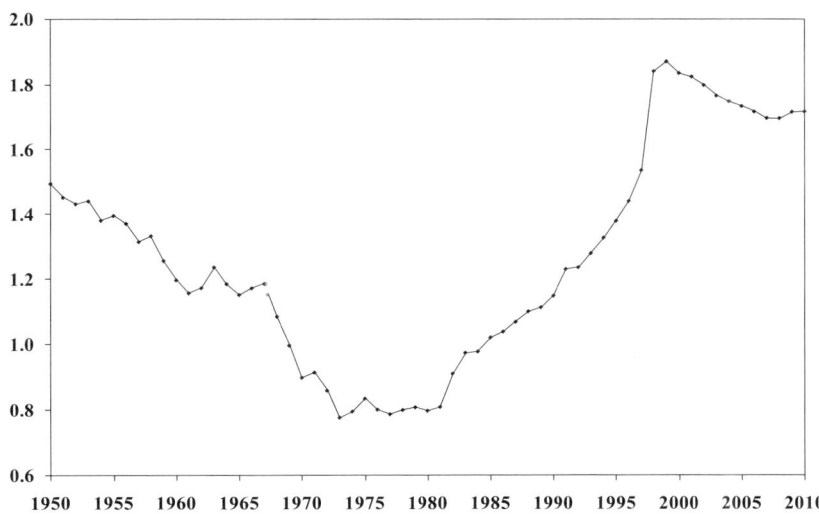

Note: Capital stock excludes residential structures.

Source: Van der Eng (2009, 2008), updated to include 2008-2010.

Figure 8.3 Capital–output ratio for Indonesia, 1950–2010

8.2.4   Employment Data

Consistent long-term estimates of employment are hampered by the fact that
the population censuses of 1961, 1971, 1980, 1990 and 2000 are the only
sources of data, and the definitions of employment in each were slightly
different. The census results were used to extrapolate the data of the National
Labour Force Surveys (*Survei Angkatan Kerja Nasional*, Sakernas),
conducted for 1976–80, 1982 and 1985–2008. The Sakernas definitions of
employment also differed over the years (Sigit 2000a, pp 28–29).

Figure 8.4 shows the interpolated employment data from the population
censuses and also the Sakernas data. The interpolations and the Sakernas data
track each other closely until 2000. The deviation in total employment since
2000 was possibly caused by the change in the Sakernas definition of
employment to exclude 10–14 year old workers, starting in 1998 (Sigit,
2000a, p 8). Many 10–14 year olds remained gainfully employed in
Indonesia and comprised 3.7 per cent, 2.9 per cent and 2.9 per cent of total
employment in 1980, 1990 and 2000 respectively, according to the census
data.

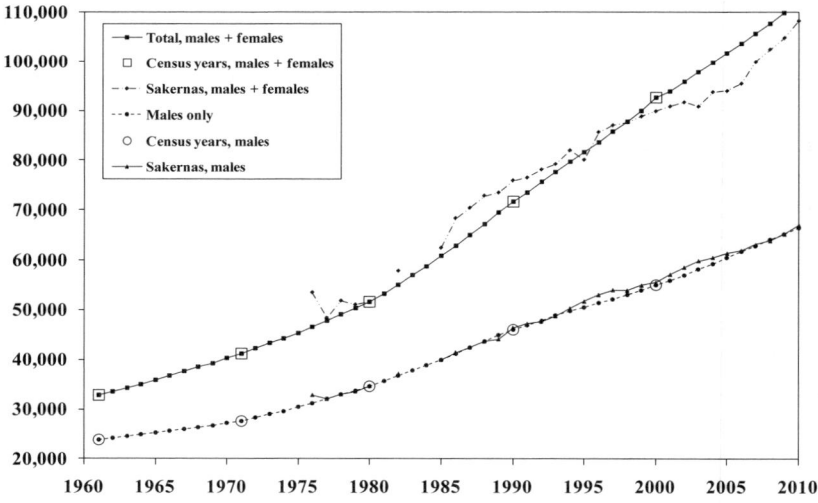

Sources: Population census data 1961, 1971, 1980, 1990 and 2000 (interpolated, taking
account of population growth 10 years previously); 1976–80, 1982 and 1985–2010 Sakernas
data.

Figure 8.4   Employment in Indonesia, 1961–2010 (thousands)

Figure 8.5 shows the participation rates of men and women in employment as percentages of both the total male/female population and the population aged 15 years and over. The significant increase in the participation rate of women from 30 per cent in 1961 to over 52 per cent in 2000 is partly due to changes in definition, but particularly a reflection of the increasing participation of women in gainful employment, rather than household-based occupations.

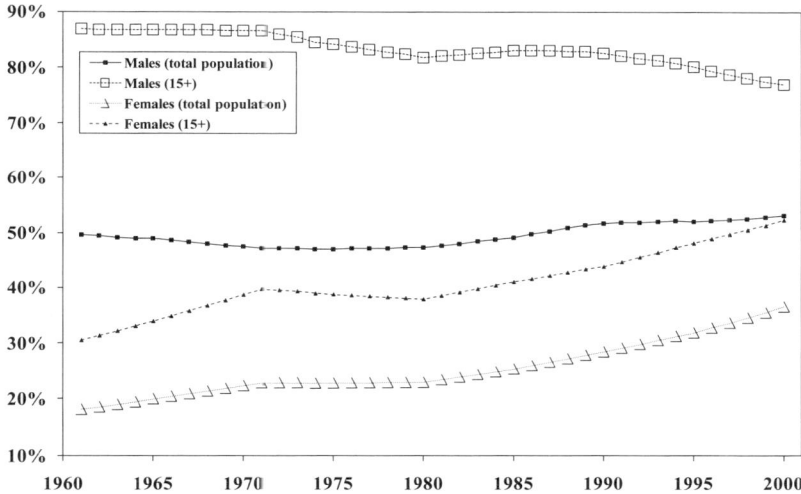

Sources: See Figure 8.4.

Figure 8.5   Crude participation rates in Indonesia, 1961–2000 (percentages)

8.2.5   Educational Attainment Data

To augment the labour force data, the chapter uses an indicator of per capita educational attainment in Indonesia, shown in Figure 8.6. It is an approximation of long-term changes based on annual enrolments in institutions for primary, secondary and tertiary education. Figure 8.6 shows that the results closely track the population census results, which suggests that they approximate the trend. Improvement in human capital was obviously a gradual process.

Educational attainment grew at a very significant rate of 5.0 per cent per year during 1950–67 and 3.0 per cent during 1967–2010. Up to the 1970s, the gains were mainly due to the expansion of primary education. The share of secondary education increased after 1970, possibly in reaction to changes in the labour market where the demand for educated labour increased. The share of tertiary education remains small in 2010. As the method used to estimate educational attainment in Figure 8.6 does not allow us to disaggregate educational attainment by age groups, the chapter uses per capita educational attainment as a proxy for the educational attainment per person gainfully employed.

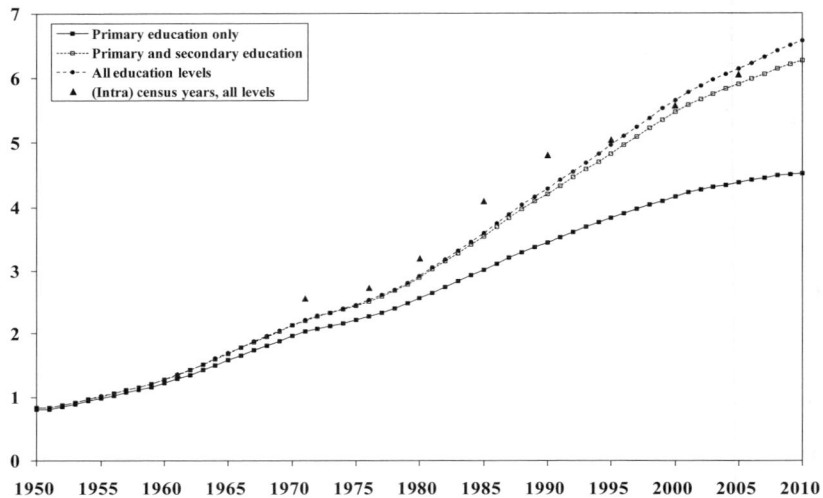

Notes: (Intra) census years calculated by assuming that those reported as having 'incomplete primary education' had an average of two years of schooling, those with primary education six years of schooling, completed secondary education nine years (six years + three years for high school), and tertiary education 15 years (six + three + two years of college + four years at university). Other estimates are derived from data on primary, secondary and tertiary education enrolments during 1870–2008. Student years were accumulated on the assumption that the working life of a primary school graduate was 50 years, that of a secondary school graduate 45 years, and of a university graduate 40 years. The series of accumulated education in terms of student years were divided by population. This procedure assumes that all enrolled students actually went to school during the year. It makes no adjustment for quality differences between the types of schooling or between public and private universities, and does not take account of overseas education.

Sources: 1961–80 census benchmarks Hugo *et al.* (1987: 282), 1990 BPS (1992: Table 11.9), 1995 BPS (1996b: 138), 2000 BPS (2002: 151), 2005 BPS (2006: 93), enrolments 1880–2010 from annual statistical publications and from the Ministry of Education in Indonesia, http://www.kemdiknas.go.id/

*Figure 8.6   Educational attainment in Indonesia (average years of
schooling per person), 1950–2010*

Data on the output elasticity of educational attainment are not available. However, Sakernas contains wage income data that are disaggregated by the highest form of education that employees completed. As the number of years for each form of education is known, it is possible to estimate the income elasticity of each additional year of education. For the years 1989–99, the income elasticity of educational attainment was a fairly constant 0.11, meaning that each additional year of education yields on average an 11 per cent increase of income.[6] This number is taken as a proxy for the elasticity of output with respect to education for the entire period. Equation 8.6 then allows the calculation of education–adjusted employment, using the extrapolated population census data shown in Figure 8.4.

8.2.6 Labour Income Share Data

Although efforts are underway to estimate national income in Indonesia from the income side of the economy (Saleh and Jammal, 2002), Indonesia's national accounts do not yet offer such estimates. The main sources on labour income are the quinquennial I–O Tables and Indonesia's System of Economic and Social Accounting Matrices and Extension (SESAME) that use the I–O tables as their 'anchor' (Keuning and Kusmadi, 2000). The income data in the I–O Tables only comprise the sum of wages and salaries received, which is generally estimated on the basis of Sakernas. They do not include in-kind incomes, particularly the incomes of unpaid household workers. The income of the self-employed and of household-based ventures is included in the total operating surplus of all companies, which is not disaggregated.[7] Non-cash labour income is, however, identified in SESAME.

The SESAME data are shown in Table 8.1, while an estimate for 1971 is added on the basis of the 1971 I–O Table. Labour income in the intermediate years was estimated by calculating labour income per employed worker for each benchmark year, using total employment shown in Figure 8.4, interpolating per worker labour income, and multiplying it with total number of employed workers.

---

[6] Collins and Bosworth (1996, p. 152) found an East-Asia average of 10.7 per cent. They assumed a flat 7 per cent in their growth accounting study involving China and India (Bosworth and Collins 2008, p 47).

[7] Osada (1994, p. 481) did not account for the income of self-employed and of household-based ventures. Sigit (2004, pp. 103–104) solved this by multiplying average income of waged employees from Sakernas with the total number of gainfully employed, expressing the total as a percentage of GDP. However, this estimation yields significantly lower labour income shares than in the SESAME tables. In addition, there is no correction for the fact that the definitions of income varied in the different Sakernas years (Sigit 2000b, pp. 7–9 and 17–18).

Table 8.1 indicates significant changes over time in the labour income share, from a peak of 54 per cent in 1978 – just before investment boom and the capital–output ratio increased significantly (see Figure 8.3) – and a maximum of 57 per cent in 2003, to a very low minimum of 28 per cent in 1998 at the height of the crisis, when wage rates were eroded by a drastic inflation spike. For most years, the labour income share moved in a band between 40 and 50 per cent of GDP.[8] As some of these fluctuations appear unreasonable, the last column shows a simple interpolation of labour income shares. For 2006–08, the labour income share was assumed to be the same as in 2005.

Total GDP at factor cost in Table 8.1 was estimated in a few steps:

i)   by deducting total net indirect taxes from GDP at current market prices from the national accounts for 1971–2000 (prior to the 2000 revision);

ii) calculating the ratio by which GDP at factor cost was underestimated in the national accounts before 2000 on the assumption that GDP at factor cost was correctly calculated in SESAME for the benchmark years;

iii) interpolating the ratio for the benchmark years and multiplying GDP at factor costs from the national accounts with this ratio; and

iv) adding net indirect taxes, which yields GDP at market prices for the intermediate years.

The data presented in this section are necessarily rough, given the difficulties in the compilation of statistical data in Indonesia in past and present. These difficulties increase the further back in time. Still, the data are based on the best possible available information and are reasonably robust.

---

[8]   A labour income share of 40–50 per cent may appear to be low, given that e.g. Bosworth et al. (1996) use a fixed 70 per cent for developed countries and 60 per cent for less–developed countries, as well as for China and India in their recent study (Bosworth and Collins 2008, p. 62), and that the share was 55–60 per cent in India during 1950–89 (Sivasubramonian 2003, p. 175). However, it should be noted that labour income shares of 70–75 per cent were only achieved after World War II in countries like the UK or France (Prados and Rosés 2003, pp. 12–13), and after 1970 in Japan (Hayami and Ogasawara, 1999, p. 3–4). Before the war, at lower levels of GDP per capita, the shares of labour income were significantly lower. In addition, capital income included the imputed income from the productive use of land, most of which was owned by small farming households. Hence, in an economy with agriculture as the most important single sector in terms of employment and income, income from land use may have been relatively significant.

Table 8.1 *Share of labour income in GDP in Indonesia, 1971–2005 (bln Rupiah, current prices)*

	Labour income			Capital income	Total GDP (factor costs)	Total GDP (market costs)	Labour income shares	
	Wages, salaries	Income in kind	Total				(1)	(2)
1971			1,918	1,991	4,260	4,270	45.0%	45.0%
1972			2,693		5,207	5,443	51.7%	43.5%
1973			3,508		7,510	7,838	46.7%	47.1%
1974			4,344		11,644	12,091	37.3%	40.7%
1975	2,853	2,393	5,245	8,097	13,342	13,686	39.3%	39.3%
1976			7,637		16,282	16,972	46.9%	39.1%
1977			10,158		20,040	20,886	50.7%	38.9%
1978			12,813		23,671	24,700	54.1%	38.6%
1979			15,609		32,867	34,172	47.5%	38.4%
1980	9,491	9,044	18,535	29,976	48,511	48,913	38.2%	38.2%
1981			21,791		57,010	58,763	38.2%	39.4%
1982			26,229		61,748	63,880	42.5%	40.6%
1983			30,960		79,525	81,976	38.9%	41.8%
1984			35,998		90,687	93,410	39.7%	43.1%
1985	22,904	19,537	42,441	53,176	95,617	98,407	44.4%	44.4%
1986			51,334		97,970	104,499	52.4%	44.9%
1987			60,818		119,341	126,471	51.0%	45.4%
1988			70,924		134,299	143,332	52.8%	45.9%
1989			81,687		167,870	180,315	48.7%	46.5%

Table 8.1 (Continued)

	Labour income			Capital income	Total GDP (factor costs)	Total GDP (market costs)	Labour income shares	
	Wages, salaries	Income in kind	Total				(1)	(2)
1990	55,738	37,049	92,787	104,570	197,357	210,867	47.0%	47.0%
1991			*111,337*		*234,449*	*249,598*	*47.5%*	*47.7%*
1992			*130,717*		*263,667*	*281,679*	*49.6%*	*48.4%*
1993	91,479	59,484	150,963	156,458	307,420	329,776	49.1%	49.1%
1994			*205,853*		*391,959*	*416,679*	*52.5%*	*50.2%*
1995	163,376	98,983	262,359	248,633	510,993	542,755	51.3%	51.3%
1996			*267,547*		*569,344*	*597,843*	*47.0%*	*50.4%*
1997			*272,865*		*626,652*	*664,481*	*43.5%*	*49.5%*
1998	168,585	109,731	278,316	700,126	978,442	989,573	28.4%	28.4%
1999			*547,299*		*1,075,489*	*1,093,439*	*50.9%*	*37.7%*
2000	397,579	244,495	642,074	725,941	1,368,015	1,379,770	46.9%	46.9%
2001			*793,041*		*1,647,865*	*1,679,291*	*48.1%*	*50.0%*
2002			*954,195*		*1,828,843*	*1,900,030*	*52.2%*	*53.4%*
2003	690,975	430,548	1,121,523	849,657	1,971,180	2,045,854	56.9%	56.9%
2004			*1,300,667*		*2,402,907*	*2,273,142*	*54.1%*	*54.7%*
2005	1,064,463	421,705	1,486,168	1,348,467	2,834,635	2,770,960	52.4%	52.4%

Note: Data in italics are estimated values, non-italic data are from the sources below. Labour income shares (1) are estimated by calculating labour income per employed worker for each benchmark year, interpolating per worker labour income, and multiplying it with total employment. Labour income shares (2) are estimated with simple interpolation of the shares, except for 1996–97, which is an interpolation of 1995 and 2000, ignoring the 1998 value.

Sources: IDE/BPS (1977), BPS (1996a: 72), BPS (1999: 27), BPS (2003: 35), BPS (2005: 11), BPS (2008: Appendix 5) and Indonesia's national accounts.

8.3 SOURCES OF ECONOMIC GROWTH

The data presented in the previous section now allow us to estimate TFP growth and its contribution to economic growth. The results are shown in Table 8.2, which reveals that TFP growth was marginally negative during 1971–2008 and contributed only −4 per cent to economic growth during 1971–2008.[9] During 1971–85, TFP growth was on average positive, but it still contributed only marginally to output growth. In all, 71 per cent of output growth during the high-growth period 1971–97 is explained by the expansion of capital stock, and most of the rest by the growth of education-adjusted employment. Only during the years of economic recovery 2000–10 did the contribution of TFP growth become positive and significant at 30 per cent, although the growth of capital stock and of education-adjusted employment together continued to explain most of economic growth.

Table 8.2   Decomposition of economic growth, 1971–2010 (annual averages)

	s_l	g_t^Q	g_t^K	g_t^L	$g_t^{L^*}$	g_t^{TFP}
1971–85	44.1%	5.7	6.5	3.0	4.1	0.2
1986–97	49.4%	7.2	10.9	2.8	4.3	-0.5
1998–99	35.4%	-6.5	2.9	2.1	3.6	-9.7
2000–10	52.1%	5.2	4.4	1.9	2.9	1.6
1971–10	47.4%	5.4	7.1	2.6	3.8	-0.1
Contributions to GDP growth:						
1971–85			64%		32%	4%
1986–97			77%		30%	-6%
1998–99			-29%		-20%	149%
2000–10			40%		30%	30%
1971–10			69%		34%	-2%

Note: The annual averages are calculated as simple averages for each period. Annual average TFP growth is estimated with labour income shares (1) in Table 8.1, 2005 shares are used for 2006–10.

Sources: See Figures 8.1–8.6 and Table 8.1.

---

[9]   The use of labour income shares in the last column of Table 8.1 made hardly any difference. TFP growth during 1971–2010 was in that case also -0.1 per cent per year and contributed -3 per cent to GDP growth.

These results are very different from the 30–40 per cent contribution of TFP growth to GDP growth in China and India during 1978–2004 recently estimated by Bosworth and Collins (2008, p. 49). The main reasons for the differences between Indonesia and China and India are that annual employment growth in Indonesia was 2.6 per cent compared with 2.0 per cent in China and India, and the apparently arbitrary assumption that the capital shares in GDP in both China and India are a flat 35 per cent. In addition, their procedure of estimating capital stock growth is opaque and may be another source of differences. Hence, without comparing growth accounting results obtained with similar assumptions and methods of estimating capital stock, it is difficult to compare Indonesia, China and India.

The same conclusion can be drawn from a comparison of TFP estimates for Indonesia in other studies. Table 8.3 compares this chapter's estimates of TFP growth and its contribution to economic growth with other studies. The table includes, as far as possible, information from the calculations in other studies in order to trace the possible reasons for the significant differences in all studies, particularly between studies 2–11 and studies 1 and 12–15.[10] The different results are due to differences in (a) the period considered; (b) the basic data used; (c) the ways in which the key variables for growth accounting (as this study identified them above) were constructed and (d) variables actually used to account for growth, or any combination of these factors.

As studies 1 and 3–11 are all multi-country studies that paid minimal attention to the intricacies of Indonesia's national accounts and their consequences for growth accounting, the results of those studies may have to be interpreted with caution. The multi-country studies often used different data sets and/or different ways to process the data, but generally without regard for the inherent problems in the underlying data sets. For example, several of the multi-country studies obtained output data from the Penn World Tables (PWT), which in turn obtained them from the World Bank's *World Development Indicators*. However, for Indonesia there are many unexplained anomalies between these data and the official data from the Indonesian statistics agency BPS. For example, PWT gives total population estimates for Indonesia as 124.7 million in 1971, 154.4 million in 1980, 188.0 million in 1990 and 224.1 million in 2000, while Indonesia's population censuses give totals of respectively 118.4, 147.0, 178.5 and 206.2 million. PWT also offers GDP in international prices, even though Indonesia only featured twice in the six benchmarks of the International Comparisons

---

[10] The information in this table is incomplete, because many studies do not give the basic data or the processed data by country, which impedes comparison and identification of the possible reasons for the different outcomes.

Project, in respectively 1980 and 1996. Hence, PWT estimated the key expenditure components of GDP for most years in its Indonesian time series on the basis of its multilateral 'shortcut approach', but without consideration of the degree of underestimation in Indonesia's national accounts data.

Other possible problems are a consequence of the creative ways in which studies resolved the unavailability of data for countries such as Indonesia. For example, multi-country studies often took capital stock data from Nehru and Dhareshwar (1993), which were based on aggregated investment data obtained from the World Bank that took no account of underestimation, and from which capital stock was estimated on the basis of arbitrary assumptions, such as a single 'decay rate' of 4 per cent for all countries in the sample. Van der Eng (2009) showed the significantly different results of estimates of capital stock in Indonesia from several studies. Different capital stock estimates feed into different TFP growth estimates. In addition, factor income shares in GDP do not exist for Indonesia, which led e.g. Sarel (1997, pp. 44–48) to estimate them for 1978–96 on the basis of data for 26 other countries, while other studies made assumptions without due acknowledgement of what income shares may have been in Indonesia. Baier et al. (2006) used Mitchell's handbooks of historical statistics as key sources, but without accounting for inconsistencies in e.g. the national accounts data, and simply interpolating years for which data were missing, without due account of the availability of other data for Indonesia.

In other words, it is difficult to check whether the different estimates of TFP growth from the multi-country studies are true differences or the consequences of measurement errors and/or the assumptions underlying the processing of the data. For the same reason it is not possible to explain in detail the differences in the results of other studies and this chapter. Only in the case of Sigit (2004) is it possible to explain the discrepancy, because Sigit over–estimated capital stock growth, which he based on an estimate of capital stock from a then unpublished BPS study, extrapolated back in time with investment data. He also underestimated the share of labour income in total income by counting only wage income from Sakernas and excluding income in kind.

Table 8.3 *TFP contribution to economic growth in Indonesia in various studies (annual averages)*

Study	Period	Unweighted			Weighted			g(Q)	Unweighted		Weighted			TFP
		g(Q/L)	g(K/L)	g(Y/L)	g(K/L)	g(Y/L)	g(TFP)		g(K)	g(L)	g(K)	g(L)	g(TFP)	contribution*
1. Baier et al. (2006: 45)	1951–2000	1.8	4.4	1.4	1.5	0.9	-0.6							-37%
2. UNIDO (Firdausy 2005: 12)	1961–2000							5.7	6.9	3.0			-1.5	-27%
3. Drysdale and Huang (1997: 208)	1962–1990							6.7			2.6	2.0	2.1	31%
4. Bosworth et al. (1996: 111)	1960–1992	3.3			2.3	0.4	0.6							17%
5. Collins and Bosworth (1996: 157)	1960–1994	3.4			2.1	0.5	0.8							24%
6. Lindauer and Roemer (1994: 3)	1965–1990	4.3						6.5					2.7	42%
7. Ikemoto (1986: 376)	1970–1980							7.7	7.4	3.6	3.0	2.2	2.5	32%
8. Young (1994: 243)	1970–1985	5.0					1.2							24%
9. Kawai (1994: 384)	1970–1990							6.2					1.5	24%
10. Sarel (1997: 29)	1978–1996	4.7	9.0				1.2							24%
11. World Bank (1993: 58)	1980–1990							5.6					1.6	29%
12. Osada (1994: 480)	1985–1990							6.3	9.7	4.0			-2.7	-43%
13. Sigit (2004: 104–5)	1980–2000	2.9	5.9		3.8			5.4	8.4	2.5	5.4	0.9	-0.8	-16%
14. Sutanto (2004: 11)	1992–2002							3.8	7.2	1.7	4.5	0.6	-1.4	-37%
15. This study	1971–2010	2.8	4.4	2.8				5.4	7.1	3.8	3.7	1.8	-0.1	-2%

* TFP contribution is to labour productivity (Q/L) growth for studies 1, 4, 5, 8 and 10, and to output (Q) growth in the other studies.

Notes: Unweighted means that no account is taken of the income shares, weighted means that growth is weighted with the income share of capital, respectively labour. g = annual average growth rate, Q = GDP, K = capital stock, L = employment, Y = human capital (generally expressed as years of education).

Sources: See references in the table.

Table 8.4   TFP growth in manufacturing industry in Indonesia in various studies

Study	Period	Annual average TFP growth	TFP contribution to output growth
1. Aswicahyono *et al.* (1996, p 357)	1976–91	1.4	11%*
2. Aswicayhono and Hill (2002, p 148)	1975–93	2.7	21%
3. Timmer (1999, pp 87–89)	1975–95	2.8	22%
4. Vial (2006, p 367)	1976–96	3.5	35%*
5. Osada (1994, p 184)	1985–90	3.6	22%
6. Hayashi (2005, pp 99, 107)	1986–96	1.9 (SMEs) 2.3 (LEs)	22% 17%
7. Ikhsan-Modjo (2006, pp 3 and 12)	1988–2000	1.6	16%

Note: * These sources do not specify manufacturing output growth, which for this table is calculated from the national accounts data.

Sources: See references in the table.

Several studies estimated TFP on the basis of the firm-level data from the annual survey among industrial firms in Indonesia employing 20 or more people. The results are shown in Table 8.4. They all suggest that in manufacturing industry TFP growth has been modest, but significant and positive, which contrasts with the economy-wide findings of this chapter.

What does it mean that the contribution of TFP growth was only -2% during 1971–2010, and why does this result contrast with the significantly positive contribution of TFP growth in manufacturing? The results in Table 8.2 do not necessarily indicate that there has been no technological change in Indonesia that contributed to economic growth. There are at least two fundamental issues that make it difficult to automatically equate the residual from growth accounting with the contribution of technological change to economic growth: (1) TFP growth is estimated as a residual and (2) the chapter's calculation assumes perfect elasticity of substitution of labour and capital.

The measurement of TFP growth as a residual means that TFP fails to account for the fact that some aspects of technological change may already have been captured in the measurement of capital stock and education–adjusted employment. As capital accumulation tends to be the main vehicle of technological change, much of the technology is embodied in the stock of capital goods. This fundamental issue is likely to be significant for Indonesia in recent decades, given the high rate of capital accumulation since the early 1980s, as Figure 8.2 showed. Hence, most of the non-residential capital stock is of recent vintage, and is likely to embody the most recent technologies. In addition, in manufacturing industry, investment in machinery and equipment was predominant and sustained most of the rapid growth of output in that sector (Timmer, 1999, pp. 83 and 89). While some technological change and efficiency gains were captured in the rates of TFP growth in manufacturing industry in Table 8.4, other gains were most likely captured in the measured industrial capital stock. On the other hand, as most investment outside manufacturing industry may have been in the form of non-residential structures, particularly investment in public infrastructure, the embodied efficiency gains may not have been as significant as was the case in manufacturing industry.

Likewise, the measurement of education-augmented employment may have captured some technological change that would otherwise be measured as part of TFP. After all, the significant improvement in educational attainment explains one-third of the 34 per cent contribution of education–adjusted employment to economic growth during 1971–2010 as Table 8.2 indicated. Several of the studies in Table 8.3 did not adjust for changes in educational attainment. Hence, without the education adjustment, TFP growth in Table 8.2 would have been positive and higher.

While this chapter only accounted for quality changes in the labour force, there is a wide range of other factors that could be included in the process, which would yield a more intricate Denison/Maddison-type exercise to account for the proximate factors of economic growth (e.g. Maddison, 1987). Such factors could be related to factor inputs, such as changes in hours worked, the age–sex composition and average skills in the case of employment, or the average age of capital stock. Or they may be other factors, such as the structural change effect, economies of scale consequences, catch-up and capacity use effects, changes in trade barriers, natural resource windfalls etc. If it is possible to quantify these for a country like Indonesia, they would help to whittle down the unexplained residual. While this methodology presupposes the availability of a wide range of reliable quantitative data, which may be difficult to obtain for a country like Indonesia, it would get the exercise of accounting for growth closer to understanding the residual, and the degree to which the residual is related to technological change.

This chapter's measure of TFP growth – and that of other studies as well – may be less a measure of technological change than simply an unexplained residual that comprises a wide range of factors related to peculiarities of Indonesia's business environment, many of which impacted on the efficiency of production. If so, marginal TFP growth during 1971–97 may rather reflect a multitude of inefficiencies in Indonesia's economy rather than the lack of technological change. If positive TFP growth was indeed a reflection of significant technological change in manufacturing industry, as the studies in Table 8.4 suggest, the inefficiencies may have largely existed in non-manufacturing sectors of the economy. They may for example have taken the form of imperfections in particularly non-tradable sectors in non-manufacturing industry and services, such as transport and communications, or in labour, capital and commodity markets, possibly due to inhibiting regulations, the lack of exposure to foreign competition, the dominance of state-owned enterprises, and/or the presence of opportunities for anti-competitive behaviour.

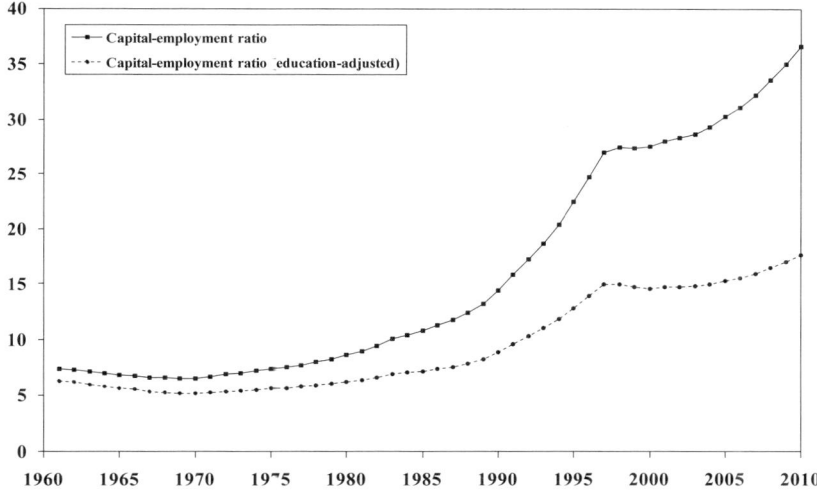

Sources: See Figures 8.2, 8.4 and 8.6.

Figure 8.7   Capital–employment ratio in Indonesia, 1961–2010 (million 2000 Rupiah per person)

A possible indication that TFP growth merely measures the residual is the fact that during 2000–10 the residual became consistently positive, explaining on average a significant 30 per cent of GDP growth, while it had been erratic and on balance only marginally positive before 1997. Of course, capital accumulation was relatively low during 2000–10, while the growth of employment decreased somewhat. In addition, there may have been productive overcapacity by 1999 that became more efficiently used during 2000–08. Still, this change may be understood as an improvement in efficiency caused by the many growth-enhancing, or rather inefficiency-decreasing institutional changes that recent successive governments have introduced in Indonesia. For example, deregulation and re-regulation in various ways enhanced competition in previously non-tradable sectors. Likewise, new capital market regulation imposed greater discipline on listed firms. While such changes may have increased uncertainty among foreign investors about investing in Indonesia, at the same time they may have been an encouragement for domestic and foreign firms in Indonesia with a more intimate knowledge of past and current idiosyncrasies and risk in Indonesia's business environment, and ways to hedge it (see Figure 8.7 above).

Secondly, and related to the first point, available growth accounting studies implicitly assume that there is perfect elasticity of substitution between labour and capital. This study did the same in equation (8.5).[11] However, as Rodrik (1998, pp. 84–8) has argued, it cannot be automatically assumed that this is the case.[12] If, for example, economic growth and technological change had either a labour-saving or a capital-saving nature, the elasticity of substitution would be more than, respectively less than 1. Hence, if technological change in Indonesia in recent decades was to a degree labour-saving and capital-absorbing, it yields a downward bias of the estimated rate of TFP growth. The bias may be in proportion to the capital-labour ratio, which indeed increased significantly in Indonesia, as Figure 8.7 shows, particularly during 1988–97. The ratio even increased for education-adjusted employment, but to a lower degree. Although this point can be readily made, it is not easy to quantify its implications for efforts to account for economic growth.

8.4   THE CONTRIBUTION OF INVESTMENT TO ECONOMIC GROWTH IN RECENT YEARS

The previous section has shown that the accumulation of capital has been the main driver of economic growth in Indonesia since 1971. As a percentage of GDP, investment (i.e. Gross Fixed Capital Formation, GFCF) has indeed increased significantly, as Figure 8.8 shows, from 4.5 per cent in 1966 to almost 30 per cent in 1996, before decreasing to 19 per cent in 2002 and recovering to 32 per cent in 2010. The chart shows that the ratio was at an unprecedented level immediately before the 1997–98 crisis and that a more 'normal' ratio was 24 per cent of GDP, the 1975–97 average according to the

---

[11] In turn, this assumption is based on a range of underlying assumptions, including perfect competition (see below).

[12] An econometric approximation of factor shares during 1971–2010 for Indonesia seems to support the suggestion that the elasticity of substitution between capital and labour is imperfect. Linear multiple regression to estimate the coefficients in equation (8.4) yielded 0.52 for s_k and a low 0.38 for s_{l*} (F (2, 38) = 29.4, adjusted R^2 = 0.59), adding up to 0.90 rather than 1.

national accounts, and the 1971–95 average according to the I–O Tables. If this ratio were the only criteria to gauge economic recovery from the 1997–98 crisis – which it is not, of course – Indonesia's recovery was achieved in 2005.

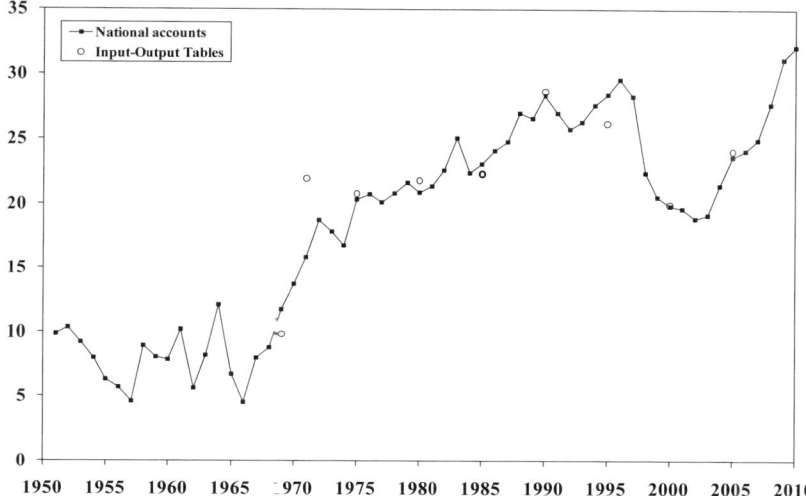

Note: The ratio is calculated form current price data.

Sources: National accounts (current prices) and Input–Output Tables of Indonesia.

Figure 8.8   Share of gross fixed capital formation in GDP in Indonesia, 1951–2010

Despite the recovery of the investment ratio to a 'normal' level in 2005, there has been considerable concern in Indonesia and in assessments of Indonesia's economy about what has been regarded as a low ratio of investment to GDP. Much of this pessimism is reflected in the very low, if not negative levels of foreign direct investment (FDI) that reached Indonesia since 1997.[13] To the extent that FDI is a key vehicle for technological change, this is indeed a concern. On the other hand it should be noted that during 1980–97 FDI contributed only 3.4 per cent to total investment, and – after excluding a non–FDI item from the notional balance of payment data on

---

[13] It is difficult to know the degree to which FDI into Indonesia decreased, as statistical data are incomplete (Lindblad and Wie, 2007, pp. 20–21). However, balance of payments data indicate that net FDI inflows were US$ -0.9 billion per year during 1997–2004, and US$ 4.3 billion per year during 2005–10.

direct investment – that number was still only about 6.5 per cent during 1998–03 (World Bank, 2005, p. 86). Hence, domestic firms in Indonesia are a much more significant source of investment than foreign firms. In addition, there are no indications that foreign firms operating in Indonesia have left the country in large numbers. For example, despite wide media coverage given to the post-1997 withdrawal of some Japanese firms from Indonesia, the number of Japanese subsidiary firms in Indonesia actually increased from 671 in 1999 to 698 in 2004 (Van der Eng, 2007). In addition, a survey among these firms indicated that about 60 per cent of Japanese subsidiary firms reported in each year that their operations were profitable, while 20–25 per cent remained at 'break-even' level.

That does not mean that foreign firms in Indonesia have no concerns about their operations in Indonesia. After all, Indonesia has gone through major economic and political changes since the onset of the crisis in mid-1997. The following is a list of several of the changes that firms in Indonesia have had to deal with.[14] In the economic sphere, for example:

- macro–economic instability, particularly high inflation and interest rates, a significant depreciation of the currency followed by exchange rate instability;
- changes in trade policy, including efforts to curb luxury imports through temporary surcharges; and
- Indonesia's involvement in trade liberalisation within AFTA and in bilateral trade agreements and its obligation to lower trade barriers, countered by domestic protectionist pressures in specific sectors.

In the sphere of public policy, for example:

- democratisation, a subsequent diffusion of political power, and increased political influence of special interest groups;
- decentralisation starting in 2001 and an increase in the authority of local governments to determine e.g. minimum wages and local taxes, sometimes amounting to increasing domestic trade barriers; and
- regulatory reforms not only affected for instance capital markets, but also some deregulated sectors such as telecommunications. While changes in competition policy increased scrutiny of collusive inter-firm relations, and campaigns to combat corruption may have decreased overt corruption in the centres of decision making but probably led to a decentralisation of corruption. Changes in the

---

[14] For more in–depth assessments of the economic and policy changes impacting on the business environment (see *e.g.* Basri and van der Eng, 2004; Hill and Shiraishi, 2007; and the triennial 'Survey of Recent Developments' in the *Bulletin of Indonesian Economic Studies*).

system of customs procedures and also tax assessment and collection added to the confusion caused by changing regulations, while changes in labour regulations enhanced uncertainty in the procedures determining the hiring and dismissing of employees. While the regulatory reforms may have increased confusion, they are also likely to have increased the cost of compliance; and

- public infrastructure delays causing problems related to poor communications and transport are an additional factor caused by the fact that budget shortages forced governments to delay infrastructure projects that depended on public investment in e.g. transport, electricity and communications.

Several surveys among firms have indicated continued concerns, often reflecting the points above, but also listing issues that were already frequently mentioned as concerns before 1997. As a consequence, foreign firms with operations in Indonesia experienced new challenges, and have expressed their concerns about them, but without necessarily concluding that a withdrawing from Indonesia would be the best option. In expressing their concerns, they may have enhanced the perception that Indonesia's business environment is complex, costly and rife with risk, which in turn may have influenced would-be new foreign investors.

For example, many international agencies place Indonesia well down the list of countries. In 2006, the Japan Center for Economic Research ranked Indonesia 45th out of 50 countries according to competitiveness (JCER, 2006), while the World Bank ranked the country 135th out of 175 countries according to the 'ease of doing business' (World Bank, 2006, p. 6). It is possible to quibble about the measures that have been used to compile these rankings and their relevance to firms already operating in Indonesia. Still, such rankings capture perceptions of Indonesia's business environment among foreign firms that could consider operations in the country. Worse, such rankings may influence foreign firms that are about to consider investing in Indonesia. At a time when other Asian countries, particularly China, are bracing themselves as major competitors to Indonesia for resource-seeking foreign investment aiming to take advantage of Indonesia's relatively low labour costs, negative perceptions about the country's business environment may be an explanation for the country's poor FDI record. FDI inflows indeed remained low compared to inflows during the 1980s and 1990s, and compared to other Asian countries. While other agencies monitoring the changes in Indonesia's business environment have indicated improvements, they also note that much remains to be done (see e.g. LPEM, 2005; JICA 2007).

It is clear that the multitude of changes, including improvements in the business environment still need to crystallise before there will be a marked change in the general perception of Indonesia's business environment. Still, that may not prevent domestic firms and foreign firms that are already in the country from increasing their investments, as they have appeared to have done since 2000, particularly during 2008–10. Hence, without fresh FDI, investment rates may nay have remained lower than what they were just before the crisis, but they were unlikely to decrease to zero.

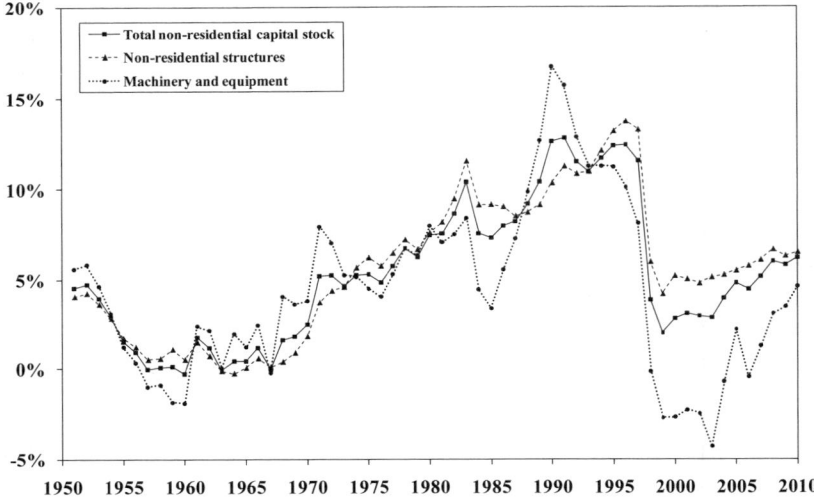

Source: Van der Eng (2009), updated to include 2008–2010.

Figure 8.9   Annual growth of non-residential gross fixed capital stock in Indonesia, 1950–2010 (percentages)

Figure 8.9 shows the rates of growth of capital stock, calculated with capital stock data after deduction of implicit depreciation of capital goods. The trend is largely determined by non-residential structures, with the growth of the stock of machinery and equipment fluctuating around it. The rate of growth increased from around 5 per cent in the early-1970s to more than 10 per cent by the mid-1990s, after which it plummeted to about 2.5 per cent when investment decreased. The increase in the investment–GDP ratio to on average 26 per cent in 2004–10 reflects investment growth, but also the sustained but modest real GDP growth, unaffected by the Global Financial Crisis. Consequently, the growth of capital stock (after accounting for implicit depreciation) only inched up to 5 per cent during 2005–10. This underlines that the contribution of capital stock growth was still a significant 40 per cent during 2000–10, as Table 8.2 showed, but not enough to contribute to achieving the kind of GDP growth that Indonesia experienced during 1971–97.

As the country achieves economic recovery, and as the dust of the economic and political uncertainties in the business environment settles and investors regain their courage, it is not implausible to assume that Indonesia will re-achieve a rate of growth of capital stock exceeding 5 per cent per year. Crucial to achieving this rate of growth will be the recovery of the rate of growth of the stock of machinery and equipment. This has been negative during 1998–2004, implying that investment was insufficient to compensate for implicit depreciation of capital goods.

8.5   CONCLUSION

This chapter estimated TFP growth as the residual growth, after accounting for the growth of capital stock and education-adjusted employment. Residual growth was on average –0.1 per cent during 1971–2010, contributing –2 per cent to GDP growth. It also estimated that most of GDP growth, 69 per cent, was explained by the growth of the capital stock and 34 per cent by the growth of education-adjusted employment. As such, the case of Indonesia appears to offer support for Krugman's 'perspiration'-based explanation of economic growth in East Asia. However, the chapter noted that the estimated capital stock in Indonesia is likely to contain embodied technology, while the education-adjustment of employment is also likely to capture part of productivity growth. Hence, residual growth is more likely a reflection of a wide range of factors that impact on economic growth, but that the chapter has not been able to account for, rather than only productivity growth. Given that the measured residual TFP growth was marginally negative, it may reflect a range of inefficiencies that existed in the Indonesian economy and that cancelled out positive productivity growth, such as in manufacturing industry.

Support for that suggestion was found in the fact that TFP growth during 2000–10 was consistently positive, contributing 30 per cent to GDP growth. This may indicate a reduction of these inefficiencies as a consequence of a multitude of changes in Indonesia's business environment, and possibly a shift from a development pattern away from accumulation-based growth towards efficiency-based growth. A down-side of the reduction of these inefficiencies may have been that the required regulatory changes increased the uncertainty that particularly would-be foreign investors perceived about Indonesia's business environment. At the same time, firms already in Indonesia were able to use their accumulated experience in the country in order to absorb the idiosyncrasies in the country's business environment. A reasonably high investment-GDP ratio during 2004–10 seems to underscore that suggestion.

The fact that increasing investment is the key to the resumption of higher levels of economic growth in Indonesia points to the urgency of improvements, or at least stabilisation of change in the country's business environment. The chapter mentioned several issues that are of concern to private enterprise and that may have impinged on domestic investment, and particularly new foreign investment. Addressing these concerns will be a major prerequisite for acceleration of economic growth to levels that will again make a very significant difference to employment and average incomes, as was the case in earlier decades.

The chapter has indicated that the intricacies of the statistical data available for Indonesia require a cautious approach for the purpose of estimating TFP growth. It confirms the caution about interpreting TFP growth estimates that Felipe (1999) expressed in his survey of the literature on TFP growth in Asia. Given that caution, the chapter underlines that the proximate results of accounting for growth are possibly useful in setting the stage for further analysis of the ultimate factors that are too often regarded as exogenous to economic growth, including the evolution of markets and the institutions that impacted on them, as well as the actual processes of innovation and technological change.

REFERENCES

Aswicahyono, H., K. Bird and H. Hill (1996), 'What Happens to Industrial Structure when Countries Liberalise? Indonesia since the mid–1980s', *Journal of Development Studies*, **32** (3), 340–63.

Aswicahyono, H. and H. Hill (2002), "Perspiration" versus "Inspiration" in Asian Industrialisation: Indonesia before the Crisis', *Journal of Development Studies*, **38** (3), 138–63.

Baier, S.L., G.P. Dwyer and R. Tamura (2006), 'How Important are Capital and Total Factor Productivity for Economic Growth?', *Economic Inquiry*, **44** (1), 23–49.

Basri, M.C. and P. van der Eng (eds) (2004), *Business in Indonesia: New Challenges, Old Problems*, Singapore: Institute of Southeast Asian Studies.

Bosworth, B.P., S.M. Collins and Yu–chin Chen (1996), 'Accounting for Differences in Economic Growth' in Kohsaka, A. and K. Ohno (eds), *Structural Adjustment and Economic Reforms: East Asia, Latin America, and Central and Eastern Europe*, Tokyo: Institute of Developing Economies, pp. 47–124.

Bosworth, B.P. and S.M. Collins (2008), 'Accounting for Growth: Comparing China and India', *The Journal of Economic Perspectives*, **22** (1), 45–66.

BPS (1992), *Penduduk Indonesia: Tabel Hasil Sensus Penduduk 1990. Seri S.2.* [The population of Indonesia: Table with the results of the 1990 population census] Jakarta: Biro Pusat Statistik.

BPS (1996a), *Sistem Neraca Sosial Ekonomi Indonesia 1993* [The system of socio–economic accounts of Indonesia in 1993]. Jakarta: Biro Pusat Statistik.

BPS (1996b), *Penduduk Indonesia: Hasil Survei Penduduk antar Sensus 1995, Seri S2.* [Indonesia's population: Results of the 1995 inter–census population survey] Jakarta: Biro Pusat Statistik.

BPS (1999), *Sistem Neraca Sosial Ekonomi Indonesia 1998* [The system of socio–economic accounts of Indonesia in 1998]. Jakarta: Badan Pusat Statistik.

BPS (2002), *Penduduk Indonesia: Hasil Sensus Penduduk Tahun 2000.* [Indonesia's population: Results of the 2000 population census] Jakarta: Badan Pusat Statistik.

BPS (2003), *Sistem Neraca Sosial Ekonomi Indonesia 2000* [The system of socio–economic accounts of Indonesia in 2000]. Jakarta: Badan Pusat Statistik.

BPS (2005), *Sistem Neraca Sosial Ekonomi Indonesia Tahun 2003* [The system of socio–economic accounts of Indonesia in the year 2003]. Jakarta: Badan Pusat Statistik.

BPS (2006), *Penduduk Indonesia: Hasil Survei Penduduk antar Sensus 2005, Seri S1.* [Indonesia's population: Results of the 2005 inter-census population survey]. Jakarta: Badan Pusat Statistik.

BPS (2008), *Sistem Neraca Sosial Ekonomi Finansial Indonesia 2005.* [The system of socio–economic–financial accounts of Indonesia 2005]. Jakarta: Badan Pusat Statistik.

Chen E.K.Y. (1997), 'The Total Factor Productivity Debate: Determinants of Economic Growth in East Asia', *Asian-Pacific Economic Literature*, **11** (1), 18–38.

Collins, S.M. and B.P. Bosworth (1996), 'Economic Growth in East Asia: Accumulation versus Assimilation', *Brookings Papers on Economic Activity*, **2**, 135–203.

Drysdale, P. and Y. Huang (1997), 'Technological Catch-Up and Productivity Growth in East Asia', *Economic Record*, **73**, 201–11.

Felipe, J. (1999), 'Total Factor Productivity Growth in East Asia: A Critical Survey', *Journal of Development Studies*, **34** (4), 1–41.

Firdausy, C.M. (2005), 'Productivity Performance in Developing Countries, Country Case Studies: Indonesia.' Report for the United Nations Industrial Development Organization (UNIDO), can be accessed on http://www.unido.org/file–storage/download/?file_id=60412.

Hayami, Y. and J. Ogasawara (1999), 'Changes in the Sources of Modern Economic Growth: Japan Compared with the United States', *Journal of the Japanese and International Economies.* **13** (1), 1–21.

Hayashi, M. (2005), *SMEs, Subcontracting and Economic Development in Indonesia: With Reference to Japan's Experience*, Tokyo: Japan International Cooperation Publishing.

Hill, H. (1999), *The Indonesian Economy since 1966: Southeast Asia's Emerging Giant*, Cambridge: CUP.

Hill, H. and T. Shiraishi (2007), 'Indonesia after the Asian Crisis', *Asian Economic Policy Review*, **2** (1), 123–41.

Hill, H., H. Aswicahyono and K. Bird (1997), '*What Happened to Industrial Structure during the Deregulation Era?*', in Hill, H. (ed.), *Indonesia's Industrial Transformation*, Singapore: ISEAS, pp. 55–80.

Hugo, G.J., T.H. Hull, V.J. Hull and G.W. Jones (1987), *The Demographic Dimension in Indonesian Development.* Singapore: Oxford UP.

IDE–BPS (1977), *Input-Output Table Indonesia, 1971.* Tokyo/Jakarta: Institute of Developing Economies – Biro Pusat Statistik (2 volumes).

Ikemoto, Y. (1986), 'Technical Progress and the Level of Technology in Asian Countries', *The Developing Economies*, **34** (4), 368–90.

Ikhsan-Modjo, M. (2006), 'Total Factor Productivity in Indonesian Manufacturing: A Stachatic Frontier Approach', *ABERU Discussion Paper No.28*. Caufield East: Department of Economics, Monash University.

JCER (2006), *Potential Competitiveness Ranking 2005*. Tokyo: Japan Center for Economic Research, http://www.jcer.or.jp/eng/pdf/potential2005.pdf

JICA (2007), *Studi Tentang Perbaikan Kebijakan Investasi di Republik Indonesia.* (Study on the improvement of investment policy in the Republic of Indonesia), Tokyo: Japan International Cooperation Agency.

Kawai, H. (1994), 'International Comparative Analysis of Economic Growth', *The Developing Economies*, **32** (4), 373–97.

Keuning, S.J. (1991), 'Allocation and Composition of Fixed Capital Stock in Indonesia: An Indirect Estimate Using Incremental Capital Value Added Ratios', *Bulletin of Indonesian Economic Studies*, **27** (2), 91–119.

Keuning, S.J. and S. Kusmadi (2000), 'SAM and SESAME in Indonesia: Results, Usage and Institutionalization' in *Studies in Methods, Series F, No.75/Vol.2, Handbook of National Accounting: Household Accounting, Experience in Concepts and Compilation, vol.2, Household Satellite Extensions*, New York: UN Department of Economic and Social Affairs, Statistics Division, pp. 355–97.

Krugman, P. (1994), 'The Myth of Asia's Miracle', *Foreign Affairs*, **73** (6), 62–78.

LPEM (2005), *Monitoring Investment Climate in Indonesia: A Report from the Mid 2005 Survey.* Jakarta: Institute for Economic and Social Research (LPEM), University of Indonesia.

Lindauer, D.L. and M. Roemer (1996), '*Legacies and Opportunities*', in Lindauer, D.L. and M. Roemer (eds), *Asia and Africa: Legacies and Opportunities in Development*, San Francisco: ICS Press, pp 1–24.

Lindblad, T. and T.K. Wie (2007), 'Survey of Recent Developments', *Bulletin of Indonesian Economic Studies*, **43** (1), 7–33.

Maddison, A. (1987), 'Growth and Slowdown in Advanced Capitalist Economies: Techniques of Quantitative Assessment', *Journal of Economic Literature*, **25**, 648–708.

Maddison, A. (1988), 'Ultimate and Proximate Growth Causality: A Critique of Mancur Olson and the Rise and Decline of Nations', *Scandinavian Economic History Review*, **36** (2), 25–29.

Nehru, V. and A. Dhareshwar (1993), 'A New Database of Physical Capital Stock: Sources, Methodology and Results', *Revista de Análisis Económico*, **8** (1), 37–59.

Oguchi, N. (2004), '*Integrated Report*' in Oguchi, Noriyoshi (ed.) *Total Factor Productivity Growth: Survey Report*, Tokyo: Asian Productivity Organization, pp. 3–29.

Osada,H. (1994), 'Trade Liberalization and FDI Incentives in Indonesia: The Impact of Industrial Productivity', *The Developing Economies*, **32**, 479–491.

Prados de la Escosura, L. and J.R. Rosés (2003), 'Wages and Labor Income in History: A Survey', *Working Papers in Economic History WP03–10*, Getafe: Universidad Carlos III de Madrid.

Rodrik, D. (1998), '*TFPG Controversies, Institutions, and Economic Performance*', in Yujiro Hayami and Masahiko Aoki (eds), *The Institutional Foundations of East Asian Economic Development*, London: Macmillan, pp. 79–101

Saleh, K. and Y. Jammal (2002), 'Towards Income Accounts for Indonesia', *Report No.14, STAT Project*, Jakarta: Badan Pusat Statistik.

Sarel, M. (1997), 'Growth and Productivity in ASEAN Countries', *IMF Working Paper No. WP/97/97*, Washington DC: International Monetary Fund.

Sigit, H. (2000a), 'Telaah Data Ketenagakerjaan di Indonesia' (Analysis of employment data in Indonesia), *Laporan No.5, STAT Project*, Jakarta: Badan Pusat Statistik.

Sigit, H. (2000b), 'Earning Data in Indonesia: A Review of Existing Sources', *Report No.10, STAT Project*, Jakarta: Badan Pusat Statistik.

Sigit, H. (2004), '*Indonesia*', in Noriyoshi, O. (ed.) *Total Factor Productivity Growth: Survey Report*, Tokyo: Asian Productivity Organization, pp. 98–133.

Sivasubramonian, S. (2003), *The Sources of Economic Growth in India, 1950–1 to 1999–2000*, New Delhi: Oxford UP.

Sutanto (2004), 'Konsep dan Aplikasi Total Faktor Produktivitas (TFP)', *Majalah Nakertrans (Departemen Tenaga Kerja & Transmigrasi)*, **24** (3) 10–11.

Timmer, M. (1999), 'Indonesia's Ascent on the Technology Ladder: Capital Stock and Total Factor Productivity in Indonesian Manufacturing, 1975–95', *Bulletin of Indonesian Economic Studies*, **35** (1), 75–89.

Van der Eng, P. (1992), 'The Real Domestic Product of Indonesia, 1880–1989', *Explorations in Economic History*, **28**, 343–373.

Van der Eng, P. (1999), 'Some Obscurities in Indonesia's New National Accounts', *Bulletin of Indonesian Economic Studies*, **35** (2), 91–106.

Van der Eng, P. (2002), '*Indonesia's Growth Performance in the 20th Century*', in Maddison, A., D.S. Prasada Rao and W. Shepherd (eds), *The Asian Economies in the Twentieth* Century, Cheltenham: Edward Elgar, pp. 143–79.

Van der Eng, P. (2005), 'Indonesia's New National Accounts', *Bulletin of Indonesian Economic Studies*, **41** (2), 253–62.

Van der Eng, P. (2007), 'Japanese Firms in Indonesia: Hard Times?' Unpublished paper.

Van der Eng, P. (2008), 'The Sources of Long-Term Economic Growth in Indonesia, 1880–2007', *Working Papers in Economics and Econometrics No.499*, Canberra: School of Economics, ANU College of Business and Economics.

Van der Eng, P. (2009), 'Capital Formation and Capital Stock in Indonesia, 1950–2008', *Bulletin of Indonesian Economic Studies*, **45** (3), 345-371.

Vial, V. (2006), 'New Estimates of Total Factor Productivity Growth in Indonesian Manufacturing', *Bulletin of Indonesian Economic Studies*, **42** (3), 357–69.

Weerasinghe, P.N. and G Fane (2005), Accounting for Discrepancies among Estimates of TFP Growth in East Asia', *Economic Papers*, **24** (3), 280–93.

World Bank (1993), *The East Asian Miracle: Economic Growth and Public Policy*, Oxford: Oxford UP.

World Bank (2005), 'Raising Investment in Indonesia: A Second Generation of Reforms', *World Bank Report No. 31708–IND*, Washington DC: The World Bank.

World Bank (2006), *Doing Business 2007, How to Reform: Comparing Regulation in 175 Countries*, Washington DC: The World Bank.

Young, A. (1994), 'Accumulation, Exports and Growth in the High Performing Asian Economies: A Comment', *Carnegie–Rochester Conference Series on Public Policy*, **40**, 237–50.

Young, A. (1995), 'The Tyranny of Numbers: Confronting the Statistical Realities of the East Asian Growth Experience', *Quarterly Journal of Economics*, **110**, 641–80.

Yudanto, N., G. Wicaksono, E. Ariantoro and A.R. Sari (2005), 'Capital Stock in Indonesia: Measurement and Validity Test', *Irving Fisher Committee on Central Bank Statistics Bulletin*, **20**, 183–198.

APPENDIX

Table A.8.1   Key data used to estimate TFP in the chapter, 1960–2008

	GDP (market prices)	Non-Residential capital stock	Employment (x 1000)	Educational attainment per person (years)	Share of Labour Income (GDP) (1)	Annual % growth rates				
		(bln 2000 Rp)				GDP	Capital stock	Employment	Education-adjusted employment	TFP
1960	197,379	236,200		1.36		4.70	-0.29			
61	207,715	240,232	32,709	1.44		5.24	1.71			
62	207,224	242,919	33,456	1.52		-0.24	1.12	2.29	3.22	
63	196,241	242,680	34,225	1.61		-5.30	-0.10	2.30	3.32	
64	205,710	243,710	35,016	1.70		4.83	0.42	2.31	3.29	
1965	212,550	244,667	35,834	1.78		3.33	0.39	2.34	3.31	
66	211,180	247,468	36,672	1.87		-0.64	1.14	2.34	3.35	
67	208,638	247,348	37,534	1.96		-1.20	-0.05	2.35	3.30	
68	231,831	251,258	38,430	2.05		11.12	1.58	2.39	3.39	
69	256,715	255,740	39,318	2.13		10.73	1.78	2.31	3.31	
1970	291,644	262,058	40,279	2.21		13.61	2.47	2.45	3.36	
71	301,470	275,712	41,261	2.28	45.0%	3.37	5.21	2.44	3.15	-0.91
72	337,703	290,177	42,377	2.33	51.7%	12.02	5.25	2.70	3.28	7.79
73	391,604	303,745	43,523	2.39	46.7%	15.96	4.68	2.70	3.39	11.89
74	402,321	319,589	44,486	2.45	37.3%	2.74	5.22	2.21	2.94	-1.63
1975	403,044	336,419	45,726	2.52	39.3%	0.18	5.27	2.79	3.60	-4.43

Table A.8.1   (Continued)

	GDP (market prices)	Non-Residential capital stock	Employment (x 1000)	Educational attainment per person (years)	Share of Labour Income (GDP) (1)	Annual % growth rates				
	(bln 2000 Rp)					GDP	Capital stock	Employment	Education-adjusted employment	TFP
76	440,522	352,660	47,000	2.61	46.9%	9.30	4.83	2.79	3.71	4.99
77	474,130	372,794	48,310	2.70	50.7%	7.63	5.71	2.79	3.86	2.86
78	497,776	397,818	49,65/	2.81	54.1%	4.99	6.71	2.79	3.99	-0.25
79	523,357	422,625	51,041	2.92	47.5%	5.14	6.24	2.79	4.09	-0.08
1980	569,647	454,004	52,421	3.05	38.2%	8.84	7.42	2.70	4.18	2.66
81	603,796	488,300	54,294	3.18	38.2%	5.99	7.55	3.57	5.09	-0.62
82	582,435	530,502	56,238	3.32	42.5%	-3.54	8.64	3.58	5.14	-10.69
83	601,227	585,570	58,254	3.45	38.9%	3.23	10.38	3.59	5.17	-5.12
84	643,944	629,553	60,347	3.59	39.7%	7.10	7.51	3.59	5.14	0.53
1985	662,041	675,301	62,519	3.74	44.4%	2.81	7.27	3.60	5.34	-3.60
86	702,645	729,203	64,774	3.89	52.4%	6.13	7.98	3.61	5.29	-0.44
87	739,186	789,056	67,114	4.03	51.0%	5.20	8.21	3.61	5.24	-1.50
88	783,491	861,528	69,543	4.16	52.8%	5.99	9.18	3.62	5.14	-1.05
89	855,027	950,963	72,064	4.29	48.7%	9.13	10.38	3.63	5.04	1.35
1990	932,354	1,070,366	74,396	4.42	47.0%	9.04	12.56	3.24	4.75	0.16
91	980,971	1,206,918	76,137	4.55	47.5%	5.21	12.76	2.34	3.88	-3.33
92	1,088,339	1,345,078	77,928	4.69	49.6%	10.95	11.45	2.35	3.87	3.26
93	1,166,346	1,491,960	79,768	4.82	49.1%	7.17	10.92	2.36	3.90	-0.30

Table A.8.1   (Continued)

| | GDP (market prices) | Non Residential capital stock | Employment (x 1000) | Educational attainment per person (years) | Share of Labour Income (GDP) (1) | Annual % growth rates | | | | |
| | | | | | | GDP | Capital stock | Employment | Education-adjusted employment | TFP |
	(bln 2000 Rp)									
94	1,255,019	1,665,386	81,660	4.96	52.5%	7.60	11.62	2.37	3.92	0.02
1995	1,356,598	1,870,199	83,311	5.10	51.3%	8.09	12.30	2.02	3.63	0.25
96	1,459,647	2,101,456	85,003	5.24	47.0%	7.60	12.37	2.03	3.59	-0.64
97	1,525,369	2,342,446	86,738	5.38	43.5%	4.50	11.47	2.04	3.68	-3.58
98	1,321,432	2,432,763	88,517	5.52	28.4%	-13.37	3.86	2.05	3.64	-17.17
99	1,326,061	2,480,786	90,342	5.66	42.4%	0.35	1.97	2.06	3.56	-2.30
2000	1,389,770	2,550,631	92,059	5.78	46.9%	4.80	2.82	1.90	3.31	1.76
01	1,441,353	2,629,659	93,818	5.88	48.1%	3.71	3.10	1.91	3.01	0.65
02	1,505,359	2,706,739	95,738	5.97	52.2%	4.44	2.93	2.05	3.05	1.45
03	1,577,171	2,783,430	97,689	6.06	56.9%	4.77	2.83	2.04	3.02	1.83
04	1,656,517	2,894,323	99,665	6.14	54.1%	5.03	3.98	2.02	2.98	1.59
2005	1,750,815	3,033,085	101,652	6.23	52.4%	5.69	4.79	1.99	2.95	1.87
06	1,847,293	3,168,553	103,635	6.30	52.4%	5.51	4.47	1.95	2.84	1.90
07	1,963,092	3,331,091	105,632	6.38	52.4%	6.27	5.13	1.93	2.78	2.37
08	2,082,105	3,530,096	107,637	6.45	52.4%	6.06	5.97	1.90	2.63	1.84
09	2,177,742	3,734,060	109,721	6.56	52.4%	4.58	5.77	1.85	2.63	0.45
2010	2,310,690	3,964,249	111,713	6.63	52.4%	6.10	6.16	1.82	2.55	1.83

Source: See the main text.

9. Explaining Success and Failure in Economic Development[1]

Adam Szirmai

9.1 INTRODUCTION

During the last 60 years many myths about development have been exploded through sober empirical analysis and measurement of development trends. Developing countries are not inevitably condemned to poverty and stagnation. Average GDP per capita has increased more than four fold. Life expectancy at birth has increased by some 25 years. Child mortality has declined and human capital has increased. Contrary to Malthusian predictions, food production has outpaced a rapidly growing global population, especially in densely populated developing countries. Developing countries are not locked into agriculture and mining. They can become powerful global players in manufacturing production and exports. The average figures in table 9.1 hide disparities in socio-economic performance. One of the most striking phenomena in the study of development is the diversity of developing country experiences. In Asia, several countries have experienced rapid growth and catch-up, including Taiwan, Korea, Singapore, Hong Kong, China, Malaysia, Thailand, Turkey, Sri Lanka, India, Indonesia and Vietnam. Latin American economies grew rapidly until 1980, though their growth momentum faltered between 1973 and 2000 and their prospects are uncertain. With the exception of tiny countries such as Mauritius and Botswana and the exceptional case of South Africa, most African countries have experienced long-run stagnation since 1973, after a period of growth between 1950 and 1973. In the Middle East, economic performance of most countries has been weak, in spite of vast oil resources. Few of the oil-rich

---

[1] An earlier version of the chapter was presented at the conference World Economic Performance. Past, Present and Future organised at the occasion of the 80th Birthday of Angus Maddison, at the University of Groningen in October 2006. A longer version is available as a working paper, A. Szirmai, *Explaining Success and Failure in Development*, UNU–MERIT Working Paper, 2008–013, Maastricht 2008.

countries have been able to use their mineral resources to generate sustainable growth in other sectors of the economy.

Table 9.1   Dynamic changes in the Developing World, 1950–2005

	1950–60	1981	2000–05
GDP per capita (1990 PPP$), 1950, 2003	854.9		3645.6
Food production per capita (1980 = 100)	88.0		147.0
Manufactured exports as % of commodity exports	6.0		53.0
Life expectancy at birth	40.8		65.4
Child mortality by age 1	180.0		65.0
Child mortality by age 5	281.0		95.0
Gross Enrolment Rate primary education	75.8		103.9
Gross Enrolment Rate secondary education	15.7		58.3
Gross Enrolment Rate tertiary education	2.1		13.0
Net Enrolment Rate primary education	48.1		82.0
Net Enrolment Rate secondary education	35.0		45.0
Percentage of population, with less than 1 dollar a day		40.4	21.1
Number of persons with less than 1 dollar a day		1481.8	1092.7
Percentage of population, with less than 2 dollars a day		66.8	52.9
Number of persons with less than 2 dollars a day		2449.8	2735.5

Sources: Szirmai (2009): www.dynamicsofdevelopment.com; GDP per capita from Maddison (2007).

As a result of these divergent trends, developing countries that had similar levels of per capita income in the 1950s, such as e.g. China, Ghana, Tanzania, Senegal, Honduras, Indonesia, Malaysia, Thailand, South Korea and Taiwan now show vast differences in levels of economic development (Lal and Myint, 1996).

It sometimes appears that it is simply success that explains further success. Once dynamic processes of economic catch-up and technological change and catch-up have been firmly established, these call forth new talents, resources and institutional changes, which contribute to further development. New opportunities create further opportunities, growth becomes path dependent and policy makers can hardly get it wrong, as in present-day China. The sources of growth in successful development experiences may differ, but whatever the sources, success feeds upon itself in what Myrdal (1968) referred to as cumulative causation. Small initial differences between countries are reinforced over time. On the other hand, once development stagnates, as a result of external shocks, misguided policies, political instability or bad luck, it may be very difficult to get the economy moving again, as evidenced by Indonesia after the Asian crisis of 1997, Latin

America during the lost decade of the 1980s and Sub-Saharan Africa after the 1973 oil shock. Failure feeds on failure, just as much as success feeds on success. But the question remains whether we can explain why and how countries embark on such different paths.

In recent years, a whole range of exciting books and articles have been published focusing on long-run growth and development (Acemoglu et al. 2001; Acemoglu and Robinson, 2006; Collier, 2007; Landes 1998; Maddison, 2001 and 2007; Sachs, 2005; Helpman 2004; Easterly, 2001; Barro 1996, Rodrik, 2003, 2006 and 2007; Lal and Myint, 1996; North, 1990 and Lomborg, 2001, to name but a few). But in fact, the search for explanations of development and stagnation is closely bound up with the history of the economic and social sciences. From Adam Smith to Max Weber, classical economists and sociologists tried to explain the mystery of the capitalist breakthrough of the West and Western offshoots starting from an initial situation of shared global poverty in the Middle Ages. Since the 1950s, attention has shifted from explaining Western development, to why developing countries have failed to develop – whether as a result of internal conditions or external exploitation – and under what conditions they could catch-up with the advanced economies in the future.

This chapter attempts to summarise and synthesise insights derived from my textbook: *The Dynamics of Socio-Economic Development* (Szirmai, 2005).[2] This book, in turn, drew much of its inspiration from Angus Maddison's lifelong attempts to quantify and analyse different aspects of economic development. Of special importance are his early book *Economic Progress and Policy in developing countries* (1970), his lecture *Notes on Developing Country Performance* (1986), his analysis of proximate and ultimate sources of growth (Maddison, 1988), his recent magnum opus The *World Economy. A Millennial Perspective* (2001) and his *Contours of the World Economy 1–2030 AD* (2007). In this essay, I would like to explore what we can learn from the diversity of country experiences and the wealth of empirical studies about them. Can we come up with systematic explanations of relative success and failure in socio-economic development?

This chapter is structured as follows. In section 9.2, I briefly discuss the failure of mono-causal and historically invariant explanations of success and failure. Section 9.3 introduces the paradox of increasing global inequality combined with the increasing fluidity of the international order. This serves as a background for the discussion of post-war development trends. Section 9.4 provides a further elaboration of Maddison's ideas about proximate and

---

[2] For the detailed references and statistical tables underpinning the argument, the reader is referred to this source and to the accompanying website (www.dynamicsofdevelopment.com).

ultimate sources of growth and development. In sections 9.5 and 9.6, I apply this framework and summarise what we can learn from post-war development experiences.

9.2   THE FAILURE OF MONO-CAUSAL EXPLANATIONS

Explaining economic development is not for the simpleminded. The first observation that one can make is a negative one: every single mono-causal explanation ever advanced for development falls down in the face of the empirical evidence.

Max Weber explained the breakthrough of capitalism in North Western Europe from the *religious characteristics* of the Protestantism. But, Max Weber's *Protestant Ethic* cannot cope with the recent economic success of countries with a Confucian tradition. Differences in degrees of *corruption* cannot explain why some countries stagnate and others develop. Some countries and regions such as present-day China or Indonesia under Suharto prosper in spite of pervasive corruption, while others suffer deeply. Some types of corruption seem to be economically sustainable. *Climatic and geographic determinists* such as Jeffrey Sachs (Sachs et al. 2004), Jared Diamond (1998) or Paul Collier (2007) cannot account for the success of landlocked economies such as Switzerland, Austria, Botswana or rapid growth in tropical regions such as Malaysia, Singapore, Thailand or Southern China.

Japan, Korea and Taiwan have shown how countries can achieve phenomenal economic development in spite of scarce *natural resources*. Oil and mineral resources have often – but again not always – even turned out to be a bane for economic development, as in the case of Nigeria, Congo or Venezuela, but less so in the case of Indonesia, Qatar or Botswana. *Capital accumulation* is an ingredient of every conceivable development strategy. But high rates of investment are no guarantee for sustained growth of per capita output or total factor productivity. *Human capital* seems to be important in successful development experiences. But many African developing countries have achieved great success in expanding their education systems, while their economic growth stagnated (Pack and Paxson, 2001).

Protection of *property rights* has often been advanced as a key precondition for innovation, technological change and economic progress (North and Thomas, 1973: Landes, 1998). But the case of China since 1978 illustrates that explosive growth and catch-up can coexist with weak intellectual property rights and weakly defined property rights in general (Qian, 2003, Rodrik, 2006, 2007). Marxist and other theories of *colonial and neo-colonial exploitation* fail to explain why some former colonies break the mould of dependence and stagnation and emerge as dynamic economies, and others do not. Why did the USA become the world productivity leader while Brazil and Argentina have remained developing countries, though their decolonisation was only a few decades apart? Much has been made of *good economic policies*. It is certainly true that disastrous policies such as those of Zimbabwe's Mugabe or Indonesia's Sukarno can wreck a country. But apart from that policy variables such as openness to foreign investment, macroeconomic policies, price distortions, financial policies, and trade openness do not have predictable and robust effects on growth rates (Rodrik, 2006).

The first insight that follows from this is that it is seldom single factors, which explain breakthroughs and successes in economic development. It is the interaction of many complementary internal and external factors and determinants and the timing of these interactions. In his still eminently readable book *Strategy of Economic Development* (1958), Alfred Hirschman argues that one cannot compile a fixed list of 'prerequisites' for economic development, which would automatically result in economic success. Different countries face different binding constraints and different initial conditions.

Nevertheless, though initial conditions differ, success is path dependent and development experiences are seldom identical, we can learn from a systematic empirical analysis of past experiences of growth and stagnation.

9.3 THE PARADOX OF INCREASING GLOBAL INEQUALITY AND ACCELERATED CATCH-UP

Economic development takes place in the context of a changing international economic order. This order can be seen as an arena for a technology race, where countries and regions compete with each other over decades and centuries in terms of technology, productivity, per capita incomes and standards of living. In the long run these phenomena are closely linked. Technological advance fuels productivity growth. Growth of productive capacity provides the potential for economic growth, poverty reduction, improvements in standards of living, health, education and welfare and the emergence of more sustainable production technologies.

In the World Economy: A Millennial Perspective (2001), and *Contours of the World Economy* (2007), Angus Maddison has charted and quantified the long-run development of the world economic order. In Europe the acceleration of growth dates back to the fourteenth century, when Europe overtook the incumbent technological leader China.[3] From the fourteenth century onwards, Europe experienced a long-run increase in per capita incomes, which also spread to the Western Offshoots. Since 1820, per capita incomes in the Western world have increased 20-fold (Maddison, 2007, p. 70). Among the characteristics of this long-run growth process are the dual nature of sustained internal growth and 500 years of external economic and political expansion of the Western world. This resulted in the creation of a single interdependent world economic order, but not a global empire. The length of the Western growth experience contrasts with earlier cyclical economic movements of growth and decline. As other regions and countries did not participate to the same extent in this growth process, global divergence increased.

Though global inequality is on the increase, country positions in the global system of inequality are not immutable. On the one hand, there are changes in economic and technological leadership. On the other hand, some technologically backward economies realise very rapid catch-up.

Technological leadership shifted from China to Southern Europe in 14th century. Within Europe leadership shifted from Italian city states to the Iberian Peninsula, then in the 17th to North Western Europe, more specifically to the Dutch Republic. In the 18th century, the UK became the leader with breakthroughs in industrial production technologies. Around 1890, leadership shifted to the USA, which pioneered standardised production for mass markets and which has retained its lead in the post-1950 period. The Iraq war has shown the limits of US military dominance. Persistent current account deficits and a declining confidence in the dollar are the first signs of faltering leadership. The twenty-first century is witnessing the emergence of the Asian Giants China and India, whose weight and importance in the world economic order is rapidly increasing.

Since 1870, accelerated catch-up processes took place in Germany, Russia (Gerschenkron, 1962) and Japan. Western European countries were catching up relative to the USA between 1950 and 1973. Japan's catch-up streak continued till 1990, followed by a long spell of sluggish growth and relative stagnation. Latin America grew rapidly from 1900 untill 1980 (Hoffman, 1998; Maddison, 2001), catching up in some subperiods, though not all.

In Asia, South Korea, Taiwan, Singapore and Hong Kong provided spectacular examples of catch-up from 1950 onwards. Since the 1980s, second-tier NICs (Newly Industrialised Countries) such as Malaysia, Indonesia, Sri Lanka and Thailand have joined the race, while growth of

---

[3] Maddison dates the overtaking of China by Europe a century earlier than previous observers have done.

output and productivity accelerated in the 1990s in China, India and Vietnam (China from 1978).

Of course, not all countries participated in catch-up. There are many examples of relative and absolute stagnation, including Latin America after 1980 and the countries of the former Soviet Union. In *The Bottom Billion*, Paul Collier (2007) has analysed the experiences of 58 poor stagnating economies, which account for more than a billion inhabitants living below the poverty line of a dollar a day. Most of these countries are located in Sub-Saharan Africa, which has been experiencing stagnation since the oil crisis of 1973.[4] These countries face four interacting development traps: the political conflict trap, the natural resource trap, landlockedness and the trap of bad governance.

With regard to catch-up, the modern international order is characterised by an interesting paradox between increasing inequality and acceleration of the rate of catch-up. The technology race has resulted in a dramatic increase in long-run inequality in per capita incomes between countries. Around 1820, Maddison estimates that rich countries such as the UK had a per capita income of twice that of India. In 2006, the richest 29 countries were 14.2 times as rich as the 48 poorest countries (World Development Indicators Online, 2008). In 2006, the ratio in PPP dollars of the richest country, the USA to the poorest country, Burundi, was over 60 to 1. However, as global income disparities increase, the speed with which individual countries change their positions in the income ranking has also accelerated. The high growth rates of present day China and India, and earlier Japan, Taiwan and Korea in the twentieth century have not yet been witnessed in economic history. In one or two generations, countries move from the very lowest positions to the middle or even the upper ranges of the global income ladder.

The acceleration of catch-up is illustrated in table 9.2. In the nineteenth century, GDP per capita in the catch-up countries was growing at between 1.4 and 1.9 per cent per year, compared to the 5–9 per cent after 1950. Prior to 1913, the ratio of per capita GDP growth in catch-up episodes, relative to the growth of the technological leader the United Kingdom was between 1.3 and 2. After 1950, the catch-up countries – most of them located in Asia – were growing on average three times as fast as the world leader the USA. The acceleration of catch-up is related to globalisation and greater possibilities for international technology diffusion.

---

[4] Growth rates in several African countries have increased after 2000, fuelled by increasing demand for primary products. Some African countries such as Ghana, Mozambique, Tanzania, Uganda and Angola have been experiencing rapid growth in the years preceding the present global financial crisis.

World Economic Performance

Table 9.2   Post-War Catch-up Episodes

Country	Period[a]	Growth of GDP	Growth of GDP per capita	Rate of Catch-up[b]
1820–1913				
USA	1820–1905	4.1	1.5	1.3
Germany	1880–1913	3.1	1.9	1.8
Russia	1900–1913	3.2	1.4	2.0
Japan	1870–1913	2.5	1.5	1.5
United Kingdom	1820–1913	2.0	1.1	
World average	1820–1913	1.5	0.9	
1950–2003				
China	1978–2006	8.1	6.9	3.6
West Germany	1950–1973	6.0	5.0	2.7
India	1994–2006	6.7	5.1	2.4
Indonesia	1967–1997	6.8	4.8	2.4
Ireland	1995–2006	6.2	6.2	2.8
Japan	1946–1973	9.3	8.0	3.6
Korea	1952–1997	8.2	6.3	3.0
Malaysia	1968–1997	7.5	5.1	2.6
Russia	1998–2005	7.2	7.2	3.9
Singapore	1960–1973	10.0	7.6	2.5
Taiwan	1962–1973	11.4	8.7	2.8
Thailand	1973–1996	7.6	5.8	3.2
Vietnam	1992–2005	7.6	6.1	2.9
World average	1950–1973	4.9	2.9	
World average	1973–1997	3.1	1.4	
World average	1997–2003	3.5	2.3	

Notes: a) The periods have been chosen so as to maximise sustained high growth rates over an extended period. b) Ratio of Growth of GDP per capita compared to growth in lead economy in corresponding period. Prior to 1913, the comparison is with the UK, after 1950 with the USA.

Sources: Country data 1990 and before, plus figures for world total from Angus Maddison, Historical Statistics, World Population, GDP and Per Capita GDP, 1–2003 AD (update: August 2007) http://www.ggdc.net/maddison/. Country data 1991–2006 and West Germany from: The Conference Board and Groningen Growth and Development Centre, Total Economy Database, November 2007, http://www.conference–board.org/economics" .West Germany from Conference Board/GGDC.

9.4 PROXIMATE, INTERMEDIATE AND ULTIMATE SOURCES OF GROWTH

The key challenge to our theoretical and empirical understanding in development economics is to understand why some developing countries experience accelerated catch-up and others become mired in stagnation. The framework of proximate and ultimate sources of growth developed by among others Angus Maddison (1988), Moses Abramovitz (1989) and more recently by Dani Rodrik (2003) is very useful for such analysis. Here, I provide some further elaboration of this framework, distinguishing proximate, intermediate and ultimate sources (see Figure 9.1).

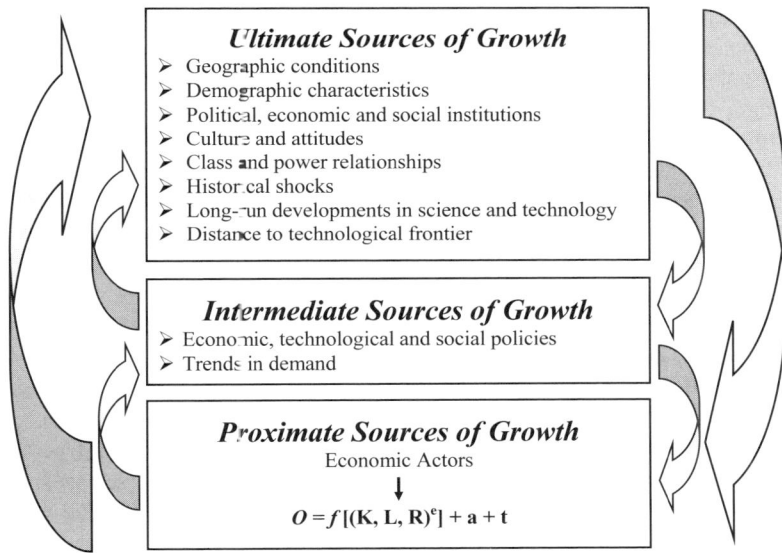

Ultimate Sources of Growth
➤ Geographic conditions
➤ Demographic characteristics
➤ Political, economic and social institutions
➤ Culture and attitudes
➤ Class and power relationships
➤ Historical shocks
➤ Long-run developments in science and technology
➤ Distance to technological frontier

Intermediate Sources of Growth
➤ Economic, technological and social policies
➤ Trends in demand

Proximate Sources of Growth
Economic Actors
↓
$O = f[(K, L, R)^e] + a + t$

Figure 9.1   Sources of growth

9.4.1   Proximate Sources

Proximate sources of growth refer to the directly measurable sources of growth of output such as

- labour input and accumulation of human capital (L),
- capital accumulation and embodied technological change (K),
- exploitation of land and natural resources (R) and

- the increasing efficiency (e) with which resources are used to produce a flow of goods and services.

The efficiency term 'e' subsumes a wide range of factors such as economies of scale and scope, utilisation rates, more effective use of existing technologies (*technical efficiency*), economically efficient combinations of capital labour and other inputs (*economic efficiency*), shifts of resources to more productive and dynamic sectors and specialisation according to comparative advantage (*allocative efficiency*). A factor of particular importance is disembodied technological change. The term 'a' refers to net factor income from abroad and the term 'p' to net voluntary and involuntary transfers (plunder, expropriation, aid flows and remittances).

In the present formulation of the framework, the proximate sources of growth also include the behaviour of the economic actors that are responsible for the changes in the proximate sources, such as saving and capital accumulation, investment in human capital, investment in technological change, efficiency improvements, innovations, and entering new economic sectors. Economic actors provide the link between the macro-economic analysis of the production function and the burgeoning micro-economic literature on firm-level analysis, household surveys, entrepreneurship and innovation studies. It also allows us to examine the relationships between proximate sources such as capital accumulation and ultimate sources such as for instance culture and institutions. Culture and institutions provide the incentives and mindsets for saving, investment and entrepreneurial behaviour by economic actors.

Disembodied technological change refers to advances in our technological knowledge concerning products and production processes. It involves the development of new production processes, new types of machinery, new forms of organisation, use of new inputs, new products and services, new ways of distributing products and services, and new knowledge that can be transferred through education. It also involves a variety of knowledge spillovers between economic actors and between countries. With regard to technological change, it is important to distinguish between technological change at the frontiers of knowledge in the lead economies and diffusion and absorption of technology in the follower countries. The latter is of vital importance for developing countries (see section 9.6 of this chapter).

Abramovitz (1989) has emphasized the importance of complementarities between the proximate sources of growth. Among the most important of these complementarities is that between capital goods embodying new technologies and improvements in skills and human capital. Without appropriate inflows of new capital, new skills will be wasted (Pack and Paxson, 2001) and vice versa. Thus, the joint effect of accumulation of human capital, and physical capital may be much larger than the sum of the separate contributions. What complicates the issue, however, is that complementarity does not necessarily mean simultaneity. There are indications that prior investments in human capital set the stage for subsequent effective deployment of physical capital (Godo and Hayami, 2002; Sandberg, 1982). The time lags involved can be substantial, up to 40–60 years.

It is long known (Abramovitz, 1989; Nelson, 1996; Rodrik, 2003) that one should be careful in giving the sources of growth equation a strong causal interpretation. As Rodrik notes for instance, capital accumulation and efficiency in the use of resources are themselves endogenous. Causality may well run backwards from growth to accumulation and productivity (Rodrik, 2003, p. 4). These circular relationships are indicated by the feedback arrows in figure 9.1. Nevertheless, the sources of growth formulation are indispensable for a systematic empirical examination of growth sources.

9.4.2 Intermediate Sources of Growth

The intermediate sources of growth refer to two types of factors: (i) trends in domestic and international demand and (ii) policies – economic policies, social policies and technology policies.

Adding demand as an intermediate source of growth is an attempt to respond to the criticism that the sources of growth framework is an exclusively supply side approach. Taking patterns of demand into account is important for the understanding of the path-dependent nature of processes of economic development. Thus, when world demand or domestic demand is growing and market shares are expanding, this motivates economic actors to accumulate human and physical capital, which results in further growth and competitiveness.

Interpreting national and international socio-economic policies as intermediate factors emphasizes that policy is in turn influenced and constrained by more ultimate factors such as economic interests and the characteristics of the power structures. This is increasingly being rediscovered in recent research in political economy (e.g. Acemoglu et al. 2001; Acemoglu and Robinson; 2006, Shleifer and Vishny, 1993; Shleifer et al. 2004), which sees policy itself as an endogenous variable, explained by more ultimate factors such as the balance of power between different classes or between elites and the mass of the population.

9.4.3 Ultimate Sources of Growth

Ultimate sources of growth refer to historical trends, external shocks, demographic conditions and trends, class structures, economic and political institutions, culture and attitudes and geographic conditions. The ultimate sources include:

- geographic location, climate and natural resources;
- demographic and epidemiological trends;
- the history of political centralisation and state formation; institutions for conflict management and maintenance of law and order, political stability and the quality of governance;
- the dynamics of class relationships and elite-mass relationships;
- the evolution of values and attitudes affecting economic behaviour;
- the development of institutions such as private property, intellectual property rights, joint stock companies, banking institutions, institutions which align economic incentives with social costs and benefits;
- developments in the international order, such as international trade regimes;
- long-run developments in science and technology;
- the distance of a country from the technological frontier, which determines its catch-up potential; and
- absorptive capacity and the evolution of technological and social capabilities.

The use of the term ultimate sources of growth is not meant to imply a linear model of causality. Causality is circular at all levels. For instance, economic growth obviously affects demographic and epidemiological transitions in well-known ways. In the long run even cultural values and institutions are shaped and reshaped in the course of economic development (Harrison, 1985; Harrison and Huntington, 2000).[5] The difference between the more ultimate and more proximate sources of causality lies mainly in the ease of quantification and the time span of the chains of causality. It also provides a research strategy, which starts with the measurable economic factors and then goes beyond them to broader social and historical determinants. It also provides a framework for multidisciplinary analysis of economic development.

9.5   PATTERNS AND EXPLANATIONS

In the following sections, I apply the framework of proximate and ultimate causes to identify common elements and patterns in successful episodes of economic development.

---

[5] Ester Boserup has argued that even the seemingly ultimate factor of 'natural' environment has been shaped by the impact of human interventions in socio-economic development.

9.5.1 Proximate Sources

Capital accumulation

Without exception successful development involves bridging the capital intensity gap and increasing domestic savings and/or foreign inflows of capital. Without rapid accumulation of capital, there can be no success in economic development. Capital accumulation and capital intensification in developing countries are linked with industrialisation (Szirmai, 2009).

Developing countries have been remarkably effective in increasing their investment rates since 1950. Savings rates in developing countries are now comparable to or higher than those in the advanced economies. China, in particular, has extremely high savings rates. Also for most of the twentieth century, developing countries have profited from net inflows of financial resources (Maddison, 1986; Szirmai, 2005). But, neither the rate of capital accumulation nor the level of capital per worker is a guarantee for a high rate of economic growth. If the efficiency of investment is low and absorptive capacity (skills, education, capability, experience, incentives) is lacking, capital productivity and total factor productivity will be low and the impact of accumulation on growth will be limited. Thus, the very substantial increases in investment rates in sub-Saharan Africa in the post-war period are not mirrored by comparable increases in the rates of economic growth.

Human capital accumulation

Investment in human capital, expansion of educational enrolment and increased literacy have been important, in one way or another, in all cases of successful development. The argument of Gerschenkron (1962) that education can be replaced by technologies which economise on skilled labour is not supported by the historical record of catch-up countries. Neither is Easterly's rather silly proposition that education does not matter (Easterly, 2001, chapter 4).

The expansion of education and human capital has been one of the greatest success stories of the post-war period (see Szirmai, 2005, tables 7.1–7.6). In many cases starting from scratch, developing countries have built comprehensive education systems which cover large segments of their populations. Though there are major problems with educational quality and the mismatch between education and the labour market and, though universal primary education has not yet been realised in all countries, progress in human capital accumulation is unmistakable. Rates of illiteracy are decreasing and human capital per worker is increasing.

The effects of education on economic development are, however, very complex. Some theorists have emphasized that expansion of education and literacy precedes acceleration of economic development by many decades.

This was the case in the Scandinavian countries, Japan, China, Taiwan and Korea (Sandberg, 1982; Nuñez, 1990; Godo and Hayami, 2002). So, expansion of education may not have immediate and direct consequences for growth, as is confirmed by the experiences of many developing countries. In an excellent analysis of the Japanese catch-up experience, Godo and Hayami (2002) combine the notions of *complementarity* and *threshold*. The early increase in education initially had little impact on growth, because capital per worker was growing slowly, so there was little complementarity. After World War II, a threshold level of education had been reached and capital accumulation and slower education advance combined to promote explosive growth.

Where educational investment was insufficient, this has generally acted as a brake on development. Thus, expansion and improvement of education in one form or another may be considered one of the important necessary conditions for development.

The concept of human capital is broader than education. It includes health and sufficient nutrition, which also contribute to productivity of households and growth of economies.

Structural change: Industrialisation as an engine of growth
Since 1950, all developing countries, that have experienced rapid growth and catch-up, have been successful industrialisers and industrial exporters (Szirmai, 2008). Countries that fell behind in aggregate terms were also the weakest industrial performers, such as countries in sub-Saharan Africa. In the past 50 years, manufacturing has been the main engine of growth and development in developing countries. In other words, the *structural change* involved in the shift from agriculture to industry has been a key ingredient of successful economic development.

The pattern of structural change in post-war developing countries differed from the earlier pattern in the advanced economies, where the share of industry increased first and the share of services increased later. In developing countries, there was a simultaneous shift from agriculture to industry and services. At an early stage, the share of services was already as high as or higher than that of industry. This has to do with the rapid expansion of the government share in GDP. It is likely that this early growth of a not very productive service sector acted as a brake on development.

Though the share of manufacturing in GDP and employment has increased in a great majority of developing countries, the increasing share of developing countries in world exports of manufacturing goods is attributable to some 12 countries (including China, India, Brazil, Mexico, Turkey, Malaysia, Indonesia, Thailand, Sri Lanka, Vietnam, Singapore and Hong Kong).

According to Arthur Lewis learning to industrialise is a lengthy process which can take up to 30–40 years (Lewis, 1978). It is worth noting that all the developing countries which were successful in industrialising after 1950, had learning experiences in industrialisation which date back to the 1930s and sometimes even to the nineteenth century, as in the case of China and India. The failed industrialisation of sub-Saharan Africa since 1950 is not due to some innate incapacity for industrial production. It is in part due to the fact that industrialisation really started from scratch in the post-colonial period.

The importance of manufacturing as an engine of growth is not undisputed. Recent empirical research (e.g. Timmer and de Vries, 2009; Chakravarty and Mitra, 2009) point to the importance of other sectors such as business services. It also indicates that the role of manufacturing in economic development may be becoming less important over time. Nevertheless, the historical record still tends to confirm the fact that success in manufacturing and success in overall development seem to go hand in hand.

Agricultural development: Decreasing shares, increasing output and productivity

In contrast to the predictions of Malthusian pessimists, developing countries have been remarkably successful in increasing the per capita output of foodstuffs in the post-war period. The increases have been most striking in large and densely populated developing countries such as India, Indonesia and China (Szirmai, 2005, table 10.1). The exception to this trend is sub-Saharan Africa where output per capita is at the same level as in 1979–81 and lower than in 1934.

These output and productivity increases have been realised through expansion of arable land, increases in cropping intensities, increases in irrigation, increases in the application of fertilizers and development and diffusion of new seeds (biotechnological change). Increases in yields per harvest (irrigation, fertilizers and technological change) account for over 70 per cent of output growth in the past 40 years (Szirmai, 2005, table 10.8).

These increases in agricultural output have been realised with shrinking shares of agriculture in total employment and shrinking shares of agriculture in GDP. Nevertheless, there is a correlation between successful development in agriculture and overall economic performance in developing countries.

Total factor productivity growth and technological change

In the context of East Asian industrialisation, there is a well-known debate between *accumulationists* emphasizing the role of capital accumulation and *assimilationists* emphasizing the role of technological change (see Timmer, 2000). Accumulationists argue that physical capital accumulation has been more important than total factor productivity growth. Their pessimistic prediction was that the growth process would run out of steam once sufficient capital had been accumulated. This has so far not occurred in South and East Asia.

There is, however, a measure of truth in the accumulationist observation that in early phases of industrial development, wasteful processes of accumulation predominate, whether in Stalinist Russia, Maoist China, Nehru's India or Nyerere's Tanzania. Industrialisation in Korea and Taiwan also started with capital accumulation in combination with cheap unskilled labour in textiles and assembly activities. This 'primitive' accumulation usually goes hand in hand with highly distorted markets, extensive government intervention, nationalisations, protection, large scale production and import substitution (Lin et al., 2000).

The key question is whether, after accumulation processes have been set in motion, an economy can upgrade its production technology, achieve shifts from low-tech sectors to medium and high tech sectors, and increase its overall efficiency. All these elements will express themselves in growth of total factor productivity. One of the typical differences between success and failure in economic development lies in this switch from accumulation to upgrading. The development experiences of both the newer and the older Asian industrialising countries demonstrate that the accumulationists have been too pessimistic and that such shifts are possible. On average, TFP growth rates since the 1990s have been higher than in the 1970s and 1980s. Growth has accelerated, human capital has been upgraded, new sectors have emerged and new technologies have been absorbed.

The assimilationists are also right in emphasizing that even the raw accumulation of physical capital requires a major effort of mastering, adapting and implementing imported embodied technologies. Thus, TFP change in developing countries is closely associated with the international transfer and acquisition of technology.

9.5.2 Intermediate Sources

Prudent macroeconomic policies

It has now become customary in both academic and policy circles to routinely sneer at the Washington consensus (Williamson, 1990) underlying the neo-liberal policy recommendations for developing countries since the 1990s. However, there is strong evidence that macroeconomic stability and prudent fiscal and monetary policies have been essential ingredients in the Asian growth performance and successful growth episodes elsewhere.

It is the inability of Latin American countries to implement sustained macroeconomic stabilisation policies over longer periods of time, which underpins the disappointing performance of Latin American policies since the oil shock of 1973. In Latin America, bursts of painful macroeconomic restructuring adjustment have been followed time and time again by populist waves of resistance against adjustment policies. Thus, it seems as if Latin America is primarily experiencing the negative side of economic orthodoxy: painful restructuring without long-term benefits following from sustained adjustment policies. This inability to realise sustained macroeconomic stability may well have to do with high degree of initial inequality in Latin America which creates political stresses and pressures that affect the economic policy stance.[6] The present re-emergence of Peronist-type policies and populist political movements in Venezuela and Bolivia bodes ill for their economic future in the longer run.

However, the critics of orthodox macroeconomic policies are right in noting that macro-economic reform is not sufficient to attain high growth rates and increased economic welfare. They also require microeconomic changes and supporting industrial and technology policies which allow for a transition from capital accumulation to technological upgrading (Westphal, 2002; Hausmann and Rodrik, 2005; see also the paragraph on industrial policies below).

Policies aimed at achieving a balance between agricultural and industrial development

Finding a good policy balance between incentives for agriculture and industry is an ingredient of successful development. Balanced growth path theory emphasizes that growth is enhanced if the different sectors grow at such rates that they do not act as a brake on growth in other sectors (Mellor, 1976). This is especially relevant for the agricultural sector. As the agricultural sector provides food to the urban population, intermediate inputs to manufacturing and a market for industrial products, policy discrimination against agriculture has a negative impact on industrial growth and development success. Between 1945 and 1960, development policies discriminated heavily against agriculture, with markedly negative results. Countries in sub-Saharan Africa, which had long been self-sufficient in food production, became more and more dependent on agricultural imports and food aid. Negative climatic conditions and droughts account for some of this impact, but man-made policies were at least as important in explaining agricultural stagnation.

From 1960 in parts of the developing world, intersectoral policies started changing. India, China, Vietnam, Thailand and Indonesia started taking a more balanced approach (Timmer, 2005). The policy bias against agriculture

---

[6] This is an example of the intermediate character of economic policy, which in turn is influenced by more ultimate conditions in a country.

continued longest in sub-Saharan Africa, until 1980 or later. It is only since the 1990s that changes have started being implemented in the context of structural adjustment programmes. These changes refer to the gradual elimination of price controls, marketing boards and similar exploitative institutions that discriminate against agriculture.

Trade regime: Outward economic orientation

The developing countries that are economically most successful are invariably those that opened up to the outside world and engaged in international trade (e.g. Sachs and Warner, 1995; Rodrik, 2003). Those countries that remained inward-oriented for too long were the countries that stagnated. The timing of the switch to export-orientation is one of the key elements distinguishing Southeast Asia from Latin America. Latin America continued inward-looking policies much longer. The outward orientation of the East Asian economies contributed to an appropriate choice of techniques, where economies made optimal use of their supply of cheap labour to become competitive in world markets.

Openness to foreign investment

Openness also refers to the role of *Foreign Direct Investment* (FDI) in the economy. Though Japan and South Korea are famous examples of countries that were able to acquire international technology, without opening up in any important ways to foreign investment, this route is no longer open to most developing countries (Westphal, 2002; Narula and Lall, 2006; Hobday, 2000, 2009). Since the 1970s, FDI is one of the key channels of technology acquisition. It has played a very positive role in countries with sufficiently developed absorptive capacities. The volume and impact of FDI have increased tremendously. The more developed its absorptive capacities and the quality of its domestic entrepreneurship, the more a country will profit from FDI. The less developed the absorptive capacity of a country, the more exploitative will the role of foreign capital be.

Trade regime: Reducing protectionism

The evidence that trade openness is positively linked to economic success is mixed. Some studies see a connection between openness and growth (Sachs and Warner, 1995; Krueger, 1998; Baldwin 2003), others (e.g. Rodriguez and Rodrik, 2001; Fagerberg and Srholec, 2006) question the direct correlation between indicators of openness and growth. This finding is not so surprising and reflects the historical poverty of cross-country regression methods. Why is the evidence so mixed?

First, in almost all cases of economic success, outward orientation was preceded by a period of closure, protectionism and import substitution. The only exceptions that come to mind are the city states of Hong Kong and Singapore, which were simply too small to depend on their domestic markets. For most successful developing countries, import substitution did provide the time required for learning the basics of industrialisation. There are few examples of developing countries which started exporting manufactured goods from scratch.

Examples of formerly inward-looking economies which turned outwards include South Korea, Sri Lanka, Taiwan, India, China and Indonesia. In this respect, the much maligned import substitution has played a positive role in the economic history of the presently economically more successful developing countries. The present emphasis in world trade negotiations on unconditional trade liberalisation by the poorest developing countries disregards the positive role that protection has played in the past (Chang, 2002).

In the second place, the outward orientation of the successful East Asian economies has not been synonymous with import liberalisation and reduced levels of industrial protection. In spite of the smoke screens thrown up in the ambiguous World Bank study, *The East Asian Miracle* (1993), policy interventions and import protection continued to play an important role in most of the successful Asian economies (except in laissez faire – Hong Kong).

On the other hand, it cannot be denied that protectionist policies nurture inefficiency, waste and economic stagnation, by reducing incentives for competition. This has had detrimental effects in both Latin America and sub-Saharan Africa. In China, the protected state enterprises continue to be a burden on the overall economy. The sooner economies exposed their firms to the discipline of the market, the more they profited from the learning effects of the preceding period of import substitution. The later the turn outwards, the more the inefficiency generating effects of protection predominated. The acceleration of growth in China and India was unmistakably accompanied by a shift towards a more-outward looking stance in trade policy, reduced protection and an increase in competitive pressures. Economic stagnation in Africa and Latin America is associated with continued protection which was conducive to inefficiency and rent seeking behaviour.

Financial openness

Not all forms of openness are beneficial for growth and development. Since the financial crises of the 1990s, in particular the Asian crisis of 1997, a convincing case has been made for retaining some measure of control over short term capital flows, to avoid extreme destabilisation in globalised financial markets (Stiglitz, 2000, 2002; Tobin, 2000; Eichengreen, 2000). Premature financial openness makes developing countries with underdeveloped financial markets and shaky banking systems more vulnerable to external shocks. The present global financial crisis has reinforced the call for more and better regulation of the international financial system.

International trade policies

In the longer run, international trade policy and reduced restrictions on international trade achieved in successive GATT negotiation rounds have had positive effects on industrialisation and growth in developing countries and have contributed in major ways to their increased access to developed country markets. The great exception has been agricultural protection, which has continued almost unabated to the present day to the detriment of the primary export prospects of developing countries, whether of the poorest LDCs in Africa or the more affluent Latin American countries.

Liberalisation and deregulation and market orientation

In long-run perspective it is unmistakable that acceleration of growth in Asia has been accompanied by economic liberalisation, deregulation, and a turn towards market incentives, for instance in countries like China, India, Indonesia, Malaysia or Thailand (e.g. Lin et al. 2000; Mani, forthcoming). In Africa, liberalisation and privatisation initially led to further economic decline, deindustrialisation and stagnation (Jalilian et al, 2000). In Latin America, the record of liberalisation has been mixed. Liberalisation of trade, finance and domestic markets led to declines in technological capabilities and increased macroeconomic instability in countries such as Argentina, Bolivia, Brazil, Mexico and Venezuela (e.g. Katz, 2000).

State-led growth was able to achieve substantial rates of capital accumulation in the post-war period in Brazil, Mexico, India and China, the Soviet Union, Tanzania, Zambia and Kenya. But it failed to deliver sustained growth, as planned economies were too inflexible and rigid to respond to increasingly rapid changes in domestic and international demand, in technology and in the global division of labour. State-led policies may be appropriate for rapid capital accumulation in the initial stages of industrial development but less for total factor productivity growth and technological upgrading. For sub-Saharan Africa, one can conclude without any hesitation that state intervention, nationalisations and forced industrialisation policies stifled growth after promising beginnings in the 1950s and 1960s (e.g. van Engelen et al., 2001).

Industrial and technology policies

The Asian Miracle (World Bank, 1993) attempted to reinterpret the Southeast Asian economic success as the result of outward orientation and market-friendly policies. But the conclusions of the study contradicted many of the interesting chapters included in the book, which gave ample evidence of the heavily interventionist nature of economic policies in most of these economies. This has been confirmed in a whole range of studies which definitively confirm the interventionist nature of East Asian economic policy (Westphal 2002; Amsden 1989; Wade 1990, Chang, 2002). Economic policy was not simply directed at import liberalisation and market liberalisation. On the contrary, high rates of protection were maintained and key sectors, conglomerates and even enterprises were supported and subsidised. The key purpose of policy interventions was technological learning.

Science, technology and educational policies acted as a important supplement to macro-economic policy. Industrial policy was oriented towards upgrading and the shift from traditional low-tech sectors such as textiles to high-tech sectors such as electronics. Technology policy was directed at improving domestic research capacity, improving human capital and acquiring international technology. Technology policy and industrial policy interacted to promote learning, acquisition of technological capabilities and absorptive capacities. Thus the choice to invest in a given sector such as electronics in Malaysia was not only determined by immediate economic prospects, but also by long-run learning prospects.

In *Kicking Away the Ladder*, Chang (2002) argues that in the present-day orthodox liberal world economic order, the developing countries in Africa and Latin America that are seeking to emulate the experiences of the Asian countries, are deprived of the tools and instruments which contributed to success in the past, such as some degree of protection and interventionist technology and industrial policies. Chang's conclusions are logical and derive from a realistic interpretation of policies in Asia. Nevertheless, his policy advice is not without risk for Latin America and even more so for sub-Saharan African countries.

In sub-Saharan Africa, we argued above that state policies themselves have been among the main sources of economic stagnation. In this context, one should be wary of anything that increases the discretionary power of the state apparatus. State policies have contributed to the destruction of agriculture in countries that had food surpluses at the eve of their independence. State policies have led to forced industrialisation strategies that have been a failure across the board and resulted in industries with a negative contribution to GDP at world prices. State policies have squandered natural resources and riches in a wide range of countries. Thirty years of industrial protection has not resulted in a significant learning experience. On the contrary, it has created deeply inefficient parastatal enterprises which were unable to compete in a liberalised setting and which melted down when protection was abolished (for Tanzania, see Van Engelen et al., 2001).

Given the institutional quality of the state apparatus in Africa, it is likely that the present trend towards liberalisation and withdrawal of the state from the economy may be the best of bad options. In the period 2000–2007, there were indications that after 10 years of deindustrialization in East Africa, some countries were starting to experience some recovery, including countries such as Zambia, Tanzania or Mozambique which profited from inflows of foreign direct investment and accelerated growth since 2000 (e.g. Portelli, 2006). At a later stage, if and when the quality of governance and government institutions has also improved in Africa, one might revisit the debate reopened by Chang. But, not at this moment.

My conclusion is that the debate concerning industrial and technology policy and the use of instruments of protection cannot be separated from the debate about the quality of government institutions. The more effective government institutions, the more scope there is for policy interventions. It is also relevant for the policy debate that the acceleration of growth in China, India and Indonesia in the 1990s was associated on balance with a marked shift towards deregulation, privatisations and a strengthening of market forces.

Avoiding aid dependence

Foreign aid is not a major determinant of successful economic growth and development. Never in economic history have inflows of aid been responsible for a country's turnaround from stagnation to growth and catch-up (Szirmai, 2005, chapter 14). Ultimately, growth and socio-economic development can only be realised through internal efforts, entrepreneurship, policies and internal dynamics. There is no doubt, that some forms of aid have had positive impacts. But at best, the impacts on growth and development are marginal. Aid can become counterproductive when aid flows allow governments to continue ineffective and economically destructive agricultural and industrial policies, which they would not have been able to sustain in the absence of aid flows. Aid also becomes counterproductive when aid flows are too large as a percentage of GDP. There is a potential negative effect of very large inflows of aid, which have a distorting influence on entrepreneurial incentives. My working hypothesis is that a sustained inflow of aid beyond a threshold level of around 5–7 per cent of GDP will sap the long-run productive potential of a country.

9.5.3   Ultimate sources of economic development

In the light of our rejection of mono-causal explanations, generalising about the ultimate sources of growth is perhaps the hardest of all. Here I discuss a number of the key factors from the literature.

Geographic conditions, climate, soil conditions and natural resources

Geographic determinists such as Sachs, Rodrik, Collier and Diamond argue that geographic factors such as climate, soil conditions, mineral resources and distance from the continental coastline are important ultimate determinants of growth and stagnation (Sachs et al., 2004, Diamond, 1998, Collier, 2007, Rodrik, 2003). Thus, moderate climate, location on the seaboard, fertile soils and resources such as coal, oil, gas or minerals are seen as positive factors in developmental success. It is very plausible that geographic conditions and resource endowments affect the path of development, as does population size (Chenery et al., 1986). They define the challenges a country's people, entrepreneurs and policy makers have to grapple with. Policies and human actions have somehow or other to take into account landlocked location, lack of resource availability, physically demanding climatic conditions or poor soil conditions.

However, the claims for geography as a factor differentiating between success and failure are heavily overstated in the twentieth century context. Geographic conditions do not determine success or failure in development. For every factor mentioned by the determinists, there are powerful counterexamples. Nowadays, many tropical countries and regions with intemperate climates show very rapid growth. Resource poor countries such as Japan and Korea have experienced spectacular catch-up. There are many examples of very prosperous landlocked economies such as Switzerland, Austria, Southern Germany or Botswana and of stagnating seaboard economies such as Eritrea or Zambia. In the post-war period, oil riches have more often been a negative source of growth than a positive one (Collier, 2007).

Demographic trends

Ester Boserup made a convincing case for the importance of demographic trends as driver of economic growth and technological change (Boserup, 1965, 1981). Her argument, in a nutshell, was that increasing population densities with given production technologies result in increasing pressure on resources and diminishing returns. They also create incentives for technological advance and intensive cultivation practices in agriculture and technological change in general, which may more than counteract diminishing returns. Success in development occurs when the localised race between technological change and population growth is won by technology. Failure occurs when the race is won by population. In many sub-Saharan African countries, population growth has exceeded growth of GDP since 1973, resulting in stagnating per capita incomes. Population growth has also exceeded the rate of technological change in agriculture. As a result, diminishing returns to traditional agricultural practices have resulted in stagnation of food production. On the other hand, in East Asia, surplus labour has contributed to the success of labour intensive manufacturing. Agricultural productivity growth in developing countries is primarily found in countries with the highest population densities in Asia (India, China, Indonesia), while agricultural productivity in low density Africa has stagnated.

More generally, the anti-Malthusian argument is that increasing pressure on resources creates incentive for technological change, and makes technological alternatives in production and energy supply more viable (Simon, 1982; Lomborg, 2001).

Scientific and technological advance
Long-run changes in science and technology are among the ultimate sources of increases in productive capacity. The locus of such change is in the most advanced economies of the world (World Bank, 1999). From there technological change spreads and diffuses to those developing countries that have sufficient absorptive capacity to profit from global technological change. But scientific and technological advance itself depends on the institutional and cultural incentives for intellectual and inventive effort and the resources invested in the progress of knowledge. It is thus entangled with other ultimate factors.

The rate of scientific and technological change is accelerating. From the perspective of developing countries this is a double-edged sword. For some countries technological change creates new opportunities for catch-up and even technological leapfrogging. Thus, rapid advances in communication and information technology in the post-war period allow for the emergence of global production chains and the rapid outsourcing of large parts of manufacturing production to developing countries. On balance, this has had tremendous advantages for developing countries. In the service sector, technological change creates unexpected new opportunities for developing countries, such as the outsourcing of call centres, administrative work and software programming which were not available in earlier periods. Rapid advances in biotechnology create opportunities for breakthroughs in agricultural production and health care from which some countries have benefitted.

But the acceleration of technological change creates increasing problems for those countries which are falling behind and do not have the absorptive capacity to tap into global change. Such countries are in danger of becoming even more marginalised and stagnant than they already were. These issues will be taken up again in the final section of this chapter.

Initial conditions: Prior productivity increases in agriculture

Prior productivity increases in agriculture are among the initial conditions facilitating the emergence of industry in a developing country. Productivity increases in agriculture create a surplus available for investment (Johnston, 1970; Timmer, 1988). Productivity increase in agriculture releases resources for industrialisation in the early stages of industrialisation, without endangering domestic food production. Countries illustrating this phenomenon include post-war Korea and Taiwan, Japan in the late nineteenth century, Britain in the eighteenth century, China after 1978. African agriculture is a negative case in point. Low productivity in traditional agriculture provided an inauspicious starting point for the African industrialisation drive in the second half of the twentieth century.

Initial conditions: Initial levels of economic and social inequality

In the post-war period, lower initial levels of economic inequality of income and land ownership created a more favourable setting for growth. Extreme inequality constrains the size of domestic markets, creates perverse economic incentives and sets the stage for political instability (Myrdal, 1968). The Iberian colonial legacy of embedded inequality in Latin America has created institutional barriers to the participation of larger proportions of the population in the growth process. This inequality is the latent source for the periodic emergence of populist movements, which have followed growth-destroying policies. On the other hand, radical land reform in both China and Taiwan created a more equal initial situation in the fifties which was conducive to subsequent growth.

Political stability and the emergence of pacified nation-states

Political pacification and the emergence of stable nation-states is one of the most important ultimate sources of economic growth. As emphasized by Max Weber, without a stable national monopoly of the means of violence, centralisation and standardisation of regulation within the nation-state, the predictability which is required for long-term investment and entrepreneurship is lacking. Political instability, wars and ethnic conflict are amongst the most important sources of economic stagnation, as evidenced by current conflicts in Somalia, Sudan, Pakistan, Iraq and Congo, to name but a few examples.

The present sources of economic stagnation in many African countries are not primarily economic in nature. Rather they refer to the absence of political centralisation, standardisation and the evolution of a stable national monopoly on the means of violence. Both cross-country regression studies and historical studies point to the overwhelming importance of the existence of a stable national political framework for economic activity (Alesina, 1996;

Collier, 2007). In Africa, borders drawn by colonial rulers in the late nineteenth century frequently did not coincide with cultural and ethnic traditions. The legitimacy of the central state institutions in multi-ethnic states is weak. The instability of present-day states in turn is also influenced by pre-colonial history of state formation. Though more and more is being discovered about ancient African empires, we may conclude that the degree of early political centralisation in sub-Saharan African history was far weaker than in the Asia.

The lack of internal stability in sub-Saharan African states has been compounded by external intervention by outside powers each supporting their ethnic clients and exacerbating internal conflict. Thus, in much of the post-war period, Africa was the arena of cold-war conflict by proxy. Since the end of the cold war, African nations themselves have increasingly intervened in other African countries.

The quality of political institutions
Where the legitimacy of state institutions and the nation-state is weak, the stage is set for the emergence of states which rule on behalf of specific ethnic groups or elite interests. In such settings, state economic policy is almost exclusively aimed at maintaining the power of the ruling elites, at the expense of other segments of society. For Africa, the term 'predatory state' has been coined for political systems which are almost exclusively oriented to keep strong men in power, such as Zaire's Mobutu or Zimbabwe's Mugabe. Other observers refer to these phenomena as the 'neo-patrimonial state' (Sandbrook, 1986; Bratton and van de Walle, 1997; Collier, 2007).

The quality of state institutions also depends on bureaucratic capabilities, the degree of insulation of the bureaucracy from pressure groups (e.g. South Korea as a positive example) and the regulative burden claimed for governments. One of the most interesting paradoxes of post-war socio-economic development is the existence of relatively weak states with disproportionately heavy economic tasks and a wide range of discretionary powers. The absence of bureaucratic traditions and experience, low remuneration of civil servants, the use of the state apparatus as an instrument for holding on to power and the discretionary powers all contributed to the institutionalisation of corruption. The present worldwide shift towards a more limited role for the state in economic development should not be interpreted solely in economic terms, but against this wider backdrop of potentially venal state institutions.

Corruption
In cross-country regressions, corruption (and institutional quality) is often identified as a key determinant of economic development (Shleifer and

Vishny, 1993). But differences in the degree of corruption cannot explain why some countries stagnate and others develop. More important is the nature of corruption. In some economies the proceeds of corruption are reinvested productively in the domestic economy. In others they are stashed in Swiss banks, or frittered away on golden shoes or golden palaces. Nigeria has been emasculated by corruption, but corruption under the new order of Suharto in Indonesia was compatible with 30 years of dynamism, between 1966 and 1997. It is a major puzzle why Suharto was able to respond so effectively to the economic crisis of 1984, in spite of widespread corruption, while corruption contributed to an inadequate Indonesian policy response to the Asian crisis of 1997 (Temple, 2003). The Texan robber barons of the nineteenth century were deeply corrupt, but nonetheless very dynamic. China's pervasive corruption does not stand in the way of its impressive economic dynamics.

Institutions

Institutions, institutional quality and good governance are increasingly mentioned as important determinants of development. But it is hard to go beyond description and examples to generalise about how institutions affect growth and development. The most general formulation is still that of North and Thomas (1973), who argue that institutions that align individual interests with social welfare are conducive to economic development. In their analysis, well-defined property rights have been crucial for Western European economic development. The extent to which property rights are protected depends in turn on the balance between state power and the power of entrepreneurial groups. State formation and state power are important in establishing and maintaining property rights, but excessive state power will stifle entrepreneurial freedoms. Other important innovations with regard to property rights focus on the emergence of joint stock companies, which limit individual risk and liabilities.

Well-defined property rights affect both rates of accumulation and rates of innovation (North, 1990). Without well-defined and well-enforced property rights, entrepreneurial individuals have little incentive to take a long view and to invest in future growth. Other studies focus in particular on intellectual property rights. Protection of intellectual property rights allows inventors to enjoy the fruits of their innovative efforts. However, the focus on protection of intellectual property rights has also been criticised. Some types of innovation are based more on collective invention, than individually patented inventions. Thus, there seem to be alternative ways to align individual interests with collective growth and dynamism. Also some types of accumulation can successfully be performed by states rather than by private entrepreneurs. Nevertheless, the focus of North and Thomas on alignment or misalignment of incentives through economic institutions continues to be a very promising line of analysis.

In the context of a discussion on policy reform, Dani Rodrik made an important distinction between initiating growth and maintaining it (Rodrik, 2006; Hausmann et al. 2008). The factors that initiate growth may not be the same as those important for maintaining growth. Pointing to the Chinese and Indian experiences, he argues that large scale institutional reform – for instance of property rights – may not be necessary to kickstart growth. In order to initiate growth, one needs to identify the binding constraints facing a specific country. These will differ from country to country, so that policies which are successful in one setting may completely backfire in another. There are no standard reform recipes for kick-starting growth. This explains why so many of the cross-country regressions with policy or institutional variables give inconclusive results.

Once growth is underway, institutional reform becomes more important to maintain long run growth momentum. Institutional improvements such as better protection of intellectual property rights or more accountable government policies, which may not have been a binding constraint for starting growth, become more important for maintaining them. One might say that growth buys time for deeper institutional reforms. In absence of such reforms, an economy for instance remains vulnerable to external shocks, which may put a country off an accelerating growth path and put it on a stagnating trajectory. For instance, corruption was not a binding constraint in Indonesia from 1966 to 1996. It became a binding constraint to an adequate response to the 1997 financial crisis (Hill, 2000).

External shocks can also have positive economic effects, such as the cataclysmic communist revolution in China or land reform in post-conflict Korea and Taiwan. They can have deep negative effects such as the impact of the debt crisis of 1982 on Latin American development, or of the Asian crisis on Indonesian economic development. Sometimes the same shock has very different effects in different countries. Most Asian economies recovered quickly from the Asian crisis, but Indonesia needed 10 years to regain to its pre-crisis levels of GDP per capita. Shocks interact with the strength and effectiveness of domestic institutional arrangements. Strong shocks combined with weak institutions and policies may have disastrous effects and put an economy on a downward growth trajectory.

Cultural Factors: Work ethic, savings and entrepreneurship
Though monocausal cultural explanations of development which relate economic development to specific religions or cultures have largely been debunked, one can nevertheless identify some common attitudes of successful developers, which are rooted in culture. These elements include a

strong work ethic and social discipline, a high value placed on education and learning, attitudes conducive to high savings rates, low levels of risk aversion and positive attitudes towards entrepreneurship. Both Protestantism and the Confucian ethic value sobriety, hard work and savings.

Thus, attitudes can evolve in very different religious and cultural contexts, such as Puritan Protestantism, modernistic Islam or Confucianism, but they do seem to be important in the context of economic development. Of course, cultural traits are neither exogenous, nor immutable. When incentives change and new opportunities arise, older cultural adaptations to economic stagnation will start to change. But, cultural traits do emerge from very long historical experience and change only slowly.

Cultural factors: Developmental drive
In historical examples of successful catch-up, a common factor is 'developmental drive' (as the Meiji reformers in Japan, the leaders of China's present capitalist drive, Suharto's new order, or a variety of post-war nationalist regimes) and feelings of national pride and resentment at the present position of the nation in the international order.

Cultural Factors: Openness to the outside world
One of the key cultural attitudes favourable to successful development is openness to the outside world. This involves a willingness and eagerness to acquire and assimilate technology and knowledge from leading countries in the world economy, whichever they are. When a society turns inwards and rejects outside influences as either inferior or too threatening, or when a society cultivates too much resentment against these influences, it will tend to stagnate. Such attitudes help explain the loss of momentum of the early European leaders Portugal and Spain from the sixteenth century onwards when religion became dogmatic and anti-scientific, the long centuries of Chinese stagnation after the fourteenth century, China's failure to catch-up in the late nineteenth, early twentieth century, as opposed to Japanese success, and economic stagnation in the post-war Middle Eastern world.[7]

But it is not clear whether the openness to the outside world is a deep-seated cultural trait of a country's whole population. Rather, openness tends to depend on cultural traits of dominant elites. When China turned inward in the fifteenth century, this was primarily the outcome of a power struggle between the court mandarins and the eunuch admirals, which was won by the former.

---

[7] In this sense, the present revival of flat-earth thinking and anti-Darwinian religious fundamentalism in the USA bodes badly for the future of US economic leadership.

Distance from the technological frontier
Distance to the technological frontier is one of the ultimate sources of growth. The greater the technology gap, the greater the potential for rapid catch-up. It defines the initial conditions for growth and stagnation in the post-war period (Gerschenkron, 1962; Abramovitz, 1989). When there is sufficient technological congruence between the technological leaders and followers and social capabilities and absorptive capacities in the follower country are sufficiently developed, it can experience explosive catch-up, due to the rapid absorption of technologies developed elsewhere. The rapidity of catch-up is related to the fact that a technologically backward country can tap into state of the art global technological knowledge without undergoing all the costs and risks of developing it.

Absorptive capacities
While lead countries need to invest in advancing the frontiers of knowledge, follower countries primarily have to invest in improving their absorptive capacities so as to profit from international technology flows. Perhaps the most important ultimate factor distinguishing successful catch-up economies from other developing countries is their capacity to absorb international technology.

9.6   ABSORPTIVE CAPACITIES AND TAPPING INTO GLOBAL TECHNOLOGICAL ADVANCE

The argument with regard to absorptive capacities can be summarised in three propositions:

1) Technological change is generated in the leading economies of the international economic order.
2) Developing countries that are able to absorb internationally generated technology can profit from the advantages of technological backwardness. They can experience accelerated catch-up. Countries that are not able to absorb technology will tend to fall behind.
3) Differences in absorptive capacity account for much of the difference between success and failure in economic development in the post-war period.

In the present international order, there is great inequality in technological efforts. An overwhelming proportion of scientific research and research and development activities takes place in the advanced economies. Technological change emanates from the lead countries in the world economy. An illustration of this is provided in tables 9.3 and 9.4.

As indicated in table 9.3, almost all patent applications in the USA originate in the advanced economies. Excluding South Korea, only 1 per cent of patents granted in the USA (the technological leader) in the post-war period originates in developing countries. Similar patterns hold for scientific publications. Large multinational companies take the lead in innovation. Thus the fifty largest multinationals alone account from 26 per cent of all patents in the United States. According to estimates by the World Health Organisation, 95 per cent of all medical research focuses on health problems of the advanced countries (World Bank, 1999).

Table 9.3   US patent activity, 1990–2006

Year	Patents granted	Share of patents granted (%)		
		Foreign patents	Developing country patents	Developing countries excl. S. Korea
1870	12,157			
1913	33,915			
1950	43,039	40.8	0.6	0.3
1973	74,139	40.8	0.6	0.3
1990	99,220	46.6	1.1	0.3
1995	113,955	43.4	2.8	0.5
2000	176,083	44.9	4.8	0.7
2004	181,322	48.1	7.0	1.0
2006	196,436	47.9	8.8	1.3

Source: United States Patent and Trademark Office, TAF Special Report, All Patents, All Types, January 1977–December 2006. Pre 1988 percentages: postwar averages.

Table 9.4   R & D Efforts, 1990–2005[a]

	R&D as % of GDP			R&D per capita PPP dollars		Researchers in R&D per 1,000,000	
	1990	1997	2005	1997	2005	1996	2005
Bangladesh	0.7	0.3	0.6			51	30
China	0.8	0.7	1.5	11.8	54.2	447	852
India	0.2	0.8	0.7	8.7	13.0	153	111
Indonesia		0.1	0.05	0.4	0.2	182	199
Malaysia		0.2	0.7		1.5	90	503
Pakistan		0.2	0.5	2.3	9.0	74	80
Philippines	0.2		0.1		3.5	157	
South Korea	2.0	2.8	3.3	366.8	643.7	2,190	3756
Sri Lanka		0.2	0.2	4.6	6.0	189	141
Taiwan	1.7	1.9	2.5	298.6	481.1	3,337	6185
Thailand	0.2	0.1	0.3	5.0	16.2	104	292
Turkey	0.2	0.4	0.7	29.6	64.9	283	536
Argentina		0.4	0.5	37.9	49.9	650	822
Brazil		0.6	1.0	42.9	67.2	168	461
Chile	0.7	0.5	0.7	42.3	76.1	390	833
Colombia		0.3	0.2	15.8	8.6	84	127
Mexico	0.2	0.4	0.5	26.6	56.2	213	464
Peru		0.1	0.2	3.9	8.7	229	
Venezuela	0.5	0.5	0.2	37.8	22.6	116	86
Congo, Dem. Rep.					1.3		
Côte d'Ivoire							68
Egypt	0.8	0.2	0.2		6.1	6.8	
Morocco			0.7		7.2	20.9	
South Africa	0.8	0.7	1.0	36.3	76.0	337	361

Table 9.4 (Continued)

	R&D as % of GDP			R&D per capita PPP dollar		Researchers in R&D per 1,000,000	
	1990	1997	2005	1997	2005	1996	2005
Zambia		0.01	0.03	0.1	0.3	47	
Average Asian countries, excl. S. Korea and Taiwan		0.3	0.5	6.3	16.8	173	144
Average Latin American countries		0.4	0.5	29.6	41.3	264	466
Average African countries							
Average developing countries, excl. S. Korea and Taiwan	0.5	0.4	0.5	16.8	26.8	413	351
Average 16 advanced economies [b]	2.1	2.3	2.5	430.5	653.0	2912	4083

Notes: a) If no data for specified year, latest year in preceding five years for which data are available; b) The definition of R&D in UNESCO statistics on developing countries is more inclusive than the statistics for OECD countries from the *Science Technology and Industry Outlook*, 1998, which conform to Frascati manual definitions.

Sources: R&D expenditures from UNESCO,home page statistics on research and development, downloaded 08–2009; UNESCO, *Statistical Yearbooks*, 1993–1999. PPP converters and GDP at basic current prices, local currency units from WDI, online, downloaded 08–2009. Population from World Population Projections, 2008 revision, downloaded 08–2009. R&D as % of GDP in advanced economies, 1990 from: OECD, *Science and Technology Outlook*, 1998; Researchers in R&D from: WDI online, downloaded august 2008, supplemented by data from UNDP, *Human Development Report*, Issues, 2001, 2005 and 2007/8. Taiwan, Taiwan, National Statistics of Taiwan, the Republic of China (http://www.stat.gov.tw/main.htm) and Republic of China (Taiwan), Statistical Yearbook, 2002, 2008. India 2001–4 from Department of Science and Technology, R&D Statistics, New Delhi, Department of Science and Technology, Government of India, 2006.

Table 9.4 provides information about R&D efforts of developing countries in 1990–2005. Developing countries invest a much lower proportion of GDP in research and development (around 0.6 per cent) than the advanced economies (around 2.3 per cent). The technological gaps in terms of R&D per head of population are even greater.

Given that technological advance is primarily generated by lead countries, technological advance in a developing country is achieved by tapping into internationally available technological knowledge. Otherwise as once argued by Veblen (1915), such absorption of technology is far from easy. It is more than simple imitation. It involves effort, creativity, organisational innovation and technological adaptation (Fagerberg and Godinho, 2006). Absorbing international knowledge and technology requires a highly developed absorptive capacity, which does not come free of charge.

One of the reasons why absorption of technology is more than simple transfer of technology is that successful technology transfer almost always involves adaptation to local circumstances, institutions and conditions. Both the mastery and the adaptation of technology require considerable effort and skill. And as economic development progresses, adaptation is replaced by upgrading and investment in technological advance, which requires even more skills.

The difficulty of absorbing technology explains why some countries are able to profit from international technological advances, while others cannot and become mired in stagnation. As a wide range of authors have emphasized, catch-up requires highly developed absorptive capabilities. These capabilities in turn depend on the size of the technology and productivity gaps. Verspagen (1991) has argued that technological potential is not simply a linear function of the size of the technology gap. If the technology gap becomes too large, technological congruence will decline almost per definition. Given a certain level of social capabilities (learning capabilities, absorptive capacity), it becomes more difficult for countries to catch-up. If the capabilities are weakly developed, it becomes even harder. Thus, a traditional agricultural economy such as Burkina Faso will find it almost impossible to absorb advanced technology from the USA, Japan or Europe because the technological distance is simply too large.

Absorptive capabilities are discussed in at least three strands of literature, each of which uses slightly different terminologies. Abramovitz (1989) has argued that successful catch-up involves the prior investment in technological and social capabilities which allow countries to acquire and master international technologies. Social and technological capabilities include national educational levels, the orientation of education, technical and financial skills, a disciplined workforce, institutions which stimulate entrepreneurship, and sufficient political and economic stability to make risk-taking worthwhile. Thus we see that many of the ultimate factors discussed in section 9.5.3 are subsumed under the concept of absorptive capacities.

There is also a more micro-oriented literature deriving from authors such as Sanjaya Lall focusing on firm level capabilities and efforts (Bell et al., 1982; Lall, 1992, 1996; Romijn, 1999; Cohen and Levinthal, 1990; Szirmai et al., 2011). Lall distinguishes: production capabilities, investment capabilities and innovation capabilities which allow firms to adapt and further develop technologies.

A third rapidly growing body of literature, which is relevant for absorptive capacity, is the literature on systems of innovation (Lundvall 1992; Nelson, 1993; Edquist, 2005). Absorptive capacity is not determined only by the sum-total of the capabilities of the micro agents. It is also determined by the nature of the interactions between actors (firms, research institutions and government agencies) and the institutions influencing these interactions. The more effective a system of innovation, the more rapidly knowledge will spread within a country and the more effectively will a country be able to absorb technology from abroad.

Given the location of technological advance, catch-up in the post–1950 globalised economy was only possible if developing countries develop the capabilities to acquire, master and adapt international technology. There is not a single example of successful catch-up since the late nineteenth century which did not involve tapping into international technology – e.g. Germany, Russia, Japan, Korea, Singapore, Taiwan, Hong Kong, China, India and Vietnam. The countries that, for some reason or other, are not able or not willing to tap into global technology flows, are those that are falling behind in the world economy.

For this reason, the romantic mythology of indigenous or traditional technology, often found amongst development practitioners and developing country ideologists, is potentially dangerous for development. The myth of indigenous technology suggests that there exists something like an appropriate, indigenous technology which is more adapted to the needs and traditions of the developing countries. Such technologies are usually small scale, environmentally friendly, integrated into traditional culture and so forth.

In the light of the forgoing analysis, this is a recipe for economic stagnation. One can think of Mahatma Ghandi's preoccupation with small-scale spinning, Mao Zedong's campaign for backyard steel ovens or the Chinese ambivalence towards Western technology around 1900. But one can also think of present day aid workers' love of small water pumps, decentralised solar panels, micro-credit and other 'appropriate' technological solutions. The myth disregards the fact that economic catch-up is a vast and

262 World Economic Performance

cataclysmic process involving rapid and disruptive economic and technological change.

9.7   CONCLUDING REMARKS

In the light of the criticism of mono-causal explanations of success and failure, it would be inconsistent to summarise this overview of a large literature in a few final sentences. I have analysed a variety of important sources of growth and have attempted to assess their importance. In the previous paragraph, I have singled out one of these sources, the concept of absorptive capabilties, for special attention. It is itself the result of a great variety of factors and but it does contribute to our better understanding of the differences between more and less successful development experiences.

In developing countries with sufficiently developed social and technological capabilities there are ample opportunities for rapid catch-up. If such capabilities are weak or absent, then countries will become increasingly marginalised and exploited. Thus one can see the technology and productivity race as the outcome of two contradictory tendencies. Innovation in the lead countries leads to increased global inequality and falling behind of developing countries. Diffusion and transfer of technology allows for explosive growth and catch-up in some of the developing countries, with sufficient absorptive capacities.

The key sources of catch-up in developing countries are absorptive capacity and ability and willingness to tap into global technology. When a country has developed the capacity to absorb and adapt technology and has the eagerness and drive to do so, it can grow at an astounding rate as evidenced by several Asian countries in the post-war period. The Gerschenkronian advantages of backwardness allow a country to profit from technological advance, without bearing many of the costs and risks.

Countries that are hesitant to open themselves to global technological change and associated outside influences, for political, cultural or religious reasons, do this at their peril, as evidenced by the divergent patterns of development of Japan and China from the late nineteenth century till 1950. Either a country goes all out in its attempts to acquire and assimilate international technology or it will stagnate.

REFERENCES

Abramovitz, M. (1989), 'Thinking about Growth', in: M. Abramovitz, *Thinking about Growth and other Essays on Economic Growth and Welfare*, Cambridge:

Cambridge University Press, 3–79.

Acemoglu, D.S. Johnson and J.A. Robinson (2001), 'The Colonial Origins of Comparative Development: An Empirical Investigation', *American Economic Review*, **91** (5), 1369–1401.

Acemoglu, D. and J.A. Robinson (2006), *Economic Origins of Dictatorship and Democracy*, Cambridge MA: MIT press.

Alesina, A. (1996), 'Political Instability and Growth', *Journal of Economic Growth*, **1** (2) 189–211.

Amsden, A. (1989), *Asia's Next Giant: South Korea and Late Industrialization*, New York and Oxford: Oxford University Press.

Baldwin, R.E. (2003), *Openness and Growth: What's the Empirical Relationship*, NBER Working Paper, No. 9578.

Barro, R. (1996), *Getting It Right: Markets and Choices in a Free Society*, Cambridge MA: MIT Press.

Bell, M., Scott-Kemmis, D. Satyarakwit, W. (1982), 'Limited learning in infant industry. A case study', in: F. Stewart, and J. James (Eds.), *The Economics of New Technology in Developing Countries*, London: Pinter, 138–156.

Boserup, E (1965), *The Conditions of Agricultural Growth*, London: Allen and Unwin.

Boserup, E. (1981), *Population and Technology*, Oxford: Basil Blackwell.

Bratton, M. and N. van de Walle (1997), *Democratic Experiments in Africa. Regime Transitions in Comparative Perspective*, Cambridge: Cambridge University Press.

Chakravarty, S. and A. Mitra (2009), 'Is Industry Still the Engine of Growth? An Econometric Study of the Organized Sector Employment in India', *Journal of Policy Modeling*, **31**, 22–35.

Chang, H-J. (2002), *Kicking away the Ladder: Development Strategy in Historical Perspective*, London: Anthem Press.

Chenery, H., S. Robinson and M. Syrquin (1986), *Industrialisation and Growth. A Comparative Study, World Bank*, Oxford University Press.

Cohen, W. and D. Levinthal (1990), 'Absorptive Capacity: A New Perspective on Learning and Innovation', *Administrative Science Quarterly*, **35** (1), 128–152.

Collier, P. (2007), *The Bottom Billion*, Oxford: Oxford University Press.

Conference Board and Groningen Growth and Development Centre, *Total Economy Database* (2007), http://www.conference–board.org/economics"

Diamond, J. (1998), *Guns. Germs and Steel. A Short History of Everybody for the Last 13,000 Years*, London: Vintage Press.

Easterly, W. (2001), *The Elusive Quest for Growth: Economists Adventures and Misadventures in the Tropics*, Cambridge: The MIT Press.

Edquist, Ch. (2005), 'Systems of Innovation: Perspective and Challenges', in: J. Fagerberg, D.C. Mowery and R.R. Nelson (eds), *The Oxford Handbook of Innovation*, Oxford University Press.

Eichengreen, B. (2000), 'Taming Capital Flows', *World Development*, **28** (6), 1105–1116.

Fagerberg, J. and M. Godinho (2006), 'Innovation and Catching Up', Chapter 19, in J. Fagerberg, D. Movery and R. Nelson (eds), *The Oxford Handbook of Innovation*, Oxford:Oxford University Press.

Fagerberg, J. and M. Srholec (2006), 'The Role of "Capabilities" in Development: How Some Countries Manage to Catch-up, Paper Globelics Conference, Trivandrum, October 4–7.

Gerschenkron, A. (1962), *Economic Backwardness in Historical Perspective*, Cambridge: Harvard University Press.

Godo, Y. and Y. Hayami (2002), 'Catching Up in Education in the Economic Catch-Up of Japan with the United States, 1890–1990', *Economic Development and Cultural Change*, **50** (4), pp. 961–978.

Harrison, L.E. (1985), *Underdevelopment Is a State of Mind, The Latin American Case*, Boston: Madison Books.

Harrison, L.E. and S.P. Huntington (eds) (2000), *Culture Matters. How Values Shape Human Progress*, New York: Basic Books.

Hausmann, R. and D. Rodrik (2005), 'Self–Discovery in a Development Strategy for El Salvador', *Economia*, **6** (1), pp. 43–101.

Hausmann, R., D. Rodrik and A. Velasco (2008), 'Growth Diagnostics', in Serra, N. and J.E. Stiglitz (eds), *The Washington Consensus Reconsidered. Towards a New Global Governance*, Oxford University Press, pp. 324–355.

Helpman, E. (2004), *The Mystery of Economic Growth*, Cambridge, MA: Belknap Press of Harvard University Press.

Hill, H. (2000). 'Indonesia: The Strange and Sudden Death of a Tiger Economy, *Oxford Development Studies*, **28** (2), 117–139.

Hirschman, A.O. (1958), *The Strategy of Economic Development*, New Haven, Yale University Press, 1988 (first published 1958).

Hobday, M. (2000), 'East versus Southeast Asian Innovation Systems: Comparing OEM- and TNC-led Growth in Electronics', in L. Kim and Richard Nelson (eds), *Technology, Learning and Innovation: Experiences of Newly Industrializing Economies*, Cambridge University Press, 129–169.

Hobday, M. (2009), Learning from Asia's Success: Beyond Simplistic 'Lesson Making', Paper presented at the international workshop: Pathways to Industrialization in the 21st Century, UNU-WIDER, UNU-MERIT and UNIDO Workshop, Maastricht 22–23 October 2009.

Hoffman, A. (1998), 'Latin American Development, A Causal Analysis in Historical Perspective', PhD thesis, Groningen.

Jalilian H., M. Tribe and J. Weiss (eds) (2000), *Industrial Development and Policy in Africa: Issues of De-industrialisation and Development Strategy*. Cheltenham, UK and Northampton, MA, USA: Elgar.

Johnston, B.F. (1970), 'Agriculture and Structural Transformation in Developing Countries: A Survey of Research', *Journal of Economic Literature*, **8** (2), 369–404.

Katz, J. (2000), Structural Change and Labour Productivity Growth in Latin American Manufacturing Industries 1970–96, *World Development* **28** (9), 1583–1596.

Krueger, A. (1998), 'Why Trade Liberalisation is Good for Growth', *The Economic Journal*, 108, September, 1513–1522.

Lal, D. and H. Myint (1996), *The Political Economy of Poverty, Equity and Growth. A Comparative Study*, Oxford: Oxford University Press.

Lall, S. (1992), 'Technological Capabilities and Industrialisation', *World Development,* **20** (2), 165–186.

Lall, S. (1996), *Learning from the Asian Tigers*, London: Macmillan Press.

Lall, S. and Narula, R. (2006), 'Foreign Direct Investment and its Role in Economic Development: Do we Need a New Agenda?', in: R. Narula, R. and S. Lall (eds.). *Understanding FDI-assisted Economic Development*, Oxford: Routledge, 1–18.

Landes, D.S. (1998), *The Wealth and Poverty of Nations. Why Some Are so Rich and Some so Poor*, New York and London: Norton and Co.

Lewis, W.A. (1978), *The Evolution of the International Economic Order*, Princeton: Princeton University Press.

Lin, J.Y., F. Cai and Z. Li (2000), 'The Lessons of China's Transition to a Market Economy', Paper for APSEM/ANU/World Bank conference, Achieving High Growth, Experience of Transitional Economies in East Asia, Canberra, 6/7 September.

Lomborg, B. (2001), *The Sceptical Environmentalist. Measuring the Real State of the World*, Cambridge University Press.

Lundvall, B.A. (1992), *National Systems of Innovation. Towards a Theory of Innovation and Interactive Learning*, London: Pinter.

Maddison, A. (1970), *Economic Progress and Policy*, New York, Norton.

Maddison, A. (1986), *Notes on Developing Country Performance*, Mimeographed, Groningen.

Maddison, A. (1988), 'Ultimate and Proximate Growth Causality: A Critique of Mancur Olson on the Rise and Decline of Nations', *Scandinavian History Review*, **2**, 25–29.

Maddison, A. (2001), *The World Economy. A Millenial Perspective*, OECD.

Maddison, A. (2007), *Contours of the World Economy, 1–2030 AD. Essays in Macro–Economic History*, Oxford: Oxford University Press.

Maddison, A. 'Historical Statistics, World Population, GDP and Per Capita GDP, 1–2006 AD' (www.ggdc.net/Maddison; Last update: March 2009).

Mani, S. (forthcoming), 'The Growth of Knowledge-Intensive Entrepreneurship in India, 1991–2007. Analysis of its Evidence and the Facilitating Factors, in: A. Szirmai, W. Naudé and M. Goedhuys (eds), *Entrepreneurship, Innovation and Development*, forthcoming 2010.

Mellor, J.W. (1976), *The New Economics of Growth*, Ithaca, Cornell University Press.

Myrdal, G. (1968), *Asian Drama. An Inquiry into the Poverty of Nations*, Harmondsworth: Penguin.

Narula, R. and S. Lall (eds) (2006), *Understanding FDI-assisted economic development*. Oxford, U.K. : Routledge.

Nelson, R. (ed.), (1993), *National Innovation Systems. A Comparative Analysis*, Oxford: Oxford University Press.

Nelson, R.R. (1996), 'Research on Productivity Growth and Productivity Differences: Dead Ends and New Departures', in R.R. Nelson, *The Sources of Economic Growth*, Cambridge, Mass.: Harvard University Press (originally published in *JEL*, September, 1981, 1029–1064).

North, D.C. (1990), *Institutions, Institutional Change and Economic Performance*, Cambridge, Cambridge University Press.

North, D.C. and R.P. Thomas (1973), *The Rise of the Western World*, Cambridge: Cambridge University Press.

Nuñez, C. (1990), 'Literacy and Economic Growth in Spain, 1860–1977', in: Tortella, G. (ed.), *Education and Economic Development Since the Industrial Revolution*, València, Generalitat Valenciana.

Pack, H. and Ch. Paxson (2001), 'Is African Manufacturing Skill Constrained?', in: A. Szirmai and P. Lapperre (eds), *The Industrial Experience of Tanzania*, Houndmills/Basingstoke, Palgrave, 50–72.

Portelli, B. (2006), *Foreign Direct Investment, Multinational Enterprises and Industrial Development. Backward Linkages and Knowledge Transfer in Tanzania*, TIK, Oslo, PhD thesis.

Qian, Y. (2003), 'How Reform Worked in China', in Rodrik (ed.), *op. cit.*

Rodriguez, F. and D. Rodrik (2001), 'Trade Policy and Economic Growth: A Skeptic's Guide to the Cross-National Evidence', in: B. Bernanke and K.S. Rogoff (eds), *NBER Macroeconomics Annual 2000*, Cambridge, MA: MIT Press for NBER, 261–338.

Rodrik, D. (ed.), (2003), *In Search of Prosperity. Analytic Narratives on Economic Growth*, Princeton and Oxford: Princeton University Press.

Rodrik, D. (2006), 'Good Bye Washington Consensus, Hello Washington Confusion? A Review of the World Bank's Economic Growth in the 1990s: Learning from a Decade of Reform', *Journal of Economic Literature*, **XLIV**, 973–987.

Rodrik, D. (2007), *One Economics, Many Recipes. Globalization, Institutions and Economic Growth*, Princeton and Oxford: Princeton University Press.

Romijn, H.A. (1999), *Acquisition of Technological Capabilities in Small Firms in Developing Countries*. London: MacMillan.

Sachs, J.D. (2005), *The End of Poverty. Economic Possibilities for Our Time*, New York: Penguin.

Sachs, J. M.L. Faye, J.W. McArthur and Th. Snow (2004), 'The Challenges Facing Landlocked Developing Countries', *Journal of Human Development*, **5** (1), 31–68.

Sachs, J. and A. Warner (1995), *Economic Reform and the Process of Global Integration*, Brookings Papers on Economic Activity, **1**, 1–118.

Sandbrook, R. (1986), 'The State as an Obstacle to Development', *World Development*, **14** (3), 309–322.

Sandberg, L.G. (1982), 'Ignorance, Poverty and Economic Backwardness in the Early Stages of European Industrialization. Variations on Alexander Gerschenkron's Grand Theme', *Journal of European Economic History*, **11**, 675–98.

Shleifer, A. and R.W. Vishny (1993), 'Corruption', *Quarterly Journal of Economics*, **108** (3), 599–618.

Shleifer, A. E. Glaeser, R. la Porta and F. Lopez-de Silanes (2004), 'Do Institutions Cause Growth?', *Journal of Economic Growth*, **9** (3), 271–303.

Simon, J. (1982), *The Ultimate Resource*, Princeton, Princeton University Press.

Stiglitz, J. (2000), 'Capital Market Liberalization, Economic Growth, and Instability', *World Development*, **28** (6), 1075–86.

Stiglitz, J. (2002), *Globalization and Its Discontents*, New York and London: Norton.

Szirmai, A. (2005), *The Dynamics of Socio-Economic Development*, Cambridge: Cambridge University Press.

Szirmai, A. (2008), *Explaining Succes and Failure in Development*, UNU–MERIT Working Paper, 2008–013, Maastricht.

Szirmai, A. (2009), *Is Manufacturing Still the Main Engine of Growth in Developing Countries?*, UNU–MERIT, Working Paper, 2009–10, Maastricht.

Szirmai, A. (2009), Website Dynamics of Socio–Economic Development, http://www.dynamicsofdevelopment.com

Szirmai, A., W. Naudé and M. Goedhuys (2011), 'Entrepreneurship, Innovation and Development. An Overview', in A. Szirmai, W. Naudé and M. Goedhuys (eds), *Entrepreneurship, Innovation and Development*, 3–32.

Temple, J. (2003), 'Growing into Trouble. Indonesia after 1966', in D. Rodrik (ed.), *op. cit.*

Timmer, C.P. (1988), 'The Agricultural Transformation', in: H.B. Chenery and T.N. Srinivasan (eds), *Handbook of Development Economics*, Vol. I, Amsterdam, North Holland, Chapter 8, 276–331.

Timmer, C.P. (2005), 'Food Security and Economic Growth: an Asian Perspective', *Asian-Pacific Economic Literature*, **19** (1), May, 1–17.

Timmer, M.P. (2000), *The Dynamics of Asian Manufacturing. A Comparative Perspective, 1963–1993*, Cheltenham: Edward Elgar.

Timmer, M.P. and G.J. de Vries (2009), 'Structural Change and Growth Accelerations in Asia and Latin America: A New Sectoral Dataset', *Cliometrica*, **3** (2), 165–190.

Tobin, J. (2000), 'Financial Globalization', *World Development*, **28** (6), 1101–1104. http://www.un.org./esa/population/publications/longrange/longrange.htm

United States Patent and Trademark Office, *TAF Special Report, All Patents, All Types*, January 1977–December 2004.

Van Engelen, D., A. Szirmai, P. Lapperre (2001), 'Public Policy and the Industrial Development of Tanzania, 1961–1995', in: A. Szirmai and P. Lapperre (eds), *The Industrial Experience of Tanzania,* Houndmills, Basingstoke: Palgrave, 11–49.

Veblen, Th. (1915), *Imperial Germany and the Industrial Revolution*, New York: MacMillan.

Verspagen, B. (1991), 'A New Empirical Approach to Catching-up or Falling Behind', *Structural Change and Economic Dynamics*, **2**, 359–380.

Wade, R. (1990), *Governing the Market: Economic Theory and the Role of Government in East Asian Industrialization*, Princeton: Princeton University Press.

Westphal, L.E. (2002), 'Technology Strategies for Economic Development in a Fast Changing Global Economy', *Economics of Innovation and New Technology*, **11** (4/5), 275–320.

Williamson, J. (1990), 'What Washington Means by Policy Reform', in J. Williamson, (ed), *Latin American Adjustment: How much has Happened?*, Washington, D.C.: Institute for International Economics.

World Bank (1993), *The East Asian Miracle. Economic Growth and Public Policy*, New York: Oxford University Press.

World Bank (1999), *World Development Report 1989/99. Knowledge for Development,* World Bank/Oxford University Press.

World Bank, World Development Indicators Online, http://web.worldbank.org/WBSITE/EXTERNAL/DATASTATISTICS/0,,contentMDK:20420458~menuPK:64133156~pagePK:64133150~piPK:64133175~theSitePK:239419,00.html

10. Past, Present and Future Economic Growth in Latin America*

André A. Hofman[1] and Francisco Villarreal[2]

10.1   INTRODUCTION

The objective of this chapter is to explore the medium-term growth prospects for Latin America. The starting point for this endeavour is the analysis of historical performance of the countries in the region. This allows us to identify some of the facts that have characterised growth in the region.

In order to evaluate future growth prospects of the region we focus our analysis on the evolution of potential output. For the purpose of this chapter potential output is defined as the level of output that would be attained in the long-run under full utilisation of installed capacity. There are many techniques for the estimation of potential output. In this chapter we use the production function approach; this provides a convenient way of investigating the sources of potential output fluctuations, and allows us to link the results obtained to those obtained in the growth accounting literature.

The strategy followed is to estimate the coefficients of each country's aggregate production function using a dynamic framework. These coefficients are used to estimate potential output for the period 1950–2005. The results are compared to those of a standard growth accounting exercise using the same data set. Although in general the productivity estimates of both approaches are qualitatively similar, the estimates of the dynamic setting are smoother and explain a smaller proportion of output fluctuations.

Using the coefficients estimated for the dynamic production function, growth prospects for the period 2005–2030 are explored under alternative

---

* The views expressed in this chapter are those of the authors and do not necessarily reflect the views of the United Nations.

[1] Director, ECLAC Review, UN Economic Commission for Latin America and the Caribbean: andre.hofman@cepal.org

[2] Economic Affairs Officer, Subregional Headquarters in Mexico, UN Economic Commission for Latin America and the Caribbean: francisco.villarreal@cepal.org

scenarios. The base scenario uses the United Nations Economic Commission for Latin America and the Caribbean (ECLAC)' s demographic projections (CELADE 1999, 2004), and assumes that capital accumulation and productivity will continue to grow at their current trends. Population growth is projected to decline over the medium-term.

However, it seems unlikely that capital accumulation and productivity will continue to grow at their current pace over the course of the next 25 years. Thus, the alternative scenarios explore the rate at which capital accumulation and productivity would have to grow, in order to yield an average per capita growth rate of 4 per cent. This rate is close to the average yearly growth rate for the selected group of countries for the period 1950–2005. Results indicate that on average, either capital accumulation would have to increase 25 per cent from its current trend; or productivity growth would have to increase by a factor of 2.5 from its current trend.

10.2 HISTORIC ECONOMIC PERFORMANCE OF LATIN AMERICA

This section provides a quantitative assessment of Latin American economic growth performance since 1950. Growth performance throughout this period is treated from a comparative perspective using growth rates of GDP, and GDP per capita. Our sample covers seven countries: Argentina, Brazil, Chile, Colombia, Mexico, Peru and Venezuela. They had in 2000, a combined population of 418 million, equivalent to 80 per cent of the region's total; and a combined output of 1,800 US trillion, equivalent to 90 per cent of the region's GDP.

First, in order to contextualise, we discuss the performance of Latin America with respect to the performance of the rest of the world in the period 1950–2001. Then, we discuss the economic performance of the seven selected countries in the period 1950–2005.

This periodisation is fundamental for correctly appraising growth performance in the last decades, and especially after the crisis of the 1980s. The variable used in this chapter to define the periods is total GDP growth. The periods are selected on the basis of fundamental turning points in growth momentum. For the global economy this corresponds to 1973, which is the date of the first oil shock. For Latin America, the dates used correspond to the base period (1950–1980), the crisis period (1980–1990) and the recovery period (1980–2005) as discussed by Hofman (2000b). Additionally we consider 1998, which for some countries in the sample marked another milestone in long-term growth, due mostly to the effects of the Asian crisis on the dynamics of growth.

Tables 10.1 and 10.2 summarise the world economic performance in the period 1950–2001. Although GDP in Latin America has grown in line with world growth over the period; in per capita terms, with the exception of 1973–1980, its performance has been systematically lower than that of the world.

Table 10.1   World: GDP 1950–2005 (average annual growth rates)

	1950–1973	1973–1980	1980–1990	1990–2001	1950–2001
West Europe	4.8	2.5	2.2	2.1	3.4
USA	3.9	2.6	3.2	3.1	3.4
Asia	6.1	4.5	5.1	4.6	5.4
Africa	4.4	4.0	2.2	2.8	3.6
Lat. America	5.4	5.0	1.3	3.0	4.0
World	4.9	3.2	3.1	2.9	3.9

Source: Authors' calculation based on Maddison (2003).

Table 10.2   World: GDP per capita 1950–2005 (average annual growth rates)

	1950–1973	1973–1980	1980–1990	1990–2001	1950–2001
West Europe	4.1	2.1	1.9	1.7	2.9
USA	2.5	1.5	2.2	1.8	2.2
Asia	3.9	2.4	3.2	3.0	3.4
Africa	2.0	1.2	-0.6	0.3	1.0
Lat America	2.6	2.7	-0.7	1.3	1.7
World	2.9	1.4	1.3	1.4	2.1

Source: Authors' calculation based on Maddison (2003).

The period 1950–1973 witnessed a great expansion in Latin America, with GDP growth averaging 5.4 per cent and growth per capita averaging 2.6 per cent a year. However, most other areas had a 'golden age' with a much greater acceleration of growth. Asian growth averaged 6.1 per cent (3.9 per cent in per capita terms), Western Europe grew at a rate of 4.8 per cent (4.1 per cent in per capita terms); and the US grew at a relatively modest rate of 3.9 per cent (2.5 per cent in per capita terms).

In the wake of the first oil-shock, the period of post-war expansion abruptly came to an end in 1973. Industrialised countries settled into a much lower pace of growth. Over this period, industrialised countries' GDP grew at an annual rate of approximately 2.1 per cent, with GDP per capita growing at 2.1 per cent in Western Europe and at 1.5 per cent in the US. In the developing world, only a mild reduction was experienced in GDP terms, in Africa and Latin America the reduction was less than half a percentage point.

In per capita terms the only region that did not experience a reduction in growth rates was Latin America. Moreover, at 2.7 per cent Latin America led per capita growth for a decade. Nonetheless, during the 1980s when the United States and Asia started accelerating, both Latin America and Africa experienced a severe growth reduction, with Latin American per capita GDP contracting 0.7 per cent annually over 10 years, truly a lost decade.

The crisis of the 1980s was triggered by the rapid increase of interest rates in the international market. This affected Latin America profoundly as many of its countries had rapidly increased their foreign debt in the 1970s when international liquidity was very high. The debt crisis forced them to rethink their development strategy and in many cases a more outward looking, private sector oriented strategy was adopted.

As a result, the 1990s were in general a period of recovery for Latin American countries, with GDP growing at a rate of 3 per cent. However, per capita GDP growth of 1 3 per cent lagged all regions in the world with the exception of Africa. Moreover, the growth experience for individual countries differed greatly. Tables 9.3 and 9.4 summarise, respectively, the evolution of GDP and GDP per capita for the seven countries for the period 1950–2005.[3]

During these 55 years, combined GDP growth averaged 4.1 per cent, while GDP per capita grew at an average annual rate of 1.8 per cent. Over the period 1959–1980, Brazil and Mexico led regional growth in terms of both GDP and GDP per capita. Over the same period, Chile lagged in terms of GDP per capita; while Peru and Venezuela experienced a sharp slowdown in their per capita growth rates after 1973.

During the 1980s, all countries except Chile and Colombia suffered a contraction in per capita GDP, ranging from contraction of 0.3 per cent in Mexico to 3.4 per cent in Peru. As mentioned above, as a result of the dismal performance during the decade, all countries implemented a number of structural reforms.

Consequently, during the period 1990–1998 growth picked up again, albeit at a slower pace than in the pre-crisis period. During this period per capita growth was led by Argentina and Chile, with Brazil and Venezuela lagging

---

[3] Differences in the data in Tables 10.1 and 10.2 with respect to the data on Tables 10.3 and 10.4 are due to discrepancies in coverage in terms of countries and years. Moreover the data sources are different.

behind. The period 1998–2005 was marked by deep crises in Argentina and Venezuela.

Table 10.3   Latin America: GDP 1950–2005 (average annual growth rates)

	1950–1973	1973–1980	1980–1990	1990–1998	1998–2005	1950–2005
Argentina	4.0	3.0	-1.1	5.7	0.8	2.8
Brazil	6.9	7.2	1.6	1.8	2.3	4.6
Chile	3.6	2.8	3.1	7.6	3.6	4.0
Colombia	5.1	5.0	3.4	3.5	2.3	4.2
Mexico	6.5	6.4	1.8	3.1	2.8	4.7
Peru	5.3	3.6	-1.2	4.6	3.5	3.6
Venezuela	6.4	4.1	0.6	2.9	1.3	3.9
Average	5.8	5.7	1.3	3.2	2.3	4.1

Source: Authors' calculation based on updated data from Hofman (2000a).

Table 10.4   Latin America: GDP per capita 1950–2005 (average annual growth rates)

	1950–1973	1973–1980	1980–1990	1990–1998	1998–2005	1950–2005
Argentina	2.3	1.5	-2.6	4.4	-0.2	1.3
Brazil	3.9	4.7	-0.5	0.2	0.8	2.3
Chile	1.3	1.3	1.4	5.8	2.5	2.1
Colombia	2.2	2.6	1.3	1.6	0.5	1.8
Mexico	3.3	3.5	-0.3	1.3	1.3	2.1
Peru	2.4	0.9	-3.4	2.7	1.9	1.1
Venezuela	2.6	0.7	-2.0	0.8	-0.5	0.8
Average	3.0	3.2	-0.7	1.5	0.9	1.8

Source: Authors' calculation based on updated data from Hofman (2000a).

As Solimano and Soto (2006) point out there are three aspects of the growth process which are worth mentioning:

- growth in Latin America has been very uneven and volatile;
- the region experienced a significant slowdown during the 1980s; and
- the relative performance of countries has changed with the larger countries (Argentina, Brazil and Mexico) leading growth before the 1980s; and smaller countries, particularly Chile and more recently Peru, leading growth after.

10.3   EVOLUTION OF POTENTIAL OUTPUT

In order to estimate potential output we utilise the production function approach. The aggregate production function provides the best composite indicator of the supply side of the economy, and is the method preferred by the majority of international organisations.[4]

The general setup for the estimation of potential output using the production function approach is provided by the seminal work of Solow (1957). This also provides the framework for growth accounting, whose objective is to decompose the growth rate of aggregate output into the contributions of growth in the productive factors (labour and capital) and changes in the available technology.

Under this setup output can be expressed as:

$$Y_t = A_t N_t^{\alpha} K_t^{(1-\alpha)} \tag{10.1}$$

where Y_t is total output, A_t is *multifactor productivity*, N_t and K_t are the labour and capital inputs, and α is the elasticity of output with respect to labour.

As is described in the appendix, from equation (10.1) the growth of multifactor productivity can be expressed as:

$$\Delta a_t = \Delta y_t - \alpha \Delta n_t - (1-\alpha)\Delta k_t \tag{10.2}$$

which constitutes the key equation in growth accounting.

Growth accounting provides a useful tool for understanding the contributions of productivity and the inputs to aggregate output. Empirical studies indicate that a large portion of differences in output per capita across countries and across time are explained by variations in multifactor productivity (see Klenow and Rodriguez-Clare, 1997; Easterly and Levine, 2001 and Loayza, et al., 2005).

However, as Jorgenson and Griliches (1967) point out, estimating multifactor productivity as a residual poses several problems. Notably, if changes in the quality of inputs or their rates of utilisation are not properly accounted for the estimates of productivity will be biased.

Thus, while the production function assumes a stable relationship, errors in the measurement of the variables in equation (10.1) may prevent its identification. As Haavelmo (1944) points out, the problem of measurement

---

[4]   See for example de Masi (1997), Giorno et al. (1995), or ECP (2001).

error is not likely to have a solution; thus we need an alternative that explicitly accounts for the errors in measurement.

Thus we follow the approach of Castle (2003) and assume that equation (10.1) holds in the long run, allowing for deviations over the short to medium term. In addition, instead of using equation (10.2) to estimate multifactor productivity growth as a residual, we posit that its evolution can be described as a function of past observations.

Under certain assumptions, which are described in the appendix, the model to be estimated can be written as:

$$\Delta y_t = \psi a_t + \gamma\left(y_{t-1} - a - \beta_1 n_{t-1} - \beta_2 k_{t-1}\right) + \theta \Delta n_t + \phi \Delta k_t + \varepsilon_t \tag{10.3}$$

$$a_t = \mu + a_{t-1} + \eta_t$$

where the growth rate of GDP (Δy_t) is modelled as a function of a time varying intercept (a_t) which is meant to capture short-run changes in multifactor productivity, and is assumed to depend on past observations; an adjustment towards the long-run equilibrium described by equation (10.1), and the growth rates of labour and capital inputs. Parameters $\psi, \gamma, \beta_1, \beta_2, \theta, \phi$ and μ are coefficients to be estimated, whereas ε_t and η_t are the regression residuals, which are assumed to have zero mean and constant variance.

Note that in order for the solution to equation (10.3) to converge to its long-run equilibrium $(y_t = a + \beta_1 n_t + \beta_2 k_t)$ the adjustment coefficient γ must be negative, so that positive deviations from the long run relationship are eventually corrected.[5]

The details of the econometric methodology used to estimate equation (10.3) are described in the appendix. Table 10.5 summarises the estimation results. We can see that both the error correction coefficient (γ) and the coefficient for multifactor productivity (ψ) have the correct signs and are statistically significant.

The adjustment coefficients indicate a relatively fast convergence towards potential output. The extreme cases are Mexico, where half of the deviation from potential output is accounted for each year; to Brazil, where practically all the deviation is corrected each year. This implies that most of the fluctuations in GDP in the region are actually movements in the trend. The rest of the estimated coefficients have the expected sign, and the residuals pass all standard tests.

---

[5] This feature explains why this class of models is known as error correction models.

Table 10.5 *Estimation results*

	Argentina	Brazil	Chile	Colombia	Mexico	Peru	Venezuela
γ	-0.7195***	-0.9476***	-0.8593***	-0.6449***	-0.5130***	-0.8282***	-0.6457**
β_1	0.9913*	0.2135	0.8815***	0.6644*	0.2670	0.3096	0.2698
β_2	0.1956	0.5198***	0.2833***	0.0354	0.1118	0.2522**	0.0784
θ	0.8472**	0.2972	1.0585***	0.4586**	0.5915***		0.7867***
ϕ	0.4180***	0.3880***	0.2502***		0.3013***	0.1877***	0.1621
ψ	0.0255***	0.0172***	0.0157***	0.0139***	0.0179**	0.0340***	0.0198**

Notes: *** denote significance at the 1 per cent, ** at 5 per cent and * at 10 per cent significance levels respectively.

Source: Author's calculations.

Table 10.6 *Long-run solution*

	Argentina	Brazil	Chile	Colombia	Mexico	Peru	Venezuela
n_t	1.3779	0.2253	1.0258	1.0303	0.5205	0.3736	0.4178
k_t	0.2719	0.5486	0.3297	0.0549	0.2180	0.3044	0.1215
tfp_t	0.0355	0.0181	0.0183	0.0216	0.0349	0.0410	0.0307

Source: Author's calculations.

By imposing the long term solution we can recover the elasticities that characterise the stable relationship described by equation (10.2). The results are summarised in Table 10.6.

The assumption of constant returns to scale implies that the sum of the coefficients on the capital and labour inputs, β_1 and β_2, should add to unity. Thus results indicate that the assumption of an aggregate production function with constant returns to scale is questionable. Moreover the long-run elasticities of output with respect to capital inputs show considerable heterogeneity across countries. While this may reflect the numerous breaks in the macroeconomic series under study, it also calls into question the assumption of constant factor shares across countries.

Next we use the model to estimate the evolution of multifactor productivity. Since multifactor productivity is not directly observable, based on the assumption that it evolves according to the autoregressive structure described in equation (10.3), we recover an estimate of its evolution using a method called Kalman filtering, which can be understood as recursive least squares. The details are described in the appendix.

Figure 10.1 shows the evolution of multifactor productivity obtained from a standard growth accounting exercise with constant factor shares (α =0.7), which are contrasted with the Kalman filter estimates.

We can see that the estimates under both methods are qualitatively similar, that is aside from short periods around the early 1980s the direction of changes is consistent across the sample for all countries.

On the other hand, noting that the estimates are on different scales, we can see that the Kalman filter estimates of multifactor productivity changes are significantly smaller. To some degree this is to be expected since the dynamic approach used explicitly accounts for measurement error. Despite this the differences in magnitude are large enough so that conclusions drawn from the respective results obtained can be very different. For example, in the case of Brazil and Mexico, standard estimates for the period 1999–2005 indicate a drop in productivity, whereas Kalman estimates indicate a deceleration for the case of Mexico and an increase in the pace of growth for the case of Brazil.

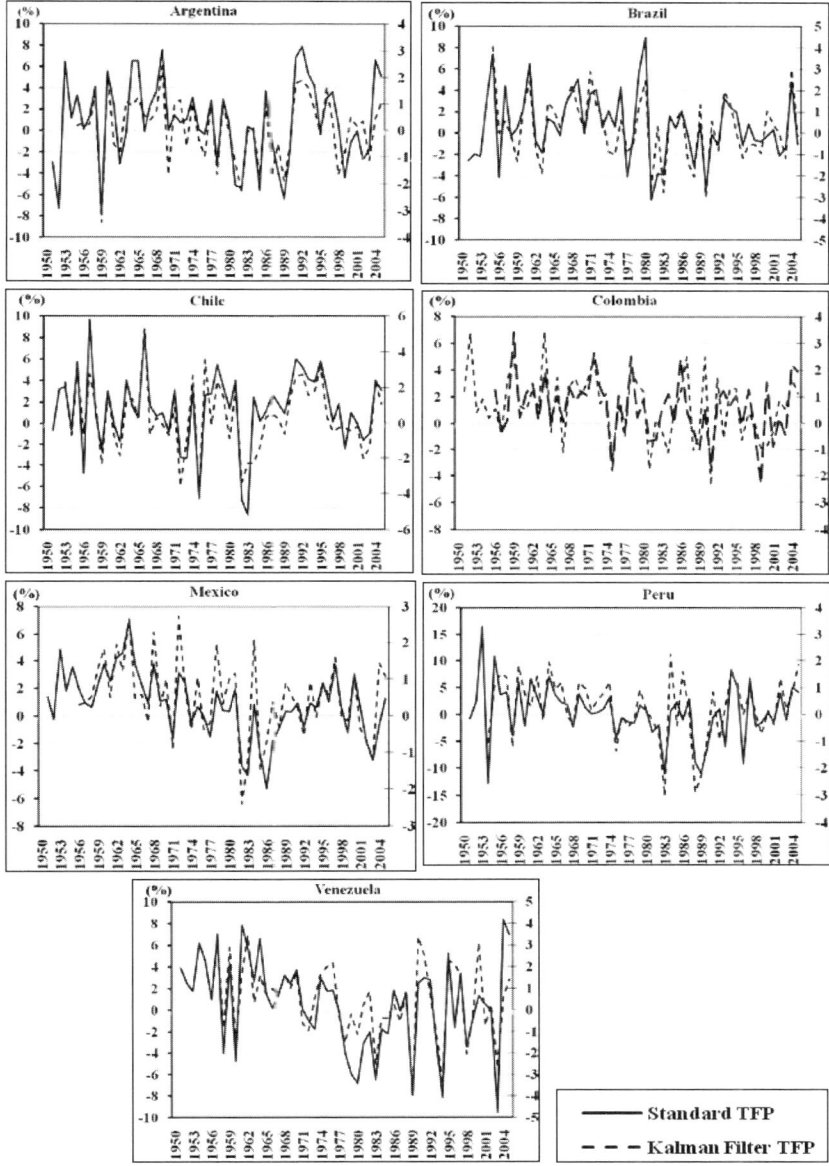

Notes: The scale of the standard estimates is shown on the left axis, whereas the Kalman filter estimated are shown on the right axis.

Source: Author's calculations.

Figure 10.1   Multifactor productivity

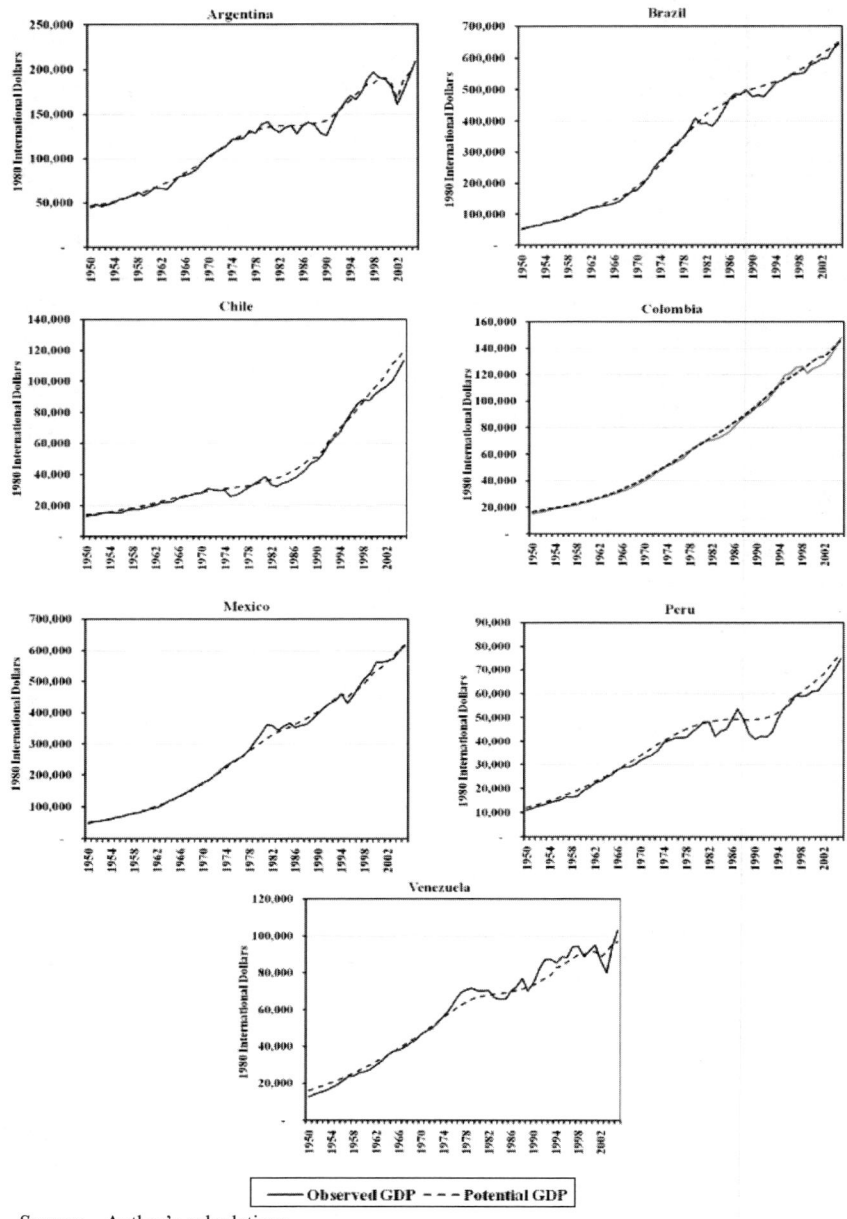

Source: Author's calculations.

Figure 10.2   Output and potential output

The advantage of using the production function approach with time-varying trend is that it allows us to characterise long-term potential output and to forecast its future evolution using a parametric model. The details of the procedure are described in the appendix. In essence we use the long term solution coefficients summarised in Table 10.6 and estimates of the potential evolution of productivity, as well as of capital and labour inputs to obtain estimates of potential output from equation (10.1). The results are shown in Figure 10.2.

There are several features worth noting. The first is that with the exception of Mexico and Venezuela, the two large oil exporters in the sample, observed GDP during the late 1970s and early 1980s was below potential. This implies that whereas the future growth prospects of Mexico and Venezuela were permanently affected by the second oil shock and the debt crisis, this was not the case for the rest of the countries of the sample.

Secondly, we can see that although the Asian crisis only had a marginal effect on the evolution of potential output of Chile, Colombia and Peru, the effect on observed output has been such that its evolution was still below potential at the end of the sample.

Finally, we can see that the Mexican financial crisis of 1995, the fallout from the attempted coup d'état in Venezuela during 2001, and the Argentinean financial crisis of 2002 had profound negative effects on the evolution of the respective countries' potential output.

10.4   FUTURE GROWTH PROSPECTS

In order to explore the future growth prospect for the countries under study, we use the estimates of the long–run coefficients obtained in section 10.3 to project the potential output under three alternative scenarios. The three scenarios are based on the same assumption regarding the evolution of the labour input. In particular we use CELADE's (1999) and (2004) forecasts for the working-age population and the refined participation rates.

The base scenario is passive in the sense that it is based on the assumption that the future evolution of productive capital and productivity remain at their current trends. In particular, the growth rates of capital stock and potential productivity are assumed to be the same as those observed over the period 1990–2005.

Table 10.7 summarises the base scenario. With the sole exception of Chile, the estimated GDP and per capita GDP average growth rates are smaller than the growth rates over the period 1950–2005.

This result reflects on the one hand the projected decline in labour input due to the reduction of population growth, and on the other the lacklustre performance of most countries over the period 1990–2005. This is clearly seen in the cases of Brazil and Venezuela, where the per capita growth rates below 1 per cent reflect an assumption of very low productivity growth in Brazil, and very low capital stock growth in the Venezuela. On the opposite side, the projected per capita growth rate of 3.5 per cent for Chile reflects the fact that over the period 1990–2005, the rate of growth of capital stock and productivity in Chile is three times the average for the remaining six countries.

Table 10.7   Growth prospects 2005–2030: Base scenario (average annual growth rates)

	Labour	Capital	Multifactor productivity	GDP	GDP pc
Argentina	1.0	1.6	23.2	2.6	1.7
Brazil	0.6	2.7	0.6	1.6	0.6
Chile	1.1	6.8	63.8	4.3	3.5
Colombia	1.7	3.3	27.5	2.4	1.2
Mexico	1.4	3.4	32.0	2.5	1.5
Peru	1.7	2.7	27.2	2.5	1.3
Venezuela	1.6	0.6	28.5	1.5	0.2

Source: Author's calculations.

The alternative scenarios consider how much either capital stock accumulation or productivity would have to grow in order to achieve a target growth rate. We consider both cases separately in order to put into perspective the feasibility of raising long-term GDP growth in a context of relatively low capital growth and a declining labour force. In particular we choose a target rate of 4 per cent per capita GDP growth.

The results for the alternative scenarios are summarised in Table 10.8. For the case of Chile, in order to achieve a long-run per capita growth rate of 4 per cent either capital stock accumulation would have to increase by 8 per cent, or productivity growth would have to double. Either of these changes would imply a GDP growth rate of 4.8 per cent.

For the case of Colombia, where the elasticity of long-term output with respect to capital inputs is relatively low (see Table 10.6) in order to achieve the target growth rate, capital accumulation would have to increase 70 per cent. For the case of Brazil which has the lowest elasticity of long-term output with respect to productivity and where the average growth rate of productivity over the period 1990–2005 is quite low due to the effects of the Asian crisis, productivity would have to increase fivefold to achieve the target growth rate.

On average, for the region to achieve per capita growth rates of 4 per cent, either capital accumulation would have to increase by about 25 per cent, or productivity growth would have to increase by a factor of 2.5.

Table 10.8   Alternative scenarios 2005–2030, average annual growth rates

	Capital	Multifactor productivity	GDP	GDP pc
Argentina	10.1	128.4	4.8	4.0
Brazil	9.1	525.9	5.0	4.0
Chile	8.3	111.2	4.8	4.0
Colombia	70.6	357.7	5.3	4.0
Mexico	15.7	165.2	5.0	4.0
Peru	12.0	141.5	5.2	4.0
Venezuela	36.2	325.1	5.3	4.0

Source: Author's calculations.

10.5   CONCLUDING REMARKS

A quantitative assessment of Latin American historic economic growth performance and its prospects for medium-term growth using a growth accounting framework indicate growth boundaries based on different scenarios. Emphasis is placed on measurable supply-side evidence involving the systematic quantification of output, human and physical capital, the role of diffusion and adaptation of technical progress and its potential in economic growth and catch-up.

The base scenario assumes that capital accumulation and multifactor productivity will continue to grow at their current trends and population growth is projected to decline over the medium-term. The alternative scenarios explore the rate at which capital accumulation and productivity would have to grow, in order to yield an average per capita growth rate of 4 per cent. Results indicate that on average, either capital accumulation would have to increase 25 per cent from its current trend; or productivity growth would have to increase by a factor of 2.5 from its current trend.

Further work should vary the periodisation as our cut-of-point is the year 2005 and therefore for example does not take into account the prosperous period of 2005–2008 nor the economic crisis of 2009. To include each of these would have influenced the result importantly. It makes clear that the exercise uses strong assumptions and conclusions need to have in mind these restrictive elements.

Future research on growth potential has to take also into account the historical and institutional context in which economic development took place, as well as the role of policy. A change in the econometric set-up would probably alter significantly the outcomes and this restriction should be taken into consideration.

REFERENCES

Castle, J. (2003), *Measuring Excess Demand and its Impact on Inflation*, M. Phil Thesis in Economics, Nuffield College, University of Cambridge, Cambridge, UK.

Centro Latinoamericano y Caribeño de Demografía (CELADE), (1999), *Boletín Demográfico No. 64 América Latina: Población Económicamente Activa 1980–2025*, UN Economic Commission for Latin America and the Caribbean, Santiago, Chile.

Centro Latinoamericano y Caribeño de Demografía (CELADE) (2004), *Boletín Demográfico No. 73 América Latina y el Caribe: Estimaciones y Proyecciones de Población 1950–2050*, UN Economic Commission for Latin America and the Caribbean, Santiago, Chile.

Costello, D.M. (1993), 'A Cross-Country, Cross-Industry Comparison of Productivity Growth', *Journal of Political Economy*, **101** (2), 207–222.

de Masi, P.R. (1997), 'IMF Estimates of Potential Output: Theory and Practice', Working Paper WP/97/177, International Monetary Fund, Washington, D.C.

Easterly, W. and R. Levine (2001), 'What have we learned from a decade of empirical research on growth? It's Not Factor Accumulation: Stylized Facts and Growth Models', *The World Bank Economic Review*, **15** (2), 177–219.

Economic Policy Committee (EPC) (2001), *Report on the Potential Output and the Output Gap,* European Union, Brussels, Belgium.

Giorno, C., P. Richardson, D. Roseveare and P. van de Noord (1995), *Estimating Potential Output, Output Gaps and Structural Budget Balances*, OECD Working Paper No. 152.

Gómez, V. (1999), 'Three Equivalent Methods for Filtering Nonstationary Time Series', *Journal of Business and Economic Statistics*, **17** (1), 109–116.

Haavelmo, T. (1944), 'The Probability Approach in Econometrics', *Econometrica*, **12**, Supplement, iii-vi+1-115.

Hamilton, J.D. (1994), *Time Series Analysis*, Princeton, NJ: Princeton University Press.

Harvey A., S.J. Koopman and N. Shephard, (2004), *State Space and Unobserved Component Models: Theory and Applications*, Cambridge, UK: Cambridge University Press.

Hendry, D.F. (1995), *Dynamic Econometrics*, Oxford, UK: Oxford University Press.

Hendry, D.F. and H.M. Krolzig (2001), *Automatic Econometric Model Selection with PcGets*, Timberlake Consultants Ltd., London, UK.

Hicks, J. (1932), *The Theory of Wages*, London, UK: Macmillan.

Hodrick, R.J. and E.C. Prescott (1997), 'Postwar U.S. Business Cycles', *Journal of Money, Credit and Banking*, **29** (1), 1–16.

Hofman, A.A. (2000a), *Economic Development of Latin America in the Twentieth Century*, Cheltenham, UK: Edward Elgar.

Hofman, A.A. (2000b), 'Economic Growth and Performance in Latin America', *Serie Reformas Económicas*, No. **54**, UN Economic Commission for Latin America and the Caribbean, Santiago, Chile.

Jofré, J.F. (2006), *Patrones de Consumo Aparente de Energias Modernas en América Latina, 1890–2003*, Research Document, Doctoral Programme in Economic History and Institutions , Universidad de Barcelona – Universidad Autónoma de Barcelona, Barcelona, Spain.

Jorgenson, D.W. and Z. Griliches (1967), 'The Explanation of Productivity Change', *The Review of Economic Studies*, **34** (3), 249–283.

Juselius, K. (2006), *The Cointegrated VAR Model: Methodology and Applications*, Oxford, UK: Oxford University Press.

Klenow, P.J. and A. Rodriguez-Clare (1997), 'The Neoclassical Revival in Growth Economics: Has It Gone Too Far?', *NBER Macroeconomics Annual 1997*, **12**, 73–103.

Loayza, N., P. Fajnzylber and C. Calderón (2005), *Economic Growth in Latin America and the Caribbean: Stylized Facts, Explanations and Forecasts*, The World Bank, Washington D.C.

Maddison, A. (2003), *The World Economy Volume 2: Historical Statistics*, Development Centre of the Organisation for Economic Cooperation and Development, Paris.

Okun, A.M. (1983), *Potential GNP: Its Measurement and Significance*, in Pechman, J.A. (ed.) (1983), *Economics for Policy Making, Selected Essays of Arthur M. Okun*, Cambridge, MA: MIT Press.

Solimano, A. and R. Soto (2006), *Economic Growth in Latin America in the Late Twentieth Century: Evidence and Interpretation*, in Solimano, A. (ed.) (2006), *Vanishing Growth in Latin America: The Late Twentieth Century Experience*, Cheltenham, UK: Edward Elgar.

Solow, R.M. (1957), 'Technical Change and the Aggregate Production Function', *The Review of Economics and Statistics*, **39** (3), 312–320.

Young, P. and D. Pedregal (1999), 'Recursive and En-bloc Approaches to Signal Extraction', *Journal of Applied Statistics*, **26** (1), 103–128.

APPENDIX

The appendix is divided into two parts. The first describes in detail the econometric methodology used to estimate the evolution of potential output, as well as the data sources used. The general setup is an error correction model. Since multifactor productivity is not directly observable, it is modelled as an unobserved component model. In order to estimate this kind of model it is necessary to cast the model in the so called state-space form and use the Kalman filter for estimation. This procedure is described in the second part of the appendix.

All computations were carried out using the E-views econometric package. Useful references for time series econometric methods in general and error correction models in particular are Hamilton (1994), Hendry (1995), and Juselius (2006). Hamilton (1994) also provides a good introduction to the Kalman filter. Finally, a book-length treatment of unobserved component models can be found in Harvey et al. (2004).

Econometric Methodology to Study the Evolution of Potential Output

As mentioned in the main text, the starting point for the estimation of potential output is the assumption of a constant returns-to-scale aggregate production function. In particular we use a Cobb-Douglas production function with Hicks-neutral augmenting productivity:[6]

$$Y_t = A_t N_t^\alpha K_t^{(1-\alpha)} \tag{A10.1}$$

where Y_t is total output, A_t is *multifactor productivity*, N_t and K_t are the labour and capital inputs, and α is the elasticity of output with respect to labour.

In order to bring the data as close as possible to the theoretical variables considered, the labour input is assumed to be comprised of both the number of actual people employed (L_t),[7] and the average number of hours worked per person (H_t); i.e. $N_t = L_t H_t$. Capital input is given by the productive capital stock (net capital stock excluding residential construction) (J_t), corrected by its rate of utilisation (U_t); i.e. $K_t = J_t U_t$.

---

[6] Hicks (1932) notes that a technological innovation is neutral (Hicks–neutral) if the ratio of the marginal products of inputs remain constant as long as the labour input ratios remain constant as well.

[7] The actual number of people employed is obtained by multiplying the working-age population (15–65 years), POP_t times the participation rate adjusted for unemployment, PR_t, i.e. $L_t = POP_t \times PR_t$.

In order to derive equation (10.2) in the main text, it is necessary to take logarithms and differentiate equation (A10.1) with respect to time. As a result the aggregate growth rate of output is given by:

$$\Delta y_t = \Delta a_t + \alpha \Delta n_t + (1-\alpha)\Delta k_t \tag{A10.2}$$

where lower case letter denote natural logarithms.

Solving equation (A10.2) yields equation (10.2) in the main text:

$$\Delta a_t = \Delta y_t - \alpha \Delta n_t - (1-\alpha)\Delta l_t \tag{A10.3}$$

As mentioned previously, equation (A10.3) is the key equation in growth accounting. Under the assumption that factor markets are perfectly competitive, the marginal product of each input should be equal to its price; thus, α and $(1 - \alpha)$ should be equal to the shares of wages and rental payments in aggregate income respectively.

Formally, to address the problem of measurement error we model multifactor productivity (a) as an unobserved component in the production function by introducing a time varying regression intercept as a proxy for the level of TFP. In particular, it is assumed that the TFP evolves as a random walk with deterministic drift.[8] This allows for permanent shifts to be picked up by TFP making the coefficient estimates robust against structural breaks.

Assuming that labour and capital are weakly exogenous with respect to output, that is assuming output does not depend on the contemporaneous valued of labour and capital inputs, the analysis of the dynamic production function can be carried out using a single equation, which in the general case can be written as:

$$y_t = \psi a_t + \Theta(L)n_t + \Phi(L)k_t + \Gamma(L)y_{t-1} + \varepsilon_t \tag{A10.4}$$
$$a_t = \mu - a_{t-1} + \eta_t$$

where $\Gamma(L)$, $\Psi(L)$, $\Theta(L)$ and $\Phi(L)$ are polynomials in the lag operator $Lx_t = x_{t-1}$, and $\varepsilon_t s$ and η_t are independent zero–mean normally distributed innovations.

Using only the first lag for expositional convenience, taking time differences and rearranging, allows equation (A10.4) to be expressed in error–correction form as:

---

[8] See the next section in the appendix for details.

$$\Delta y_t = \psi a_t + \gamma \left(y_{t-1} - a - \beta_1 n_{t-1} - \beta_2 k_{t-1} \right) + \theta \Delta n_t + \phi \Delta k_t + \varepsilon_t$$

$$a_t = \mu + a_{t-1} + \eta_t \qquad\qquad\qquad\qquad\qquad\qquad (A10.5)$$

which is equation (10.3) in the main text.

In order to estimate the coefficients in (A10.5), the model is cast into state-space form and estimated using the Kalman Filter, which is described in the next section of the Appendix. The dynamic structure is identified using a general to specific modelling strategy based on Hendry and Krolzig (2001) using a maximum lag-length of four periods.

For estimation, the following data sources are used:

- GDP (Y_t), productive capital stock (J_t), and average work hours estimates (H_t); are obtained from an updated version of Hofman (2000a).
- Working-age population (POP_t) and refined participation rates (PR_t) estimates are from CELADE (1999) and CELADE (2004).
- Following Costello (1993); the capital utilisation rate (U_t), is derived from Jofré's (2006) estimates of apparent energy consumption.[9]

Long-term potential output is obtained by plugging the long–run solution coefficients summarised in Table 10.6 into equation (A10.1), and evaluate it using the potential level estimates of inputs. These estimates are obtained as follows: For the capital input, full utilisation is assumed, i.e. $K_t^* = J_t$. For the labour input; actual working population and the average hours worked are assumed to represent their respective long-term trends, i.e. $POP_t^* = POP_t$ and $H_t^* = H_t$; while the potential refined participation rate, PR_t^*, is derived using an unobserved components model assuming a local-level model, i.e. $N_t^* = POP_t PR_t^* H_t$. Finally, potential productivity, A_t^t, estimates are also derived using an unobserved components model assuming a local–level model. Thus, (log) potential output is given by:

$$y_t^* = \psi a_t^* + \kappa_1 l_t^* + \kappa_2 k_t^* \qquad\qquad\qquad\qquad (A10.6)$$

---

[9] To obtain a proxy for the utilisation rate; (log) energy consumption is detrended using the Hodrick–Prescott filter. Then, differences from trend are rescaled so that the mode of positive deviations is equal to 1, i.e. $U_t = 1 + \left[(e_t - \bar{e}_t) - mode\left((e_t - \bar{e}_t) \right) \right]$, where e and $\bar{e}$ denote, respectively, (log) energy consumption and its trend.

Unobserved Component Models, the State–Space Form and the Kalman Filter

The general Unobserved Components (UC) model considered is given by:

$$y_t = \mu_t + \gamma_t + \varepsilon_t \tag{A10.7}$$

$$\mu_t = \mu_{t-1} + \delta_t + \eta_t \tag{A10.8}$$

$$\delta_t = \delta_{t-1} + \zeta_t$$

$$\gamma_t = \Psi(L)\varepsilon_t$$

where $\varepsilon_t \sim (0, \sigma_\varepsilon^2)$, $\eta_t \sim (0, \sigma_\eta^2)$, $\zeta_t \sim (0, \sigma_\zeta^2)$ and $\varepsilon_t \sim (0, \sigma_\varepsilon^2)$ are zero-mean stochastic processes with finite variances.

Equation (A10.7) is known as the signal or observation equation, and it says that the observable variable, y_t, can be decomposed as the sum of up to three unobserved components: a trend component, μ_t; a cyclical component, γ_t; and an irregular component, ε_t.

Equations (A10.8) are known as the state equations, and they determine the dynamic behaviour of the unobserved components. In the most general case, the trend, μ_t, is modelled as a random walk with random drift, δ_t, which is modelled as a random walk. The cycle, γ_t, is modelled as a generalised ARIMA process, equivalently it can be modelled as a sinusoidal function. Finally, the irregular component, ε_t, is modelled as white noise.

A number of restrictions can be imposed on the parameters of the system defined by (A10.7)–(A10.8) to yield different models which have been regularly used in the signal extraction literature. Of particular interest is the assumption that the cyclical component is equal to zero and a non-zero drift term in the trend, $\delta \neq 0$. These assumptions yield the local-level linear trend model used to obtain the potential estimates for the participation rate and productivity.

It is worth noting that when the trend follows an integrated random walk, i.e. $\sigma_\eta^2 = 0$, and it is assumed that the signal to noise ratio is equal to a constant, i.e. $\lambda = \sigma_\varepsilon^2 / \sigma_\zeta^2$, then it can be shown[10] that the model is equivalent to the Hodrick--Prescott (1997) filter with smoothing parameter λ.

Equations (A10.7)–(A10.8) constitute a state–space model, which in general can be expressed as:

---

[10] See Gómez (1999), or Young and Pedregal (1999) for details.

$$y_t = A' x_t + H' \xi_t + w_t \tag{A10.9}$$

$$\xi_t = F\xi_{t-1} + v_t \tag{A10.10}$$

where y_t is the observed variable, x_t is a vector of exogenous variables,[11] ξ_t is a vector of unobserved state variables, A, H and F are parameter matrices, while w_t, y_t, v_t are innovation vectors which obey the following processes:

$$w_t \sim N(0, R) \tag{A10.11}$$

$$v_t \sim N(0, Q) \tag{A10.12}$$

It is usually assumed that the vectors w_t and v_t, are independent for all t, i.e. $E(w_t v_\tau) = 0 \ \forall t , \ \forall \tau$.

The Kalman filter algorithm exploits the linear structure of the state–space representation, as well as the fact that the innovations are assumed normal, to project for each t the first two moments of ξ_t, conditional on the available information at $t-1$. Then, it updates the projection for moment t incorporating the information available at t minimising the projection squared error in each step.

In particular, the Kalman filter can be summarised in the following steps:

i)   The Kalman filter is initialised with the first two unconditional moments of ξ_1 :[12]

$$\xi_1^* = E(\xi_1) \tag{A10.13}$$

$$P_1^* = E\left[(\xi_1 - \xi_1^*)'(\xi_1 - \xi_1^*) \right]$$

ii) Then for $t = 1,...,T$, we iterate over the following equations to obtain the first two conditional moments:

---

[11] By exogeneity it is meant that x_t does not contain information about ξ_{t+s}, w_{t+s} for $s = 0,1,2,...$ beyond that contained in y_{t-1}, y_{t-2}, ..., y_1. For example, it can include lags of y_t or variables not correlated with ξ_t nor with w_t, for all t.

[12] Usually, it is assumed that the initial value of ξ_1^* is equal to zero, while the initial value of covariance matrix P_1^* is obtained from the following relationship: $(P_1^*) = [I - (F \otimes F)]^{-1} vec(Q)$ where I is the identity matrix, $\otimes$ is the Kronecker product, and $vec()$ is the vector stacking operator.

$$\xi_{t-1}^* = F\xi_t^* + K_t(y_t - A'x_t - H'\xi_t^*) \qquad \text{(A10.14)}$$

$$P_{t-1}^* = (F - K_t H')P_t^* F' + Q$$

where the matrix K_t, known as the Kalman gain matrix, is given by:

$$K \equiv FP_t^* H(H' P_t^* H + R)^{-1} \qquad \text{(A10.15)}$$

iii) Finally, the projection of the observable series is computed, y_t^*:

$$y_t^* = A'x_t + H'\xi_t \qquad \text{(A10.16)}$$

which has mean squared error given by:

$$MSE_{y_t} = H' P_t^* H + R \qquad \text{(A10.17)}$$

11. Europe's Productivity Performance in Comparative Perspective: Trends, Causes and Projections*

Bart van Ark, Mary O'Mahony and Marcel P. Timmer

11.1 INTRODUCTION

The benefits of the modern knowledge economy differ greatly between advanced economies. The EU–15, that is the 15 European Union countries that constituted the Union up to 2004 that is the focus of this chapter, experienced a slowdown in GDP growth from an annual rate of 3.5 per cent during the period 1973–1995 to 2.3 per cent during the period 1995–2008. At the same time productivity growth (measured as GDP per hour of work) slowed from an annual rate of 2.7 per cent to 1.5 between these two time periods. At the same time, average annual GDP in the United States slightly accelerated from 2.9 to 3.3 per cent and labour productivity sharply increased from 1.3 per cent to 2.1 per cent between 1973–1995 and 1995–2008 respectively. While differences in the timing of business cycles in the United States and the European Union may have some effect on this comparison, they do not explain these divergent trend growth rates.

* This chapter is an updated and extended version of our article 'The Productivity Gap between Europe and the United States: Trends and Causes', *Journal of Economic Perspectives*, Vol. 22(1), Winter 2008, pp. 25–44. It includes estimates from the EU KLEMS growth accounting databases which are updated from 2004 to 2007. The final section of the chapter includes projections for future growth which are newly added to the original paper. We are grateful to Robert Inklaar for his contribution to several parts of this chapter. The research for this chapter is based is part of the EU KLEMS project on Growth and Productivity in the European Union. This project was supported by the European Commission, Research Directorate General as part of the 6th Framework Programme, Priority 8, 'Policy Support and Anticipating Scientific and Technological Needs.

The slower output and labour productivity growth rates in Europe compared to the United States since 1995 reverse a long-term pattern of convergence. This chapter first reviews the growth and productivity performance in Europe since 1950, considering three periods characterized by different drivers of productivity. In the period 1950–1973, European growth was characterized by a traditional catch-up pattern based on the imitation and adaptation of foreign technology, coupled with strong investment and supporting institutions. However, the traditional postwar convergence process came to an end by the mid 1970s (Crafts and Toniolo, 1996; Eichengreen, 2007). Then, in the period from 1973 to 1995, output and productivity growth in both Europe and the United States began to slow. However, while the gap in output (and average per capita income) growth rates narrowed between the two regions, Europe's productivity growth remained much faster than in the United States. During this time, Europe experienced a strong decline in labour force participation and a fall in hours worked, which in turn triggered a substitution of capital for labour bringing capital-labour ratios in some major European economies to levels well above those of the United States by the mid 1990s. Finally, during the period since 1995, U.S. productivity growth accelerated until around 2004, after which it began to slow, whereas the rate of productivity growth in Europe fell throughout the period, with the exception of two brief positive spells during the peaks of the business cycle at the end of the 1990s and around 2006–2007.

In the third section of the chapter we focus on the European growth experience, especially in the period since 1995, using a new and detailed database called the EU KLEMS Growth and Productivity Accounts. The level of detail in this database allows explicit consideration of a number of issues: changes in patterns of capital-labour substitution; the increasing importance of investment in information and communications technology; the use of more high-skilled labour; the different dynamics across industries, like industries producing information and communications technology, or manufacturing and services more generally; and the diversity of productivity experience across the countries of Europe.

We show that the slowdown since the mid-1990s is mainly attributable to the slower emergence of the knowledge economy in Europe compared to the United States. In the fourth section we consider various explanations which are not mutually exclusive: for example, lower growth contributions from investment in information and communication technology in Europe, the relatively small share of technology-producing industries in Europe, and slower multifactor productivity growth (which can be viewed as a proxy for advances in technology and innovation). Underlying these explanations are issues related to the functioning of European labour markets and the high level of product market regulation in Europe. The chapter emphasizes the key role of market service sectors in accounting for the productivity growth divergence between the two regions.

Finally, we consider whether Europe will be able to accelerate its productivity growth. We argue that a strengthening in the use of knowledge inputs as a source of growth and an improved productivity growth in European market services will be needed to avoid a further widening of the productivity gap. To grasp the significance of this challenge we illustrate a few growth scenarios, making use of the historical productivity performance estimates. The slowing growth and faltering emergence of the knowledge economy in Europe since the mid-1990s has led to an ambitious action program of the European Commission, called the 'Lisbon Agenda', which was launched in 2000. Its goal was to make Europe by 2010 'the most competitive and dynamic knowledge-based economy in the world'. It aimed to raise private and public spending on research and development (leading to an 'official' target that research and development expenditures should rise to 3 per cent of GDP) and the creation of more jobs (raising the employment rate among adults to 80 per cent), especially high-skilled jobs. It also stressed the need to open up sheltered and protected sectors to greater competition, to improve the climate for enterprise and business, to reform labour markets, and to move toward environmentally sustainable growth. The Lisbon Agenda, however, has not lived up to its ambition, which has left Europe's long term productivity trend to continue on a downward trend.

Although we do not identify a silver bullet to revive growth, we argue that the issue for European productivity growth is centered around the European services sector. The nations of Europe need to find their own ways of adjusting to the opportunities and dislocations of the new information and communications technologies. Thus, within the broader growth and competitiveness agenda, we emphasize greater labour mobility and flexibility of service product markets within and across countries as being especially important.

11.2   EUROPEAN PRODUCTIVITY: 1950–2008

Europe's growth performance relative to the United States since 1950 can be usefully divided into three periods: 1950–1973, 1973–1995, and 1995–2008. The comparative European experience in GDP per capita and in GDP per hour is illustrated in Figure 11.1. The measures are compared relative to the U.S. levels and are adjusted for differences in relative price levels using the GDP-based purchasing power parities for 2005 from the OECD.

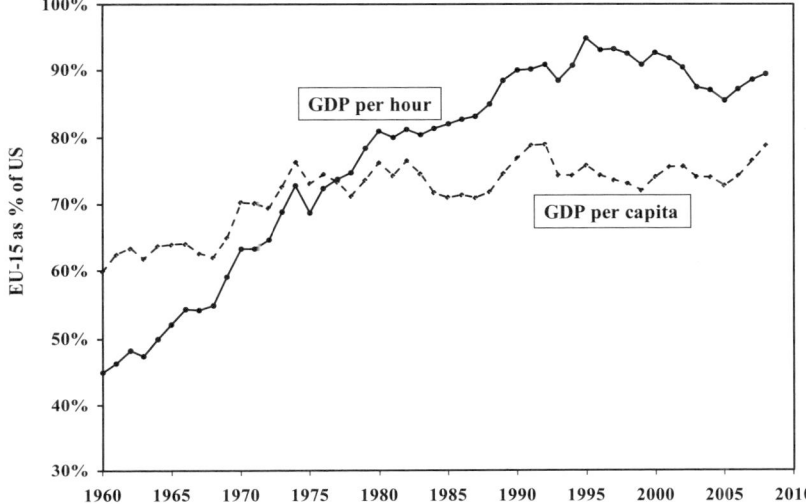

Notes: EU–15 refers to the 15 countries constituting the European Union before 2004 and include Austria, Belgium, Denmark, Finland, France, Germany, Greece, Ireland, Italy, Luxembourg, the Netherlands, Portugal, Spain, Sweden, and the United Kingdom. The EU has expanded to include ten new member states mainly in Central and Eastern Europe in 2004 and another two in 2007; the new members are not included here. Relative levels are based on purchasing power parities for GDP for 2005 from the OECD.

Source: The Conference Board Total Economy Database, Jan. 2010, http://www.conference-board.org/ economics/database.cfm.

Figure 11.1   Total economy GDP per hour worked and GDP per Capita in EU–15, 1960–2008 (relative to the United States)

11.2.1   European Catch-Up: 1950–1973

During the first period, from 1950–73, rapid labour productivity growth in the European Union went together with catching-up in terms of per capita income levels with the United States. The reasons for this dual catching-up process during the 1950s and 1960s have been extensively discussed in the literature and can broadly be divided into two groups: technology imitation and new institutions (for example, Boltho, 1982; Crafts and Toniolo, 1996; Eichengreen, 2007).

Imitation of technology and incremental innovation allowed European countries to speed up growth and productivity quite rapidly following the Depression of the 1930s and the devastation of Europe's economies during World War II. Many European countries could draw upon their legacy as industrializing nations during the nineteenth and early twentieth century.

Compared to other parts of the world, Europe after World War II already had a relatively well-educated population and a strong set of institutions for generating human capital and financial wealth, which allowed a rapid recovery of investment and absorption of new technologies developed elsewhere, notably in the United States.

This process was strengthened by the emergence of a new set of institutions in the area of wage bargaining (Eichengreen, 2007). Although there were important differences between countries, essentially these arrangements involved limiting wage demands in exchange for a rapid redeployment of profits for investment. Through this arrangement, a consensus was developed between workers and capitalists that benefited both productivity and per capita income. In addition, European capital markets favored the emergence of large 'national champion' companies while at the same time (notably in Germany) supporting a strong system of small- and medium-sized enterprises. In several northwest European countries, the education system tended to emphasize technical and vocational training. These characteristics of European institutions largely lasted until the end of the 1960s, after which labour markets became increasingly tight, leading to substantially higher wage demands.

11.2.2   The Productivity Slowdown: 1973–1995

The 'golden age' of post-World War II growth came to an end rather abruptly in the early 1970s, followed by a period of significantly slower growth lasting almost two decades on both continents (Maddison, 1987). Table 11.1 shows that while U.S. GDP growth slowed from 3.9 per cent on average per year in the period 1950–1973 to 2.9 per cent in the period 1973–1995, EU–15 growth slowed substantially more from 4.9 per cent in the period 1950–1973 to only 3.5 per cent in the period 1973–1995. However, average growth rates of per capita income between the United States and the EU–15 became quite similar at 1.8 per cent (for the EU) and 2.0 per cent (for the U.S.) between 1973 and 1995. Further details on the growth slowdown during this period are provided by Crafts and Toniolo (1996), Baily and Kirkegaard (2004), and Eichengreen (2007).

Looking back at Figure 11.1, one striking observation is that while per capita income in Europe hovered around between 70 to 80 per cent of the U.S. level between 1973 and 1995, the productivity gap between Europe and the United States continued to narrow. Indeed, average annual labour productivity growth in the EU–15 was still more than twice as fast as in the United States, at 2.7 per cent in the EU–15 against 1.3 per cent in the United States from 1973 to 1995. Thus, the labour productivity gap virtually closed from more than 30 percentage points in 1973 to only 5 percentage points in

1995, as shown in Table 11.1. In some European countries, including Belgium, France, Germany, and the Netherlands, GDP per hour worked was even higher than the U.S. level in 1995. In Europe, the combination of an unchanged gap in per capita income and a narrowing gap in labour productivity was related – by accounting identity – to a decline in labour force participation rates and a fall in working hours per person employed. Working hours per capita in the European Union countries declined from slightly above the U.S. level in 1973 to only 80 per cent of the U.S. level by 1995, as shown in Table 11.2.

Table 11.1   Average annual growth rates of GDP, GDP per capita, and GDP per hour worked, EU–15 and United States, 1950–2008 (in per cent)

	GDP	GDP per capita	GDP per hour worked
1950–1973			
EU–15	4.9	4.2	4.9
U.S.	3.9	2.5	2.6
1973–1995			
EU–15	3.5	2.0	2.7
U.S.	2.9	1.8	1.3
1995–2008			
EU–15	2.5	2.2	1.7
U.S.	3.0	1.9	2.1

Notes: See Figure 11.1. The growth rates are presented as differences in the log of the levels of each variable instead of a percentage change in the actual level in order to facilitate aggregation to regional averages and a decomposition of growth sources.

Source: Calculations based on The Conference Board Total Economy Database, January 2010, at http://www.conference-board.org/ economics/database.cfm.

A substantial literature has explored why Europe's labour market institutions have led to less work, in particular during the period 1973–1995. Blanchard (2004) stresses how the trade-off between preferences for leisure and work developed differently in Europe and the United States. Prescott (2004) estimates that the role of income taxes can account for virtually all of the difference in labour participation rates across European countries. Nickell (1997) shows that besides high payroll taxes, other labour market issues, such as generous unemployment benefits, poor educational standards at the bottom, and high unionization with little coordination also play an important role in accounting for Europe's rise in unemployment since the mid 1970s.

Europe's welfare state rapidly expanded in the 1970s, causing an increase in labour cost, a strong bias towards insiders in the labour market, and an increase in structural unemployment, in particular among youth and elderly workers.

Table 11.2   Levels of EU–15 relative to the United States, 1950–2008 (in per cent)

	1950	1973	1995	2008
GDP per capita	49.2	72.5	75.7	78.7
Hours worked per capita	120.6	105.4	79.8	88.0
GDP per hour worked	40.8	68.8	94.8	89.4
Capital input per hour worked*		82.3	97.0	88.1

Note: Output and capital levels are converted by GDP purchasing power parities for 2005.
* Measured as capital services per hour worked. Entry for 1973 refers to 1980.

Source: Calculations based on The Conference Board Total Economy Database, January 2010, at http://www.conference-board.org/ economics/database.cfm

One result of Europe's slowing growth in labour input was a rapid increase in capital intensity, as the rise in wages supported the substitution of capital for labour. Table 11.2 shows that Europe's capital stock per hour worked was at 82 per cent of the U.S. level in 1973, but had reached almost equality with the U.S. level by 1995. Some European countries had a higher capital stock per hour worked than the U.S. in 1995, including Austria, Belgium, Finland, France, Germany, and the Netherlands. As a result, the high labour productivity levels in the European Union by the mid 1990s should be interpreted with care. Economists draw a distinction between labour productivity, which can be measured by GDP per hour worked, and multifactor productivity, which relates to the level of output after accounting for labour as well as capital inputs. As we will argue in more detail below, even though Europe experienced relatively strong growth in labour productivity, the growth in multifactor productivity was much lower. This indicates that Europe's higher labour productivity growth during this period may not have been so much the result of catch-up, access to superior technology, or even faster innovation, but can be largely attributable to accumulated labour market rigidities.

11.2.3   Europe's Falling Behind: 1995–2008

Since the mid 1990s, the patterns of productivity growth in Europe and the United States changed dramatically. In the EU–15, annual GDP growth declined from 3.5 during the period 1973–95 to 2.3 per cent during 1995–2006, and labour productivity growth from 2.7 to 1.5 per cent for the same periods. In the United States, GDP slightly strengthened to 3.3 per cent from 1995–2008, relative to 2.9 per cent from 1973–95, and the productivity acceleration in the U.S. was quite sharp from 1.3 to 2.3 per cent between the two periods. By 2008, GDP per hour worked in the EU was more than 10 per cent below the U.S. level. Europe's capital intensity levels have also come down significantly, from 97 per cent of the U.S. level in 1995 to 88 per cent in 2008 (Table 11.2).

The slowdown in labour productivity may be related to the rapid growth in labour input in many European countries. During the late 1980s and 1990s, several European countries introduced labour market reforms and instigated active labour market interventions to bring long-term unemployed people to work and raise the participation rate. The slowdown in productivity growth and the decline in relative capital intensity in Europe since 1995 suggest the possibility that just as limited employment growth accompanied higher labour productivity in Europe in the 1973–1995 period, perhaps that pattern reversed itself in the more recent time period (Gordon, 2004). While in the short run, labour productivity growth might decline due to the dampening of real wage growth and consequent reduction in the rate of substitution of capital for labour, it is unlikely that the elasticity of labour input on productivity would be large in the medium and long term. According to Blanchard (2004), the employment-productivity trade-off would only exist under the assumption of stagnant output growth, which is an unlikely assumption for the medium and long run. Indeed, despite slowing productivity growth, the European Union has not experienced a large slowdown in GDP growth since 1995. A related argument is that increases in employment have raised the share of low-skilled workers in the workforce, causing labour productivity to decline. However, there are no signs of a significant slowdown in the skill level of the labour force, which would presumably arise if the underlying cause was a strong rise in low-skilled labour in Europe. On the contrary, the average skill-level of the employed labour force continued to improve since the mid-1990s. Thus, the labour market is unlikely to be the main explanation for the slowdown in productivity growth.

When put into a comparative perspective, the productivity slowdown in Europe is all the more disappointing as U.S. productivity growth accelerated since the mid 1990s. The causes of the strong U.S. productivity resurgence have been extensively discussed (see, for example, Jorgenson, Ho, and Stiroh, 2008). In the mid 1990s, there was a burst of higher productivity in industries producing information and communications technology equipment, and a capital-deepening effect from investing in information and communications technology assets across the economy. In turn, these changes were driven by the rapid pace of innovation in information and communications technologies, fuelled by the precipitous and continuing fall in semiconductor prices. With some delay, arguably due to the necessary changes in production processes and organizational practices, there was also a multifactor productivity surge in industries using these new information and communications technologies – in particular in market services industries (Triplett and Bosworth, 2006).

In Europe, the advent of the knowledge economy has been much slower since the mid 1990s. In the next section, we exploit a new database on industry-level growth accounts to develop a better view of how inputs and productivity have contributed to the change in the growth performance of European countries since 1995, in particular in comparison with the United States.

11.3 GROWTH ACCOUNTING FOR EUROPE AND THE UNITED STATES

To assess the contribution of various inputs to GDP growth, we apply the neoclassical growth accounting framework pioneered by Solow (1957) and further developed by Jorgenson and associates (Jorgenson and Griliches, 1967; Jorgenson, Gollop, and Fraumeni, 1987). Using this framework, measures of output growth can be decomposed into the contributions of inputs and productivity within a consistent accounting framework. This approach allows researchers to assess the relative importance of labour, capital, and intermediate inputs to growth, and to derive measures of multifactor productivity growth. The output contribution of an input is measured by the growth rate of the input, weighted by that input's income shares. Under neoclassical assumptions, the income shares reflect the output elasticity of each input, and assuming constant returns to scale, they sum to one. The portion of output growth not attributable to inputs is the multifactor productivity residual. Multifactor productivity indicates the efficiency with which inputs are being used in the production process, and includes pure technological change, along with changes in returns to scale and in mark-ups. Multifactor productivity, as a residual measure, also includes measurement errors and the effects from unmeasured output and inputs, such as research and development and other intangible investments, including organizational improvements (Corrado, Hulten and Sichel, 2009; van Ark et al., 2009).

Our growth decompositions are based on the November 2009 release of the EU KLEMS database. This database provides harmonised measures of economic growth, productivity, employment creation, and capital formation at a detailed industry level for European Union member states, Japan, and the United States from 1980 to 2007. In particular, this database contains unique industry-level measures of the skill distribution of the work force and a detailed asset decomposition of investment in physical capital. Labour input reflects changes in hours worked, but also changes in labour composition in terms of age, gender, and educational qualifications over time. Physical capital is decomposed into six asset categories, of which three are information and communications capital – including information technology hardware, communication equipment, and software – and three are capital that does not involve information and communications technology – machinery and equipment, transport equipment, and nonresidential structures. Residential capital, which does not contribute in any direct way to productivity gains, is excluded from the analysis.

The EU KLEMS database makes it possible for the first time to compare and analyze the role of high-skilled labour and information and communications technology capital for productivity growth at an industry level between countries. Our focus here is on the market economy, which means that we exclude health and education services, as well as public administration and defense. This exclusion implies a faster acceleration of output growth in both the European Union and the United States since 1995 than for the total economy reported in the previous section, but the difference in pace of acceleration between the two regions does not change. Also, in the remainder of this discussion, the European Union only includes 10 countries, excluding Greece, Ireland, Luxembourg, Portugal, and Sweden from our original 15, because no industry-level accounts back to 1980 were available for these five countries.

Table 11.3 provides a summary of the growth contributions of factor inputs and multifactor productivity to labour productivity growth in the market economy in the ten European Union countries and in the United States for the periods 1980–1995 and 1995–2007. When comparing the period before and after 1995, the annual growth rate of output in the European Union accelerates, and the growth differential relative to the United States drops from 1.2 percentage points (2.1 per cent in Europe versus 3.3 per cent in the United States) to 1.0 percentage point (2.5 per cent in Europe versus 3.5 per cent in the United States). As described in the previous section, hours worked in the European Union grew rapidly after 1995, to some extent making up for the shortfall in the earlier period. In contrast, the growth in hours worked slowed down substantially in the United States – in particular after 2000 – even though the average growth rate in hours was comparable to that of the European Union between 1995–2007. As a result, labour productivity growth in the U.S. market economy increased significantly compared to a large slowdown in Europe after 1995.

Table 11.3   Contributions to growth of real output in the market economy, European Union and the United States, 1980–2007 (annual average growth rates, in percentage points)

	European Union*		United States**	
	1980–1995	1995–2007	1980–1995	1995–2007
1 Growth rate of market economy output	2.1	2.5	3.3	3.5
2 Hours worked	-0.5	0.8	1.3	0.9
3 Labour productivity	2.5	1.6	2.0	2.6
Contributions from				
4 Labour composition	0.3	0.2	0.2	0.3
5 Capital services per hour	1.2	0.9	1.0	1.2
6 ICT capital per hour	0.4	0.5	0.7	0.9
7 Non-ICT capital per hour	0.8	0.4	0.3	0.3
8 Multifactor productivity	1.1	0.6	0.7	1.2
Contribution of the knowledge economy to labor productivity (4)+(6)+(8)	1.8	1.3	1.7	2.4

Notes: * excludes 5 member states of EU–15: Greece, Ireland, Luxembourg, Portugal and Sweden; Data for European Union refers to ten countries: Austria, Belgium, Denmark, Finland, France, Germany, Italy, the Netherlands, Spain, and the United Kingdom.
** based on USA old standard industrial classification.
'ICT' is information and communications technology.

Source: EU KLEMS database, see O'Mahony and Timmer (2009).

Table 11.3 shows that changes in labour composition contributed 0.2–0.3 percentage points to labour productivity growth both in the European Union and the United States during this entire time period. Even though this contribution is small, its positive sign implies that the process of transformation of the labour force to higher skills has proceeded at roughly equal rates in Europe and the United States, thus confirming the observation above that Europe has not raised its share of low-skill workers. Instead the upward trend in the skill-content of the employees shows that newcomers on the labour market have had on average more schooling than the existing labour force.

Concerning the total contribution of capital deepening to labour productivity growth, measured by capital services per hour, Table 11.3 shows somewhat larger differences between the European Union and the United States compared to labour composition. This contribution declined in Europe while rising in the United States between the two time periods. The specific contribution of information and communications technology per working hour in Europe has been lower than in the United States, and since 1995, it accelerated more slowly (Timmer and van Ark, 2005). This slower uptake in deepening of information and communications technology capital is in part related to the overall decline in capital-labour ratios across Europe since the mid 1990s, as European employment grew rapidly.

The largest difference between the European Union and the United States shown in Table 11.3 is in the contribution of multifactor productivity growth. Whereas multifactor productivity growth in the United States accelerated by half a percentage point from 0.7 per cent from 1980–1995 to 1.2 per cent from 1995–2007, it fell by the same degree from 1.1 to 0.6 per cent between these two periods in the European Union. As a residual measure, multifactor productivity has multiple interpretations, but in some way it does reflect the overall efficiency of the production process. Its reduced growth rate is therefore a major source of concern across Europe.

It should be stressed that the growth differential between the EU and the U.S. was especially strong between 1995 and 2004. The differences became significantly smaller after 2004 when Europe saw a slight acceleration in multifactor productivity growth in the market economy from 0.4 per cent (from 1995–2004) to 1.2 per cent (from 2004–2007) due to a cyclical peak, whereas U.S. MFP growth began to slow from 1.4 per cent to 0.4 per cent between the two periods.

When looking at these growth accounts from the perspective of the emerging knowledge economy, one might focus on the summed contributions of three factors: direct effects from investments in information and communication technology; changes in labour composition mostly driven by greater demand for skilled workers; and multifactor productivity growth, which – as indicated above – might include the impact of intangible investments such as organizational changes related to the use of information technology. Table 11.3 shows that the combined contribution of these three factors to labour productivity growth declined by 0.5 percentage points in Europe between the two time periods, from 1.8 percentage points from 1980– 1995 to 1.3 percentage points from 1995–2007. In contrast, in the U.S. economy the contribution of these three knowledge economy components increased from 1.7 percentage points from 1980–1995 to 2.4 percentage points from 1995–2007.

There is a large variation in labour productivity growth across European countries. Similar to the rows in Table 11.3, the first column of Table 11.4 shows the growth rate of output for ten European countries over the 1995– 2007 time period. The second and third columns divide that growth in output into changes in hours worked and changes in output per hour, or labour productivity. Columns 4–7 divide up the growth in labour productivity into the contributions from four factors: changes in labour composition; investments in information and communication technology capital; other types of physical capital; and multifactor productivity.

One key observation to be drawn from this table is that the main difference in labour productivity growth between individual European economies and the United States is to be found in multifactor productivity, not in differences in the intensity of the production factors. Indeed the bottom row shows that the standard deviation for multifactor productivity growth across the set of countries is by far the largest, ranging from minus 0.6 per cent in Spain to plus 2.8 per cent in Finland. By way of illustration, the difference in the contribution of capital deepening in information and communications technologies between a high investor like the United States and a low investor like Italy explains 0.5 percentage points out of a labour productivity growth difference of 2 percentage points between those two countries during 1995–2007. The remaining 1.5 percentage point difference is (more than) accounted for by the differences in multifactor productivity growth. Differences in multifactor productivity seem to have driven the divergence in labour productivity between European countries too. In Belgium multifactor productivity growth has been close to zero per cent per year, and in Denmark, Italy, and Spain, it is even negative. Only Finland exceeds the U.S. growth rate of multifactor growth in the market economy, and Finland is a special case that will be discussed in more detail in the next section.

How should we explain the large differences in multifactor productivity growth across countries? In the next section, a division of the aggregate market economy measures by industry focuses attention on the performance of the market services sector.

Table 11.4 Contributions to growth of real output in the market economy, EU economies and the United States, 1995–2007 (annual average growth rates, in percentage points)

	Growth rate of output	Output contribution from		Labour productivity contributions from				Labour productivity contribution of the knowledge economy
		Hours worked	Labour productivity	Labour composition	ICT capital per hour	Non-ICT capital per hour	MFP growth	
	1 = 2+3	2	3=4+5+6+7	4	5	6	7	4+5+7
Austria	2.8	0.6	2.2	0.1	0.5	0.0	1.5	2.2
Belgium	2.5	0.8	1.7	0.2	0.9	0.4	0.1	1.3
Denmark	2.3	1.3	1.0	0.1	1.0	0.1	-0.1	0.9
Finland	4.6	1.3	3.3	0.1	0.5	-0.1	2.8	3.5
France	2.5	0.5	2.0	0.3	0.3	0.4	0.9	1.6
Germany	1.4	-0.3	1.7	0.0	0.5	0.5	0.7	1.2
Italy*	1.5	1.1	0.4	0.1	0.2	0.4	-0.4	0.0
Netherlands	3.1	1.0	2.1	0.4	0.5	0.0	1.1	2.0
Spain	3.7	3.0	0.6	0.4	0.4	0.5	-0.6	0.1
United Kingdom	3.2	0.6	2.6	0.4	0.8	0.4	1.0	2.2
European Union**	2.5	0.8	1.6	0.2	0.5	0.4	0.6	1.3
USA***	3.5	0.9	2.6	0.3	0.9	0.3	1.2	2.4
standard deviation****	0.9	0.8	0.9	0.1	0.3	0.2	1.0	1.0

Notes: 'ICT' is information and communications technology. 'MFP' is multifactor productivity. * Data for Italy excludes agriculture and private households. ** Data for the European Union excludes 5 member states of EU–15: Greece, Ireland, Luxembourg, Portugal and Numbers may not sum exactly due to rounding. *** based on USA old standard industrial classification U.S. **** Standard deviation for EU countries and the United States.

Source: Calculations based on EU KLEMS database, see O'Mahony and Timmer (2009).

11.4   STRUCTURAL CHANGE AND SECTORAL PRODUCTIVITY GROWTH

During the postwar period Europe has experienced a large shift of production and employment from manufacturing and other goods-producing industries (such as agriculture and mining) towards services. Market services include a wide variety of activities, ranging from trade and transportation services, to financial and business services, and also hotels, restaurants, and personal services. Over the period 1980–2007, the share of labour input going to manufacturing has typically declined by one-third or more in most countries. Market services now account for almost half of the market economy employment in all countries and the share of total labour hours going to market services is not much lower in Europe than in the United States. While there are differences across European countries, even in Germany, a country in which manufacturing traditionally plays an important role, the number of hours worked in market services is now more than 2.5 times larger than in manufacturing.

The growing importance of market services is the result of a number of interacting forces (Schettkatt and Yocarini, 2006). Higher per capita income leads to higher demand for services. There is also an increasing marketization of traditional household production activities, including services like dining outside the home, cleaning, and care assistance. Finally, many manufacturing firms are outsourcing aspects of business services, trade, and transport activities. Whatever the underlying causes of the shift from manufacturing to services, it has important implications for productivity growth. Traditionally, manufacturing activities have been regarded as the locus of innovation and technological change, and thus the central source of productivity growth. For example, more productive manufacturing was the key to post-World War II growth in Europe through a combination of economies of scale, capital intensification, and incremental innovation. More recently, rapid technological change in computer and semiconductor manufacturing seemingly reinforces the predominance of innovation in the manufacturing sector. In contrast, the increasing weight of services in output was thought to slow aggregate productivity growth. Baumol (1967) called this the 'cost disease of the service sector'. The diagnosis of the disease argues that productivity improvements in services are less likely than in goods-producing industries because most services are inherently labour-intensive, making it difficult to substitute capital for labour in service industries. Although Baumol originally mainly referred to services activities like education, health, and public services, it was widely believed to hold for many other services sectors as well. This hypothesis has subsequently been disputed in the literature (for example, Triplett and Bosworth, 2006) and, as the following discussion will show, is not supported by the evidence from the EU KLEMS data.

Table 11.5   Major sector contribution to average annual labour productivity growth in the market economy, 1995–2007 (annual average growth rates, in percentage points)

	Market Economy 1=2+3+4+5	Contributions from			
		ICT production 2	Goods production 3	Market services 4	Reallocation* 5
Austria	2.2	0.3	1.7	0.2	-0.1
Belgium	1.7	0.3	0.9	0.6	-0.1
Denmark	1.0	0.3	0.4	0.4	-0.1
Finland	3.3	1.7	1.3	0.5	-0.1
France	2.0	0.4	0.8	0.7	0.0
Germany	1.7	0.5	0.9	0.4	0.0
Italy	0.4	0.2	0.2	0.0	-0.1
Netherlands	2.1	0.4	0.6	1.2	-0.2
Spain	0.6	0.1	0.2	0.3	-0.1
United Kingdom	2.6	0.5	0.7	1.6	-0.2
European Union**	1.6	0.4	0.7	0.6	-0.2
USA***	2.6	0.8	0.3	1.8	-0.2

Notes: * The reallocation effect in the last column refers to labour productivity effects of reallocations of labour between sectors. ** The European Union aggregate refers to ten countries in the table. *** based on USA old standard industrial classification. Information and communications technology production includes manufacturing of electrical machinery and post and telecommunications services. Goods production includes agriculture, mining, manufacturing (excluding electrical machinery), construction, and utilities. Market services include distribution services; financial and business services, excluding real estate; and personal services. Numbers may not sum exactly due to rounding.

Source: Calculations based on EU KLEMS database, see O'Mahony and Timmer (2009).

To evaluate the effect of structural changes on productivity growth, we need to look at the contributions of individual sectors on the aggregate economy. Table 11.5 shows overall labour productivity growth for the market economy split into contributions from labour productivity growth in the information-and-communications technology production sector (including production of electrical machinery and telecommunication services), goods production (including agriculture, mining, manufacturing other than electrical machinery, utilities, and construction), and the market services sector (including trade, hotels and restaurants, transport services, financial and business services, and social and personal services), each weighted by its share in value added, along with an adjustment in the final column for the reallocation of hours between industries with different productivity.

Table 11.5 shows that slow productivity growth in market services is not a universal truth, even among advanced countries with large service sectors. First, productivity growth in market services has been much faster in the United States than in Europe. At an average annual labour productivity growth rate of 1.2 per cent, market services contributed only 0.6 percentage points to labour productivity growth in Europe from 1995–2007. In contrast, labour productivity in market services increased at 3.0 per cent in the United States, contributing 1.8 percentage points to U.S. productivity growth. Secondly, within Europe two countries – the Netherlands and the United Kingdom – also showed rapid productivity growth in market services. Market services in the United Kingdom contributed almost as much to aggregate labour productivity growth as in the United States, mainly due to strong performance in trade and business services industries. Incidentally, market services also appear to exhibit rapid productivity growth in other Anglo-Saxon economies, such as Australia and Canada (Inklaar, Timmer, and van Ark, 2007). In contrast, Italy and Spain show almost zero contributions from market services to aggregate labour productivity growth. Previous studies on the growth differential between Europe and the United States also stressed the differentiating role of market services (O'Mahony and van Ark, 2003; Losch, 2006; Inklaar, Timmer, and van Ark, 2008).

The importance of market services for the productivity growth gap between Europe and the United States dwarfs the differences for other major sectors. Even though the United States has a somewhat bigger share in information and communications technology-producing sectors, the productivity growth rates in these sectors are not dramatically different. As a result, the effect on the aggregate growth differential is only 0.4 percentage points (0.8 per cent in the United States compared to 0.4 per cent in Europe). Goods production seems to be somewhat more important for aggregate productivity growth in Europe than in the United States. The contribution from labour productivity growth in goods production in Europe is about the same as that of market services, despite the former's relative size of only one-third of market services value added. For example, in France and Germany, manufacturing industries like machinery and car manufacturing are still important sources of productivity growth. In Spain and Italy, lackluster performance is not only due to slow growth in market services, but also in manufacturing, as traditional labour-intensive sectors have faced a particularly tough challenge from increasing low-wage competition from eastern Europe and China.

Table 11.6   Contributions of sectors to average annual labour productivity growth in market services, 1980–2007 (in percentage points)

	European Union*		United States**	
	1980–1995	1995–2007	1980–1995	1995–2007
Market services labor productivity	1.4	1.2	1.6	3.0
Contributions from:				
Distribution services contribution	1.1	0.7	1.2	1.3
of which from factor intensity growth	0.4	0.4	0.4	0.5
of which from multifactor productivity growth	0.7	0.3	0.8	0.8
Finance and Business services contribution	0.1	0.3	0.0	1.3
of which from factor intensity growth	0.5	0.4	0.8	1.0
of which from multifactor productivity growth	-0.4	-0.1	-0.8	0.3
Personal services contribution	-0.1	-0.1	0.2	0.2
of which from factor intensity growth	0.1	0.1	0.1	0.1
of which from multifactor productivity growth	-0.2	-0.2	0.1	0.1
Contribution from labor reallocation	0.3	0.2	0.2	0.2

Note: * European Union aggregate refers to 10 countries, as listed in Table 11.5. ** based on USA old standard industrial classification. Factor intensity relates to the total contribution from changes in labour composition and in capital deepening of information and communications technology (ICT) and non–information and communications technology (non–ICT) assets. The reallocation effect refers to the impact of changes in the distribution of labour input between industries on labour productivity growth in market services. Numbers may not add up due to rounding.

Source: Calculations based on EU KLEMS database (O'Mahony and Timmer, 2009).

A more in-depth focus on market services reveals that cross-Atlantic growth differences were especially large in distributive trade and in financial and business services. In Table 11.6 we focus on the contribution of three major groups of market services industries – namely distributive trade (including retail and wholesale trade, and transport services); financial and business services; and personal services (including hotels and restaurants, and personal, community, and social services) – to labour productivity growth in aggregate market services. In Europe, the distribution sector contributed 0.7 percentage points to average annual labour productivity growth in market services from 1995 to 2007, compared to 1.3 percentage points in the United

States. In finance and business services, the gap was even bigger, at a 0.3 percentage point contribution in Europe relative to 1.3 percentage points in the United States. Drilling more deeply into the data, it turns out that for both sectors, multifactor productivity and not factor intensity was the key to the productivity growth differential between Europe and the United States. Differences in 'factor intensity', which include the total contribution from changes in labour composition and deepening of all types of capital, appear very small. The fuelling of U.S. multifactor productivity growth from trade, finance, and business services is confirmed in studies by Jorgenson, Ho, and Stiroh (2005) and Triplett and Bosworth (2006).

11.4.1   The Productivity Dynamics of the Retail Sector

Because multifactor productivity growth represents a multitude of factors which are not explicitly measured in a growth accounts framework, it is useful to look at what might lie behind this growth. While the factors may differ across sectors, the example of the retail sector may serve as an illustration of the complex interactions between productivity, investment, and regulations. Over the past 25 years, the retail sector has undergone a substantial transformation due to benefits from the increased use of information and communications technology, commonly referred to as the 'lean retailing system' (Abernathy, Dunlop, Hammond, and Weil, 1999). The retail industry has changed from a low-tech industry where workers mainly shift boxes from the producer to the consumer depending on availability in stock, into an industry whose main activity is trading information by matching the production of goods and services to customer demand on a continuous basis. Various studies, including McKinsey Global Institute (2002), Baily and Kirkegaard (2004), Gordon (2004), and McGuckin, Spiegelman, and van Ark (2005) have discussed the reasons for superior performance in the U.S. retail industry relative to Europe.

   While there is significant evidence of a faster rise in information and communications technology capital in the U.S. retail sector compared to Europe, the productivity impact of the greater use of barcode scanners, communication equipment, inventory tracking devices, transaction processing software, and similar equipment may be understated when focusing solely on the contribution of investment as directly measured in growth accounts. The use of information and communications technology also provides indirect benefits for growth as measured by multifactor productivity through increasing the potential for other kinds of innovation. These innovation effects should in part be realized through 'softer' innovations, such as the invention of new retail formats, service protocols, labour scheduling systems, and optimized marketing campaigns (McKinsey Global Institute, 2002).

Others have emphasized the role of 'big box' formats, as exemplified most notably by the emergence of Wal-Mart, as the engine of productivity growth in U.S. retailing (Basker, 2007). From this perspective, Europe's lagging behind in productivity is due to more restrictive regulations like store-opening hours; to land zoning and labour markets; and to cultural differences that inhibit a rapid increase in market share of new large-scale retail formats. These new large-scale retail formats have been a main driver of growth in the United States, both because of increased competitive pressures on incumbent firms and the higher productivity levels of new entrants (Foster, Haltiwanger, and Krizan, 2006). In addition, deregulation in upstream industries such as trucking in the 1980s was necessary for the lean retailing model to work, because it allowed for more efficient ordering and shipping schedules.

11.4.2   The Productivity Dynamics of the Financial Services Sector

As a result of the financial crisis which started in 2008, there have been largely anecdotal claims that the financial services sector has perversely driven U.S. output and productivity growth during the decade or so before. The reasoning has been that a relatively strong emphasis on measuring the rapid increase in the monetized value of financial instruments, especially in securities trading, has inflated output and productivity growth. In practice, however, measured labour productivity growth in financial services has been fairly moderate in both the U.S. and Europe at between 2.5 and 3 per cent. And while it accelerated in Europe between 2004–2007, it did not do so in the United States. Part of this is related to the slow growth in insurance output which offset faster growth elsewhere in the financial sector. In fact, MFP growth in financial services improved in both regions since 2004.

There is considerable empirical evidence that a better-developed financial system enhances economic growth and financial institutions can help to select the most profitable investment projects. However, at the same time a more efficient financial system may not stimulate growth beyond a certain level of financial development. In other words, advanced economies may not gain much in terms of growth benefits from a more efficient financial system. It therefore remains questionable whether the estimates of productivity growth in the financial sector adequately reflect the performance of the financial sector (Inklaar and Koetter, 2008). Current statistical practices do not seem to be up to the task of measuring output and productivity adequately and there is some circumstantial evidence that measured growth, especially in European banking, has been overstated in recent years due to an overreliance on measures which are traditionally based on interest margins. By the same token, the benefits of financial innovation are often called upon in discussions of regulation in the financial sector, but their quantitative importance is generally unknown.   Before we are able to measure these factors, we need more clarity on what services banks and other financial institutions actually provide: is it mostly transaction services; or does it also involve other intermediation services, such as information on for example risk profiles, and to what extent is bearing risk a 'productive service'?

11.5   THE FUTURE OF EUROPEAN PRODUCTIVITY GROWTH

Since the mid 1990s, the European Union has experienced a slowdown in productivity growth, at a time when productivity growth in the United States accelerated significantly. The resurgence of productivity growth in the United States appears to have been a combination of high levels of investment in rapidly progressing information and communications technology in the second half of the 1990s, followed by rapid productivity growth in the market services sector of the economy in the first half of the 2000s. Conversely, the productivity slowdown in European countries is largely the result of slower multifactor productivity growth in market services, particularly in trade, finance, and business services. This pattern holds true for Europe as a whole, and also for many individual European countries.

European economies therefore face a major challenge if they are to increase economic performance and living standards through productivity growth. To grasp the significance of this challenge we illustrate a few growth scenarios, making use of current projections of labor force growth, historical MFP performance, and related projections for ICT and non-ICT capital. The key to our scenarios are projections of multifactor productivity growth. Figure 11.2 illustrates a number of possible scenarios. The baseline scenario for both the U.S. and Europe assumes that the industry growth rates of multifactor productivity growth for 1995–2007 will be maintained for the period 2010–2020, using the 2005 value added shares to compute market economy growth. This implies a widening productivity gap between Europe and the U.S. since U.S. MFP growth in market services was quite rapid over this period, while it was close to stagnation in Europe.

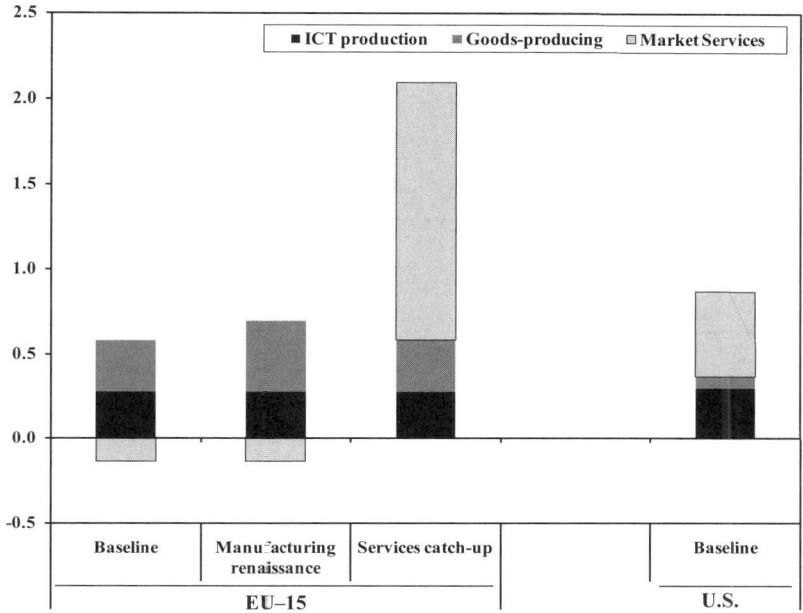

Note: Baseline scenario assumes MPF growth rates for 1995–2007. 'Manufacturing renaissance' assumes 1980–1995 productivity growth rates in manufacturing. 'Services catch–up' assumes MFP growth in market services that close aggregate MFP gap by 2020.

Source: Timmer et al. (2010), with historical estimates (on which scenarios are partly based) updated to 2007.

Figure 11.2 Growth scenarios for multifactor productivity growth in the market economy, 2010–2020 (in percentage points)

We also look at two alternatives for European MFP growth. In the first alternative, labelled 'manufacturing renaissance', we assume that Europe regains its competitiveness in manufacturing production, which has been an important driver of growth during the late 20th century. We therefore assume that MFP growth in manufacturing industries in Europe would return to their 1980–1995 rates, which considerably raises the contribution of the manufacturing sector to aggregate MFP growth. However, since manufacturing makes up a shrinking part of Europe's economies, market economy MFP growth in the U.S. would still outpace that of Europe. The other, more optimistic, alternative scenario assumes that Europe will be able to close the 2005 EU–U.S. gap in total factor productivity of 20 per cent by 2020 by way of faster MFP growth in market services. As the figure shows, this would require aggregate MFP growth in the market economy in Europe to increase to almost double the U.S. growth rate.

Table 11.7   Growth Scenarios for GDP Growth, 2010–2020 (in percentage points)

	European Union-15				United States	
	1995– 2007	2010– 2020	2010– 2020	2010– 2020	1995– 2007	2010– 2020
	historical estimates	base scenario	manufacturing renaissance	services catch-up	historical estimates	base scenario
GDP Growth	2.1	1.2	1.6	3.1	2.9	2.0
Contribution of:						
Labour Quantity	0.5	-0.2	-0.2	0.0	0.6	0.5
Labour Quality	0.2	0.1	0.1	0.1	0.2	0.1
Non-IT Capital	0.9	0.7	0.8	0.7	1.3	0.7
IT Capital	0.2	0.2	0.3	0.3	0.4	0.2
MFP Growth	0.3	0.4	0.6	2.0	0.5	0.8

Note: Employment projections based on demographic measures. Assumptions on MFP growth from Figure 11.2.

Source: Calculations based on forward projection from historical estimates derived from The Conference Board Total Economy Database, January 2010, at http://www.conference-board.org/economics/database.cfm.

Table 11.7 merges the MFP growth scenarios derived above with a growth accounting framework for 2010–2020. This required assumption on labor force growth and capital intensity. Labor force growth rates are obtained from demographic projection and assumptions on participation rates. Capital intensity largely depends on incentives provided by technology and innovation, which underpin the MFP estimates. To arrive at growth for the aggregate economy, we had to make assumptions for MPF growth in the non-market economy, in addition to the market economy estimates derived in Figure 11.2. In particular, we assumed that the negative MFP growth rates in non-market services would reduce to zero MFP growth rates for 2010–2020. As a result of these assumptions the base scenario shows slower GDP growth in both the United States and the European Union from 2010–2020 than from 1995–2007, mainly as the result of a slowing in investment in the U.S. and a slowdown in labour growth in Europe. The two alternative scenarios for Europe, 'manufacturing renaissance' and 'services catch-up' raise MFP growth by 0.2 and 1.6 percentage points respectively, bringing GDP growth in Europe up from 1.2 per cent according to the base scenario, to 1.6 and 3.1 per cent according to the alternative scenarios.

It should be stressed that neither the baseline scenario nor any of the other scenarios in Table 11.7 represents our most preferred or most likely scenario. Projecting output and productivity growth is a hazardous business, and the focus on scenarios should only be seen as helping us better understand the range of possible growth paths rather providing a point estimate that might be treated as a most likely outcome.

The prospects for accelerating growth in Europe do not look very promising from this scenario analysis. One negative factor is the projected slowdown in labour growth during the 2010–2020 period, which is the result of the rapid ageing of the population and limited attraction for skilled immigration. The large slowdown in productivity means that Europe needs to find mechanisms to exploit innovations for greater multifactor productivity growth, especially in services. Unfortunately, the traditional catch-up and convergence model of the 1950s and 1960s may not help Europe get back on track. First, because Europe had reached the productivity frontier by the mid 1990s, it now may require a new model of innovation and technological change to make better use of a country's own innovative capabilities (Acemoglu, Aghion, and Zilibotti, 2006). Arguably innovations in services are more difficult to imitate than 'hard' technologies based in manufacturing. The greater emphasis on human resources, organizational change, and other intangible investments are strongly specific to individual firms. Moreover, the firm receives most of the benefits of such changes, which reduces the legitimization for government support such as research and development and innovation subsidies to support 'technology' transfer in services. Service activities also tend to be less standardized and more customized than manufacturing production; they depend strongly on the interaction with the consumer and are therefore more embedded in national and cultural institutions. In this situation, the spillover of technologies across firms and nations becomes much more difficult. Recent work by Bloom and Van Reenen (2007) links corporate management practices to productivity. They find significant cross-country differences in corporate management practice, with U.S. firms being better managed than European firms on average, as well as significant within-country differences with a long tail of badly managed firms. In other words, a simple 'copying' of practices from other countries – or even from other firms within the same country – is not the most likely way for European service companies to attain greater productivity growth.

Second, a more flexible approach towards labour, product, and capital markets in Europe would allow resources to flow to their most productive uses. Crafts (2006) discusses the increasing evidence that restrictive product market regulations, in particular those limiting new entry, hinder technology transfer and have a negative impact on productivity, although most studies relate only to manufacturing industries. The diversity in productivity growth across European countries shows that some countries have been addressing these issues relatively successfully, while others have not. Even though most European countries have begun to make changes to institutional arrangements that increase flexibility and competitiveness in labour and product markets, such changes vary greatly across countries. The changes that have occurred depend, for example, on the size and maturity of the industry, the industry concentration, the nature of the education system, the availability of capital for startups, the sophistication of the consumer, and the characteristics of the legislative framework. More research is needed to understand the determinants of the differences in country experiences regarding innovation and regulations, in particular in services industries.

Finally, many service industries in Europe could benefit from a truly single market across Europe, in which competition can be strengthened and scale advantages may be realized. Of course, the European 'single market' program has since the 1980s aimed at removing the barriers to free movement of capital, labour, and goods, but the effect on the services industry is generally seen as limited. The present drive in Europe towards a greater openness of service product markets, for example through the adoption of a Services Directive in 2006 specifically aimed at creating a common market for services across the European Union, may hold the potential to increase productivity growth across Europe in the coming decade.

REFERENCES

Abernathy, F.H., J.T. Dunlop, J.H. Hammond and D. Weil (eds.) (1999), *A Stitch in Time: Lean Retailing and the Transformation of Manufacturing – Lessons from the Apparel and Textile Industries*, Oxford: Oxford University Press.
Acemoglu, D., P. Aghion and F. Zilibotti (2006), 'Distance to Frontier, Selection, and Economic Growth', *Journal of the European Economic Association*, **4** (1), 37–74.
Baily, M.N. and J.F. Kirkegaard (2004), *Transforming the European Economy*, Washington, DC: Institute for International Economics.
Basker, E. (2007), 'The Causes and Consequences of Wal-Mart's Growth', *Journal of Economic Perspectives*, **21** (3), 177–98.
Baumol, W.J. (1967), 'Macroeconomics of Unbalanced Growth: The Anatomy of Urban Crisis', *American Economic Review*, **57** (3), 415–26.
Blanchard, O. (2004), 'The Economic Future of Europe', *Journal of Economic Perspectives*, **18** (4), 3–26.
Bloom, N. and J.V. Reenen (2007), 'Measuring and Explaining Management Practices across Firms and Countries', *Quarterly Journal of Economics*, **122** (4), 1351–1408.

Boltho, A. (1982), *The European Economy: Growth and Crisis*, Oxford: Oxford University Press.

Crafts, N. (2006), 'Regulation and Productivity Performance', *Oxford Review of Economic Policy*, **22** (2), 186–202.

Crafts, N. and G. Tonio.o (1996), *Economic Growth in Europe since 1945*, Cambridge: Cambridge University Press.

Corrado, C., C. Hulten and D. Sichel (2009), 'Intangible Capital and U.S. Economic Growth', *The Review of Income and Wealth*, **55** (3), 661–685.

Eichengreen, B. (2007), *The European Economy since (1945): Coordinated Capitalism and Beyond*, Princeton: Princeton University Press.

European Commission (2004), *The EU Economy 2004 Review* (European Economy No. 6), Luxembourg: Office for Official Publications of the EC.

Foster, L., J. Haltiwanger and C.J. Krizan (2006), 'Market Selection, Reallocation, and Restructuring in the U.S. Retail Trade Sector in the 1990s', *Review of Economics and Statistics* **88** (4), 748–58.

Gordon, R.J. (2004), 'Why Was Europe Left at the Station When America's Productivity Locomotive Departed?' Center for Economic Policy Research Discussion Paper 4416, London: Center for Economic Policy Research.

Inklaar, R. and M. Koetter (2008), 'Financial dependence and industry growth in Europe: Better banks and higher productivity', GGDC Research Memorandum, GD–100, University of Groningen.

Inklaar, R., M.P. Timmer and B. van Ark. (2007), 'Mind the Gap! International Comparisons of Productivity in Services and Goods Production', *German Economic Review*, **8** (2), 281–307.

Inklaar, R., M.P. Timmer and B. van Ark (2008), 'Market Services Productivity across Europe and the U.S', *Economic Policy*, January, **53** (1), 141–94.

Jorgenson, Dale W., Frank M. Gollop and Barbara M. Fraumeni (1987), *Productivity and U.S. Economic Growth*, Cambridge, MA: Harvard University Press.

Jorgenson, D.W. and Z. Griliches (1967), 'The Explanation of Productivity Change', *Review of Economic Studies*, **34** (3), 249–83.

Jorgenson, D.W., M.S. Ho and K.J. Stiroh (2005), *Information Technology and the American Growth Resurgence*, Cambridge, MA: MIT Press.

Jorgenson, D.W., M.S. Ho and K.J. Stiroh (2008), 'A Retrospective Look at the U.S. Productivity Growth Resurgence', *Journal of Economic Perspectives*, **22** (1), 3–24.

Losch, M. (2006), *Deepening the Lisbon Agenda: Studies on Productivity, Services and Technologies*, Vienna: Austrian Federal Ministry of Economics and Labour.

Maddison, A. (1987), 'Growth and Slowdown in Advanced Capitalist Economies: Techniques of Quantitative Assessment', *Journal of Economic Literature*, **25** (2), 649–98.

McGuckin, Robert H., Matthew Spiegelman and Bart van Ark (2005), '*The Retail Revolution: Can Europe Match the U.S. Productivity Performance?*', New York: The Conference Board, Research Report R–1358.

McKinsey Global Institute (2002), *Reaching Higher Productivity Growth in France and Germany – Retail Trade Sector*, Washington, DC.

Nickell, S. (1997), 'Unemployment and Labour Market Rigidities: Europe versus North America', *Journal of Economic Perspectives*, **11** (3), 55–74.

O'Mahony, M. and M.P. Timmer (2009), 'Output, Input and Productivity Measures at the Industry Level: The EU KLEMS Database', *Economic Journal*, Royal Economic Society, **119** (538), F374–F403.

O'Mahony, M. and B. van Ark (eds) (2003), *EU Productivity and Competitiveness: An Industry Perspective: Can Europe Resume the Catching–up Process?*, Luxembourg: Office for Official Publications of the European Communities.

Prescott, E.C. (2004), 'Why Do Americans Work So Much More Than Europeans?', *Federal Reserve Bank of Minneapolis Quarterly Review*, **28** (1), 2–13.

Schettkat, R. and L. Yocarini (2006), 'The Shift to Services Employment: A Review of the Literature', *Structural Change and Economic Dynamics*, **17**(2), 127–47.

Solow, R. (1957), 'Technical Change and the Aggregate Production Function', *Review of Economics and Statistics*, **39** (3), 212–20.

Timmer, M.P. and B. van Ark (2005), 'Does Information and Communication Technology Drive EU–US Productivity Growth Differentials?', *Oxford Economic Papers*, **57** (4), 693–716.

Timmer, M.P., R. Inklaar, M. O'Mahony and B. van Ark (2010), *Economic Growth in Europe, A Comparative Industry Perspective*, Cambridge: Cambridge University Press (forthcoming).

Triplett, J.E. and B.P. Bosworth (2006), ''Baumol's Disease' Has Been Cured: IT and Multifactor Productivity in US Services Industries', in Jansen D.W. (ed.), *The New Economy and Beyond: Past, Present and Future*, 34–71. Cheltenham: Elgar.

Van Ark, B., J.X. Hao, C. Corrado and C. Hulten (2009), 'Measuring intangible capital and its contribution to economic growth in Europe', *EIB Papers*, European Investment Bank, **14** (1), 62–99.

12. Revisiting U.S. Productivity Growth over the Past Century with a View of the Future[1]

Robert J. Gordon

12.1 INTRODUCTION

This chapter looks ahead 20 years and predicts future growth rates of U.S. labor productivity and potential real GDP. Yet we know nothing about the future unless we understand the past, and this chapter provides a new interpretation of the growth of labor productivity and of multi-factor productivity (MFP) since 1891. Everything in this chapter refers to the U.S. and the reader is referred elsewhere for an interpretation of the divergence of productivity growth in the U.S. and Europe in the postwar period, with a European catching up process through 1995 and a falling back since then (see Dew-Becker and Gordon (2008) and Timmer et al. (2010)).

The chapter begins with the short-run facts by providing up-to-date productivity and potential GDP trends based on U.S. quarterly data through the fourth quarter of 2009 (henceforth 2009:Q4). The trends and deviations from trends (i.e., 'gaps') are new and constitute an update with improved methodology of my paper (Gordon, 2003) on the 2001–04 'explosion' in U.S. productivity growth. We learn that the productivity explosion in 2001–04 unraveled rapidly in 2004–07 prior to another explosion in 2009. Both the 2004–07 slowdown and the 2009 explosion reinforce themes long

---

[1] This chapter is a revised version of the original paper presented at Workshop on the Occasion of Angus Maddison's 80th Birthday, World Economic Performance: Past, Present, and Future, University of Groningen, the Netherlands, October 27, 2006. This chapter is dedicated not only to the 80th birthday of Angus Maddison but also to the memory of Robert McGuckin of the Conference Board. The 2006 conference version of this paper was made possible by the creative research assistance of Robert Krenn. Jesse Wiener brought new insights to this revision and extension of the data.

emphasized in my research going back more than three decades (see Gordon 1979), that productivity growth is weakest in the final stages of the business cycle expansion ('the end-of-expansion slowdown') and is most rapid in the early stages of the economic recovery ('the early recovery productivity bubble').

Next, we turn to a medium-term horizon. Relying entirely on the work of others, especially that of Steve Oliner and Dan Sichel, and of Dale Jorgenson, Mun Ho, and Kevin Stiroh, we summarize what is known about the contribution of ICT (Information-Communication-Technology) investment to the post-1995 revival of U.S. productivity growth. These authors find that, while ICT was central in the 1995–2000 revival, in contrast ICT investment plays a much smaller role in the volatile ups and downs of productivity growth between 2000 and 2008. In most of this literature the sources of the 2001–04 explosion remain mysterious and unexplained. In this section we revisit our own previous suggestions (Gordon, 2003) centering on profit pressure and intangible capital and expand these ideas to apply to the 2008–09 recession.

When forecasting the future over 20 years, a longer time horizon is necessary than just the most recent five or ten years. The core sections of this chapter revisit growth in labor productivity and MFP over the entire 20th century. In the decade since my 'One Big Wave' paper (Gordon, 2000a) on U.S. twentieth century economic growth, two events have occurred that warrant a reassessment. First, another decade of data has emerged in which U.S. productivity growth has revived and, at least for a few years has surged ahead of any similar period in recorded history. Second, and perhaps more important, the 1999 conversion of the U.S. National Accounts to chain-weighted price and quantity indexes resulted in a major upward revision in U.S. real GDP growth during 1929–48, and this adds further support to the previous 'big wave' hypothesis that productivity growth during the middle of the twentieth century was historically unique. The analysis of long-term labor productivity and MFP growth begins with BLS estimates of MFP for the period since 1948 and extends those back to 1891, developing adjustments for labor and capital composition and for changes in the quantity of capital. The capital quantity adjustments are also extended into the post-1948 era.

The last section of the chapter develops the implications of the historical analysis for future forecasts. What span of history is relevant for a 20-year forecast, just the past 20 years or a longer horizon? How can we take advantage of forecastable components of future economic growth, such as the plateau of educational attainment that already has occurred? Jorgenson and colleagues, as well as economists at the U.S. Congressional Budget Office (CBO) have provided forecasts going out at least over the next ten years, and we attempt to learn from their forecasts in developing our own.

The chapter develops an internally consistent set of forecasts for output, output per capita, labor productivity, the capital deepening effect, labor quality, and MFP growth The outcome is a projected annual growth rate for 2007–2027 for total-economy labor productivity of 1.7 per cent per year, slower than the actual 2.02 per cent for 2000–2007 or the actual 1.79 per cent for 1987–2007, but faster than the 1.36 per cent for 2004–07 or the 1.25 per cent for 1972–95. The implied growth rate of 2007–2027 real GDP is 2.4 per cent, slightly slower than the 2.5 per cent consensus in several recent projections. However, the implied 1.4 per cent growth rate of real GDP per capita represents a significant slowing in the projected advance in the American standard of living from the 2.16 per cent annual growth rate achieved over 1929–2007.

12.2 TREND PRODUCTIVITY AND GDP GROWTH IN QUARTERLY DATA, 1954–2007

Distinguishing features of the U.S. quarterly postwar growth performance are relatively rapid growth in labor productivity from the late 1940s through 1973, much slower growth through 1995, and a revival after 1995 that further accelerated in 2001–04. As many had predicted, productivity growth slowed in 2004–07 to be followed by an unexpected resurgence during the recession and early recovery of 2008–09. This section disentangles trend from cycle in the U.S. data for aggregate output, labor productivity, and aggregate hours of work.

The U.S. performance contrasts starkly with that in Europe, particularly the original 15 members of the EU prior to the 2004 enlargement (the 'EU–15'). After growing more rapidly than the U.S. throughout the postwar period and almost catching up to the level of U.S. labor productivity, Europe stalled after 1995; its productivity growth rate declined while that in the United States revived. By one set of PPP weights, the ratio of labor productivity in the EU–15 relative to the U.S. was 77 per cent in 1979, reached 91 per cent in 1995, and by 2008 had slipped back to 83 per cent.[2] To limit its scope, this chapter has no further discussion of European performance regarding productivity or per-capita income. Readers are referred to parallel papers by Dew-Becker and Gordon (2008), Gordon (2010a), and the book by Timmer et al. (2010). However, hypotheses suggested to explain the long-period fluctuations in U.S. productivity growth should always refer to the quite opposite European experience; for instance slow productivity growth in the

---

[2] Details are provided in Gordon (2010a), which in turn is based on data from the Groningen web site.

U.S. during the 1973–95 period can hardly be blamed on high oil prices when Europe's productivity continued to grow rapidly despite experiencing the same oil prices.

12.2.1   The Output Identity

In this section we examine the dimensions of post-war growth in U.S. output, productivity, and aggregate hours. We develop statistical elements of trend growth in these three variables that help us to illuminate changes over time in cyclical and long-run behavior. The output identity decomposes real GDP (Y) into output per hour (Y/H), aggregate hours per employee (H/E), the employment rate (E/L), the labor force participation rate or LFPR (L/N), and the working-age population (N)[3].

$$Y \equiv \frac{Y}{H} \cdot \frac{H}{E} \cdot \frac{E}{L} \cdot \frac{L}{N} \cdot N \qquad (12.1)$$

The identity in equation (12.1) requires that we define labor productivity using not the standard published measures of output per hour in the private non-farm business sector (NFPB), but rather output per hour in the total economy. This shift in definition requires use of unpublished BLS data on aggregate hours of work in the total U.S. economy (H). Most work on productivity growth refers only to the NFPB sector and cannot be compared to economywide trends in employment, the labor force, and the working-age population without the introduction of cumbersome additional terms in (12.1), as has been previously analyzed in Gordon (2003). Here we limit the analysis of short-term behavior to equation (12.1), in which output per hour (Y/H) is defined as real GDP divided by aggregate hours of work for the total U.S. economy.

12.2.2   Actual and Trend Growth in Output, Hours and Productivity, 1952–2009

To distinguish long-run trends from cyclical movements, we develop trends based on the Kalman filter method. Unlike the more frequently used method of Hodrick and Prescott, which produces trends that are excessively sensitive to business cycle movements, the Kalman technique allows the cycle to be purged from the trend growth estimates through the use of a cyclical feedback variable (see Hamilton, 1994). The particular technique of

---

[3] The employment rate E/L is simply unity minus the unemployment rate, that is *(1-U/L)*

developing the cyclical feedback variable for our trend estimates is based on separate research on the relationship between U.S. inflation and the gap between the actual and natural rates of unemployment, as summarized in Gordon (2010b). Here we skip over the details and present the results, which reveal a problem in extending trend estimates past the U.S. business cycle peak of 2007:Q4 to the most recent data in 2009:Q4.

Our examination of trends and cycles begins in Figure 12.1, which displays the eight-quarter change of real GDP and its Kalman filtered trend growth rate. The eight-quarter actual changes capture the magnitude and timing of the major and minor business cycles over the postwar period. The depth and duration of the 2007–09 recession are comparable to the previous 1980–82 double recession episode. Because the Kalman filter uses the estimated unemployment gap (backed out of the inflation equation) to control for the business cycle, the trend displayed in Figure 12.1 flattens out the variability at the business cycle frequency and reveals almost no response of the trend to the marked business cycles of 1974–75, 1980–82, or other recession episodes.

Notice that after 2002 the trend estimates diverge. The line that surges up after 2005 is an unconstrained estimate based on the data estimated through 2009:Q4. To obtain some perspective on the role of the 2008–09 recession in creating this trend output growth resurgence, the dashed line shows the growth rate of trend GDP estimated freely through 2007:Q4 and then forced to remain constant after that quarter.

Why do the trend estimates diverge as they do in the 2008–09 period? The key to understanding this phenomenon is the shift in labor-market behavior documented by Gordon (2010b). During the 2008–09 recession employment and unemployment responded with a much higher elasticity to the output cycle than in earlier cyclical downturns. As a result, the use of the unemployment gap as a cyclical feedback variable in the Kalman detrending technique leads the trend estimation procedure to conclude that the output gap in 2008–09 was much larger than actually occurred. To explain actual real GDP behavior in light of this large (but exaggerated) output gap based on the unemployment gap, the Kalman estimation technique translates this large assumed output gap into an increase in the trend growth rate of output as required to make the trend compatible with the exaggerated output gap and the actual data on real output growth. For 2009:Q4 the freely estimated Kalman trend growth rate is 3.7 per cent per year, much higher than the constrained 2.8 per cent per year, and we reject the higher rate as an implausible byproduct of the structural change discussed above.

Because all trends estimated from data after 2007 are contaminated by structural change in the relationship between output and labor markets, the analysis of this chapter sets the end of the relevant sample period in 2007:Q4 rather than 2009:Q4. The resulting trend growth series for real GDP is quite stable over the entire postwar period, ranging between 3.5 and 4.0 per cent from 1952 to 1974, and then in the range between 2.7 and 3.5 per cent from 1975 to 2007.

Figure 12.2 displays the actual and trend behavior of aggregate hours in the same format as Figure 12.1, and Figure 12.3 does the same for total-economy productivity growth. Figure 12.2 for aggregate hours displays a peak in the growth trend in 1978 of 1.9 per cent per year as a result of the rise in labor force participation of females (and also the peak entry of baby-boom teenagers). There is little difference in the trend estimates for 2008–09 based on free estimation and a constrained extrapolation of the estimates through 2007:Q4; the former is 0.90 per cent per year and the latter 0.96 per cent per year. What remains unexplained and quite unique in the history of aggregate hours growth is the marked decline in both hours per employee and in labor-force participation in the 2001–05 period. This weakness in the position of labor relative to management that was evident in the aggregate hours data for 2001–03 also may have an impact on the economic recovery of 2010 and beyond (see Gordon, 2010b).

Figure 12.3 provides a parallel presentation of output per hour in the total economy, not the standard published data for the NFPB sector. The growth trend for productivity varies substantially more than the output trend in Figure 12.1. The trend declines from a peak of 2.8 per cent per year in 1961 to 1.2 per cent in 1979. The influx of inexperienced females and teens is often cited as a factor for slow trend productivity growth in the late 1970s. Then the trend fluctuated in a narrow range between 1.4 and 1.6 per cent per year between 1980 and 1995, before surging up to its unconstrained peak of 2.4 per cent in 2002.

In parallel with Figure 12.1, an alternative estimate of trend productivity growth is presented in Figure 12.3 that estimates the Kalman trend procedure freely through 2007:Q4, the end of the previous 2001–07 business expansion, and assumes that the 2008–09 productivity growth trend persists at the trend growth rate observed for 2007:Q4. The 2009:Q4 trend growth is 2.9 per cent for the unconstrained trend and 1.9 per cent for the constrained trend. While rejecting the unconstrained trend as an artifact of the above-discussed structural change in labor market behavior in 2008–09, we admit that this poses a dilemma in making future forecasts. What will be the path by which the unexplained 'excess productivity' of 2009 will be eliminated? We return to that question in the final section of the chapter.

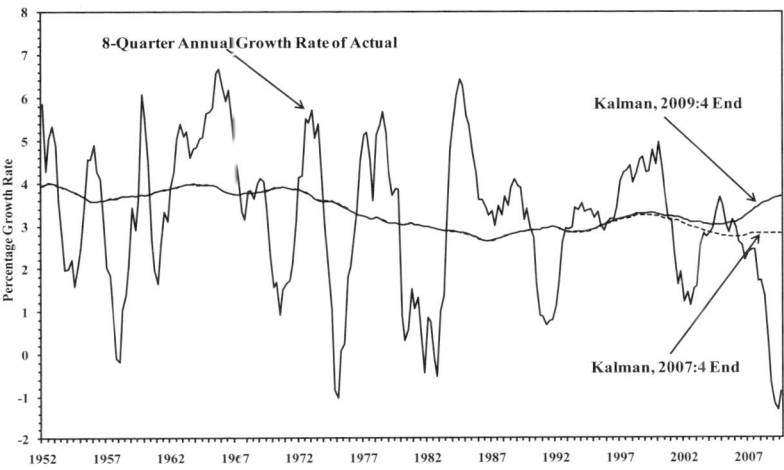

Figure 12.1   Annual growth rate of actual and trend real GDP, quarterly data, 1952: Q1 – 2009: Q4

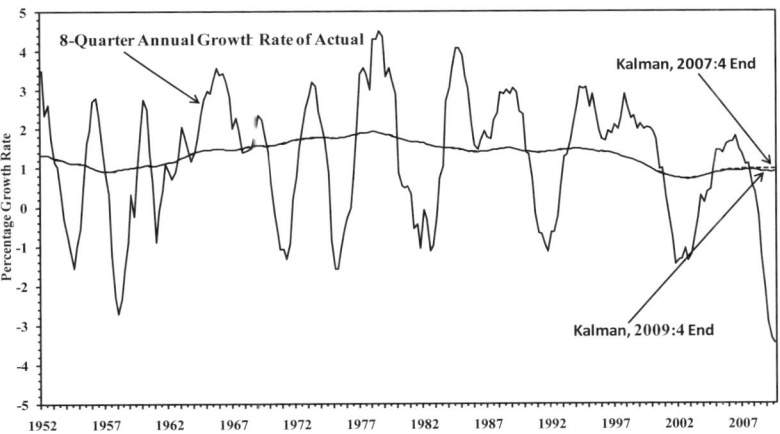

Figure 12.2   Annual growth rate of actual and trend total economy hours, quarterly data, 1952: Q1 – 2009: Q4

Sources: Refer to sources listed under Table 12.1

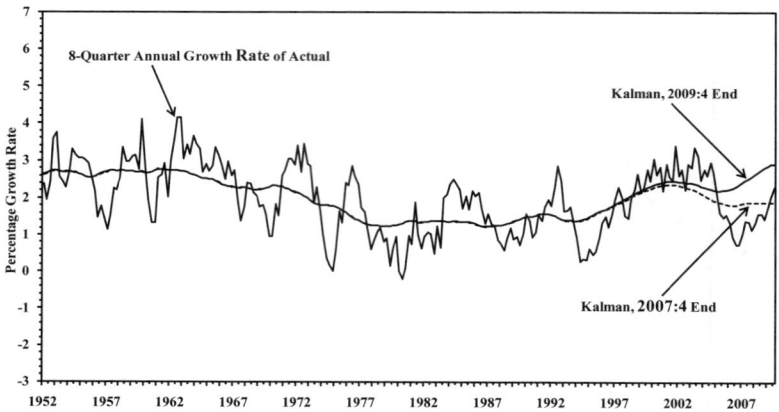

Figure 12.3   Annual growth rate of actual and trend total economy output per hour, quarterly data, 1952: Q1 – 2009: Q4

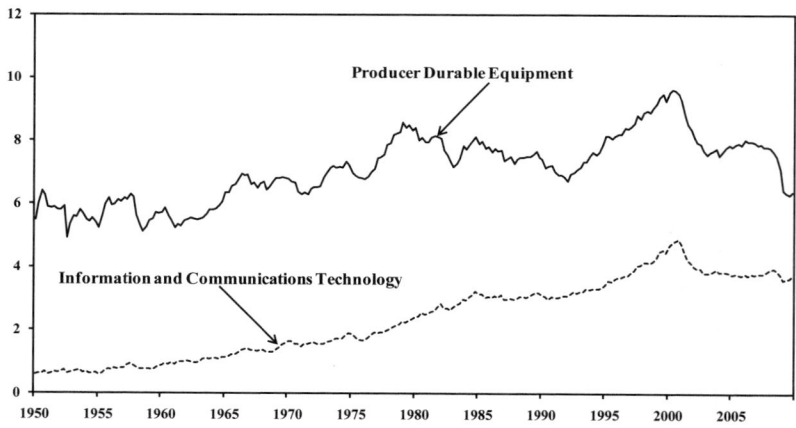

Figure 12.4   Shares in nominal GDP of investment in producer durable equipment and in information communication technology, 1950: Q1 – 2009: Q4

Sources: NIPA Tables 1.1.5 and 5.3.5.

share of capital, we obtain the standard relationship between MFP growth, labor productivity growth, and the contribution of capital deepening.

$$m = y - bk - (1 - b)n = y - n - b(k - n) \qquad (12.2)$$

Thus MFP growth can be written either as the growth rate of output minus the weighted growth rate of the two inputs, labor and capital, or alternatively as the growth rate of labor productivity $(y - n)$ minus the growth rate of the capital-deepening effect $(b(k - n))$.

12.3.1 Growth Accounting for the 1995–2000 Revival and the Post-2000 Aftermath

The literature on the post-1995 productivity growth revival goes beyond equation 12.2 by distinguishing between the contribution of capital deepening in ICT and non-ICT capital, and MFP growth in ICT and non-ICT capital. It is also conventional to estimate the component of MFP growth due to higher labor quality and to list that contribution separately. An important recent contribution is the November, 2008, update by Oliner and Sichel of their 2000 and 2002 papers (see reference list).[4]

These authors devote careful attention to the contribution of the several important categories of ICT capital. They divide up the different contributions of capital deepening by type of capital and as well subdivide the growth of MFP between the contributions of the ICT-producing sectors and the rest of the economy. Their latest calculation is displayed in Table 12.2 for three periods, the slow productivity growth period of 1973–95, the initial revival period of 1995–2000, and the subsequent interval that started with the 2001–04 productivity 'explosion' but then was followed by very slow productivity growth between 2004 and 2007. All data in both Tables 12.2 and 12.3 refer to the NFPB sector, in contrast to Table 12.1 which covers the entire economy.

Starting at the top of Table 12.2, we first observe on line 1 the upsurge of U.S. productivity growth from 1.47 per cent in 1973–95 to 2.51 per cent in the initial 'revival' in 1995–2000 and then back down only slightly to 2.48 per cent in 2000–07. The next section of the Oliner–Sichel table subdivides the total contribution of capital deepening in the three periods (i.e., the $b(k - n)$ term in equation 12.2 above) into the contributions of ICT and non-ICT capital. The 1995–2000 period was remarkable in that ICT capital contributed almost all of the capital-deepening effect, whereas ICT capital contributed about two-thirds of the capital-deepening effect prior to 1995 and after 2000.

---

[4] Table 12.2 was provided to me by Dan Sichel on February 12, 2010.

The absolute contribution of ICT capital deepening after 2000 (0.87 per cent per year on line 2) was only slightly higher than before 1995 (0.77 per cent).

Table 12.2   Decomposition of labor productivity growth and MFP percentage points, annual rate

	1973–1995	1995–2000	2000–2007
1. Output per hour	1.47	2.51	2.48
2. Capital deepening	0.77	1.13	0.87
3. ICT	0.46	1.09	0.60
4. Hardware	0.25	0.60	0.27
5. Software	0.13	0.34	0.19
6. Communications	0.07	0.15	0.13
7. Other	0.31	0.04	0.28
8. Labor quality	0.27	0.26	0.35
9. Aggregate MFP	0.43	1.13	1.26
Contribution of:			
10. ICT	0.29	0.76	0.47
11. Computer Hardware	0.12	0.19	0.09
12. Semiconductor Hardware	0.09	0.45	0.22
13. Software	0.04	0.08	0.11
14. Communications	0.04	0.04	0.04
15. Other	0.14	0.37	0.79
16. Sum of ICT Contribution (3+10)	0.75	1.85	1.07
17. Share of ICT in Total (16/1)	0.51	0.74	0.43
18. Memo: ICT Investment as % of GDP	2.67	4.19	3.95
Nominal Value-added Shares of:			
18. Computer Industry	1.10	1.50	1.01
19. Semiconductor Industry	0.40	0.90	0.61
20. Software Industry	1.00	2.40	2.60
21. Communications Industry	1.50	1.90	1.31
22. Other Sectors	96.40	94.20	94.97
MFP Annual Growth Rate in:			
23. Computer Industry	11.00	12.80	8.84
24. Semiconductor Industry	27.20	49.80	33.64
25. Software Industry	4.20	3.70	4.30
26. Communications Industry	2.40	1.90	3.29
27. Other Sectors	0.14	0.39	0.83

Sources: Unpublished update of Oliner and Sichel (2002), obtained from Daniel Sichel on February 15, 2010. Line 18 from NIPA Tables 1.1.5 and 5.3.5.

The contribution of ICT to overall productivity growth also includes the contribution of growth of MFP in the ICT industries. This also surged after 1995 and after 2000 remained substantially higher than before 1995. In particular the contribution of semiconductors and of software to overall MFP growth was substantially higher after 2000 than before 1995, while communications was the same and the contribution of computer hardware actually lower.

Oliner and Sichel's headline result is that the sum of the ICT contribution to overall productivity growth fell from 74 per cent in 1995–2000 to 43 per cent during 2000–07, a lower percentage contribution than before 1995 (see line 17). However, the absolute contribution of ICT for 2000–07 on line 16 was substantially greater than in the pre-1995 interval. The total contribution of the ICT sector to explaining the post-2000 productivity growth was negative in the sense that the ICT contribution both to capital deepening and to MFP growth declined substantially while the overall growth rate of productivity, the phenomenon to be explained, was basically flat. By definition, this implies that the continuing rapid rate of labor productivity growth after 2000 resulted from a combination of faster growth in labor quality (line 8), of capital deepening in non-ICT capital (line 7), and especially in MFP growth in the non-ICT industries.

Table 12.3   Sources of output and productivity growth, 1959–2006

	1959– 1973	1973– 1995	1995– 2000	2000– 2006
1. Private Output	4.18	3.08	4.77	3.01
2. Hours worked	1.36	1.59	2.07	0.51
3. Average labor productivity	2.82	1.49	2.70	2.50
4. Contribution of Capital Deepening	1.40	0.85	1.51	1.26
5. Information Technology	0.21	0.40	1.01	0.58
6. Non-information Technology	1.19	0.45	0.49	0.90
7. Labor Quality	0.28	0.25	0.19	0.31
8. Multi-factor Productivity	1.14	0.39	1.00	0.92
9. Information Technology	0.09	0.25	0.59	0.38
10. Non-information Technology	1.05	0.14	0.42	0.54
11. Contribution of Information Technology	0.30	0.65	1.60	0.96
12. Share Attributed to Information	0.11	0.44	0.59	0.38

Source: Jorgenson, Ho, and Stiroh (2008), Table 1.

Dale Jorgenson and co-authors (2008) arrive at similar conclusions using similar techniques. Table 12.3 displays their results in a format that is as close as possible to that of Table 12.2. Their share of ICT in explaining growth in average labor productivity is less than that of Oliner–Sichel in each period, but they concur that the share of ICT was lower after 2000 than before 1995. Their results extend back from 1973 to 1959 and show that ICT capital made virtually no contribution to economic growth before 1973, but made a greater relative contribution during 1973–95 than during 2000–06, although the absolute contribution was higher in the later period.

The most important difference between Tables 12.2 and 12.3 is that the Jorgenson team estimates the total effect of capital deepening to have been much higher in 1995–2000 (their 1.51 per cent vs. 1.09 per cent in Table 12.2) and also after 2000 (their 1.26 per cent vs. 0.87 per cent in Table 12.2). All of this difference is attributed to the non-ICT part of the economy, with post-2000 non-ICT capital deepening 0.90 per cent in Table 12.3 vs. 0.28 per cent in Table 12.2. Offsetting the higher estimate of the capital deepening effect are lower estimates of MFP growth especially after 2000 (0.92 per cent in Table 12.3 vs. 1.26 per cent in Table 12.2).

Whatever the reason for Oliner and Sichel's larger estimates of MFP growth and the Jorgenson et al. larger estimates of the capital-deepening effect outside of the ICT sector, there remains the task of explaining why productivity growth remained robust after 2000 despite the collapse of the ICT investment boom. What caused MFP growth in the non-ICT part of the economy to grow so rapidly in 2000–2006/7 relative to its much slower growth prior to 1995?

12.3.2   Substantive Explanations of What Happened after 2000

The upsurge of productivity growth between late 2001 and mid-2004, and its much more moderate growth rate during 2004–07, supports the interpretation offered in Gordon (2003). This explanation had two key components. First, I argued that the most important cause of the productivity growth upsurge in 2001–03 was an unusual degree of downward pressure on profits that led to aggressive cost cutting by business firms. A second explanation was the role of intangible capital that contributed a source of lagged response of productivity growth to the ICT boom of the late 1990s.

The first explanation (see Gordon, 2003, pp. 247–49) relies on the unusual trajectory of corporate profits in 1992–2003 that was initially examined by Nordhaus (2002). While National Income (NIPA) profits peaked in 1997 and declined after that as a share of national income, the stock market focused on the measure of profits compiled by the Standard and Poors (S&P) corporation as part of their compilation of the S&P 500 stock market average. S&P

profits grew by 70 per cent between early 1998 and early 2000 and then declined by more than half between early 2000 and early 2001. Nordhaus attributes a substantial role in this 'most unusual pattern' to a wide variety of shady accounting tricks to which corporations turned as they desperately attempted to pump up reported profits during 1998–2000 in an environment in which true profits were declining. In Nordhaus' words, these tricks led to the 'enrichment of the few and depleted pension plans of the many'. The stock market bubble between 1997–2000 can be explained in part by the divergence between NIPA and S&P profits.

The unusual trajectory of S&P reported profits in 1998–2001 placed unusual pressure on corporate managers to cut costs and reduce employment after 2000. During the 1990s corporate compensation had shifted to relying substantially on stock options, leading first to the temptation to engage in accounting tricks during 1998–2000 to maintain the momentum of earnings growth, and then sheer desperation to cut costs in response to the post-2000 collapse in reported S&P earnings and in the stock market. The stock market collapse had an independent effect on the pressure for corporate cost cutting, beyond its effect on the stock-option portion of executive compensation, by shifting many corporate-sponsored defined-benefit pension plans from overfunded to underfunded status.

A plausible interpretation of the unusual upsurge of productivity growth in 2001–03, then, is that it was the counterpart of an unusual degree of pressure for corporate cost cutting, in turn caused by the role of accounting scandals and corporate write-offs that led to the unusual trajectory of reported S&P profits relative to NIPA profits. The unprecedented nature of corporate cost cutting was widely recognized at the time. As the Wall Street Journal put it:

> The mildness of the recession masked a ferocious corporate profits crunch that has many chief executives still slashing jobs and other costs.   Many CEOs were so traumatized by last year's profits debacle that they are paring costs rather than planning plant expansions (Hilsenrath, 2002, 1st April, A1).

After I had suggested the 'savage cost–cutting hypothesis' in my 2003 paper, Oliner, Sichel and Stiroh (2007) suggested an interesting test. They showed with cross-section industry data that those firms that had experienced the largest declines in profits between 1997 and 2002 also exhibited the most significant declines in employment and increases in productivity. While it is difficult to translate a concept like 'draconian cost cutting' into the context of time-series macro analysis, the Oliner et al. evidence using micro data across industries does lend credibility to the basic idea.

This chain of causation from the profits debacle to the 2002–03 productivity surge seems plausible as the leading explanation of the unusual productivity behavior that cannot, as we have seen in Tables 12.2 and 12.3, be explained by ICT investment. But it raises a central question: How were corporate managers able to maintain output growth while cutting input costs so aggressively? One explanation is that the heady atmosphere of overstated profits and an accompanying stock market boom in the late 1990s caused corporations to become overstaffed with layers of unproductive employees. A complementary explanation is that some of the productivity benefits of the ICT investments of the late 1990s had delayed effects that lasted into the years (2001–03) after ICT investment itself collapsed.

The idea that some of the benefits of ICT investment were delayed is compatible with the influential Paul David (1990) 'delay' hypothesis that he applied in parallel to the development of electricity generating (when the payoff in manufacturing productivity in the 1920s was delayed 40 or more years after the invention) and to the development of the computer. The Oliner–Sichel and Jorgenson et al. estimates in Tables 12.2 and 12.3 require that the full productivity payoff from the use of ICT capital occurs at the exact moment that the computer is produced. Assuming no delay between production and installation, the computer produces its ultimate productivity benefit on the first day of use.

Subsequent research after David's insightful paper has suggested that the full impacts of great inventions like electricity, the internal combustion engine, and in this case the marriage of personal computers with the internet, may take a substantial time to come to fruition (see Gordon 2000b). The full impact of electricity took more than 50 years to occur, waiting on the complementary inventions of consumer appliances, radio, TV, and air conditioning. The full impact of the internal combustion engine required the complementary inventions of supermarkets and superhighways. Similarly, many of the complementary innovations made possible by the invention of the internet came to fruition in 2001–04 after the investment boom had collapsed, including the notable example of the airport lobby electronic check-in kiosk that barely existed in 2000 but by 2005 was universal. Several authors have gone further than David's 'delay' hypothesis by modeling the role of business learning, that they call 'intangible capital', in shifting the time path of the investment and the payoff of those investments.[5]

12.3.3   Implications of Explanations for Future Growth

To speculate in 2003 about the causes of the then-evolving productivity growth explosion was risky, but as the data evolved between 2003 and 2007 those hypotheses seem more plausible. The pressure on costs and to layoff

---

[5]   See Basu, Fernald, Oulton, and Srinivasan (2003); and Yang and Brynjolfsson (2001).

workers reached a peak in 2001–2002, and productivity growth exploded. After 2003 profits have increased rapidly and productivity growth slowed dramatically. The 'intangible capital' hypothesis is also inherently temporary unless a second era of rapid increases in ICT investment occurs, but that did not happen after 2001.

Viewed in retrospect the 2001–04 productivity growth explosion increasingly looks like a one-off, unique, temporary phenomenon. In particular, I find ever less plausible the view, common in the late 1990s, that ICT investment had a magic quality that would break through all previous boundaries set by the scarcity of economic resources. Doubtless the invention of the internet has revolutionized industries ranging from university libraries to bookshops, but that revolution is over. University libraries have already replaced card catalogues by computer terminals, and Amazon (together with Barnes and Noble and Borders) has already achieved its goal of pushing independent bookshops out of business. In turn, Amazon has come close to pushing Borders out of business.

My interpretation of the ICT revolution is that it is increasingly burdened by diminishing returns. The push to ever-smaller devices runs up against the fixed size of the human finger that must enter information on the device. Most of the innovations since 2000 have been directed to consumer enjoyment rather than business productivity, including video games, DVD players, and iPods. iPhones are nice, but the ability to reschedule business meetings and look up corporate documents while on the road already existed by 2003. Readers of this chapter who actively create economic research might ask themselves what has happened to improve their productivity since the invention of 'Office 97' (including MS Word and Excel), other than the arrival in their home offices of broadband internet in contrast to the feeble dial-up connections of the late 1990s?

And what about Europe? Europeans use cell phones and web connections as much or more than Americans (admittedly with substantial variation between Scandinavia and the Olive Belt). But what good has this done? As they have adopted their desktops and laptops equipped with Intel processors and Microsoft software. Europeans have experienced a steady slowing in the growth rate of their output per hour, and indeed of their output per capita. The failure of Europeans to achieve accelerated growth in productivity after 1995, as occurred in the U.S., shifts the focus of causal explanations away from universal technological advances such as the internet, to country-specific environmental factors that encourage or discourage growth. The Groningen research (see especially Timmer et al. 2010) that has made us aware of the enormous difference between productivity growth in U.S. vs. EU retailing, despite the universal adoption of bar-code scanning, has pointed to non-electronic sources of cross-country differences, starting with land-use restrictions and planning.[6] This author walks around the central cities of Europe and notices many things, but particularly the protection of ancient inner-city shopping districts in which basic commodities are sold in cramped aisles and with less self-service than in the median American retailer.

The goal of this chapter is to make forecasts 20 years ahead of growth in US output per hour and potential GDP. So far interesting issues have been identified without resolution. The first section devoted to the quarterly data and output identity leaves open whether the unique 2008–09 gap between a repeat explosion of actual productivity growth and the constrained trend growth in productivity will be followed by a subsequent radical slowdown, just as the 2001–04 explosion was followed by the subsequent 2004–07 slowdown. The second section which identified the disconnect between ICT investment and the post-2000 U.S. productivity growth experience makes the 2001–04 'explosion' look temporary rather than permanent and adds urgency to our need to determine which part of pre-1995 history is relevant to forecasting productivity growth into the future. This suggests a strong motivation to re-examine the twentieth century history of growth in output, labor productivity, and MFP.

12.4   A RE-EXAMINATION OF TWENTIETH CENTURY HISTORY

We now turn to a longer-term perspective on economic growth since the late nineteenth century. We begin with a simple calculation of output, conventional inputs, and MFP growth for 1891–2007, dividing up those 115 years into nine subintervals between benchmark years that are chosen to be cyclically neutral and thus to skip over years influenced by war, recessions, or depressions. These data are then compared for the postwar period with the BLS computations of MFP growth that implement adjustments for capital composition, the so-called 'capital quality' correction that has long been advocated by Dale Jorgenson and his co-authors. Building on earlier research in Gordon (2000a), we attempt to extend adjustments for capital and labor quality back before 1948 and in addition to make additional adjustments to the quantity of capital input.

---

[6] The first policy recommendation in Baily and Kirkegaard (2004, p. 7–8) is to reform land–use planning in Europe.

12.4.1   BEA and Kendrick Data for MFP since 1891

The results of our initial data exercise are displayed in Table 12.4 for the non-farm private non-housing economy. The concept of labor is total hours and for capital is the total capital stock, with structures and equipment weighted equally using inflation-adjusted dollar weights. There are no adjustments for changes in labor or capital quality. Benchmark years are chosen to be 1891, 1913, 1928, 1950, 1964, 1972, 1979, 1988, 1996, and 2007. Current NIPA data are linked to Kendrick's (1961) data in 1929 for output, in 1948 for labor input, and in 1925 for capital input.

The top section of Table 12.4 exhibits our newly calculated results with NIPA data current as of February, 2010. The middle section displays results for the same concepts and time intervals in the 'old' (pre-1999) data used by Gordon (2000a, Table 12.1), and the bottom section displays the difference between the growth rates based respectively on the new and old data. The theme of the earlier paper was the 'one big wave' of US MFP growth that began around the time of World War I, peaked in the 1928–50 interval, and then ebbed after 1972. One notes in the old data that MFP growth increased after 1913 and again after 1928 and then slowed successively after 1950, 1964, and 1972.

There are three important differences in the new data. First, the crescendo in 1928–50 is substantially stronger than before, with MFP growth in that interval 1.85 points higher than in 1913–28 (compared with 0.48 points in the old data) and 1.61 points higher than in 1950–64 (compared with 0.43 points in the old data). In the bottom section we note that data revisions have increased the growth rates for the 1928–50 interval by 1.33, -0.24, 1.26, and 1.46 for output, labor, capital, and MFP, respectively.[7] Second, for the period after 1964 output growth has been revised upwards more than the data on labor and capital, implying substantial upward revisions of MFP growth. Third, and most obviously, we now have 11 more years of data after the previous terminal year of 1996, and the resulting rate of MFP growth in 1996–2007 is faster than in any other interval shown but the 1928–50 'big wave' period, although MFP growth in 1996–2007 is only moderately faster than the third–place interval 1950–64.

---

[7]   The NIPA revisions for 1929–48 were introduced in the benchmark revision of August, 1999. They combine the influence of chain-weighted deflators that increase more slowly than the previous fixed-weight deflators, and in addition the growth rate of nominal GDP was revised upwards.

Table 12.4 Output, inputs, and MFP growth, non-farm non-housing private economy, new and old data, 1891–2007

Years	Output	Labor	Capital	MFP
New data				
1891–1913	4.48	2.68	4.46	1.26
1913–1928	3.13	1.10	2.84	1.51
1928–1950	4.08	0.67	0.86	3.36
1950–1964	3.51	1.16	3.18	1.75
1964–1972	4.18	1.85	4.52	1.53
1972–1979	3.70	2.34	3.63	0.98
1979–1988	3.06	1.47	3.40	1.01
1988–1996	2.92	1.47	2.38	1.18
1996–2007	3.60	1.15	2.82	1.95
Old data				
1891–1913	4.43	2.92	3.85	1.14
1913–1928	3.11	1.42	2.21	1.42
1928–1950	2.75	0.91	0.74	1.90
1950–1964	3.50	1.41	2.89	1.47
1964–1972	3.63	1.82	4.08	0.89
1972–1979	2.99	2.38	3.46	0.16
1979–1988	2.55	1.09	3.35	0.59
1988–1996	2.74	1.74	2.26	0.79
Difference between new and old data				
1891–1913	0.05	-0.24	0.61	0.12
1913–1928	0.02	-0.32	0.63	0.09
1928–1950	1.33	-0.24	0.12	1.46
1950–1964	0.01	-0.25	0.29	0.28
1964–1972	0.55	0.03	0.44	0.64
1972–1979	0.71	-0.04	0.17	0.82
1979–1988	0.51	0.38	0.05	0.42
1988–1996	0.18	-0.27	0.12	0.39

Sources: Private non-farm non-housing Output: From 1929 the source is non-farm private business output in 2005 dollars from NIPA Table 1.3.6 minus gross housing value added from line 14 of the same table. For 1891–1929 the source is Kendrick (1961), Table A–III, p. 298 for GDP minus government and farm output, but not excluding housing output.
Labor Input: From 1948 the source is hours worked in the non-farm private business economy from NIPA Table 6.9 minus hours worked in real estate, where the latter takes real estate persons engaged from NIPA Table 6.8 and applies hours worked per employee for the broader finance, insurance, and real estate sector from Table 6.9. For 1891–1948 the source is private non-farm manhours from Kendrick (1961), Table A–XXIII p. 338.
Capital Input: From 1925 the source is Tables 4.1 and 4.2 of the Fixed Assets section of the BEA web site. For 1891–1925 the source is non-farm private non-residential capital stock from Kendrick (1961), Table A–XVI, p. 323.
Multifactor Productivity Growth: This is calculated from output, labor input, and capital input, by using uniform weights of 0.7 for labor and 0.3 for capital.

12.4.2 BEA Data Compared with BLS MFP Data, with and without Composition Adjustments

If we were interested only in the growth of labor productivity and of MFP for the postwar years, we would not need to put together data series from the BEA and Kendrick sources, because the BLS has already done the job for us for the years since 1948. Our previous examination of the BEA–Kendrick series originates in our interest in what happened to growth in labor productivity and in MFP for the years before 1948.

The BLS calculates MFP by subtracting from output growth not only the growth of labor hours and growth in the capital stock, but it also subtracts the contribution of changes in labor and capital composition. Its labor composition adjustment is based on subdividing the labor force into cells by age, gender, and educational attainment, and then weighting by the labor compensation earned in each cell. Thus a shift in composition toward more educated workers yields a positive labor composition adjustment, while the increase in the share of teenagers in the 1960s and 1970s caused by the baby boom creates a negative labor composition adjustment. The BLS capital composition adjustment results from aggregating different components of the capital stock (structures, ICT equipment, non-ICT equipment, inventories, and land) using weights based on the user cost of capital. Because of rapid depreciation, one dollar of ICT equipment receives a higher weight than one dollar of non-ICT equipment, which in turn receives a higher weight than one dollar of structures.

The basic series released by the BLS contain data only on their composition-adjusted 'labor input' (as contrasted to labor hours) and 'capital services' (as contrasted to the capital stock). However, the BLS web site has extensive information that allows us to create Table 12.5 and to compare BLS series with their BEA counterparts used in Table 12.4. The middle section of Table 12.5 simply copies the BEA post-1950 growth rates of output, inputs, and MFP from the top section of Table 12.4. Then the top section of Table 12.5 reports BLS growth rates for output and for labor and capital inputs *without composition adjustments*. Except for measurement and definitional issues, these should be the same as their BEA counterparts in the middle section. Also reported is the growth rate of BLS 'non-adjusted MFP', using the BLS income shares to calculate MFP growth by subtracting growth in unadjusted labor hours and the unadjusted capital stock.

Table 12.5   BEA and BLS Data on output, inputs, and MFP growth, non-farm non-housing private economy, 1950–2007

BLS MFP Data

Years	Output	Labor hours	Capital stock	non-Adj MFP	Contributions of		Adj MFP
					Labor composition	Capital composition	
1950–1964	3.70	1.03	1.99	2.36	0.27	0.43	1.66
1964–1972	4.22	1.68	3.27	2.05	-0.01	0.53	1.54
1972–1979	3.69	2.19	3.09	1.23	0.00	0.45	0.78
1979–1988	3.15	1.63	3.06	1.08	0.33	0.60	0.15
1988–1996	2.97	1.32	1.98	1.44	0.42	0.50	0.52
1996–2007	3.32	0.84	2.47	1.95	0.23	0.53	1.19

BEA Data

Years	Output	Labor	Capital	MFP
1950–1964	3.51	1.16	3.18	1.75
1964–1972	4.18	1.85	4.52	1.53
1972–1979	3.70	2.34	3.63	0.98
1979–1988	3.06	1.47	3.40	1.01
1988–1996	2.92	1.47	2.38	1.18
1996–2007	3.60	1.15	2.82	1.95

BLS minus BEA

Years	Output	Labor	Capital	MFP
1950–1964	0.19	-0.13	-1.19	0.62
1964–1972	0.04	-0.16	-1.25	0.52

Table 12.5 (Continued)

BLS minus BEA

Years	Output	Labor	Capital	MFP
1950—1964	0.19	-0.13	-1.19	0.62
1964—1972	0.04	-0.16	-1.25	0.52
1972—1979	-0.01	-0.15	-0.54	0.26
1979—1988	0.09	0.16	-0.34	0.07

Sources: All data were obtained from the BLS web site. Growth rates for 1950–88 were calculated from a text file "mfp2ddod.txt" available for the discontinued SIC-basis data for 1948–2002, and growth rates for 1988–2007 were calculated from a downloadable Excel file "mfptables.xls", except for those associated with capital stock, which was acquired through the efforts of Randy Kinoshita of the BLS. These tables provide separate series on hours, composition-adjusted labor input, and the size of the labor composition adjustment. They also provide separate series on capital services and the size of the capital composition effect, allowing the capital stock to be calculated indirectly for 1950–1966. The income shares of labor and capital are included, allowing MFP to be calculated either with unadjusted labor hours and the capital stock, or the adjusted series on labor input and capital services.

The three right-hand columns of the top section report the contributions to output growth of the labor and capital composition adjustments. Note that the labor composition adjustment is essentially zero during 1964–79, when the baby-boomers entered the labor force as inexperienced teenagers. The labor composition adjustment was also held down between 1964 and 1988 by the entry of females into the labor force. Given the increasing importance of computers in recent years, it is somewhat surprising that the capital composition contribution was roughly similar in each of the six periods.[8] Presumably the shift from structures to equipment in the early part of the postwar years was as important as the shift from long-lived non-ICT equipment to short-lived ICT equipment in the period since 1988.

The final column in the top section reports the 'adjusted' growth rate of MFP, that is, the officially reported BLS series on MFP growth that incorporates the composition adjustments. Because the composition adjustments sum to a positive number ranging between 0.52 percentage points to 0.93 per cent, the adjusted MFP growth rate is always lower than the unadjusted MFP growth rate.

The bottom section of Table 12.5 subtracts the BEA-based numbers from the unadjusted BLS numbers, and we find differences that are surprisingly large. While differences for output and labor hours are quite small, differences for growth in the capital stock are relatively large and always negative, while differences for MFP are always positive and relatively large in the first two periods, 1950–64 and 1964–72, albeit nearly zero in the intervals 1979–88 and 1996–2007. Some part of the differences may be due to a differing treatment of residential capital, since our BEA series exclude all residential capital while the BLS includes residential income-generating rental property.

12.4.3   Adjustments for Labor Composition Prior to 1950

This section develops composition adjustments for labor and capital in the period prior to 1950 and also calculates additional adjustments to the quantity of capital. Each of the adjustments made in this section is based on the analysis of Gordon (2000a, pp. 61–73), and there is no new research here other than to apply the previous research to the revised data summarized above in Table 12.4.

---

[8] The numbers shown in the top right section of Table 12.5 are not the composition adjustments themselves but rather their contributions, calculated by multiplying the labor and capital composition adjustments by the income shares of labor and capital, respectively.

The first adjustment is for labor quality and is based on the extensive analysis carried out by Edward F. Denison in his well-known books on the sources of U.S. economic growth. We reject two of Denison's (1962) controversial assumptions, first that effort per hour increased as hours per week decreased between 1909 and 1957, and second that part of the reward to educational attainment reflects innate ability rather than the contribution of education itself. While either assumption is debatable, neither is adopted by the BLS in their postwar data on MFP growth, and we want to adhere as closely as possible to the BLS approach.

Table 12.6   Adjustments for changes in labor composition, selected intervals

	1913 –28	1928 –50	1950 –64	1964 –72	1972 –79
1. Denison composition adjustment for hours	0.39	0.42	0.18	0.19	0.14
2. Denison composition adjustment for education	0.57	0.62	0.60	0.67	0.75
3. Denison composition adjustment for age, gender	0.11	0.02	-0.06	-0.45	-0.47
4. Alternative education adjustment	0.49	0.48	0.54	0.71	0.84
5. Alternative total labor composition adjustment (equals line 3 + line 4)	0.60	0.50	0.48	0.25	0.37
6. BLS composition adjustment			0.39	-0.01	0.00

Sources: The Denison adjustments were copied from Gordon (2000a), Table 3. The BLS composition adjustments were taken from the same sources as Table 12.5.

The first line in Table 12.6 shows the Denison hours adjustment, based on the assumption that the elasticity of productivity (i.e., the effectiveness of an hour of work) to declining labor hours declined steadily from a negative unity in 1913–28 to about -0.2 in 1972–79. The second line shows his adjustment for educational attainment which includes two components that are not part of current BLS practice. First, he adjusts for increasing educational attainment using earnings weights but then multiplies the result by 0.6, assuming that the remaining 0.4 of earnings differences reflects innate ability rather than the contribution of education. Second, he assumes that any percentage increase in the number of school days per year has the same effect on productivity as a similar percentage increase in the number of school years per person. Our alternative education adjustment displayed on line four eliminates Denison's adjustments for the length of the school year and for ability.[9]

Our alternative labor composition adjustment includes the alternative education component and Denison's age–gender effect, that is, line five is the sum of lines three and line four. For comparison we show the BLS labor composition adjustments for the post-1950 and note that they are uniformly lower, perhaps because their data (obviously more recent than Denison's) places more importance on the negative age–sex adjustment and less importance on the positive correction for educational attainment.[10]

12.4.4   Adjustments for Capital Composition before 1950

The BLS makes adjustments for the composition of capital in its postwar MFP data by weighting each type of capital by its user cost. Pending further research on the user cost of capital prior to 1950, we calculate a capital composition adjustment in this section by a rough approximation. The BLS capital composition effect reflects both the rising share of short-lived equipment to structures, and the rising share of short-lived ICT equipment within the total of capital equipment. To determine the relative importance of the composition effect before 1950, we have recalculated our BEA capital stocks alternatively with equal dollar weights and with a weight of three dollars on each dollar of equipment and one dollar for each dollar of structures.

In Table 12.7 the first column shows that the growth rate of capital with the 3:1 recalculation in 1928–50 is 0.27 per cent faster than with the basic 1:1 calculation. Comparing the average growth rate of the 3:1 effect in the 1950–2007 interval with the BLS capital composition effect, we find that the average growth rate of the 3:1 correction in Table 12.7 is 0.50 per cent per year, much lower than the BLS capital composition adjustment that averages 1.57 per cent per year over the same 1950–2007 period. Accordingly, we backcast the BLS capital composition adjustment from 1950 back to 1891 by multiplying column (1) for that period by 1.57/0.50. The result is shown on the first three lines of column (2) in Table 12.7.

---

[9] Eliminating the ability adjustment for 1913–28 in Denison (1962) requires dividing his adjustment for increasing school years by 0.6, whereas after 1928 the correction is applied to another book, Denison (1979), and involves dividing through by 0.8.

[10] A labor composition effect of 0.5 is applied to the pre-1913 period to reflect increasing educational attainment, particularly at the elementary school level, as explained in Gordon (2003), pp. 65–66.

Table 12.7 Adjustments to capital input growth for changes in capital composition, variable retirement, and highway/GOPO capital, selected intervals

	Reweight equipment 3–to–1 (1)	Backcast BLS comp. adjustment (2)	Effect of variable retirement (3)	Add GOPO capital (4)	Add highway capital (5)	Total capital adjustment (6)
1891–1913	-0.29	-0.97				-0.97
1913–1928	0.09	0.31			0.35	0.66
1928–1950	0.27	0.92	0.86	0.14	0.18	2.09
1950–1964	0.32	1.33	-0.98	-0.12	0.29	0.52
1964–1972	0.72	1.64	-0.64	-0.09	0.24	1.15
1972–1979	0.75	1.41	-0.21	-0.07	-0.12	1.00
1979–1988	0.18	1.89	-0.16	-0.05	-0.23	1.45
1988–1996	0.47	1.56	0.22		-0.08	1.70
1996–2007	0.67	1.67				1.67

Sources by Column:

(1) The BLS capital composition adjustment comes from the same sources as Table 12.5 for 1950–2007. The capital composition adjustment for 1913–50 computed in column (1) is divided by the 1950–2007 ratio of column (1) to column (2), namely 0.30.

(2) The stock of BEA equipment and nonresidential structures used to compute the capital stock in Table 12.4 was reweighted by multiplying the real dollar value of equipment by three. The difference between the annual growth rate of the reweighted and unweighted capital stocks is the capital composition effect in column (2).

(3) The ratio of the variable retirement capital stock to the fixed retirement capital stock was taken separately for structures and equipment from Gordon (2000a), p. 72. These ratios were applied to the revised BEA capital stock data used in the calculations of Table 12.4.

(4) GOPO capital was taken from Wasson, Musgrave, and Harkins (1970), Table 7 and restated from 1958 to 2000 dollars.

(5) Highway capital data for 1921 to 1995 was provided by Barbara Fraumeni

(6) Column (6) is the sum of columns (2) through (5).

12.4.5 Revising the Quantity of Capital

An important error in standard measures of capital input is the assumption that service lifetimes are fixed. Yet Feldstein and Rothschild (1974) have argued from a theoretical perspective that a fixed retirement pattern is not optimal, and Feldstein and Foot (1971) showed on the basis of firm-level data that retirement patterns are variable and depend on firm cash flow and on the state of the economy-wide business cycle. The issue of variable retirement was mainly important between 1930 and 1950 when gross fixed investment was very low. Standard capital measures assume that structures and equipment were being retired during 1930–50 on a fixed schedule even though nothing was being built or purchased to replace the capital that was allegedly being retired. Yet Chicago's Loop and Manhattan's Midtown were not littered with vacant lots during the 1930s and 1940s; the old buildings were still there, and so was the old equipment which made such a contribution to America's production achievement during World War II.

The method developed in Gordon (2000a) is to make the ratio of retirements to capital, relative to its historic mean, depend on the ratio of gross investment to capital, also relative to its historic mean. This procedure implies that retirements are reshuffled among the years between 1925 and 1996, but that the average retirement rate over the entire period is maintained at the same level as in the BEA data. The effect as shown in column (4) of Table 12.7 is substantially to raise the growth rate of capital in the 1928–50 period and to reduce it thereafter. The data for this adjustment are taken from Gordon (2000a) and no further calculations have been made for the period since 1996.

Two types of capital financed by the government enter the production function of the private business economy and should be included in private capital input. Part of the sharp rise in U.S. output during World War II was made possible by government-owned privately-operated (GOPO) capital. Initially the government did not keep track of this stock of capital, but after I studied this phenomenon and estimated its magnitude (Gordon, 1969), the BEA began to keep track of GOPO capital and provides estimates that we can use in this historical retrospective (see Wasson, Musgrave, and Harkins, 1970). GOPO capital makes a small addition to the growth of capital input in 1928–50 and then reduces it after 1950 as the wartime plants (many of which were converted to civilian use in the late 1940s) were eventually retired.

A related problem is that a substantial part of government-owned infrastructure serves as an unmeasured input to production in the private sector. Over the twentieth century there was a gradual shift over time in the transportation sector from privately-owned railroad capital to government-owned highways, airports, and air-traffic control facilities. We rely on Fraumeni's (2007) estimates of highway capital. As shown in column (5) of Table 12.7, highway capital added to the growth rate of capital input in each period before 1972 and reduced capital input growth thereafter.

The total adjustment to capital input varies over time but reaches by far its highest impact in the 'big wave' period of 1928–50, due to the combined effects of capital composition, variable retirement, GOPO capital, and highway capital. The effect was smallest in 1950–64 when the variable retirement effect was being reversed. The capital adjustment was substantially higher in 1988–2007 than in 1950–88, mainly because the negative impact of variable retirement and GOPO capital by then had faded away.

12.4.6   Alternative Measures of MFP Growth

The end result of the research in this section has been to develop several adjustments to the growth of labor and capital input. For the period since 1950 the labor and capital composition effects are taken from the BLS, and we develop composition effects by similar methods that are applied to the period 1891–1950. In addition we make three adjustments to the growth of capital input that go beyond the BLS methodology by adjusting for variable retirement, GOPO capital, and highway capital.

Table 12.8 displays the results. Column (1) shows the same unadjusted growth in MFP as was displayed in the top section of Table 12.4. Column (2) incorporates the labor composition adjustments from Table 12.6, line five for 1913–50, with the average of 1913–50 backcast to 1891. For 1950–2007 the contribution of the labor composition adjustment is taken directly from the top section of Table 12.5, where the BLS source has already multiplied by labor's income share. Columns (3–5) further adjust for the corrections in capital input growth from Table 12.7, multiplied by a capital income share of 0.32.

Column (5) shows the growth in MFP with the full set of adjustments, and column (6) shows the difference made by the full set of adjustments. The largest downward adjustments are in the 'big wave' period when unadjusted MFP growth was the highest, but there is no consistent tendency for the adjustments to be negatively correlated with unadjusted MFP growth. The 'big wave' period 1928–50 retains its first place in column (5) by a substantial margin. The adjustments tend to create a rough uniformity in MFP growth across five of the remaining periods including 1891–1928, 1950–72, and 1996–2007, with an average adjusted MFP growth rate in these intervals of 1.12 per cent per year.

These successful periods for adjusted MFP growth contrast with the dismal slowdown years of 1972–96 when adjusted MFP growth was only 0.33 per cent per year. A difficult problem in forecasting into the next decade or two is to determine which of the previous time intervals are relevant.

Table 12.8 Alternative measures of MFP growth for non-farm non-housing business GDP, annual growth rates for selected intervals, 1891–2007

	Standard inputs (1)	Add labor composition adjustment (2)	Add capital composition adjustment (3)	Add variable retirement (4)	Add GOPO and highway capital (5)	Total impact of labor and capital adjustments (6) = (5) - (1)
1891–1913	1.26	0.92	1.23	1.23	1.06	-0.20
1913–1928	1.51	1.10	1.01	1.01	0.89	-0.62
1928–1950	3.36	3.02	2.72	2.45	2.35	-1.01
1950–1964	1.75	1.48	1.06	1.37	1.32	-0.43
1964–1972	1.53	1.53	1.00	1.21	1.16	-0.37
1972–1979	0.98	0.98	0.52	0.59	0.65	-0.32
1979–1988	1.01	0.68	0.08	0.13	0.22	-0.79
1988v1996	1.18	0.77	0.27	0.20	0.18	-1.00
1996–2007	1.95	1.72	1.19	1.25	1.25	-0.70
1891–2007	1.79	1.50	1.25	1.25	1.19	-0.60

Sources: Column (1) is identical to MFP growth in the top section of Table 12.4. Column (2) is equal to column (1) minus the labor income share times the labor composition adjustment, from the BLS after 1950 and as reported in line 5 of Table 12.6 before 1950. Column (3) is equal to column (2) minus the capital income share times the capital composition adjustment, from Table 12.7, column (1). Column (4) is equal to column (3) minus the capital income share times the effect of variable retirement as calculated in Table 12.7, column (3). Column (5) is equal to column (4) minus the capital income share times the effect of GOPO and highway capital as calculated in Table 12.7, columns (4) and (5).
Note that in Table 12.8 the capital income shares are taken from the BLS MFP sources used in Table 12.5 for each interval of the postwar period and are extrapolated before 1950 by taking the 1950 shares of roughly 0.68 for labor and 0.32 for capital.

What do these results for MFP growth imply for labor productivity growth? A glance back at the BLS data in Table 12.5 show that the difference between unadjusted growth in output per hour and BLS-adjusted MFP growth over the full 1950–2005 period is 1.07 per cent with relatively little variation across periods. Over the past 116 years the adjusted growth rate of MFP from Table 12.8, column 5, has been 1.19 per cent per year, which added to the 1.07 would yield a 'normal' growth rate in unadjusted labor productivity of 1.07+1.19 or about 2.26 per cent per year. By coincidence this is very close to the actual growth rate of NFPB output per hour of 2.23 per cent between 1997 and 2007.

The results on adjusted MFP growth raise numerous questions about which vast amounts have been written. Why was adjusted MFP growth so low between 1972 and 1996 and so high between 1928 and 1950? Should we accept a 'normal rate' of adjusted MFP growth of 1.12 per cent as occurred in five of our nine intervals? These issues are discussed in the next section as we attempt to forecast the main magnitudes for the next 20 years.

Table 12.9   Alternative estimates of MFP growth in the NFPB sector, 1972–2007

	Slowdown period	Revival period
BLS from Table 12.5 (1972–96 and 1996–2007)	0.46	1.19
Oliner–Sichel from Table 12.2 (1973–95 and 1995–2007)	0.43	1.21
Jorgenson–Ho–Stiroh from Table 12.3 (1973–95 and 1995–2006)	0.39	0.96
Gordon from Table 12.8 (1972–96 and 1996–2007)	0.33	1.25

How does the adjusted BLS growth rate of MFP for the post-1972 period in Table 12.8 compare for similar time intervals with the Oliner–Sichel estimates reported in Table 12.2 and the Jorgenson et al. estimates reported in Table 12.3? Table 12.9 has four lines reporting in order: the official BLS estimates from Table 12.5, the Oliner–Sichel estimates from Table 12.2, the Jorgenson et al. estimates from Table 12.3, and our adjusted estimates from Table 12.8. The exact years covered by each source are shown in the row labels. The range of estimates for 1972/73 to 1995/96 is quite narrow between 0.33 per cent and 0.46 per cent. The range of estimates for 1995/96 to 2006/07 is wider, but if the low Jorgenson numbers are excluded the range between 1.19 and 1.25 per cent is very narrow. Table 12.9 serves as background to our attempt to pull hints from historical data that are relevant to our task of creating forecasts for 2007–27.

12.5   LEARNING FROM THE PAST TO FORECAST THE FUTURE: PRODUCTIVITY AND REAL GDP GROWTH 2007–2027

One stands on relatively solid ground when talking about the past, but at least initially feels as if floating in a haze when looking out 20 years into the future. But an examination of data in this chapter going back to 1891 yields several possible criteria to bound the likely growth rates of labor productivity and of MFP in the future.

12.5.1   Aspects of the Record, 1987–2007 as contrasted with 2000–2007

Our forecasts are developed in steps within the format of Table 12.10. The left two columns record annual growth rates of the central variables for 1987:Q4 to 2007:Q4, and the two middle columns record growth rates for 2000:Q4 to 2007:Q4. Two columns are shown for each time interval, the first reporting data on the total economy as displayed in Table 12.1, and the second reporting current BLS data for the NFPB sector. We are particularly interested in any similarities or differences between the two overlapping intervals, and we will make use both of the total-economy data and of the NFPB data in arriving at our future forecasts. The longer 20-year period has contained many surprises up and down in the history of growth in labor productivity and in MFP. The 20-year average of these surprises should be highly relevant to what happens over the next 20 years.

Interest in the seven-year interval 2000:Q4 to 2007:Q4 originates in the fact that both quarters were at or near business cycle peaks. This interval can be viewed as more 'normal' than 1987–2000, which combined a period when total-economy productivity growth was slower than anyone could explain (1.19 per cent for the total economy), and then productivity revived more rapidly than anyone had predicted (2.42 per cent). The 1987–95 interval was best described by Solow's famous paradox that 'we can see the computers everywhere but in the productivity statistics'. But the 1995–2000 revival period was unusual as well. This was the famous 'dot.com' era, when by general consensus there was too much investment in computers and communication infrastructure, and this five-year interval may also have been unique in that one could only invent the internet once.

Table 12.10   Actual and predicted growth rates of components of real GDP and related variables, total economy and non-farm private business (NFPB) sector – actual for 1987–2007 and projected for 2007–2027

	Actual 1987:Q4–2007:Q4		Actual 2000:Q4–2007:Q4		Projected 2007:Q4–2027:Q4	
	Total economy	NFPB sector	Total economy	NFPB sector	Total economy	NFPB sector
Output (Y)	2.93		2.38		2.40	
Components						
Output per hour (Y/H)	1.79	2.23	2.02	2.48	1.70	2.05
Hours per employee (H/E)	-0.13		-0.54		-0.10	
Employment rate (E/N)	0.05		-0.13		0.00	
Labor-force part. rate (L/N)	0.02		-0.21		-0.20	
Working-age population (N)	1.19		1.24		1.00	
Related Variables						
Aggregate hours (H)	1.14		0.36		0.70	
Household employment (E)	1.26		0.90		0.80	
Labor force (L)	1.21		1.04		0.80	
Output per capita (Y/N)	1.74		1.14		1.40	

Table 12.10 (Continued)

	Actual 1987:Q4-2007:Q4		Actual 2000:Q4-2007:Q4		Projected 2007:Q4-2027:Q4	
	Total economy	NFPB sector	Total economy	NFPB sector	Total economy	NFPB sector
Decomposition of NFPB labor productivity growth						
Output per hour		2.23		2.48		2.05
Capital deepening		0.96		0.87		0.85
ICT		0.71		0.60		0.60
non-ICT		0.25		0.28		0.25
Labor quality		0.32		0.35		0.15
Multi-factor productivity		0.96		1.26		1.05
ICT		0.50		0.47		0.45
non-ICT		0.45		0.79		0.60
Share of ICT investment in GDP		3.69		3.95		4.00

Sources: Actual data in top section, same sources as Table 12.1 above. Actual data in bottom section, same sources as Table 12.2 above, adjusted as explained in the text. Forecasts as explained in the text.

The 20-year period 1987–2007 combines the inexplicably slow productivity growth of 1987–95, the temporarily ebullient period 1995-2000, and the interesting 2000–07 period that in some dimensions looks like more normal behavior. The seven years between 2000:Q4 and 2007:Q4 were neatly divided in half, with extremely rapid productivity growth between 2000:Q4 and 2004:Q2 (2.68 per cent), and much slower growth from 2004:Q2 to 2007:Q4 (1.36 per cent), averaging out to 2.02 per cent for the seven-year interval. As argued above the productivity growth 'explosion' of 2001–04 rested on a combination of savage corporate cost cutting and delayed learning from the internet revolution. Once profits had recovered the pressure for cost cutting disappeared, and eventually the delayed learning subsided as well.

Unfortunately, the relevance of the 2000–07 period is tainted by the bizarre behavior of the labor-market variables. Given that the unemployment rates were similar at the beginning and end, there was an unprecedented drop in hours per capita, with aggregate hours *(H)* growing at only 0.36 per cent per year while the working-age population grew at 1.24 per cent per year. Hours per capita fell by 0.88 per cent per year, or a cumulative exponential 6.4 per cent decline between 2000 and 2007.

The sharp decline in hours per capita in 2000–07 to some extent reduced output growth but it also raised productivity growth, in that some of the reduction of labor hours represented a permanent transition to a more aggressive stance of management against labor (Gordon, 2010b). To this extent that 2.02 per cent growth in total-economy output per hour in 2000–07 may be misleading as an indicator for future forecasts. Since forecasts of future growth of aggregate hours are bunched together at 0.7 per cent (see for instance Jorgensen et al. 2008, Table 2), we anticipate that at least half of the return from 0.38 in 2000–07 to 0.70 on average after 2007 will be offset by slower productivity growth.

This argument that the 2000–07 growth rate of total economy labor productivity was unsustainably high, due to the role of cost-cutting in boosting productivity as offset to a sharp decline in labor hours, suggests that the long-run growth rate of productivity in the total economy is likely to be closer to the 1.79 per cent of 1987–2007 than the 2.02 per cent of 2000–07. By the same reasoning, the growth rate of NFPB sector productivity, shown in Table 12.10 to be 2.48 per cent in 2000–07, is more likely to be closer to the 2.23 per cent of 1987–2007.

12.5.2 Reconciling Labor Productivity and MFP in the Forecasts

One possible criterion lies in a coincidence that two key numbers are the same. As shown in Table 12.10, the average annual growth rate of NFPB labor productivity between 1987:Q4 and 2007:Q4 was 2.23 per cent per year.

The coincidence comes from the historical analysis in this chapter. The average growth rate of adjusted MFP over the past 116 years (Table 12.8, column 5) has been 1.19 per cent. Add to this the average excess of actual (unadjusted) labor productivity growth over adjusted MFP growth in the BLS postwar data from 1950 to 2007, which is 1.07 per cent. Lo and behold, these two numbers add up to 2.26, almost identical to the actual rate of productivity growth for 1987–2007.

Do we have any good reasons to suspect that the next 20 years will deliver a significantly faster growth rate of unadjusted labor productivity than the last 20 years? Similarly, is there any good reason to think that adjusted MFP growth will exceed the rates that were achieved over the past 116 years? When we add those realized adjusted MFP growth rates to the recorded relationship since 1950 of average labor productivity to adjusted MFP growth, we keep coming back to a NFPB productivity growth rate of roughly 2.25 per cent per year.

The lower section of Table 12.10 reports the decomposition of labor productivity growth into capital deepening, the labor quality effect, and the growth rate of MFP. This is shown both for 2000–07 using the Oliner–Sichel data reported in Table 12.2, and also for 1987–2007 creating weighted averages of the Oliner–Sichel data and assuming that growth rates observed in Table 12.2 over 1973–95 apply for 1987–95 as well. Note that the capital-deepening effect declined from 1987–2007 to 2000–07 by about 0.10 percentage points and that all of this decline was in the ICT sector. Growth in labor quality stayed roughly constant, while MFP growth outside of the ICT sector increased markedly.

Our forecasts for the capital-deepening effect are almost identical to the actual record of 2000–07, and we expect the share of ICT investment in GDP to be roughly stable. This share, displayed in Figure 12.4, shows that during 2001–07 the share of neither ICT investment or PDE investment ever came close to reaching the levels achieved in the temporary investment bubble of 1998–2000. With no reason to expect this bubble to happen again, there is no reason why the rapid growth rate of the capital-deepening effect in 1995–2000 should be relevant to forecasts.

The next line in the bottom section of Table 12.10 shows that we expect the contribution of labor quality growth to fall by roughly half over the next 20 years. Jorgenson et al. (2006), show that educational attainment has reached a plateau in the U.S., in their estimates implying that the improvement in labor quality (the BLS labor composition effect) will gradually decline toward zero over the next 10 to 15 years. Similarly, Goldin and Katz (2008) both lament and explain the plateau in U.S. educational attainment. They point out (2008, Figure 9.1, p. 327) that unlike most European nations, where a catching-up process has made the 25–34 age group much better educated than the 55–64 age group, in the U.S. the educational attainment of both age groups is the same, the very definition of a plateau.

Since the continuation of the labor quality adjustment depends largely on increasing educational attainment, yet this increase seems to have disappeared, Table 12.10 cuts in half the labor quality adjustment for 2007–2027 as compared to its average value of 1987–2007. The difficulties of further increasing U.S. educational attainment are well documented by Goldin and Katz, including a rapidly increased relative price of higher education and a paucity of opportunities for less privileged students to gain fellowship support.

What growth rate should we choose for MFP? This is the wild card in any forecast of future productivity behavior. As summarized above, the average growth rate of adjusted MFP for the U.S. economy since 1891 has been 1.19 per cent. The respective figures for 1987–2007 and 2000–07 from Table 12.10 are 0.96 and 1.26 per cent respectively. My inclination is to lean toward a number closer to the 1987–2007 experience than the unusual 2000–07 period. The fundamental driver of adjusted MFP growth is innovation, which exhibits ebbs and flows over time. The 'Great Inventions' of the late nineteenth century, especially electricity and the internal combustion engine, propelled MFP growth through most of the twentieth century until those inventions had been exploited, at least in the U.S., around 1970. By the early 1970s the country was electrified, air conditioning had allowed manufacturing and service industries to spread across the south and southwest, consumer appliances had liberated women, radio and TV had ended isolation and brought the world into the living room, the interstate highway system was largely built, and the population had moved to the suburbs.

Perhaps it is not so surprising that the opportunities to exploit technology were limited between 1972 and 1995. Then came the upsurge of the contribution of ICT capital to economic growth, and according to the results in Tables 2 and 3 from Oliner–Sichel and Jorgenson–Ho–Stiroh, the duration of the contribution of this invention was surprisingly short–lived, leading to the skepticism I have previously expressed (Gordon 2000b) as to whether the invention of the PC and internet deserves to be called a 'Great Invention' of the magnitude of electricity and the internal combustion engine, or something in the next category of greatness.

The MFP forecast for 2007–27 in Table 12.10 of 1.05 per cent is relatively optimistic. It is faster than the 0.96 for 1987–2007 and much faster than the lamentable growth rates of 0.33 to 0.46 per cent recorded for 1972–2005 in the four estimates summarized in Table 12.9. In 1972–95 the subsidiary innovations from the Great Inventions of the late nineteenth century were depleted. The same could happen again over the next 20 years. ICT technology in the last ten years has mainly taken the form of miniaturization, not a true transformation of function as occurred in the 1990s. Without a set of new and transforming inventions, there is more likelihood that MFP growth may drift below the projected 1.05 per cent than rise above it.

12.5.3   Implications for Future Growth in Real GDP and Output per Hour for the Total Economy

When the components of NFPB labor productivity growth in the lower right section of Table 12.10 are summed, we arrive at a projected growth rate of 2.05 per cent, slower than the 2.48 per cent of 2000–07 and even slower than the 2.23 per cent of 1987–2007. Nevertheless this relatively pessimistic estimate is much more rapid than the 1.47 per cent for 1973–95 in Table 12.2.

Once the future growth rate of NFPB labor productivity is established, it becomes relatively easy to set out the future growth rates of the other components of the output identity. We take our forecasts of future growth in population and the other labor variables from recent articles projecting to the period 2008–18 by Toossi (2009) and Wyatt and Byun (2009). The projected growth rate of aggregate hours is 0.7 per cent, the same as forecast by Jorgenson et al. (2008). Projected growth in total economy labor productivity of 1.70 is slower than the 2.05 per cent estimate for the NFPB sector – as usual, the gap between productivity growth in those two sectors is positively correlated with NFPB productivity growth (the slower the NFPB growth, the smaller the gap between NFPB growth and total economy growth). The implied growth rate for GDP is 2.40 per cent, almost exactly the same as for 2000–07 and the slowest growth in potential real GDP of any period in recorded American history since at least 1870.

Does the explosion of labor productivity growth in 2009 require a significant qualification of these projected growth rates for 2007–27? While total-economy growth in output per hour between 2008:Q4 and 2009:Q4 was a robust 3.78 per cent, growth in the preceding four quarters was a minimal 0.8 per cent. The annual growth rate over the eight quarters between 2007:Q4 and 2009:Q4 was 2.29 per cent, and this implies that for total-economy productivity growth to average 1.7 per cent per year for 2007–27, given what has already occurred, productivity growth for 2009–2027 will be only slightly slower at 1.63 per cent per year. The productivity growth explosion of 2009 has been impressive (at least in part a consequence of panicked cost cutting in late 2008 and early 2009) and reinforces the view of Gordon (2010b) that labor hours are now more responsive to output fluctuations than before the 1990s, while productivity no longer exhibits procyclical fluctuations at all. However, the overall magnitude of the 2007–09 productivity growth achievement is not large enough to require any qualifications to the growth rate forecasts of Table 12.10. The implied growth rate for 2009–2027 of 1.63 per cent is still higher than the 1.36 per cent actual growth rate between 2004:Q2 and 2007:Q4 and even higher than the 1.25 per cent actual growth rate between 1972:Q4 and 1995:Q4.

12.6   CONCLUSION

This chapter provides a novel combination of perspectives on the behavior of growth in both output per hour and of MFP at high frequencies for the past 50 years, at low frequencies dating back to 1891, and in forecasts of the likely outcome over the 20-year period 2007–2027. The history of U.S. productivity behavior in the past 116 years is characterized by significant upward and downward shifts in growth rates. To make sensible forecasts, we must understand the past.

This chapter contributes to that understanding initially by decomposing the growth of total-economy output, aggregate hours, and labor productivity from 1952–2007 into actual changes, changes in a statistical trend that is defined to exclude business-cycle movements, and the residual or deviation from trend growth. The growth rate of trend real GDP has fluctuated in a narrow range between 3 and 4 per cent since 1952, while the trend in aggregate hours for the total economy has ranged from 0.7 to 1.9 per cent. The peak period for output growth was in the 1950s and 1960s, while the peak period for hours growth was in the late 1970s as teenagers and females entered the labor force at a rapid rate. The low 0.7 trend growth rate of hours reached in 2002–03 reflected an unprecedented reduction in work hours that was the counterpart of superheated productivity growth in this interval. This chapter interprets both as inherently temporary.

The statistical trend for growth in total economy labor productivity ranged from 2.75 per cent in early 1962 down to 1.25 per cent in late 1979 and recovered to 2.45 per cent in 2002. Our results on productivity trends identify a problem in the interpretation of the 2008–09 recession. The unprecedented decline in labor hours, employment, and labor-force participation in 2008–09 lead the statistical detrending technique to the conclusion that productivity was doing quite well, given the historical weakness of productivity in recessions. As discussed in Gordon (2010b) this represents a shift in labor-market behavior rather than an unexplained upsurge in the productivity growth trend, and for the discussion of short-term responses we hold constant the trend of real GDP, aggregate hours, and total economy labor productivity after 2007 at the trend growth rate reached in 2007:Q4.

The medium-term analysis of changes in U.S. labor productivity and MFP begins with the familiar decompositions of labor productivity growth into the contributions of capital-deepening, labor quality, and MFP, further divided into the contributions of ICT and non-ICT investment. These results show that the 1995–2000 productivity growth revival was primarily driven by ICT investment, while the subsequent relatively rapid growth in productivity during 2000–07 was primarily driven by an upsurge of MFP growth in non-ICT industries. We have provided an interpretation of the temporary productivity growth explosion of 2001–04 based on Gordon (2003, 2010b): a sharp decline in profits and in the stock market in 2000–01 motivated firms to cut all costs, and particularly labor costs, more deeply than had previously occurred for a given change in the output gap. Employment continued to decline while output rose in 2001–04 not only because the pace of the output recovery was weak, but because delayed learning how to use the late–1990s invention of the internet caused some of the benefits of that invention to spill over from the 1990s to the 2001–04 interval. Once the cost-cutting had been digested and the delayed benefits from the internet invention had been realized, productivity growth slowed in 2004–07 to a pace little faster than in 1972–95.

An important contribution of the chapter is to provide an updated decomposition of productivity growth over the 'long century' extending between 1891 and 2007. By far the most rapid MFP growth in U.S. history occurred in 1928–50, a phenomenon that I have previously dubbed the 'one big wave'. This chapter presents numerous corrections to the growth of labor quality and to capital quantity and quality, leading to significant rearrangements of the growth pattern of MFP, generally lowering the unadjusted MFP growth rates during 1928–50 and raising them after 1950.

The chapter approaches the task of forecasting 20 years into the future by extracting relevant precedents from the growth in labor productivity and in MFP over the last seven years, the last 20 years, and the last 116 years. Its conclusion is that over the next 20 years (2007–2027) growth in real GDP will be 2.4 per cent (the same as in 2000–07), growth in total economy labor productivity will be 1.7 per cent, and growth in the more familiar concept of NFPB sector labor productivity will be 2.05 per cent. The implied forecast 1.40 per cent growth rate of per-capita real GDP falls far short of the historical achievement of 2.17 per cent between 1929 and 2007 and represents the slowest growth of the measured American standard of living recorded during the past two centuries.

Despite their pessimism, the conclusions of this chapter are not wild guesses but rather emerge from discipline in distinguishing between the NFPB sector and the total economy, in distinguishing between labor productivity and MFP, and in providing a unique interpretation of twentieth history based on a revision to conventional measures of pre-1948 MFP growth.

And the conclusions of this chapter, even if they are bolstered with a greater reliance on historical precedents, are not wildly deviant from contemporary forecasts. Maddison (2009) predicts that growth in U.S. real GDP will be at a rate of 2.5 per cent until 2030, not far from our estimate of 2.4 per cent through 2027. Jorgenson et al. (2008) reports several estimates of future real GDP growth at 2.5 per cent, including mine in the original 2006 version of this chapter. Further consideration has required me to reduce the 2.5 number to 2.4, not a major change. For those who may disagree about the pessimistic conclusions of this chapter, there is an obligation to pick out the numbers that are wrong or dubious and to suggest a more convincing set of numbers to propel the discussion.

REFERENCES

Aaronson, S., F. Bruce, P., A. Figura, J. Pringle and W. Wascher (2006), 'The Recent Decline in the Labor Force Participation Rate and Its Implications for Potential Labor Supply', *Brookings Papers on Economic Activity*, **2**, 69–134.

Baily, M.N. and J.F. Kirkegaard (2004), *Transforming the European Economy*, Washington, DC: Institute for International Economics.

Basu, S., J.G. Fernald, N. Oulton and S.Srinivasan (2003), 'The Case of the Missing Productivity Growth, or Does Information Technology Explain Why Productivity Accelerated in the United States but not in the United Kingdom?' *NBER Macroeconomics Annual*, 9–63.

David, P.A. (1990), 'The Dynamo and the Computer: An Historical Perspective on the Modern Productivity Paradox', *American Economic Review Papers and Proceedings*, **80** (2), 355–61.

Denison, E.F. (1962), *The Sources of Economic Growth in the United States and the Alternatives Before Us*, Supplementary Paper no. 13. New York: Committee for Economic Development.

Denison, E.F. (1979), *Accounting for Slower Economic Growth: The United States in the 1970s*, Washington: Brookings.

Dew-Becker, I, and R.J. Gordon (2008), 'The Role of Labor Market Changes in the Slowdown of European Productivity Growth', *NBER Working Paper 13840*, Also *CEPR Discussion Paper 6722*.

Feldstein, M.S. and D.K. Foot (1971), 'The Other Half of Gross Investment: Replacement and Modernization Expenditures', *Review of Economics and Statistics*, **53**, 49–58.

Feldstein, M.S. and M. Rothschild (1974), 'Towards an Economic Theory of Replacement Investment', *Econometrica*, **42**, 393–423.

Fraumeni, B.M. (2007), 'Productive Highway Capital Stocks and the Contribution of Highways to Growth in GDP', **1**, *Federal Highway Administration, U.S. Department of Transportation*.

Goldin, C. and L.F. Katz (2008), '*The Race between Education and Technology*', Cambridge MA: Belknap Press of Harvard University Press.

Gordon, R.J. (1969), '$45 Billion of U.S. Private Investment Has Been Mislaid', *American Economic Review*, vol. **59**, 221–38.

Gordon, R.J. (1979), 'The End-of-Expansion Phenomenon in Short-run Productivity Behavior', *Brookings Papers on Economics Activity*, **1**, 447–61.

Gordon, R.J. (2000a), 'Interpreting the 'One Big Wave' in U.S. Long-term Productivity Growth', in van Ark, B., S. Kuipers, and G. Kuper (eds.), *Productivity, Technology, and Economic Growth*, Boston: Kluwer Publishers, 19–65.

Gordon, R.J. (2000b), 'Does the New Economy Measure Up to the Great Inventions of the Past?', *Journal of Economic Perspectives*, **14** (4), 49–74.

Gordon, R.J. (2003), 'Exploding Productivity Growth: Context, Causes, and Implications', *Brookings Papers on Economic Activity*, **2**, 207–79.

Gordon, R.J. (2010a), 'Controversies about Work, Leisure, and Welfare in Europe and the United States', in E.S. Phelps and H.W. Sinn (eds), *Perspectives on the Performance of the Continental Economies*, Cambridge MA: MIT Press, forthcoming.

Gordon, R.J. (2010b), 'Okun's Law, Productivity Innovations, and Conundrums in Business Cycle Dating', *NBER Working Paper*, A much shorter version with the same title is published in the *American Economic Review Papers and Proceedings*, **100** (2), 11–15.

Hamilton, J.D. (1994), *Time Series Analysis*, Princeton NJ: Princeton University Press.

Hilsenrath, J.E. (2002), 'While Economy Lifts, Severe Profit Crunch Haunts Companies; Nervous CEOs Could Slow Recovery by Continuing Layoffs, Plant Closings', *Wall Street Journal*, April 1, A1.

Jorgenson, D.W. (2010), 'Growth and Crisis in the World Economy', presentation at AEA Meetings, Atlanta, January 3.

Jorgenson, D.W. and K.J. Stiroh (2000), 'Raising the Speed Limit: U.S. Economic Growth in the Information Age', *Brookings Papers on Economic Activity*, 2000, **1**, 125–211.

Jorgenson, D.W., M.S. Ho, and K.J. Stiroh (2006), 'The Sources of the Second Surge of U.S. Productivity and Implications for the Future', working paper, March.

Jorgenson, D.W., M.S. Ho and K.J. Stiroh (2008). 'A Retrospective Look at the U.S. Productivity Growth Resurgence', *Journal of Economic Perspectives*, **22** (1), 3–24.

Kendrick, J.W. (1961), *Productivity Trends in the United States*. Princeton: Princeton University Press for NBER.

Maddison, A. (2009), 'The World Economy in 2030: A Quantitative Assessment', paper presented to International Economic Association meetings, Utrecht, August.

Nordhaus, W.D. (2002), 'The Recent Recession, the Current Recovery, and Stock Prices', *Brookings Papers on Economic Activity*, **1**, 199–220.

Oliner, S.D., and D.E. Sichel (2000), 'The Resurgence of Growth in the Late 1'990s: Is Information Technology the Story?', *Journal of Economic Perspectives*, **14** (4), 3–23.

Oliner, S.D., and D.E. Sichel (2002), 'Information Technology and Productivity: Where Are We Now and Where Are We Going?', *Federal Rese4rve Bank of Atlanta Economic Review*, **87** (3), 15–44.

Oliner, S.D., D.E. Sichel, E. Daniel and K.J. Stiroh (2007), 'Explaining a productive decade', *Journal of policy Modeling*, **30** (4), 633–673.

Timmer, M.P., R. Inklaar, M. O'Mahony and B. van Ark (2010), *Economic Growth in Europe – A comparative industry perspective*, Cambridge UK: Cambridge University Press.

Toossi, M. (2009). 'Labor Force Projections to 2018: Older Workers Staying More Active', *Monthly Labor Review*, **132** (11), 30–51.

Wasson, R.C., J.C. Musgrave and C. Harkins (1970), 'Alternative Estimates of Fixed Business Capital in the United States', *Survey of Current Business*, April, 18–36.

Wyatt, I.D. and K.J. Byun (2009), 'The U.S. Economy to 2018: From Recession to Recovery', *Monthly Labor Review*, **132** (11), 11–29.

Yang, S. and E. Brynjolfsson (2001), 'Intangible Assets and Growth Accounting: Evidence from Computer Investments', Working Paper, MIT, May.

Epilogue

Life and Work of Angus Maddison

1926–2010

Confessions of a Chiffrephile

Angus Maddison[*]

FAMILY INFLUENCES

My interest in economics started early. Until I was six, I lived in Newcastle-on-Tyne, where the main industries were shipbuilding and coal-mining. A large proportion of the work force were unemployed throughout the 1920s, and unemployment was massive in 1929–33. My father had a steady job as a railway fitter but I had two unemployed uncles, and there were many unemployed neighbours. The unemployed were not only poor but depressed. Many loitered aimlessly at street corners, looked haggard, wore mufflers and cloth caps and smoked fag-ends. Their children were often sickly or tubercular.

My father took me to Gateshead every Sunday to see my grandmother. The double-decker bridge across the Tyne had openwork iron girders with a long drop to a dirty river that flowed between laid-up ships and a long line of derelict factories. The bleak image of the dead economy was sharpened by the noise and vibration above. Trams rattled down the middle of the roadway, and trains rumbled ominously overhead. At the Gateshead end, the buildings were blacker, and the clusters of unemployed thicker than in Newcastle. I saw nowhere so depressing until visiting Calcutta 30 years later.

In 1933, the railway workshops were relocated in Darlington. We only moved 30 miles but it was a different world with much less unemployment. I was also aware of other improvements, as I knew that food prices had fallen and that mortgages were affordable.

My parents both left school when they were 12 and were interested in improving their education and mine. My mother used to read to me at an early age, she taught me to play golf, we had competitions in spelling or guessing the title of operatic music we heard on the radio. She took me to movies with dancing or singing (Shirley Temple, Fred Astaire, Nelson Eddy and Jeannette McDonald) and later we graduated to the Sadlers Wells ballet

---

* Confessions of a Chiffrephile by Angus Maddison was published in *Banca Nazionale del Lavoro Quarterly Review*, no. 189, June 1994.

and opera when they appeared locally. My father had been in France from 1914 to 1918 as a paramedic, giving first aid and comfort to the wounded and dying. He continued this interest as a first aid instructor in evening classes for railwaymen. When I was young I often went along as the accident 'victim' and was bandaged and splinted by the class. At the time I was an adolescent both my parents were active in the education activities of the Cooperative Movement which ran 'weekend schools' once a month where my father was often the chairman. When I was about 12 I started to go with them to these sessions. The speakers gave lectures on British political or economic issues or on international affairs. Those I remember best were Hamilton Fyfe, Principal of Aberdeen University, J.M. (later Lord) Peddie, a Coop economist, Sir Walter Citrine, the trade union leader, and Bruno Halpern, an Austrian economist. About 30 regulars attended these sessions, and the discussions were usually animated. The people who came were nearly all industrial workers or their wives, who were active in trade unions or local labour politics.

One of these meetings, in 1940, was concerned with the political and economic consequences of the war. There were a couple of speakers, Cyril Joad, a philosopher, who dealt with the political issues, and Jack Hemingway, my history teacher, who explained how the war could be financed, basing himself on Keynes' new book, *How to Pay For the War*, which my father bought. This was the first book I read on economics and was more or less intelligible to a 13 year old. It advocated a compulsory levy to prevent inflation, and rationing to provide fair shares. The annex on national income put the macroeconomic options in a simple quantitative framework. It was then that I began to realise that economics was a useful discipline for solving serious problems and wondered why peace-time economic problems could not have been solved by the same approach Keynes applied to those of wartime. I followed up Keynes' reference to Colin Clark and read his *Conditions of Economic Progress* in the public library and was fascinated at the way it quantified what was going on in so many countries. This first exposure to economics had a lasting effect on my subsequent research agenda and the contact with adult education gave me the idea that you get educated by forming your own networks and setting your own programme. I was never subsequently very respectful of formal curricula.

My mother was one of 10 children, a boisterous Scottish family, who bubbled with self-confidence. My most colourful relative was my Uncle David who had some kind of chest trouble he had developed in the army. He had a small military pension and could not work at his trade as a French-polisher. He became a street corner politician, giving occasional talks on Fabian socialism on a soapbox on the Newcastle town moor. He always welcomed an audience and was quite willing to use a small boy as a foil for his skeptical ideas on politics and religion. My mother regarded him as a sage, so he became my guru. I imbibed a good deal of what he said without fully understanding it, and he got me to read Shaw and Voltaire.

SCHOOL

When I was 11, I passed the examination to go to the grammar school. At that time, it was not free. The fees were equivalent to about six weeks of my father's take home pay, so it involved significant parental sacrifice. If I had not been the only child, they probably would not have been able to afford it.

At the grammar school, I was a successful pupil, and specialised in history, English and foreign languages when I entered the sixth form. I was also the editor of the school magazine and secretary of the debating society. There was no economics teaching, but a significant amount of economic history. During the war we had many women teachers, only a few years older than their pupils. My history teacher was Jack Hemingway. He was a friend of my father and took me under his wing. He had been a liberal parliamentary candidate and was active in adult education. He stressed that history was not a set of facts about kings and queens, but that there were different schools of historians, and different layers of past experience which could be examined. He got me to read Adam Smith, Tawney, Cole, Postgate, the Hammonds and the Webbs. Joan Clapton was also a strong influence. She taught English literature and special history subjects to sixth formers. She was a radical intellectual of 1930s vintage, who roused my interest in Marxist literature, not so much the economics, but the materialist interpretation of history, the notion of exploitation and of class conflict.

My German teacher, Stephanie Hawthorn, fresh from Oxford, helped turn us into Europeans. The sixth form classes were small – for German there were usually three of us. My two classmates were dedicated entirely to language studies and were deep into comparative linguistics. With the four languages we had studied, English, French, German and Latin, we found we had a quick key to learning related European languages. They dabbled in more exotic tongues and I took an evening class in Russian. I improved my speaking knowledge of German by listening to the BBC German service and to the German radio. I also frequented a German-speaking Club for Austrian, German, and Czech refugees who were released from internment to join the Pioneer Corps of the British army.

One of the learning problems in a provincial town is access to books, but I did not do too badly. There were the school and public libraries, and I had a friend, Scottie (J.R. Scott) with a second-hand book business. He had a very large stock of books on history and economics, and he let me borrow books, or gave me big discounts when I could afford to buy them.

UNIVERSITY STUDIES

At the end of 1944, I won a scholarship in history to go to Cambridge University (Selwyn College). I went in January 1945, rather than wait for the next academic year, by which time I expected to be in the army.

Student numbers were greatly reduced because the war was still on, but the London School of Economics was evacuated to Cambridge and added a large mix of female and foreign students. The array of scholars offering lectures was impressive, and one was free to go or stay away from all of them. The University Library was near my college and there was open access to millions of books.

The most exciting of the economic history lectures were those of Michael Postan. He covered British history from medieval times to the nineteenth century. We used the same analytical tools for the whole period – a framework in which the size of the capital stock, changes in technology and demography figured large. He presented empirical evidence of a quantitative kind, made bold hypotheses where information was lacking, and managed to convey the impression that these were contentious topics of major interest. All this delivered with exotic Bessarabian showmanship.

I also attended R.H. Tawney's lectures on economic history at LSE. These were delivered without panache but their analytic content was as sharp as Postan's. Tawney covered very broad themes – how the institutions of the American and Russian economies differed from those of the UK, why peasants had not disappeared from European agriculture as Marx had predicted.

The most crowded lectures were those of Harold Laski, who was Professor of Political Science at LSE, and chairman of the Labour Party. Laski was a great raconteur, with a droll humour. He dealt with the evolution of British political institutions like parliament, the crown, local government etc. stressing that the way they worked depended on the locus of political and economic power.

At the beginning of June 1945 I went home and worked actively in the General Election of 5th July for the Darlington Labour candidate who won with a majority of more than 8,000. In the neighbouring constituency of Stockton, my friend George Chetwynd (the husband of one of my school teachers), defeated Harold Macmillan by nearly 9,000. The sweeping victory of the Labour party, the successful outcome of the war and the creation of the UN gave me a strong sense that the big issues that had preoccupied my parents were on their way to solution.

When I went back to Cambridge in 1945 the atmosphere was very different. The LSE had gone back to London, but the university was much more crowded. It was full of people demobilised from the armed forces, and generally speaking those with the highest academic merit had been released first. It was a stimulating peer group. To add to the variety, there were about 150 American and a few Canadian soldiers including Harry Johnson (1). There was a reflux of dons from the war. Bertrand Russell came back from America, and replaced Laski as the star lecture room attraction.

I was more prosperous, as my grant had risen and I had two part-time jobs – teaching an evening class in one of the Cambridge village institutes and lecturing to German prisoners of war for the Foreign Office. In the summer I had passed the American examination for translation work at the War Crimes Tribunal at Nuremberg, but the British Foreign Office persuaded the Americans not to recruit British nationals. As compensation they gave me a job lecturing in POW camps. Both of these lecture series were on problems of reconstruction in European countries.

I spent most of the summer of 1946 on European political issues. The Cambridge Labour Club held a conference for about 30 European social democrats organised by Robin Marris, Wat Tyler and myself in conjunction with Denis Healey, who was then international secretary of the Labour Party. At that time there was still a social democratic movement in East Europe, so the geographic scope was very wide. Then I went abroad for the first time, for six weeks. First to Tirol, where the Austrian students and the four occupying powers organised a two week seminar, then to Prague, Switzerland and Italy. In Paris I attended a meeting of the International Union of Socialist Youth, organised by Healey and Per Haekerrup, who was later Danish foreign minister. We stayed in the Ecole des Arts et Metiers in Montrouge, and were roused by a militant French activist in a blue shirt who shouted 'c'est l'heure' so dramatically that we thought there was at least a fire if not a revolution.

In 1946, I switched from history to economics. This was a much tougher discipline than history and was made more challenging by the competition between different schools of thought. Dennis Robertson, the professor, gave an elegant and whimsical introductory course on pre-Keynesian lines, and Joan Robinson made most of the running for the Keynesians. She also ran a huge discussion group, which was a bit intimidating as she loved a fight and tended to demolish opponents. The hottest topics were theoretical, and almost entirely concentrated on what Cambridge economists had said. As Dharma Kumar paraphrased Joan Robinson, 'time is a device to prevent everything happening at once, space is a device to prevent it all happening in Cambridge'. There was not much attention to what people thought in Oxford, or LSE, in Scandinavia or the USA, and almost nothing on problems of economic growth, business cycles, the European economy, or economic development which later became my major interests.

Austin Robinson was an honourable exception to the neglect of the real world and gave a highly quantitative course on current problems of planning and resource allocation. He was one of the few lecturers who permitted the audience to ask questions.

My supervisor was Morris Dobb, a scholarly Marxist who was the only prominent Cambridge economist interested in long run capitalist development. I used to read my weekly essays to him, and I often took the initiative in suggesting topics. He had the demeanour of a discreetly agnostic bishop who certainly did not push his own views. He was not very interested in the mainstream Cambridge controversies, but had a very wide range of interests in history and economics and a broad international perspective. He was a close friend of Piero Sraffa. They had been to Russia together, and at that time were editing Ricardo's correspondence. Sraffa would occasionally enliven the supervision by bursting in with a dazzling smile and a new discovery.

Economic students were generally much more dedicated to their subject than historians. Interaction with this peer group was as important in the learning process as the lectures and supervision. The two people who contributed most to my education in this respect were Wilfred Beckerman and Robin Marris.

There was some scope for discussion of non-Cambridge type topics in the Marshall Society where I remember impressive presentations by Arthur Lewis on the nature of the innovative process and by Nicky Kaldor on how he had revamped Hungarian economic policy. I was also impressed by the style and content of Lionel Robbins' Marshall Lectures in 1947 which were about policy problems of war economics, postwar planning and the transition to market economies.

I was a member of the Political Economy Club set up by Keynes, and continued by Robertson, who selected the membership of about 20. It was the only seminar where students gave papers which were subject to discussion. I gave a paper on Anglo-American differences in industrial productivity, basing myself largely on Laszlo Rostas' new book which came out in 1948 (2). This was the topic on which I wanted to do my graduate work, so I was grateful for Robertson's hospitality.

In July 1948 I went into the Royal Air Force to do my military service. This was more interesting than I had expected. I became an education officer at a Group headquarters in York, giving talks on current affairs to airmen, and lecturing on strategy to officers taking promotion examinations. I made them read Julius Caesar, von Clausewitz, Eisenhower, and the strategic bombing survey where a bunch of economists (3) identified mistakes in British wartime strategy which my pupils found hard to swallow.

In October 1949 I sailed to Montreal in a crowded Cunarder, and started graduate study at McGill University. The graduate school had useful courses on new topics like game theory or linear programming, but students got little guidance or supervision. However there was expertise on output and productivity measurement at the Dominion Bureau of Statistics in Ottawa where official statisticians were both accessible and helpful, so I managed to to do the basic statistical part of my research which was intended to enlarge the Rostas comparison of UK and US industrial performance to include Canada. It was fashionable to attribute a good deal of the large US productivity advantage over the UK to economies of scale, and I hoped to test this by looking at Canada, where productivity was higher than in the UK, but where the scale of production was smaller.

In December 1949 I went to the meetings of the American Economic Association in New York, which was a huge affair, with many simultaneous sessions, about 1,000 economists, and the great stars of the time including Schumpeter who was the chairman. I had bought his Capitalism Socialism and Democracy in 1945, and was fascinated by its breadth of vision and originality. It was interesting to experience his wit and sparkle. He introduced Seymour Harris, the great anthologist of the epoch, by saying to the audience 'many of you have read his works, most of you have written them'.

In 1950 I moved to Johns Hopkins University in Baltimore. There were about 20 graduate students in economics, with close supervision of research and compulsory graduate courses. The faculty included Fritz Machlup, Evsey Domar, Clarence Long and Al Harberger, and there was a steady stream of visitors including Bergson, Kuznets and Viner. There was also a large US government research programme on Soviet economic performance.

My research supervisor was Clarence Long, who had lengthy experience with the National Bureau of Economic Research, and followed their policy of intensive manuscript criticism. I wrote a 20 page paper on Canadian industrial productivity and a few days later, to my astonishment, he gave me 15 typewritten pages of commentary, with fully documented criticism of my sloppy reasoning, weak evidence, poor table layout, vague headings, inadequate sources and woolly conclusions. I had never previously been subjected to such close scrutiny, but it was, of course exactly what graduate students need and usually do not get. Another person who was extremely helpful was Irving Siegel, who worked on the Russian project and had done a good deal of work on productivity in government agencies before the war.

Machlup gave the compulsory graduate course twice a week. He not only lectured but cross-examined his class, and gave us written tests to find out if we had absorbed his message. He was an eclectic and original economist with enormous charm and dedication. His main concern was to inculcate the virtues of clarity and precision.

Although I found the discipline at Hopkins very useful, I did not think I would profit much from another year of it, nor did I want to settle in the USA, so I got an academic job in the UK, at the University of St. Andrews in Scotland, where I had very light duties teaching a course in American economic history. I was able to write up the research I had done as a graduate student and published three articles.

In September 1952, I got a temporary three month assignment with the Food and Agriculture Organisation of the United Nations in Rome. I worked for Gerda Blau in the economics department on problems of the world wheat market, and she also sent me to GATT for three weeks to analyse non tariff barriers to agricultural trade. I could probably have stayed in FAO where I earned more than five times what I was paid as a lecturer in Scotland, but as the horizons were limited to agricultural problems I moved to Paris in January 1953, where the salary was lower, but the work promised to have wider scope.

OEEC: ANALYSING PERFORMANCE OF ADVANCED CAPITALIST COUNTRIES

OEEC was created in 1948 to foster economic recovery in Western Europe. It was a major instrument in assessing requirements for American aid under the Marshall Plan and coordinating its distribution. When I came, the character of the Organisation had changed. There was clearly scope for further activity in liberalising trade and in provision of liquidity through the European Payments Union, but part of the original raison d'être had disappeared with the termination of Marshall Aid.

Up to 1952, the emphasis had been on the establishment and monitoring of detailed quantitative goals – rebuilding iron and steel capacity, creating transport networks, improving up energy supplies etc. The OEEC had a large network of 'vertical' committees with a sizeable secretariat for consideration of these problems in individual industrial sectors, in energy and agriculture. This was the area where the loss of momentum was most perceptible, but this was also true to some extent of the Economic Committee (4) serviced by the Economic and Statistics Directorate which I had joined.

In 1953 the Economic Committee had three regular jobs: (a) annual reviews of economic policy in individual Member countries, (b) an annual report on the European economy and (c) vetting the annual reports of the committees covering industrial, agricultural and energy problems. The country reviews involved experts from capitals on lines which are still followed. This was not true of the two areas where my own work was concentrated.

My boss was François Walter, the Director of Economics. He was a French civil servant on secondment (from the Cours des Comptes), without formal training in economics. He had spent the war in England and his anglophilia extended to writing in English. He had feverish energy and needed a factotum with the stamina to check his economic arguments and polish his English. Wilfred Beckerman had done this before I came, and was glad to move on to the National Accounts Division. In theory we worked five and a half days a week, but Walter didn't believe in squandering Saturday afternoons on leisure pursuits. In these conditions I learned to work hard and draft quickly, and constant contact with Walter improved my French a good deal.

The worst chore was the annual report where every paragraph was subject to detailed scrutiny and approval by the Economic Committee. Walter did not draft the whole report before presenting it, but gave the committee a chapter at a time. The result was a great deal of rewriting and a patchy structure. However, it was a good training exercise for me, because one had to try to capture the essence of what was happening in the European economy as a whole and at the same time accommodate the often discordant points made by members of the national delegations.

My second task was as secretary of the subcommittee which vetted the annual reports of the industry committees. We had to eliminate the expression of protectionist views, try to inculcate some of the virtues of liberalism into the chairmen of the committees and the respective parts of the secretariat and check the validity of their economic reasoning. Although this was a laborious and sometimes painful process, it was reasonably effective. The chairman, Dr. Horst Robert, read all the reports carefully, and was meticulously briefed. There were occasional crises, e.g. when the textiles committee wanted to publish a strongly protectionist report, but we won these battles, as we had strong support from Robert Marjolin, the Secretary General.

There was clearly a need for a more sophisticated forum than the Economic Committee to monitor the macro-economic conjuncture, to assess growth performance, to exchange ideas on policy options and to improve the diagnostic quality of our statistics. All of these tasks were undertaken successfully in the course of the next few years, but there was no grand design – the improvement happened gradually. It is clear from Marjolin's memoirs (5) that he did not see progress in this direction as a priority. His mind was concentrated on progress towards a European customs union.

An opportunity for improving our policy analysis occurred when the Group of Economic Experts was created. The first meeting was intended mainly as an encounter between the economic side of the new US administration and the Europeans. The first session was not enlightening from an analytical point of view, but it was clear that the Eisenhower team was interested in regular exchange of views on economic policy options and the interaction of the American and European economies at a reasonably high level. The US delegate was Gabriel Hauge, who had been on Eisenhower's political campaign staff and was his personal economic assistant. The French delegate was Paul Delouvrier, then the the chief French official for economic cooperation and later Governor General of Algeria. The other members were high level economic professionals, notably Robert Hall from the UK and Otmar Emminger from the Bundesbank (or Bank deutscher Länder as it then was). It was agreed to follow up on a regular basis, under Hall's Chairmanship. He was economic advisor to the UK government, a slow speaking Australian of great wisdom and professional competence. He was a master of the meaningful grunt and an excellent chairman of the Group until 1961.

The core of the group was Robert Hall, Otmar Emminger, Etienne Hirsch, head of the French Plan from 1952 to 1959 (later Pierre Uri or Jacques Donnedieu de Vabres), Jan Tinbergen (later Jan Pen or and Pieter de Wolff) from the Netherlands, Arthur Burns (later Raymond Saulnier) from the US Council of Economic Advisors, and varying representation from the Bank of Italy. In the long run the type of dialogue they developed revolutionised the character of our work and strengthened the Organisation substantially.

There was a very wide range of views in the Group. Tinbergen was a social engineer and model builder. Hirsch was a planner but a very flexible one. Hall was a pragmatic Keynesian. Emminger was the most articulate. He was primarily concerned with financial stability and payments equilibrium. He was not interested in microeconomic questions which were to be solved by market mechanisms set in train by macro-policy. The German position was not one of laisser-faire and was concerned with employment as well as price stability. This was certainly the case for Alfred Mueller-Armack, Erhard's state secretary in the Ministry of Economics. The Germans were usually very well briefed on business conditions as they had five conjuncture institutes. Burns was least concerned with employment and growth. He pushed the US government away from Keynesian activism in favour of price stability and budget balance. Nevertheless, Burns with his NBER background was interested in close monitoring of performance of the leading economies and their mutual interaction. Hall avoided methodological confrontations. It was agreed that the best way to develop the dialogue was to set up future sessions with an analytical paper from the Secretariat on the nature of current conjuntural problems, to analyse the policy options for stability and growth, and discuss issues where the interaction of the economies was likely to cause problems. The emphasis was almost entirely macroeconomic. It marked a complete change from the detailed allocation problems which had preoccupied OEEC in earlier years.(6)

In 1955 there was a major change at the top of the Organisation when Marjolin and his two deputies resigned. Marjolin was a man of luminous intelligence. He believed in using the force of ideas to change the world by pragmatic action. Starting from very humble origins, leaving school at fourteen, he restarted his formal education when he was 20 and attained high academic honours. He was a successful economic journalist in prewar France, had an important wartime role as Jean Monnet's Deputy in Washington, was a major actor in implementing the Marshall Plan and later in creating the European Community. His successor René Sergent (an Inspecteur de Finance, and previously Deputy Secretary General of NATO) did not have Marjolin's intellectual power, vision and drive. However, Sergent was an agreeable and intelligent man with a disarming humility and willingness to take advice. He responded very positively to our initiatives to strengthen the analytic work of the Organisation, particularly as his period of office was wracked by unsuccessful attempts to use the OEEC as a vehicle for a Europe wide free trade area.

François Walter left at the same time as Marjolin. He was replaced by Eivind Erichsen, a Keynesian economist with wide experience in the Norwegian Ministry of Finance. Milton Gilbert, the director of Statistics and National Accounts, became the overlord of Economics as well as Statistics.

The change brought a big improvement in the quality of our work and the efficiency of our Directorate. Milton was an economist and statistician of the highest calibre. He had played a major part from 1940 in organising and defining the scope of the official US national accounts.(7) Marjolin took him on around 1950 to introduce national accounting techniques to OEEC countries and he was the only American in the OEEC Secretariat. He worked closely with Richard Stone in Cambridge in training a new breed of official statistician and establishing a standardised system of accounts. He had built up a highly competent National Accounts division under Geer Stuvel to check the procedures followed in the different countries in implementing the new system and to produce standardised accounts for all Member countries. He had also inaugurated a series of pathbreaking comparisons of purchasing power of currencies and comparability of real product levels.(8) This national accounts work was the bedrock on which our future analysis of comparative growth performance was based. It provided a yardstick for assessing the success of policy which had never existed before. Gilbert was also active in the creation of the International Association for Research in Income and Wealth, where Simon Kuznets stimulated academic researchers in many countries to create a historical counterpart to the postwar national accounts. Apart from his work on national accounts, Milton had once been editor of the

Survey of Current Business in the US Department of Commerce, so he was well qualified for the work on policy issues and the monitoring of the short term economic situation in the OEEC area, to which he now switched his attention.

Gilbert had a relaxed easy-going manner and did not write much himself; but when we had to prepare discussion papers for the experts, we would spend hours trying to clarify the major issues. I gave him a draft on the lines we had agreed, he went over it slowly, carefully and orally, making the text as succinct as possible, trying to find words with the exact nuance of meaning in order to get a document that was lucid and creatively pungent with regard to policy options. He had an eagle eye for tables, making sure that they were the most appropriate we could produce, and elegantly presented (9). Over the next five years I learned a good deal from these long sessions. Under the new dispensation we could also prepare much better annual reports, with some thematic unity (10), and we got a better chairman, Roger Ockrent, for the Economic Committee.

In the Summer of 1958 I spent a month on leave of absence (as a NATO Fellow) in Washington and New York where I was able to brief myself rather fully on US techniques of policy analysis and pick up ideas for improving our analytical work. I had long talks with Paul McCracken and David Lusher in the Council of Economic Advisors, with Julie Shiskin who prepared their business indicators, with George Terborgh and Raymond Goldsmith on measurement of capital stock, with Ed Denison on techniques of analysing economic performance and Senator Paul Douglas on the work of the Joint Economic Committee of Congress of which he was then the chairman. In New York I saw Sol Fabricant and Geoffrey Moore in the NBER, Sanford Parker of *Fortune* magazine and Bill Butler of the Chase Manhattan Bank on techniques of monitoring US economic performance. I also started a fruitful relationship with the team of economists at United Nations headquarters who wrote the part of the UN's *World Economic Report* on advanced capitalist countries.

We sharpened our analysis of long-term growth potential and productivity performance by using the national income statistics and our new publication on manpower statistics to create a more systematic framework of growth accounts. We first made use of these macro accounting techniques in a major study on growth problems and prospects which was published in the 8th annual report. The quality of our business cycle analysis was substantially upgraded. Our current economic indicators were improved through introduction of US seasonal adjustment techniques. In 1960 the Department started a new publication, *Main Economic Indicators*, incorporating about 100 seasonally adjusted series, which was a much more sophisticated vehicle for short term conjunctural analysis than we had previously had.

These analytic improvements were fed into our work for the Economic Experts which was gradually transformed into the Economic Policy Committee in 1959. This had a higher status than the Economic Committee, it met every four months and consisted of fiscal and monetary policy officials from all Member countries. In April 1961 it was further augmented by the creation of a working party on policies to stimulate economic growth, and another (more influential but with a restricted membership) on payments issues and the fiscal monetary mix-with Emile van Lennep (11) as chairman. A little later another working party was created to deal with problems of inflation and production costs. The impetus for the new working parties came from new Kennedy administration. Walter Heller and Jim Tobin from the Council of Economic Advisors created a new atmosphere of intellectual cooperation, Bob Solow was a very effective contributor to the new work on growth, and Bob Roosa to the discussions on payments issues.

This committee structure is still the hard core of OECD's economic policy work. The analyis was strengthened later when the Economic Department developed forecasting models, quarterly national accounts, and created the twice yearly Economic Outlook, but the work we did in 1955–60 was of fundamental importance in strengthening cooperation between the advanced capitalist economies, and in creating an articulate dialogue which helped them avoid the mistakes of diagnosis and policy they made in the interwar years of conflict and beggar your neighbour policy. It was important that the USA was fully involved in this process. It strengthened OEEC in a period when it was under great strain on the trade front.

In the course of 1960–1there were major changes in preparation for the creation of a new organisation. The US and Canada were to join as full members, and procedures for Japanese entry were begun. There was pressure from the USA to instigate work on development, with a view to persuading European countries to increase or initiate aid to developing countries. The time was propitious as the process of decolonisation was reaching completion and there was increasing competition from the USSR to win the allegiance of the third world, with notable success in the case of Egypt and Cuba.

I became the secretary of the Development Assistance Group, a forerunner of the development aid activities to be carried out by the new organisation. The first task was to set up a comprehensive statistical monitoring system to measure the flow of different categories of financial resources to developing countries (official loans and grants, private credits and direct lending, export credit guarantees etc.) from each of the 14 countries which were deemed to be developed. Most of the countries had no comprehensive view of such flows. We could get a rough aggregate crosscheck from balance of payments statistics but we had to go to central banks, finance ministries, export credit agencies, the World Bank and IMF to break down the different categories.

The results were sometimes unexpected, e.g. the flow from France was very much bigger proportionately than in the USA, but as expected the flows were small from Germany, Japan and Scandinavia. This first report *(The Flow of Financial Resources to Countries in Course of Economic Development)* was carried out at breakneck speed and published in April 1961. It set the main guidelines which the Development Assistance Committee still uses for collecting data from its Member countries.

At that time it seemed to me that the basis for analysing growth and stability in advanced capitalist countries had been reasonably firmly established, and that the problem of development was an exciting new field. I therefore decided to switch jobs, but I first took six months leave of absence in the second half of 1962 to write my first book, *Economic Growth in the West*, Allen and Unwin, 1964, where I tried to explain the postwar acceleration of growth in Western Europe, and the greater stability of the growth path. I pushed the historical perspective back to 1870, using the same type of quantitative national accounting evidence we had been using in OEEC for the postwar period. When I was writing it, I realised how far my horizons had widened over the research agenda I had as a graduate student. I was still trying to explain why some countries achieved faster growth or higher income levels than others, but I had a broader view of causality (particularly the role of domestic and international policy), a firmer and bigger array of macroeconomic evidence for a wider group of countries, and a longer time horizon. I also had a strong belief in the usefulness of the type of international cooperation in which I had been engaged, and in the efficacy of postwar macroeconomic policy in improving capitalist economic performance.

ECONOMIC DEVELOPMENT

I worked almost exclusively on development problems from the early 1960s to 1971. In 1963 I was director of the OECD's technical assistance programme which mainly involved economic advisory assistance to Greece, Portugal, Spain, Turkey and Yugoslavia. In 1964–6 I was a Fellow of OECD's new Development Centre. In 1967, I left OECD for five years, first on a research project for the Twentieth Century Fund, and then in 1969–71 to work for Harvard University's Development Advisory Service in Pakistan and Ghana.

The Development Centre was created to involve OECD more directly with developing countries in order to understand their policies better and to operate as some sort of intellectual intermediary between them and the OECD.

The first President was Robert Buron, a French politician with wide connections in the third world, who regarded politics as 'le plus beau des metiers'. After a prewar career in the Chamber of Commerce for chocolate makers and wartime public relations for the French movie industry, he became an MRP politician and held a number of ministerial posts in the Fourth and Fifth Republic – notably Minister of Colonies (d'Outre Mer) for Mend`es France and Minister of Transport for de Gaulle. Buron was not interested in research but in seminars for ministers and senior officials in countries where there was scope for a dialogue on development problems and policies. Raymond Goldsmith was made Vice-President to oversee research. He had made pioneering theoretical contributions to the study of capital, wealth, savings and financial flows and had produced a massive flow of comparative empirical studies in these fields. He picked a very good librarian for the Centre and helped start work on national accounts for developing countries in order to monitor their economic growth (12), but in most respects he was a loner. He did not create a research team but got on with his own work. He let the Fellows choose their own topics, insisting only that they be related in some way to foreign aid.

My first instinct was to attempt a general survey explaining comparative development experience in quantitative and historical perspective in the way I had done for the OEEC countries. I decided to postpone this for several reasons. In the first place the statistical basis for such a venture did not then exist. A second reason was that the developing world was much more heterogeneous in institutions, ideologies, policy objectives and weaponry, cultural and political heritage, social structure and level of real income. Given the huge range of these countries and my relative ignorance of them, it seemed sensible to familiarise myself with problems of countries where I had sufficient entr'ee to get a feel for the policy making process and which would represent different types of political-institutional heritage. The Centre offered plenty of scope for this and it was quite compatible with my official commitment to research on foreign aid (13).

BRAZIL

Brazil was the country where I developed the widest range of contacts and saw most of the policy-making process. I went to Rio in October 1964 at the invitation of Roberto Campos, Minister of Planning in the military regime which had just overthrown the populist government of Goulart. Campos was an economist-diplomat with very wide experience. He was born in a monastery in the backwoods of Matto Grosso and was a seminarist before he joined the foreign ministry in 1939 as a junior consul. On his way up, he got a Ph.D. in economics from Columbia University, was one of the Brazilian delegates to Bretton Woods, helped make the development plan of President Kubitschek, was head of the Brazilian Development Bank and Ambassador to the United States. Campos was by far the most powerful minister, strongly supported by Octavio Bulhoes as Minister of Finance. Campos had a team of outstanding young economists in his ministry, including Mario Simenson and João Paulo dos Reis Velloso who later became ministers. The mentor of both Campos and Bulhoes was Eugenio Gudin (1886–1986), a laisser-faire liberal of penetrating intellect and irreverent humour, who had founded the academic study of economics in Brazil after a career as an engineer.

The main preoccupation of the economic team was a stabilisation exercise to put a halt to hyperinflation, reduce the budget deficit, reform the tax system, get rid of a distorted set of price controls and subsidies, liberalise foreign trade, create a new exchange rate mechanism and reform financial institutions. The stabilisation exercise was an outstanding success in laying the foundations for a subsequent decade of very fast economic growth and it was carried out in gradualist fashion in 1964–7, without pushing Brazil into recession. I was able to observe this operation at close quarters in the research department of the Planning Ministry where I was a consultant. I also had contact with the research group in the Vargas Foundation, which performed some of the functions of a statistical office, producing both the national accounts and the price indices as well as providing short term business cycle analysis in its journal *Conjuntura*. I went to Brazil six times in 1964–7, visited a good many parts of the country, acquired some modest competence in Portuguese, as well as learning the samba and bossa nova.

I was very impressed by the vigour and originality of Brazil. The population has cosmopolitan roots, with significant immigration of Italians, Germans, Japanese, Lebanese as well as the original mix of Portuguese settlers and African slaves. As there are several very large cities, its intellectual life is multipolar. It has been blessed with much gentler political transitions than most of Latin America, so the tone of discussion on economic policy issues was less bitter than in some other places. It is a frontier country with a high degree of self confidence without a chip-on-the-shoulder feeling of exploitation by powerful neighbours. Added to this was the fascination of the economic problems they were tackling. I had had no previous experience of such an inflationary economy, such boldness in institutional innovation, or such an elaborate set of institutions for coexistence with inflation. The Campos approach to these problems was basically liberal and (except for his gradualism) not too different from that of the World Bank and IMF in the 1980s, but at that time it went counter to the prevailing policy views in other Latin American countries.

The most disconcerting thing about Brazil was the very high degree of inequality. Regional variance in per capita income in the twenty states ranged from nine to one, and the horizontal variation of income was also very sharp and noticeable, particularly in Rio with its impoverished ramshackle favelas poised on slippery hillsides behind luxurious beachfront apartments. It was also very noticeable that the black population was completely absent from the seats of power or any well paid activity except sport and entertainment (14).

GUINEA

In January 1965, four of the Development Centre fellows, Edmond Janssens, Nino Novacco, Göran Ohlin and I, went to Conakry for a month with Buron and Goldsmith. In the first week, we talked to Sekou Touré, the President, Ismael Toué his brother, who was Economic Development Minister, Saifoulaye Diallo, the Minister of Finance and Planning, who appeared to be second man in the regime, and Keita Fodeba, a professional dancer and founder of the national ballet, who had become a highly original Minister of Defence. Buron made a speech to the national assembly and then we had all the senior economic officials in a seminar for three weeks.

In the colonial period, Sekou Touré, who started life as a postal worker, had been a Communist (CGT) trade union leader and a member of the French parliament. He was the great grandson of a warrior chief, Samory, who fought the French between 1879 and 1898. In the 1950s, he went to Czechoslovakia to a school for party cadres. In Guinea he had organised political life on a single party basis. Virtually all adults were expected to join. The party had nearly 8,000 committees and when we visited outlying regions we found roomfuls of villagers who had come to palaver – often with very searching questions such as why a colonial power like Portugal was in OECD. One of the functions of the party was to reduce the significance of ethnic divisions which were physically very marked. Sekou was a very dark skinned stocky Malinke, whereas Saifoulaye was a tall lanky Peul with light brown skin and semitic features.

The Guinean situation was unique in Africa as the French had abandoned the country when it opted for independence in 1958 (15). There was no neocolonial apprenticeship as there was elsewhere in French Africa which became independent in 1960. In a population of 3 million, there were less than 50 Guineans with higher education. There had been 600 Frenchmen in government service, several thousand French soldiers, and about 2500 expatriates in productive and service enterprises who all left abruptly. As a result, the administration, health services and modern economy had collapsed. The country was excluded from the franc area to which its neighbours belonged. Ministers (virtually all without higher education) had had to improvise an administration from scratch, getting technical assistance from wherever they could. The radio, (La Voix de la Revolution) was run by a beautiful Hungarian lady. The only newspaper, Horoya, had a circulation of 8,000 every 2 or 3 days but the East Germans had built the Patrice Lumumba printing plant with a capacity of several hundred thousand newspapers a day. Military advice and incompatible equipment came from China, Czechoslovakia, and the German Federal Republic. The military effectiveness of the army seemed doubtful, but they did useful work on development projects. They made shoes, clothing and suitcases, mended roads and trained rural animateurs. The Defence Minister was also responsible for security and police. It had a crack unit of glamorous women who served as traffic police in Conakry and doubled as a night club orchestra. Before we came, the army had had visit from Franz Joseph Strauss, the German Defence Minister, and when we were there they had another from Che Guevara, the Cuban specialist on guerilla warfare.

The Guinean ministers and civil servants were friendly, without guile, ready to answer all questions, and several of them dressed in traditional Muslim robes. We visited the big bauxite and aluminium operation in Fria, a banana and pineapple plantation, a match factory and a model state farm run by a group of ministers. The farm was littered with Soviet tractors and other machinery, but had no visible output. When I asked the Minister of Planning about this, he replied 'Tu sais, jai pas la tête pour les chiffres' (I have no head for figures). The state trading organisation had taken over French shops, which were almost completely empty, and plantation agriculture was faltering. In spite of the chaos, it was a lively and interesting place. It survived by virtue of a robust subsistence economy, widespread smuggling by ethnic groups with relatives in neighbouring countries, and rich deposits of bauxite and iron ore which attracted foreign investment. The mixed bag of foreign aid was quite sizeable, and, on balance, was probably helpful but some of the projects seemed very dubious, e.g. the Chinese match factory imported huge Chinese trees to provide its raw material.

In July 1965 there was a seminar on supposedly similar lines in Teheran, but it was totally different from Guinea. We met elegant officials and junior ministers with sleeked hair and expensive suits, who listened politely and said little. Hoveida (later executed by Khomeini) was the only interesting one, but we did not learn much about the country. When I tried to discuss the oppressive atmosphere of the place with Buron, he shut me up, as he suspected that his chauffeur might be listening and reporting on us.

MONGOLIA

In January and early February 1967 I undertook a bizarre and picaresque mission for my friend Herbert Philips of UNESCO. I visited Outer Mongolia and Cambodia to investigate the role of science in economic development. I was mainly interested in the Mongol part of the trip, as I had taken a course on Mongol history at Johns Hopkins, where Owen Lattimore had a project including the exiled head of the Mongolian buddhists, the Gegen Dilowa Hutuktu, and two Mongol princes. My companion on the trip was Ratchik Avakov, a Soviet Armenian who had worked in IMEMO in Moscow and who was then working in UNESCO. At first he was a bit suspicious of me but after a month together and 30,000 miles of travel in climates ranging from 30 degrees below zero to about 80 above, we ended up like brothers.

I began to realise Ratchik's value in Moscow when he got the Mongol ambassador out of bed early in the morning and demanded that he give me a visa. That way we got an Aeroflot plane the same day that landed at Omsk and Tomsk and finally deposited us in Irkutsk, where we waited a long time for the two engined Antonov of Mongol Air. By mistake I picked up what I thought was the only British passport in Irkutsk and met its owner, the wife of the British ambassador to Mongolia, who was on the same plane.

There was only one hotel in Ulan Bator, a city where a large proportion of the population still lived in yurts (felt tents). The adult inhabitants had deeply lined faces from constant exposure to the extreme climate. A large proportion were bow–legged–having spent a good deal of their lives in the saddle in a country with two and a half million horses and only a million people. They drank fermented mare's milk (kumiss) which they boiled with tea, and they ate a good deal of horsemeat, often steaks sliced off the haunch of a living animal. The food in the hotel was abysmal. The Yugoslav cook had gone insane trying to improve the local diet. There had been a big expansion in cereal output, so he had put bread on the menu, but it came in damp, heavy, unsliceable chunks. Fortunately, Heath Mason, the British Ambassador, invited me to dinner a couple of times. The Embassy was in the hotel, and he got a regular monthly supply of Yorkshire steak and kidney puddings, delivered in the diplomatic pouch by two Queen's messengers who helped eat them.

The country had broken away from Chinese rule in the early 20th century and had been in the Soviet sphere of influence since the 1920s as a buffer state. The princely class, and the large population of Lamaistic Buddhist monks had been obliterated. The old cursive script, written in vertical columns was replaced by cyrillic, written horizontally. The political system was organised on the Soviet model, with large amounts of Soviet aid and technical assistance, and there was a large Soviet military presence. In the Summer of 1939, these Soviet forces had repulsed a Japanese invasion in the battle of Khalkhin-Gol.

Chirendev, the head of the Academy of Sciences, was an atomic physicist and told us about its major research projects. The biggest was on agriculture, a second on mathematical and natural sciences, with a much smaller commitment to social sciences. There was also research activity in the University of Ulan Bator and in the geological institute. In all, there were 9,000 people with higher education and a 1,000 of these were in research institutes. We also talked to the ministers of labour and education, the rector of the university, the planning ministry and the statistical office. It was difficult to assess the impact of science and technical change on growth, but there had clearly been large changes over the previous 40 years. Communication was sometimes a bit difficult. I asked Mrs. Lchamsoryn, the president of the State Commission on Labour and Wages, how many people were unemployed. The interpreter told me it was a silly question. I persisted, and was told that 'under socialism there can be no unemployment'.

We made a field trip about 30 kilometres out of Ulan Bator to a collective farm where there were a lot of yurts huddled together surrounded by wooden fences to mitigate the cold wind. Here as elsewhere, there were hundreds of horses. We went to an outlying brigade, a kilometre or so from the farm headquarters, to have some boiled tea and interview an old peasant. I asked him what difference socialism had brought, and he said, echoing Lenin, that socialism meant electricity. It was only then that I noticed an electric wire from the main camp to his yurt. As Mongols move their herds and yurts around to different pasture in the course of the year, I wondered if the electricity moved with them.

We managed to get enough statistical material for our report and left after a week. Getting out was difficult as the electrical system in the aircraft failed just after take off. We managed to glide back and the elderly pilot spent several hours unsuccessfully working on it with a spanner. Eventually he borrowed the presidential plane, which looked the same outside, but inside had a salon and a bedroom configuration rather than serried rows of seats. We got to Irkutsk about 10 hours late. After the usual halts in Omsk and Tomsk, we spent a freezing day in Moscow visiting IMEMO, then flew to Delhi and Bangkok for stop-offs before going on to Pnom Penh for our next mission, where we swapped our fur covering for straw coolie hats.

USSR AND JAPAN

In mid-1965 Goldsmith was replaced as Vice President of the Centre by Ian Little. Ian brought in a new team of Fellows (Tibor Scitovsky and Maurice Scott) to work together on a common project on industrialisation and trade. As I was not part of this project, I was able to spend a good deal of time on a study of Japanese and Soviet growth. Both of these countries had attempted to accelerate their growth performance and catch up with the advanced countries, so it seemed useful to assess what they had achieved and how they did it.

In 1964 I had visited Moscow and Leningrad to collect material for work on Soviet growth. I contacted IMEMO (the Institute for World Politics and Economics) in Moscow (which was the main institute of the Academy of Sciences for studying western economies), and found myself unexpectedly welcome as their Deputy Director, Manoukian, had just translated my book, *Economic Growth in the West*. The most outspoken and interesting of their economists was Stanislav Menshikov, who became a good friend.

It was more difficult to meet economists working on the Soviet economy, but with some difficulty I got the telephone number of Gosplan and contacted Valentin Kudrov who had translated the OEEC real income studies into Russian. Kudrov came, with a minder, to meet me at the Metropole Hotel. In his halting English and my very limited Russian, we managed to have a dialogue in which I sounded his opinion of several US Kremlinologists whose work was my main quantitative source, and we had an exchange of views on problems of measuring real product and growth which we still continue.

Apart from this I managed to take in something of the flavour of Soviet society, being accosted by people wanting Beatles records, looking at museums, watching the May Day parade in Red Square, with Kruschev, Ben Bella and Oginga Odinga on Lenin's tomb.

In 1965, I visited Japan for a few weeks to collect material on Japanese growth. Here it was possible to have a much deeper dialogue than in Moscow, and statistical information was readily available. I already had friends in Hitotsubashi University, particularly Kazushi Ohkawa, who was starting to publish 13 volumes on Japanese quantitative economic history. Saburo Okita opened the doors of government agencies such as the Bank of Japan, the Economic Planning Agency, the Ministry of Agriculture, and the Ministry of Education where one could often find ten economists in a room all fresh and eager to talk after their morning callisthenics. Apart from the sophistication of these people, I was struck by the strong discipline and an organisation that operated like clockwork. I had had the same impression about Japanese industry on my first trip in 1961 when I had visited the Sony radio factory, and found the foremen had Ph.D's and all the operatives had high school education.

During 1966, when I was writing up the Japan-Russia study, I was fortunate in having fairly frequent contact with Arthur Lewis. I visited him a couple of times in Princeton, he spent six weeks in the Centre in the Summer of 1966 and we met from time to time afterwards as members of an OECD expert group on technical assistance. Arthur was probably the brightest economist to work on development and as a West Indian, had a lifetime familiarity with the problems. I profited greatly from contact with him, both in our daily luncheon sessions in Paris, and from his written comments on my drafts which were always forthright, penetrating and enlightening.

ECONOMIC PROGRESS AND POLICY IN DEVELOPING COUNTRIES

At the beginning of 1967 I left OECD, and wrote the general survey of postwar development experience I had considered doing three years earlier. This was financed by the Twentieth Century Fund of New York. For the next two and a half years I worked at home in Paris, with a couple of brief spells as a visiting academic, in Berkeley in 1968, and in Montreal in 1969.

At that time, I became strongly influenced by Edward Denison's comparative growth accounting approach which incorporated the theoretical insights of Bob Solow and Ted Schultz. I made some departures from Denison in giving a bigger weight to capital and introducing domestic policy and foreign aid as part of the explanatory framework. The book covered 29 countries and involved a great deal of statistical groundwork, to estimate comparative levels of real GDP, stocks of physical and human capital as well as comparable estimates of growth of GDP and for major sectors. One of the main chapters is included above as essay one.

The rest of the book dealt largely with policy issues concerning reasons for instability of the growth path, problems in agricultural, industrial and trade policy and attitudes to population growth. Although country performance varied widely, the tone of the book was optimistic about the significant acceleration in postwar growth. A major shortcoming was that it neglected the social impact of growth, something I felt should be next on my research agenda.

SOCIAL POLICY IN PAKISTAN AND GHANA

Pakistan

I went to Pakistan for the Harvard Advisory Group (16) at the end of June 1969, to work on social problems in the Planning Commission in Islamabad.
I already had some knowledge of the country. I had met Chief Economist, Mahbub ul Haq, in Bangkok in 1962 when we were members of a UN expert group which produced a report on *Methods of Long Term Projections*. He arranged a visit I made to Pakistan in May 1965 when I met several other very bright and well trained Pakistani economists, notably Nurul Islam, Sartaj Aziz and Khalid Ikram and I attended a conference in Harvard in 1965 on Pakistani economic development where I met American economists who had

worked on Pakistan including Edward Mason, Hollis Chenery, Gus Papanek and Kenneth Galbraith.

As Pakistan got a good deal of foreign aid, its administration was more open to foreign advisors than most. Indeed part of the advisory work was to brief the continuous stream of World Bank missions. There was a political change shortly before I went which seemed to promise some scope for advance in social policy.

From 1958 the military government of Ayub Khan had had a doctrine of functional inequality: 'The underdeveloped countries must consciously accept a philosophy of growth and shelve for the distant future all ideas of equitable distribution and welfare state. It should be recognised that these are luxuries which only developed countries can afford' (17).

Ayub was toppled in March 1969 by workers and students in a climate of social unrest. Political opposition was gathering strength in East Pakistan because of the uneven allocation of foreign aid and the fruits of development. The new military dictator, Yahya Khan, took a number of measures to appease discontent, suspending 15 per cent of high level civil servants for corruption, raising the minimum wage, chastising business tax evaders, promising more resources to education and to East Pakistan.

The Planning Commission was the central agency coordinating economic policy and foreign aid in the new capital, Islamabad (designed by Doxiadis). It was part of the Presidential Secretariat, the President being the Minister to whom we reported, with M.M. Ahmad as Deputy Chairman. Ahmad was a moderate, doleful, and reserved chap who was hereditary leader of a small religious sect, the Ahmadiyas. I had the impression that he carried less weight than his predecessor Said Hasan who had worked for Ayub. Mahbub had a very powerful role with direct access to the President when necessary. The defender of the corporate interests of the old bureaucracy was Qamar-ul-Islam, a top member of the Civil Service of Pakistan (CSP), an elite group descended directly from the Indian Civil Service (ICS) of colonial days.

In the Commission my main job was to scrutinise policy proposals for education, health, housing, urban water supply, and family planning that came from the relevant ministries and the regional planning agencies in Dacca and Karachi. I had to get a perspective of what was feasible from whatever documentary evidence I could collect, cross-examining my colleagues, and occasional visits to hospitals or public works projects. Apart from Nafees Sadek, who produced a brilliant report on family planning, the Commission was not rich in expertise on these matters, but Charles Benson of the Ford Foundation was a knowledgeable colleague on education.

My work did not involve particularly sophisticated comparisons of costs and benefits but it provided fascinating insight into the social situation and the systematic biases in resource allocation which derived from the character

of the power elite. I never had any problem with Mahbub in being forthright
on such issues, and parts of my drafts emerged in several chapters of the plan.
Whether I had much impact on what happened is another issue, but I may
have contributed something to checking programmes I thought were
misguided.

Pakistan's social structure was still strongly influenced by the heritage of
the British raj. The nationalist forces which had created Pakistan had no
element of socialism or social reform as in India, nor were they particularly
religious. Their religious content was primarily anti-Hindu and certainly not
Islamic in any fundamentalist sense. The Pakistan Jinnah created was
Viceregal and the primary locus of power was the bureaucratic-military elite.
The organisational framework of this group was still the one created by the
British and their working language was English. Their houses, clubs,
cantonments, life style and idioms were British colonial. The group was
much bigger than in colonial days. The armed forces numbered 300,000 with
7,000 officers compared with 100 Muslim officers in the smaller Indian army
of the British period. There were 500 members in the elite CSP and about
1,150 Class I officers under them. This was more than ten times the number
of top Muslim officials under the British. These people got the major benefits
of government housing expenditure. Urban improvements were concentrated
in their cantonment areas. They benefitted substantially from expenditure on
secondary and higher education. The benefits also went to the new class of
businessmen who also got subsidised loans, licenses to import scarce goods
and other perquisites. The traditional landlord elite was virtually untouched
by land reform except in East Pakistan where most landlords had been
Hindus. Landlords in West Pakistan were major beneficiaries of government
expenditure on irrigation, particularly the new waters that became available
after the construction of the Tarbela dam on the Indus river – a World Bank
project intended to replace potential water losses to the Indian Punjab.

The bulk of the population were extremely poor. The average weight of an
adult Pakistani was 120 lbs, i.e. about 30 lbs less than the average European.
Their average haemoglobin count was two thirds of that in Europe, and in
this anaemic state they were readily prone to tuberculosis, pneumonia and
influenza. At any one time, a third of the population suffered from intestinal
disorders, the rural population was infected by hookworm, and prone to
typhoid. Eighty five per cent of the population were illiterate and most
women had a very low status, hidden behind veils with very few
opportunities to get a job.

Many of the proposals we got would have bypassed these people, i.e.
major expansions in secondary and higher education, medical training for
doctors who emigrated on graduation, housing and urban facilities for the
bureaucracy and military. There had been some progress in areas where

welfare gains were cheap. Malaria, dysentery, and smallpox eradication programmes, together with access to simple drugs had prolonged average life expectation from 30 to 50 years in the two decades since independence, and there was plenty of scope for further cheap gains by expanding and improving primary education, better water and sewerage, birth control programmes, better trained teachers and nurses, better rural health centres.

At the beginning of 1970, political criticism of the government increased, particularly in East Pakistan. The Jama'at-i-Islami party (a fundamentalist group advocating violent forms of action) alleged that the Harvard Advisory Group were foreign spies. After this we adopted a lower profile, our workload dropped considerably, and in mid 1970, the Group was discontinued.

In this period of increased leisure, I started a history of India and Pakistan, *Class Structure and Economic Growth*, Allen and Unwin, London, 1971. This explained the emergence of the postcolonial elite from the heritage of Hindu, Moghul and British rule, and showed how the new distribution of power had affected the character of postwar policy and the nature of economic growth. I visited East Pakistan and India for a few weeks to gather more material. Then I went to Harvard for six months, to write up the book and collect further material in the Widener Library. There I attended Alexander Gerschenkron's economic history seminar regularly and went occasionally to lectures by John Fairbank on Chinese history, and by Simon Kuznets on economic growth.

I was more satisfied with the book on India and Pakistan than with most of the other things I had written on development because I had worked for much longer in the country, had had the daily experience of running a household (Harvard gave me a large house and five servants) and had close access to the policy making process. Even the workaday environment of the Commission was enlightening with its four segregated lifts for different categories of civil servant, stairs which only the sweepers used, the bearers who lost documents because they couldn't read the names of the addressees, the all-male group of one-finger typists.

Most members of the Harvard Group were congenial colleagues. There were very interesting places to visit, Lahore (a Moghul capital), Harappa (the seat of the Mohenjo Daro civilisation), Taxila (a town built by Alexander the Great), old British hill stations like Murree and Abbottabad, and the road up the Khyber to Kabul, with stop-offs in Peshawar, Landi Kotal, and Jallalabad.

GHANA

At the end of 1970 I went to Ghana to work in the Ministry of Finance and Planning on social policy. I had been interested in broadening my knowledge of Africa, which, apart from a brief visit to Nigeria, was confined largely to ex-French colonies.

Ghana was the first British African colony to become independent, in 1957, about a year before Guinea broke away from France. Ghana had the same aspirations to break with colonial tradition and create a variety of African socialism. The transition to independence was much easier in Ghana, which inherited large sterling balances from the colonial administration, had a very much larger stock of educated people, and some political experience before independence (with Kwame Nkrumah as prime minister). It was not cut off from the rest of the commonwealth or aid from the metropole as Guinea had been. The Gold Coast had been run as a coherent entity, whereas Guinea was carved out of a much larger French administrative area on the eve of independence.

Ghana was unusual in Africa in having built up a very large export sector of relatively prosperous peasant cocoa farmers. White settler agriculture was virtually non-existent, because the climate is extremely unattractive. It was a rather egalitarian country as access to land was easy, and there were no barriers of religion or caste to impede social mobility. Women were much freer in Ghana than was the case in Pakistan or in Islamic Guinea. Conjugal ties are informal, and it was quite common to find successful businesswomen with several children who had never had a husband. Because of the relative abundance of land and the steady nature of the climate, hunger was not a significant problem.

Nkrumah had expanded the government sector of the economy considerably. There had been a big push for industrialisation. In agriculture he created state farms, there was large investment in infrastructure projects, e.g. the large new port in Tema, the highway between Accra and Tema, and lavish conference facilities for Pan African conferences. He provided aid to some other African countries, Guinea in particular. He greatly extended the education network and the size of the administration. He spent the sterling balances, accumulated foreign debt, and squeezed the income of cocoa farmers. Many of the investment projects were ill conceived, and some were disastrously wasteful. The result was economic stagnation, substantial inflation, balance of payments crisis, and allocation of resources by licensing which led to inefficiency and corruption.

In 1966, Nkrumah was overthrown by the armed forces and went into exile in Guinea. The military have ruled the country off and on ever since, but I went there during a brief interval when Kofi Busia was prime minister, after elections in August 1969.

The objectives of economic policy were not very clear when I was there. It was felt that Nkrumah had made major errors and that his thrust in policy should be stopped. However, there was no policy to remedy the balance of payments problems, there had been little reduction in the state's economic commitments, and there was still a large network of administrative controls. Official interest in the social sectors was desultory and the Finance Minister, Mensah, took decisions without much reference to his staff. Busia, the Prime Minister exercised little control over his ministers. He was a mild mannered ex-professor, in rather poor health. He was keen on European advisors, particularly if they came from Oxford, and he did not trust his own people much.

I found the government's housing policy had the same bias as in Pakistan. The top civil servants and army officers aspired to colonial style bungalows on quarter acre plots with two car garages. Most of governmental expenditure on housing went into buildings which approached these standards. There were about 60,000 government houses. They represented only about 6 per cent of the total housing stock but 60 per cent of the houses which did not have mud walls. They were allocated by the state housing corporation, the armed forces and police, the Tema Development Corporation, Ministries of Education, Health etc. All these authorities were making big losses because they charged only 7 per cent of the occupants' salaries in rent. Gross rents from these houses were about 5 million cedis whereas I estimated a private developer would need 40 million cedis to make a reasonable return.

I recommended a large cutback in building of such houses, an increase in rents and diversion of the money to better provision of water and sewerage, and research on improved ways of building and roofing the mudwalled tin-roofed housing in which 90 per cent of the population lived.

As I could find no way to get the Minister of Finance to read my report, I gave it to the Prime Minister, who, to the consternation of the civil service and army, decided to implement my recommendation to double the rents of government owned housing. I had suggested that the increase be phased in gradually, but he did it at one swoop. This was probably the greatest influence I ever had as an advisor, but its implementation helped to topple Busia.

At about the same time my Harvard colleagues persuaded the PM not to implement the 30 per cent increase in government salaries which he was well known to be contemplating, on the grounds that such a policy would raise prices rather than real incomes.

The juxtaposition of two unpopular decisions in one prime ministerial speech sparked off riots and Busia's fall seemed increasingly probable. On the 10th July, he gave a banquet for top level officials of the central and provincial government, the police and the military. He told them they should work harder, be less corrupt, and pointed with pride to a tiny enclave of foreign advisors who were serving him so well. At this time, I resigned, partly for health reasons, and partly because of the obvious dangers of foreign advisors giving advice which was subject to virtually no filtering processes before being implemented. The organisational and policy basis for putting the country back on its feet seemed extremely feeble. Busia was deposed by the military about six months later, the economy went downhill over the next decade, and in spite of some recent gains, per capita income is still below the 1950 level.

SOCIAL POLICY IN OECD COUNTRIES: EDUCATION

In August 1971 I returned to OECD and to the end of 1978 worked on social policy issues, mainly education, income distribution and employment problems.

The notion of education as human capital analogous to physical capital had been put forward by Schultz in 1961 and received a warm welcome from economists. The idea was also taken up enthusiastically by educationists who found its central argument a useful support in bolstering educational budgets. However by the 1970s, serious doubts had started to arise about the private and the social returns obtained from the very rapid expansion of education in the 1960s.

The sceptics included those who argued that education was to an important degree a screening device, that there was overemphasis on formal credentials, that it was difficult to distinguish the role of intelligence, family background and education in determining earnings, and there were people with new and radical policy messages (such as Jencks and Illich) who cast strong doubts on the contribution of formal education.

In this complex field there is a paucity of sharp evidence, and unlike the OECD economic committees where there is some degree of professional discourse, meetings on education involved civil servants and policy makers with very diverse background and training. As a result, it seemed to me that new policy initiatives sometimes involved reckless experimentation.

I felt my most useful contribution to rational policy making would be to improve the quality and comparability of the quantitative evidence on earnings and education, on educational costs and benefits, on levels of formal educational achievement and enrolment. In pursuit of this aim we created a committee on educational statistics which produced the first *OECD Yearbook of Education Statistics* in 1974. This was designed to show the flow of pupils through different levels of formal education in the framework of demographic accounts, so that one could easily compare the enrolment situation in the different countries by sex and age. It also showed stocks of educated people in the population broken down by age, and public expenditure on education. The analysis was backed by a standardised classification of education in OECD countries which appeared in 10 volumes from 1972 to 1975 ard provided a detailed basis for comparing equivalent levels of educational provision. We made pilot studies of total public and private expenditure by level of education (including earnings foregone of students in postcompulsory education) and made a beginning in assessing of participation in and expenditure on training and adult education (18).

The major gap in the indicators was a measure of the cognitive performance of pupils over time and at different levels. The IEA (Institute of Educational Achievement) had gathered a great deal of useful comparative evidence by organising a massive series of tests in 22 countries for secondary education, but was reluctant to consolidate its findings to provide an aggregate picture of educational performance (19). There was in fact a good deal of resistance in educational circles to studies which might make it possible to judge the quality of teachers and curricula.

At that time, governments were concerned with the distributional impact of education, but it was clear that people had very different conceptions of its equalising potential. Some had meritocratic goals in mind and wanted to achieve a gradual downward expansion of opportunity, giving bright children from poorer families a chance to rise in the social hierarchy. Others saw expansion of education as a process for changing the social structure, and reducing income dispersion by a massive increase in the proportion of people with higher education. Some were primarily interested in changing attitudes. They wanted to use the education system as a vehicle of fraternity-reducing status differentials and other kinds of social distance. I tried to assemble evidence on these issues and organised a major conference which involved a confrontation between eminent economists, sociologists and educationalists (20). On the whole I found education a disappointing field for effective international cooperation because of the difficulties of measuring performance and the power of interest groups to resist the production of relevant evidence (21).

THE WELFARE STATE

In 1974–5, there was a sharp recession which affected the USA and Japan as well as virtually all the European countries. This was accompanied by a burst of inflation whose intensity was unparalleled in peacetime. In the event, it turned out that the Western economies had entered a new phase of development, where growth was much slower and less stable than in the postwar golden age.

These unprecedented developments led to a disturbing reorientation in the macroeconomic policy objectives and armoury of OECD countries, but they also led to a reexamination of the size and structure of government social spending and social tranfers.

By the early 1970s, government spending in European countries had risen to an average of about 40 per cent of GDP. The bulk of this went on social programmes. Further expansion in these was triggered automatically in recession as payments for income support rose and indexed benefits kept pace with inflation. There were also large expenditures on industrial subsidies.

These programmes had expanded in the earlier period of rapid economic growth in response to mixed policy objectives, some of which were redistributive, some of an insurance character, some simply a response to the pressure of interested lobbies. In order to finance these programmes, governments had increased their revenue mainly by a large increase in social security levies with a regressive incidence. There was a substantial degree of income churning in which governments collected taxes and paid out transfers to the same people without much net effect on income distribution.

Nevertheless, the welfare state had strengthened the forces making for economic growth and stability. It had also made capitalist property relations and the operation of market forces more legitimate by removing most of the grievances which motivated proponents of a socialist alternative. As a result the 'socialist' parties in these countries had generally abandoned the aim of nationalising industry or significantly interfering with the operation of market forces.

Between 1974 and 1978 I spent a good deal of time on problems of the equity and efficiency of tax-transfer systems. We created a committee on social aspects of income transfer policy with Ian Byatt, of the UK Treasury, as chairman. The committee explored a wide range of distributive issues: incomes policies, poverty traps, incentives, unemployment compensation, minimum wages, distribution of income and wealth, tax and social security reform. We also did a pilot survey of the tax transfer systems of France, Italy, the Netherlands and the UK.

The time was propitious for such research. The OECD fiscal committee put out a number of very useful comparative studies on the structure of taxation, tax incidence by income level and its effect on incentives. The economics directorate published a series of studies on various kinds of public expenditure, and income distribution (22). In the UK, the Royal Commission on the Distribution of Income and Wealth put out eight major reports from 1976 to 1979, and the Swedish Low Incomes Commission had put out a 12 volume report in the early 1970s. In the USA, the Brookings Institution (animated by Joe Pechman and Henry Aaron) carried out a vast array of studies on tax incidence and social security. Together with Alice Rivlin as Director of the new Congressional Budget Office they worked as an effective pressure group for reform in these areas. In France, the Giscard government gave prominence to distributive issues in its early stages, particularly in the preparations for the seventh plan.

In the 1980s, political attitudes on these issues changed a good deal. The Thatcher governments in the UK and the Reagan-Bush administrations in the USA rejected the egalitarian bias in the distributive policy of earlier governments, made big reductions in the incidence of direct taxes and succeeded in bringing substantial increases in inequality. The policy switch in other countries was less extreme, but the political interest in monitoring these problems was sharply diminished, and the results of several of our studies were not published (23). In fact the size of the welfare state has risen since the 1970s. Popular support for it is very firmly embedded in European countries, so there were 'automatic' increases in benefits when unemployment rose and there was an influx of poor immigrants from outside the area. Furthermore governments tended to cushion the social impact of anti-inflationary macro-policy by expanding programmes to disguise unemployment (such as the large expenditure on early retirement in France or the huge expansion in the number of people drawing 'handicapped' benefits in the Netherlands). Hence the problems of balancing equity and efficiency in social spending are just as sharp as they were in the 1970s, and the usefulness of internationally comparable monitoring exercises are rather clear.

UNEMPLOYMENT AND LABOUR MARKET ANALYSIS

The recession and slowdown in economic growth in the OECD economies in the 1970s had major implications for the labour market. Unemployment had been at frictional and seasonal minima in the 1960s, and cyclical unemployment had virtually disappeared. But by 1978, European unemployment was two and a half times as large as in 1973 and would have been significantly higher if governments had not taken measures to check immigration, to entice people to leave the labour force or to work part-time. The OECD Committee on Manpower and Social Affairs therefore found its agenda full of new and pressing problems and the importance of the issues caused it to be raised to Ministerial level in 1976.

There was clearly a need to improve comparative monitoring of the situation in the labour market. OECD already had a regular publication (Labour Force Statistics) which I had always used for analysing labour input in comparative macroeconomic accounts, but the definitions of unemployment differed considerably from one country to another. They were derived from different sources (mostly administrative as labour force sample surveys were then far from general) and governments sometimes changed the definitions for political purposes.

As a first step in improving the situation, I asked the US Bureau of Labor Statistics in 1975 to lend us one of their experts (Connie Sorrentino) to examine the inter-country variance in definitions of unemployment and make recommendations for standardisation. We then set up a committee of labour statisticians to consider more closely the possibilities for improved labour market monitoring. BLS provided the chairmanship of the committee. We followed up the Sorrentino report by a more detailed study, *Measuring Employment and Unemployment* (1979) which analysed in full detail the scope of the different national unemployment and employment statistics. This provided a basis for improved monitoring for the ministerial committee, but there was a need to push the analysis further by looking at dimensions of labour 'slack' other than unemployment, e.g. measures to encourage a reverse flow of immigrant workers, reductions in activity rates through increased provisions for early retirement, classification of less efficient workers as handicapped, incentives to promote short time working and cut working hours, or incentives to firms to hoard workers. Germany was a rather extreme case where unemployment in 1978 was 3.8 per cent of the labour force, but 'labour slack' was 8.6 per cent. I therefore proposed the adoption of a systematic set of labour market accounts which would put labour market participation into a demographic framework (24) and measure labour input in terms of total hours worked. The advantage of this for labour market analysis was obvious, and the measure also had more general application for growth and productivity accounts. Such accounts necessarily involve merger of data from different sources, and in their full version also involve assessment of deviations of actual labour input from 'normal' (for migration, activity rates, working hours, and unemployment). Labour statisticians are much less used to data merger and imputations of this kind than are national accountants, so progress in this area has been slow. Nevertheless, several countries now have accounts of this kind, e.g. Finland, France, Germany and Sweden.

My basic feeling about the social policy issues on which I worked in OECD was that the analytical basis for policy decisions was rather poor. Consequently decision-making relied too much on hunches or reactions to interested pressure groups. There was a need for monitoring frameworks analogous to the growth accounts and cyclical indicators available for macroeconomic policy, and I tried to develop something appropriate in each of the three fields. What I did was slow to make an impact, but not without long term influence. There were frustrations when one was rowing against the stream, but there were also opportunities for doing something new if one took the right initiatives, used the appropriate networks and picked the right chairperson for intergovernmental committees. The possibilities for freewheeling initiatives and conjuring up research funds were in fact greater than in OECD macropolicy work where governmental interests and perceptions were more clearly focussed.

ACADEMIC LIFE IN GRONINGEN

My main reason for leaving the OECD and entering academic life was to have more freedom to pursue my own research agenda. The University of Groningen was the ideal spot for me. It was founded in 1614, and has over 20,000 students in a picturesque old town of 150,000, with canals, a sixteenth century cathedral and a night life which can compete with the boulevard St. Michel and the rue St. Denis in Paris. There are about 200 economists teaching in the faculties of economics, econometrics and business science. Most of the teaching I did has been at graduate level on economic growth and development in different parts of the world economy. There is plenty of scope for interdisciplinary cooperation with economic historians and sociologists who are also part of the economics faculty. The graduate students are exceptionally well qualified for comparative quantitative work, as they are computer literate, fluent in two or three languages and willing to learn more. There is a research school for Ph.D. students. I have supervised 12 of them, and most of their theses have been published. (25)

Since I went there in 1978, I have written two books which covered the development of 16 advanced capitalist countries in a comparative framework of historical growth accounts. I tried to analyse both the supply side possibilities and to see the influence of policy and the international economic order in determining economic performance. The analytical frame work of these books and associated articles (26) was strongly influenced on the supply side by John Kendrick, Edward Denison, and Moses Abramovitz with whom I have had frequent contact in various ways.

I continued to work on lower income countries in a comparative economic context, both to quantify their economic performance and to assess the influence of indigenous institutions and colonialism in explaining their relative economic backwardness. I extended my analysis to cover world economic performance in two books published by the OECD Development Centre. (27)

In the past 10 years or so, the Groningen research programme in my field has had two main branches: (a) growth analysis; (b) level analysis.

In the first field I created a network of researchers on historical growth accounts in the Club des Chiffrephiles (28). We organised four international workshops on quantitative economic history in Groningen in 1984, 1985, 1989 and 1994 and I also persuaded the International Association for Research in Income and Wealth to renew its interest in historical national accounts in seminars in 1987 and 1992. More recently we started to reexamine the long-run estimates of growth performance of the East European economies and China. In this way it has been possible to widen the scope of historical national accounts to cover the bulk of the world economy well back into the nineteenth century, and some of our associates have pushed back the quantification much earlier.

In comparative economic history, it is necessary to measure levels of performance as well as growth. The second major focus of our Groningen research effort has therefore been on international comparisons of real product by industry of origin. This is a complement to the expenditure side estimates initiated by Kravis, Heston and Summers, and it is more useful for growth and productivity analysis. The analytical statistics we get from such work help to sharpen analysis of the causes of economic growth, catch-up and convergence, lead-country/follower-country phenomena, and the locus of technical progress. Since 1983, this ICOP (International Comparisons of Output and Productivity) programme has produced more than 60 publications. The history and methodology of the approach are set out in Maddison and van Ark 1988 and 1994 (29). The basic data on value added, productivity and purchasing power are derived from censuses of production. Our interests have been worldwide, but we did not aspire to comprehensive coverage. We were satisfied to concentrate our efforts on relatively large countries which provide a representative picture of world population and output covering a very wide range of income levels. The estimates have so far covered 13 countries for agriculture and mining and 21 countries for manufacturing. For the core countries Argentina, Brazil, China, France, Germany, Indonesia, Japan, Korea, Mexico, Netherlands, the UK and USA we have developed a network of associated researchers, and more recently have extended the work to East European countries. As the methodology has been clearly articulated and our worksheets are as transparent as possible, the basic approach is now rather easy to replicate and such comparisons have attracted visiting researchers from Australia, Bulgaria, China, Finland, Russia and Portugal.

NOTES

1. H.G. Johnson, 'Cambridge in the 1950s, Memoirs of An Economist', *Encounter*, January 1974, pp. 28–39.
2. L. Rostas, *Comparative Productivity in British and American Industry*, Cambridge University Press, 1948.
3. U.S. Strategic Bombing Survey, *The Effects of Strategic Bombing on the German War Economy*, October 1945 (the authors included Kenneth Galbraith, Paul Baran, Edward Denison, Tibor Scitovsky, and Nicholas Kaldor).
4. See Eric Roll, *Crowded Hours*, Faber and Faber, London, 1985, Chapter 6 on the work of the Programmes Committee of which he was chairman. The Programmes Committee was the predecessor of the Economic Committee.

5. Robert Marjolin, *Architect of European Unity, Memoirs 1911–1986*, Weidenfeld and Nicolson, London, 1989.
6. See the (May 5th 1955) comment of Hall in A. Cairncross, ed., *The Robert Hall Diaries 1954–61*, Unwin Hyman, 1991, p.35 on the significance of the expert group: 'These meetings are really something quite exceptional for economists and I should think are quite new in the history of the world, in the sense that economic experts, if they existed at all as Government advisers, were not generally very important people until Keynes's ideas had been commonly accepted in the West. So that there were not the people to meet as we do: now we have 7 or 8 or 9 people who are by and large the chief professional advisers of the main Western Governments except Canada – all have more or less the same professional training in that they understand how to maintain the level of activity and what forces operate on it.'
7. See S. Kuznets, 'Discussion of the New Department of Commerce Income Series. National Income: A New Version', and 'Objectives of National Income Measurement, A Reply to Professor Kuznets', by M. Gilbert, G. Jaszi, E.F. Denison, and C.F. Schwartz in *Review of Economics and Statistics*, August 1948. For Gilbert's role in developing the accounts, see C.S. Carson, 'The History of the United States National Income and Product Accounts', *Review of Income and Wealth*, June 1975.
8. M. Gilbert and I.B. Kravis, *An International Comparison of National Products and the Purchasing Power of Currencies*, OEEC, Paris, 1954; M. Gilbert and Associates, *Comparative National products and Price Levels*, OEEC, Paris, 1958; D. Paige and G. Bombach, *A Comparison of National Output and Productivity*, OEEC, Paris, 1959.
9. See comments on Gilbert's style in Murray Rossant's foreword to M. Gilbert, *Quest for World Monetary Order*, J. Wiley and Sons, New York, 1980, p. viii.
10. *Europe Today and in 1960*, OEEC, 1957; *A Decade of Cooperation: Achievements and Perspectives*, OEEC, 1958; *Policies for Sound Economic Growth*, OEEC, 1959; *Europe and the World Economy*, OEEC, 1960.
11. See E. van Lennep, *Herinneringen van een internationale Nederlander*, Stenfert Kroese, Leiden, 1991.
12. The Development Centre started to collect national accounts information from developing countries in 1964, held a few seminars on their comparability, and produced its first regular estimates in 1968, *National Accounts of Less Developed Countries 1950–1966*.
13. My contribution to the Centre's work on aid consisted of two books, A. Maddison, *Foreign Skills and Technical Assistance in Economic Development*, OECD Development Centre, 1965, and A. Maddison, A. Stavrianopoulos and B. Higgins, *Foreign Skills and Technical Assistance in Greek Development*, OECD Development Centre, Paris, 1966.
14. See A. Maddison and Associates, *The Political Economy of Poverty, Equity and Growth: Brazil and Mexico*, Oxford University Press, New York, 1992.
15. See Elliott J. Berg, 'Socialism and Economic Development in Tropical Africa', *Quarterly Journal of Economics*, 1964, for an excellent analysis of the roots of African socialism.
16. See George Rosen, *Western Economists and Eastern Societies: Agents of Change in South Asia 1950–1970*, Johns Hopkins, Baltimore, 1985 for a description of the Harvard Group's experience in Pakistan.
17. Mahbub ul Haq, *The Strategy of Economic Planning: A Case Study of Pakistan*, OUP, Karachi, 1966, p. 30.

18. L. Lévy Garboua, S. Newman, T. Noda, A. Peacock, T. Watanabe, and M. Woodhall, *Educational Expenditure in France, Japan, and the United Kingdom*, OECD, 1977). The work on educational statistics has been institutionalised on a somewhat irregular basis. The latest report is Education in OECD countries 1987–88, Paris, 1990. However, the work on statistics of the stock of educated persons, which is particularly useful for growth accounts, has now been dropped.

19. See my comment on IEA in A.C. Purves and D.U. Levine, *Educational Policy and International Assessment: Implications of the IEA Surveys of Achievement*, McCutchan, Berkeley, 1975.

20. See OECD, *Education, Inequality and Life Chances*, OECD, Paris, 1977.

21. See A. Maddison, 'What is Education For', *Lloyds Bank Review*, April 1974, for a general survey of educational objectives.

22. M. Sawyer, 'Income Distribution in OECD Countries', *OECD Economic Outlook, Occasional Studies*, July 1976.

23. I set out my own views in 'Origins and Impact of the Welfare State', *Banca Nazionale del Lavoro Quarterly Review*, March 1984.

24. See 'Monitoring the Labour Market: A Proposal for a Comprehensive Approach in Official Statistics (illustrated by recent developments in France, Germany and the UK)', *Review of Income and Wealth*, June 1980. My proposals for a functional classification of manpower and employment budgets can be found in my Shell Lecture 'Why Do Unemployment Rates Differ?', University of Buckingham Employment Research Centre, October 1983. In 1988, the – (pp. 84–114) for the first time OECD published comparative labour market budgets for 22 OECD Member countries, with a functional breakdown not unlike that which I had suggested.

25. The most recent are C. de Neubourg, *Unemployment, Labour Slack and Labour Market Accounting* , 1987; T. Elfring, *Service Employment in Advanced Economies*, 1988; E. Bax, *Modernisation and Cleavage in Dutch Society*, 1988; J. Reijnders, *The Enigma of Long Waves*, 1988; S. Manarungsan, *The Economic Development of Thailand 1850–1950*, 1989; van B. Ark, *International Comparisons of Output and Productivity*, 1993; D. Pilat, *The Economics of Catch-Up, The Experience of Japan and Korea*, 1993; and P. van der Eng, *Agricultural Growth in Indonesia since 1880*, 1993.

26. See *Phases of Capitalist Development*, Oxford University Press, 1982, *Dynamic Forces in Capitalist Development*, Oxford University Press, 1991, 'Growth and Slowdown in Advanced Capitalist Economies: Techniques of Quantitative Assesment', *Journal of Economic Literature*, June 1987, 'Ultimate and Proximate Growth Causality: A Critique of Mancur Olson on the Rise and Decline of Nations', *Scandinavian Economic History Review*, No.2, 1988.

27. See A. Maddison, *The World Economy in the Twentieth Century*, OECD Development Centre, Paris, 1989; A. Maddison and G. Prince, *Economic Growth in Indonesia 1820–1940*, Foris, Dordrecht and New York, 1989, A. Maddison and Associates, *The Political Economy of Poverty, Equity and Growth: Brazil and Mexico*, Oxford University Press, New York, 1992; A. Maddison, *Monitoring the World Economy 1820–1992*, OECD Development Centre, 1994.

28. 'Chiffrephile' is a word I invented to characterise economists and economic historians, who, like myself, have a strong predilection for quantification.

29. My interest in this kind of comparative work goes back a long way, see 'Productivity in Canada, the United Kingdom and the United States', *Oxford Economic Papers*, October 1952, *Economic Progress and Policy in Developing Countries*, Norton, New York, 1970. The ICOP work began with 'A Comparison

of Levels of GDP Fer Capita in Developed and Developing Countries 1700–1980', *Journal of Economic History*, March 1983. The ICOP methodology is set out in A. Maddison and B. van Ark, *Comparisons of Real Output in Manufacturing*, World Bank, 1988, and A. Maddison and B. van Ark, 'The International Comparison of Real Product and Productivity', Research Memorandum, Groningen Growth and Development Centre, 1994. See also A. Szirmai, B. van Ark, and D. Pilat (eds), *Explaining Economic Growth: Essays in Honour of Angus Maddison*, Elsevier, North Holland, 1993 for the nature of Groningen research activity.

Research Objectives and Results, 1952–2002

Angus Maddison[*]

INTRODUCTION

My major objective has been to explain differences in the growth performance and income levels of nations. I developed a comparative and historical perspective, using a quantitative macroeconomic approach in the tradition of Colin Clark and Simon Kuznets. The influence of my work (15 books and 120 articles) is attested by frequency of citation and translation, and its impact on other scholars trying to measure and understand processes of economic growth, convergence and divergence.

I have played a major part in building up a quantitative historical record of economic growth performance and the causal influences which are measureable. I have developed a network of former students and other researchers in different parts of the world who have constructed or improved macroeconomic accounts for many countries. I have tried to promote consistency and comparability in statistical treatment, with transparent description of sources and methodology.

My work covers three fields: (1) interpretation of the economic performance of advanced capitalist countries; (2) explanation of economic backwardness, retardation and catch-up in the rest of the world and (3) analysis of the pace and pattern of world economic development, and interaction between major parts of the world economy.

INTERPRETING THE DEVELOPMENT OF ADVANCED CAPITALIST COUNTRIES

My early years were spent in the north of England in the 1920s and 1930s where there was massive unemployment and poverty, and the outlook for

---

[*] Mimeographed, Groningen Growth and Development Center.

capitalism seemed bleak. This aroused my interest in economics and an urge to understand processes of economic growth, stagnation and collapse (see my autobiographical essay. '*Confessions of a Chiffrephile*', 1994). Until the early 1960s, my interest was concentrated on the advanced capitalist countries.

In the 1950s and early 1960s, I worked in Paris, as head of the economics division of OEEC and OECD. My first book, *Economic Growth in the West* (1964) was an analysis of the postwar performance of West European capitalism, when growth of output, consumption, productivity, investment and employment surpassed any recorded historical experience. In this period, there was substantial reduction in the income gap between Europe and the world productivity leader, the United States. I attributed this in large part to improvements in domestic economic policy, reduction of barriers to international trade, and effective institutions for close international cooperation. Their impact was reinforced by the increasingly euphoric expectations of investors as the potential for rapid growth became apparent. I developed a detailed supply-side analysis of the special opportunities for catch-up in European countries, emphasising the difference between their growth potential and that of the lead country (the USA), which operates closer to the technological frontier. This approach remained a basic feature of my subsequent assessment of growth in other parts of the world.

This first book contained detailed appendices presenting standardised and comparable estimates of output, investment, labour force participation, employment, working hours and productivity for 12 countries back to 1870. A similar framework of comparable historical statistics has remained a hallmark of my work. I hoped that transparency of this kind would facilitate the research of others in this field.

A major purpose of *Phases of Capitalist Development* (1982) was to find the reasons for the sharp deterioration in Western performance after 1973. The emphasis was again historical and comparative, but went further back in time. It identified five 'phases' of development within the capitalist epoch since 1820, with a scrutiny of earlier epochs in order to highlight their specific features. In interpreting the nature of the marked slowdown after the 1950–73 'golden age', I refined my earlier analysis by use of synchronous and standardized annual indicators. This was an advance on the work of Kuznets, who often used broader comparisons of overlapping decades for somewhat different periods, with less detailed emphasis on comparability and synchronicity. I explained the relation between my approach and that of earlier interpreters of the broad sweep of economic development (Smith, Malthus, Ricardo, Marx and Schumpeter), differentiating my 'phase' analysis from the business cycle approach of Juglar, Tugan-Baranowsky and the National Bureau of Economic Research. I also emphasised the difference between my approach and the long wave analysis of Kondratieff,

Schumpeter's cyclical schema and Kuznets' 'secondary secular movements'. The indicators I use are more representative of macroeconomic performance than the partial indicators of output and prices used by earlier analysts.

After careful scrutiny of the historical record, I found very little evidence for accepting the Kondratieff notion of long waves, and rejected Schumpeter's schema of major clusters of innovation in favour of a more gradualist interpretation of the diffusion of technology. In interpreting breaks in the momentum of development, I emphasised the role of 'system shocks' which were in some degree historical accidents, but whose impact was reinforced by changes in expectations, and fashions in economic policy.

A significant finding of the study was the rejection of the idea of staggered 'take-offs' throughout the nineteenth century which had been espoused earlier by Rostow and Gerschenkron. The improved array of historical national accounts now available suggests that the acceleration in growth in the capitalist epoch was much more synchronised than had hitherto been thought, and that earlier stress on an industrial revolution in the eighteenth century was exaggerated.

The 1982 study devoted greater attention than Maddison (1964) to the interaction between lead and follower countries in the process of technological transfer and catch-up. It analysed the historical succession of lead countries: the Netherlands, the UK and the USA, and the changes in the nature of leadership.

My third major contribution to analysis of advanced capitalist countries, *Dynamic Forces in Capitalist Development* (1991), was an update of the 1982 study. Inspired by the work of Ed Denison, it incorporated a more sophisticated growth accounting exercise, exploiting greatly improved estimates of capital stock to refine the analysis of productivity change and the pace of technological progress. It made a closer analysis of the impact of system shocks on official policy objectives in relation to inflation, employment and exchange rates. My 1995 paper, 'Standardised Estimates of Fixed Capital Stock: A Six Country Comparison' (published in *Explaining the Economic Performance of Nations*) was a major improvement on Appendix D of Maddison (1991). It included annual figures on different types of investment and capital stock for a much longer time period.

I published four contributions to growth accounting methodology which analyse the role of 'proximate' measurable influences and their interaction with deeper layers of causality. The first was 'Explaining Economic Growth', *Banca Nazionale del Lavoro Quarterly review*, September 1972. This was a detailed assessment of Denison's *Why Growth Rates Differ* (1967) and an exploration of its intellectual history. The second was 'Growth and Slowdown in Advanced Capitalist Countries', *Journal of Economic Literature*, 1987, which explained my growth accounting approach and its application to the economic history of six advanced capitalist countries. A third piece was 'Ultimate and Proximate Growth Causality: A Critique of Mancur Olson on the Rise and *Decline of Nations*', *Scandinavian Economic History Review*, 1988 These three concentrated on interpretation of the performance of advanced capitalist countries. The fourth 'Causal Influences on Growth Performance' (chapter 2 of *Monitoring the World Economy, 1820–1992*) is discussed in section 3 below.

EXPLANATION OF ECONOMIC BACKWARDNESS IN THE NON-WESTERN WORLD

From the early 1960s to the early 1970s, I worked mainly on problems of economic development. As Secretary to the Development Assistance Group in OEEC, I organised the first comprehensive statistics on capital flows (*The Flow of Financial Resources to countries in Course of Economic Development, 1956–59*, 1961), was engaged in economic advisory work in Greece, Turkey, Brazil, Mexico, Pakistan and Ghana, and in research in the OECD Development Centre, the Twentieth Century Fund and the Harvard Advisory Service.

The major aim of my work in this field was to understand why the rest of the world is poorer than Western countries and to distinguish different types of non-Western experience.

As in the work on advanced countries, I attached great importance to establishing a corpus of historical statistics on growth performance and comparative levels of development. Differences in the level of development in the non-Western countries are very wide and there is great heterogeneity in their institutional heritage. In interpreting the reasons for 'backwardness', I explored the role of colonialism, indigenous social forces, institutions, property rights, religion and ideology.

My field experience of the complexity and variety of country situations made me chary of stylised generalisations about 'the third world'. For this reason, I concentrated first on country studies. I produced five of these, covering seven large non-western countries, which include more than half the world's population.

The first of these was *Economic Growth in Japan and the USSR* (1969). This combined a comparative quantitative survey of their development, with an analysis of their very different catch-up strategies between the 1860s and the 1960s. In preparing this study, I visited the USSR and Japan to see what material I could collect and to exchange views with policy analysts and statisticians. I was able to make contact with IMEMO (Institute for World Politics and Economics) and Gosplan in Moscow, where I had very fruitful discussions with Stanislav Menshikov and Valentin Kudrov. I spent longer in

Japan where I had friends in Hitotsubashi University, particularly Kazushi Ohkawa, who was starting to publish 13 volumes on Japanese quantitative economic history. Saburo Okita (later Foreign Minister) opened the doors of government agencies such as the Bank of Japan, the Economic Planning Agency and the Ministry of Agriculture.

In 1996–98, I followed up my earlier work on the USSR with an article, 'Measuring the Performance of a Communist Command Economy: An Assessment of CIA Estimates for the USSR', *Review of Income and Wealth*, September 1998 (which also appears on the website). In preparing this I benefitted from a fascinating seminar organised by the Groningen Growth and Development Centre in 1996 on the *Productivity Performance and Potential of the Former Soviet Union*. Papers were presented by six Soviet economists (including Yuri Ivanov from Goskomstat, Grigory Khanin an outspoken critic of Soviet statistics from the University of Novosibirsk, and my old friend Valentin Kudrov from the Russian Academy of Sciences), two American Kremlinologists formerly with the CIA (Gertrude Schroeder and Jim Noren), and two leading European experts (Mark Harrison and Alistair McAuley) and my colleagues from Groningen. Unfortunately most of the proceedings were not published.

Class Structure and Economic Growth: India and Pakistan Since the Moghuls (1971) was a study with greater historical depth, analysing religious traditions, property relations and the social fabric in India over the past five centuries. It analysed the successive socioeconomic regimes in the Moghul empire, the British colonial period, and in India and Pakistan since independence. It showed the impact of different components of this heritage on the nature of economic policy since independence and its limited success in promoting economic growth and social welfare. When collecting material for the book, I lived in Pakistan for a year as an advisor on social policy to the Economic Planning Commission, and I spent several weeks in India. I wrote it in Harvard University, under whose auspices I had gone to Pakistan.

When I became a professor in the University of Groningen, I taught a course on Asian economic history. From an earlier visit to Java in 1967, I had the impression that there was little quantitative material on Dutch colonialism and Indonesian history. However, in 1982, on my first visit to the School of Pacific Studies at the Australian National University (the first of several short sabbaticals) I discovered an active group of historians in this field, and found there was a wealth of detailed quantitative information in Dutch archives, which was being processed by the KIT (Royal Tropical Institute) in Amsterdam. With help from Ann Booth in Canberra and Peter Boomgaard in Amsterdam, I used the historical evidence to produce my own brand of macroeconomic accounts. The modest outcome was 'Dutch Income in and from Indonesia, 1700–1938', *Modern Asian Studies* (1989) which analysed the economic impact of Dutch colonialism in Indonesia, and compared it with that of the British in India. This was followed by a conference volume, *Economic Growth in Indonesia, 1820–1940* (1989), which I edited with my colleague, Gé Prince.

The Political Economic of Poverty, Equity and Growth: Brazil and Mexico (1992) applied a similar mix of quantitative and socioinstitutional scrutiny, analysing changes in economic policy and their impact, with main emphasis on experience since the 1920s. It was published by the World Bank, one of ten comparative volumes on Latin America, Asia and Africa. Originally, I had intended a much deeper temporal perspective, examining historical roots of economic backwardness in the centuries of colonial rule, and the impact of Spanish and Portuguese colonialism compared with that of the British in north America. Experience in the colonial period is examined in 'Historical Roots of Modern Mexico, 1500–1940' in Maddison, *Explaining the Economic Performance of Nations* (1995) and in the unpublished paper, 'Brazil 1500–1929', which appears on my website. My work on Brazil and Mexico was long in gestation. I went first to both countries in 1964, as an advisor on education, international skill transfers and manpower problems. In Brazil, I was invited by Roberto Campos, the Minister of Planning, who was effectively in charge of economic policy in 1964–67. I went to Rio frequently in these years and to Mexico City where I was a consultant in the Bank of Mexico working with Victor Urquidi. In both countries I had good access to statisticians constructing the national accounts and to the architects of economic and social policy. I renewed these contacts in 1987–91, when the World Bank study was in preparation.

The Chinese Economy in the Long Run (1998) covered a much longer period than my earlier books. It deals with three epochs of Chinese development: 1) Dynastic China (Tang, Sung, Mongol, Ming and Ching) from the seventh century to the early nineteenth; 2) the century of colonial agression and civil war from the 1840s to the 1940s and 3) the resurrection of China in two phases of communist rule, under Mao and in the reform period since 1978.

For thirteen centuries, Chinese rulers entrusted the administration of the country to a powerful bureaucracy. This educated elite, recruited on a substantially meritocratic basis and schooled in the Chinese classics, was the main instrument for imposing social and political order in a unitary state with twice the territory and more than twice the population of Western Europe. This system of government was cheap compared with the complex military feudalism of Tokugawa Japan and the multistate polity of Europe where political control and elite claims on income were dispersed amongst an array of countervailing forces. The bureaucracy, military and 'gentry' represented about 2 per cent of the population in China in the early nineteenth century compared with 6.5 per cent for the shogunal, daimyo and samurai elite in Japan. Fiscal levies were about 5 per cent of GDP in China compared with 20–25 percent in Tokugawa Japan.

The bureaucracy had a very positive effect on Chinese agriculture. They nurtured it through hydraulic works. They helped develop and diffuse new seeds and crops by providing technical advice. They settled farmers in promising new regions. They developed a public granary and canal transport system to ensure imperial food supplies and mitigate famines. They commissioned and distributed illustrated agricultural handbooks, calendars etc. Land use was very intensive, with no common or fallow land. There was a heavy concentration on crops, with much less use of animal products than in Europe. Land allocation relied mainly on market forces with relatively free purchase and sale and an early disappearance of feudal restrictions. The most dynamic agricultural advances occurred in the Tang-Sung period when there was a massive shift in the regional centre of gravity, with a big rise in the proportion growing rice south of the Yangtse, and a relative decline in dry farming (millet and wheat) in the north.

Outside agriculture, the bureaucratic system had negative effects. The bureaucracy were quintessential rent-seekers. They dominated urban life. They prevented the emergence of an independent commercial and industrial bourgeoisie on the European pattern. Entrepreneurial activity was insecure in a framework where legal protection for private activity was so exiguous. Anything that promised to be lucrative was subjected to bureaucratic squeeze. Larger undertakings were limited to the state or to publicly licensed monopolies. Use of China's sophisticated shipbuilding and navigational knowledge to engage in international trade was forbidden early in the fourteenth century.

The other feature of this bureaucratic civilisation which had long-term repercussions on economic development, was the official Confucian ideology and education system. By comparison with the situation in Europe in the middle ages, its pragmatic and secular bias gave it the advantage. Official orthodoxy was probably most benign during the Sung dynasty. After the European Renaissance and the development of Galileian and Newtonian science, the balance of advantage changed. China failed to react adequately to the Western challenge until the middle of the twentieth century, mainly because the ideology, mindset and education system of the bureaucracy promoted an ethnocentric outlook, which was indifferent to developments outside China.

I estimate that Chinese per capita income rose by about a third from the tenth to the end of the thirteenth centuries. There was a significant rise in land productivity but the advance required higher per capita labour inputs. From the fourteenth to the mid nineteenth century, the evidence suggests that per capita output stagnated, but there was extensive growth as China was able to accommodate a large increase in population, introduce new crops from the Americas (maize, potatoes, peanuts, sweet potatoes, and tobacco) and get futher gains in land productivity.

My judgement on the contours and chronology of dynastic China's development (i.e. the rise in per capita income in the Sung and its stagnation from the fourteenth to the mid nineteenth century) is not unlike that of Mark Elvin, R.M. Hartwell, Eric Jones and Justin Lin. However, they do not attempt macroquantification, and their qualitative judgement probably implies a bigger leap in the Sung than I find. Some of them suggest that Sung China was trembling on the verge of an industrial revolution, which seems exaggerated. Some tend to overstate the degree of stagnation and the decline in 'creativity' from 1300 to 1850. In this period, China managed (with some interruptions) to sustain per capita income levels, whilst increasing its population more than fourfold (compared with less than threefold in Europe). 'Extensive' growth on this scale is not the same as stagnation.

My analysis suggests that the average West European level of per capita income drew level with the Chinese in the fourteenth century and was twice as high at the beginning of the nineteenth century. Recently, Kenneth Pomeranz (2000) has suggested that Europe did not overtake the Chinese level until after 1800. He is not alone in taking this position, which was first advanced by Paul Bairoch, but he provides a much wider variety of evidence to support his case. Pomeranz's evidence is mainly microeconomic. There are only four tables in his book with no attempt at macroquantification. He does not provide a chronological profile of development in Europe or China before and beyond his point of comparison. He has one passing reference to Needham, and no discussion of the forces affecting the divergent development of technology in China and Europe. I find Pomeranz's judgement unconvincing. In 1800, the degree of urbanisation was three times higher in western Europe than in China, the proportion of the population employed in agriculture was a good deal smaller, though the European diet included a much higher proportion of meat and dairy products. Chinese life expectation was two-thirds of that in Western Europe. Pomeranz stresses western Europe's benefits from international trade, which augmented its supply of food and raw materials from the 'ghost acreage' of distant lands. He treats this benefit as if it were a windfall gain. In fact, China turned its back on international trade early in the fourteenth century, and the Ching dynasty forbade settlement on its own ghost acres in Manchuria

Between the 1840s and 1940s China's experience was catastrophic. Its economy suffered from a series of disasters, the Taiping rebellion, wars with British and French colonialists, three major invasions by Japan and civil war between the Kuomintang and Mao's communists. As a result per capita income in 1950 was less than one tenth of that in Western Europe, and threequarters of what it had been in 1300.

Since 1950, the Chinese economy has been transformed, and there has been significant catch-up in the reform period since 1978. A considerable part of the book is devoted to providing improved measures of performance in the Communist period. There is a detailed critique of Chinese official statistics which exaggerate growth but understate the level of real income. With appropriate purchasing power adjustment, I concluded that China is now the world's second largest economy, after the United States.

My five country studies provided an essential underpinning for comprehensive analysis of performance in different parts of the world economy – my third main venture into analytical economic history.

ANALYSIS OF THE PACE AND PATTERN OF WORLD ECONOMIC DEVELOPMENT AND INTERACTION BETWEEN MAJOR PARTS OF THE WORLD ECONOMY

I published several surveys of the world economy between 1962 and 2001, gradually broadening the statistical coverage and depth of historical perspective.

The first venture was 'Growth and Stagnation in the World Economy 1870-1960', *Banca Nazionale del Lavoro Quarterly Review* (1962) which was concerned with the transmission of cyclical fluctuations in trade and the impact of trade on growth. It involved the construction of annual estimates of GDP, trade volume and unit values for the main trading countries, revising earlier trade volume estimates by Hilgerdt, and by Arthur Lewis.

Economic Progress and Policy in Developing Countries (1970) was an overall survey of postwar performance in the non-Western world, which provided the same kind of historical depth and comparative perspective as in Maddison (1964). At the time it was written, systematic estimates of real expenditure and purchasing power parity existed for only a handful of Western countries and none for non-Western countries. It included a major exercise to develop alternative measures of levels of economic performance, productivity and purchasing power from the output side for 29 countries. These estimates broke new ground and helped to illuminate the range of variance within a 'developing' world whose characteristics were then often assumed to be relatively homogeneous.

In 1983 I compared the results of my 1970 output approach, which I called ICOP (international comparisons of output and productivity) to contrast with the ICP results of Kravis, Heston and Summers from the expenditure side. I argued that the ICP approach tended to exaggerate levels of output in poorer countries, and that manipulation of ICP expenditure results to produce proxy measures of real output by sector were misleading. Since then, members of the ICOP group at the University of Groningen have developed this approach much further (see 'A Comparison of Levels of GDP Per Capita in Developed and Developing Countries, 1700–1820', *Journal of Economic History*, 1983, *Comparisons of Real Output in Manufacturing,* with Bart van Ark, 1988, and the eight papers in Maddison, Prasada Rao and Shepherd (eds.) *The Asian Economies in the Twentieth Century*, Elgar, 2002).

The World Economy in the Twentieth Century (1989) was an essay in comparative economic history, using quantitative growth accounts to marshal much of the evidence. It involved a systematic confrontation of levels of performance and rates of growth across countries as well as an attempt to give an aggregate picture and examine interrelations between different parts of the world economy. Although there was heavy emphasis on measureable supply-side influences, strong emphasis was also given to the role of policy and institutions, both national and international. The sample of 32 countries covered about four-fifths of world output and population.

Monitoring the World Economy (1995) had a much longer temporal scope, and was much more comprehensive in its coverage of the world economy. The three analytical chapters provided: 1) a broad survey of economic growth and levels of performance in different parts of the world economy since 1820; 2) a review of causal influences on growth and techniques of growth accounting; 3) an analysis of changes in the momentum of growth and the role of economic policy in different parts of the world economy since 1820. There was also a set of statistical appendices of much greater scope than in my earlier books which was intended to help and encourage basic research into quantitative economic history. It demonstrated what had already been accomplished by a whole generation of scholars in making intertemporal and interspatial comparisons for a large fraction of world economic activity, and indicated the types of problem where further research and sensitivity testing was needed.

Charles Feinstein's review in the *Journal of Economic Literature*, pp.1378–1380, (1996) indicates the scope and likely impact of the book:

'the publication of this volume represents a magnificent extension of historical national accounts both in time and by region. In a prodigious sequel to his previous studies Angus Maddison now provides consistent estimates of GDP, population and GDP per capita for the period from 1820 to 1992. The main data set is based on 56 countries which together accounted in 1992 for 93 per cent of world output. The richness of this banquet can be contrasted with the thin gruel which was all that was available when Maddison published his first study of comparative growth (*Economic Growth in the West*: Allen and Unwin, 1964). At that time he was able to include estimates for only 12 countries, ten in Europe and two in North America: there were no data prior to 1870 and many omissions after that, and the supplementary information was similarly restricted. His splendid volume will surely stimulate subsequent studies in both theory and history and will thus contribute both to further advance in the coverage and reliability of national accounts data, and to better understanding of the processes of economic growth and of international convergence and divergence'.

The World Economy: A Millennial Perspective (2001) provides a much deeper temporal perspective than Maddison 1995. It analyses changes in world income and population over the past two millennia in a comprehensive way, identifies the forces which explain the success of the rich countries, explores the obstacles which hindered advance in regions and countries which lagged behind, and scrutinises the interaction between the rich countries and the rest. As with my earlier books, the causal analysis is supported by an extensive framework of macroeconomic statistics.

There are three analytical chapters : 1) the contours of world development over the past two millennia; 2) the impact of Western development on the rest of the world from the eleventh century, illustrated by the successive experience of Venice, Portugal, the Dutch Republic and the UK as pioneers in navigation, international trade, and capitalist development and 3) a survey of the world economy in the second half of the twentieth century. For the period 1820–1950, chapters 2 and 3 of Maddison (1995), are a useful supplement to Maddison (2001), where this period is covered in less detail.

Appendix B describes the statistical sources and procedures for quantifying levels of world population and income before 1820. The other five appendices deal in more detail with evidence for 1820–1998. In the past, quantitative research in economic history has been heavily concentrated on the ninetenth and twentieth centuries when growth was fastest. To go back earlier involves use of weaker evidence and greater reliance on clues and conjecture. Holes in the evidence have to be filled by proxy estimates in order to arrive at world totals. Nevertheless it is a meaningful and useful exercise because differences in the pace and pattern of change in major parts of the world economy have deep roots in the past. Quantification clarifies issues which qualitative analysis leaves fuzzy. It is more readily contestable and likely to be contested. It sharpens scholarly discussion, sparks off rival hypotheses, and contributes to the dynamics of the research process. It can do this only if the quantitative evidence and proxy procedures are described transparently, so that dissenting readers can augment or reject parts of the evidence or introduce alternative hypotheses.

The strongest and most comprehensive evidence is that for population, and the population component is of greater proportionate importance in analysis of centuries when per capita income growth was exiguous. Demographic material is also important in providing clues to the movement of per capita income over the long term. One striking example is the urbanisation ratio. When countries are able to expand their urban ratios, it indicates a growing surplus above subsistence in agriculture. Indicators of changes in or inter-country variance in life expectancy also throw light on changes in or inter-country differences in real income.

Another major purpose of the book was to revise, augment and update the analysis of world economic development since 1950. Maddison (1995) provided annual estimates of population and GDP for 56 sample countries representing 93 per cent of world output in 1992. Appendix C of Maddison (2001) shows annual estimates for 1950–98 for 117 countries, 7 regions and world totals. For Western Europe and Western Offshoots, the coverage is the same, for Latin America the annual coverage rose from 7 to 23 countries; Asia from 12 to 31; Africa from 10 to 42. For Eastern Europe and the former USSR, where many new countries have emerged, coverage rose from 7 to 27 countries (see Appendix D for the years 1990–98).

Maddison (2001) retains the 1990 international dollar as the temporal and spatial anchor for measuring levels levels of GDP over time and between countries. This was also the benchmark in Maddison (1995), but there were significant revisions in all regions except Eastern Europe and the former USSR. The derivation of the revised 1990 level estimates is shown on pp.189–90, 199, 219–220 and 228.

For 1820–1950, I relied mainly on the time series for population and GDP in *Monitoring the World Economy* in 1995 (with revisions for the Netherlands, Portugal, India, Indonesia, Japan and Vietnam). Maddison (2001) gives estimates before 1950 only for benchmark years. Readers who want annual GDP figures for 1870 or 1900 onwards can merge the two sources as indicated on p. 267 of Maddison (2001). However, I have already done this for 21 advanced capitalist countries in the Historical Statistics section of this website.

WORK IN PROGRESS

At present I am preparing a book, *Contours of the World Economy and the Art of Macromeasurement*, which should be published in 2003. The first part will be a long essay on the contours of the world economy, with a rather extensive treatment of African history since the Roman empire. The rest will be essays of the art of macromeasurement since the political economists of the seventeenth century (William Petty, Gregory King, John Graunt and Charles Davenant). The material is drawn from the Kuznets lectures I gave in Yale in 1998, the Wendt lecture at the American Enterprise Institute and the Abramovitz lecture at Stanford University in 2001.

A Story Behind Each Number – Angus Maddison (1926–2010)

Derek Blades, Bart van Ark and Harry X. Wu[*]

Just as the global economy is experiencing one of the biggest economic crises of the past century, the economics profession lost one of the world's most gifted scholars ever to document economic performance over long periods of time. Angus Maddison died from complications arising from leukemia on April 24, 2010 at the American Hospital in Paris. He was buried in the church graveyard in Chevincourt, a village near Compiègne where he had lived with his wife Penny for the latter part of his life. He is also survived by his two sons, George and Charles, his daughter Lizzy, and five grandchildren.

Angus Maddison has been an active member of the International Association for Research in Income and Wealth since 1968. He has participated in at least a dozen conferences of the Association, was a member of the editorial board of *The Review of Income and Wealth* from 1990 to 1997, and has published five articles in the *Review* since 1980. His last two articles in the *Review* were, respectively, drawn from the first Ruggles Keynote Lecture on measuring world economic performance which he delivered at the 28th General Conference of the Association in 2004 in Cork, Ireland (Maddison, 2005), and from his introductory lecture on measuring economic performance in China for the 2007 Beijing Special Conference on Transition Economies (Maddison, 2008). Angus also played an important role in organizing several sessions in the area of measuring long-term growth at conferences and stimulated the participation of many scholars in this area.

Angus Maddison's fascination with the big questions of what drives economic growth and development goes back to his youth. He encountered the perils of economic depression on his doorstep in the town where he was born. Newcastle upon Tyne, a shipbuilding and mining city in the North-East

[*] Review of Income and Wealth, Series 56, Number 3, September 2010 Review of Income and Wealth © 2010 International Association for Research in Income and Wealth, Published by Blackwell Publishing, 9600 Garsington Road, Oxford OX42DQ, UK and 350 Main St, Malden, MA, 02148, USA.

of England, was among the worst to suffer from the mass unemployment of the interwar years. In his endearing autobiography, 'Confessions of a Chiffrephile' (Maddison, 1994),[1] Angus recalls a visit with his father to neighboring Gateshead where 'the buildings were blacker, and the clusters of unemployed thicker than in Newcastle. I saw nowhere so depressing until visiting Calcutta 30 years later'. The first book he read on economics was Keynes' *How to Pay for the War*, finding it 'more or less intelligible to a thirteen year old'. A reference in Keynes led him to Colin Clark and his *Conditions of Economic Progress*, and he was 'fascinated at the way it quantified what was going on in so many countries'. Perhaps it was at this moment that Angus became a chiffrephile. This, he explained many years later, was 'a word I invented to characterize economists and economic historians who, like myself, have a strong predilection for quantification'.

In 1944, Angus won a scholarship to Cambridge University, initially to read history but soon switching to economics. He found economics a much tougher discipline and the students more dedicated to their subject. But economics teaching at Cambridge was distinctly parochial and Angus found discussions more to his liking at the Marshall Society and the Political Economy Club, originally set up by Keynes, both of which recognized the existence of other universities in Britain, Continental Europe, and even America.

Angus started his graduate studies at McGill University and later at John Hopkins in Baltimore. His thesis was a comparative study of productivity in the U.S., the U.K. and Canada and he found the Canadian statisticians at what is now Statistics Canada particularly well-informed and helpful. He returned to Europe for a teaching job at St Andrews University in Scotland and later an assignment in Rome at the Food and Agriculture Organization. In 1953 he moved to Paris to join the Organisation for European Economic Cooperation (OEEC) where he was to spend a good part of his working life.

Angus worked initially in the Economics Department, supporting the work of the Group of Economic Experts whose chairman, Robert Hall, was described by Angus as a 'slow speaking Australian of great wisdom and professional competence' and a 'master of the meaningful grunt'. An important development at this time was the strengthening of the statistical basis to allow quantitative monitoring of the economies of member countries. Milton Gilbert was recruited to work with Richard Stone to develop standardized national accounts for OEEC countries and was active in establishing the International Association for Research in Income and Wealth. Around this time, Wilfred Beckerman, Angus's close friend from

---

[1] Unless noted otherwise, the quotations below are all taken from this article.

Cambridge, was recruited by the OEEC to help member countries improve their national accounts statistics.

When the OEEC was enlarged to bring in the United States and Canada, it became the Organisation for Economic Co-operation and Development (OECD). Aid to developing countries was added to the agenda and Angus was appointed secretary to what later became the Development Assistance Committee. His first task was to set up a statistical monitoring system to measure aid flows. Around this time Angus concluded that the 'theoretical and statistical basis for analyzing growth and stability of the advanced capitalist countries' had been fairly well established, and in 1964 he moved to the OECD's Development Centre which was looking at development issues outside the OECD area. Before doing so, however, he took six months' leave to write *Economic Growth in the West*, the first of the ten major books and numerous articles on long-term economic growth that he published in his lifetime. Angus's work on development issues took him as an economic advisor for the Twentieth Century Fund and Harvard University's Development Advisory Service to Brazil, Guinea, Mongolia, Ghana, and Pakistan. In the last two of these Angus was advising on social policy issues including income distribution, and health and education policy.

In pursuit of his interest in social issues, Angus returned to the OECD in 1971 to work in the social affairs department. One of his major achievements was the publication of the first OECD *Yearbook of Education Statistics* in 1974. For the first time this brought together comparable statistics to assess the costs and benefits of education. A problem Angus noted then, and which continues today, was that 'There was in fact a good deal of resistance in educational circles to studies which might make it possible to judge the quality of teachers and curricula'. The 1974–75 recession highlighted problems of government spending on social security. Angus established a new committee to look at social aspects of income transfer policy which explored a wide range of distributive issues. Unemployment was another issue addressed by Angus. Typically his first concern was to assemble a database of comparable statistics and to this end he set up a committee of labor statisticians with key inputs from Connie Sorrentino and her colleagues at the U.S. Bureau of Labor Statistics. The committee established the standardized definitions of employment and unemployment that are used to this day by the International Labour Organization, but just as important, Angus developed an additional range of measures of 'labor slack' by correcting for government attempts to disguise unemployment through early retirement schemes and loose definitions of workers' disability.

Angus was particularly helpful to the first author of this obituary (Derek Blades), who had just been made responsible for the OECD's rather stodgy annual, *Labour Force Statistics*. Even though he worked in a different department and strictly speaking it was none of his business, he was very helpful in putting together a much more readable version and added quarterly supplements.

Looking back, Maddison's work from 1971 to 1978 can be seen to have established the OECD's statistical credibility as an impartial advisor on the many social issues of equality, education and unemployment that still dominate the agenda of most Western governments. In addition to all this, Angus continued to write, and acquired a Doctorate from the Université d'Aix-Marseille III in preparation for his next career move in 1978 – to the University of Groningen as Professor of Economic Sociology.

Angus moved to Groningen because he liked the academic atmosphere in this typical university town. It provided him with a lot of academic freedom to pursue his research agenda on economic growth and development. In an interview with the university's newspaper, at the time of his retirement in 1997, he said that Groningen (which is situated in the north of the Netherlands) is 'as close to heaven as I can get'. He trained and guided a dozen PhD students, most of whom are still actively working on aspects of growth and development in academia or in the policy research world. It was a delight for Angus's students to work with him. He was not only learned but had also travelled widely around the world and never hesitated to help his students do the same. Walking with him through the streets of Prague just after the Velvet Revolution in 1991, the second author of this obituary (Bart van Ark) remarked how much the city had changed in just a decade, to which Angus answered that it still looked much worse than during the late 1940s when he visited Prague, which then was still one of the most prosperous cities in the midst of war-ridden postwar Europe.

During the first half of his time in Groningen, Angus continued his broadly based research on growth and development. Following several earlier books he had written on this topic, he published two major monographs in 1982 and 1991 and a seminal article on growth accounting in 1987 in the *Journal of Economic Literature*. These writings explained his understanding of the dynamics and sources of growth and development. His characterization of development in terms of secular phases rather than the Kondratieff notion of long waves led to a more gradualist interpretation of the diffusion of technology and innovation, and a greater emphasis on 'system shocks'. These shocks were in part historical accidents, but their impact was reinforced by changes in expectations, and fashions in economic policy. These views, based on strong quantitative support, challenged scholars who had advanced the notion of a more abrupt 'industrial revolution' in the late eighteenth century, or traditional development economists who supported the Rostovian view of the need for an economic 'take-off' to generate growth. Angus was also an early advocate of the need to take economic institutions much more seriously by developing a model that distinguished between proximate (directly measurable economic inputs, such as labor, physical and human capital, and land) and ultimate (institutional, political, social, and cultural) sources of growth. The complex interaction of these proximate and ultimate sources, for example, was the key to the rise of a multipolar Europe after the dark Middle Ages.

Maddison also returned to the topic of measuring economic performance beyond the Western world, but began to place it more strongly in an international comparative perspective. In the early 1980s he criticized Paul Bairoch's view that the industrialization of the Western European countries took place at an average standard of living below that of contemporary less developed countries, which was very different from the conjectures by David Landes and Simon Kuznets, who believed that by that time Western Europe was already much richer than the rest of the world. To Angus Maddison these remarkably different quantitative conclusions had very important analytical implications: 'If Bairoch is right, then much of the backwardness of the third world presumably has to be explained by colonial exploitation, and much less of Europe's advantage can be due to scientific precocity, centuries of slow accumulation, and organisational and financial prosperity' (Maddison, 1983). Although he used the existing evidence at the time to show that Bairoch and his epigoni probably overstated the contemporary income gap and understated per capita income growth in the developing world, it motivated him to pursue the topic of international comparisons more intensively. Following his later work on China (see below), he returned to the topic of comparative performance between East and West at the time of the Industrial Revolution, when other scholars, notably Kenneth Pomeranz, argued that China stayed at a much higher level of development until the end of the eighteenth century than Europe – a viewpoint which Maddison strongly criticized on the basis of his reconstruction of China's macroeconomic accounts back to the year 960.

During the second half of the 1980s, Angus started a series of benchmark studies of output and productivity aimed at strengthening the basis for international comparisons. This led to a project on International Comparisons of Output and Productivity (ICOP), which focused on measuring levels of performance from the industry-of-origin side rather than the expenditure side (such as in the International Comparisons Program at the World Bank and Penn World Tables). He found that generally expenditure-based studies had a tendency to overstate the comparative output level of developing economies, because the expenditure based approach did not take sufficient account of the low output level of service sector activities in those countries (Maddison and van Ark, 2002). Several of his students did their PhD theses as part of the ICOP project.

During the final years of his time in Groningen, Maddison focused his attention even more on quantifying economic growth for longer time spans and in a broader range of countries. An important part of that endeavor focused on a quantitative assessment of China's long-run economic performance. Angus's early work on China relied mainly on quantitative research by scholars such as Dwight Perkins and Ta-chung Liu and Kung-chia Yeh as well as studies commissioned by the U.S. Congress Joint Economic Committee, which he used in his discussion of the debate between Bairoch and Landes-Kuznets. Following this, he substantially extended his investigation of Chinese economic history, exploring the literature on quantitative assessments of China's economic growth. With new research by himself and by working with others, he eventually published *Chinese Economic Performance in the Long Run* (1998).

The work on China was not only important because of China's historical role in the world economy, but it was also a key part in the puzzle of positioning economies in a comparative perspective. For example, Maddison spent considerable effort in comparing China with Japan rather than with Western Europe as in other studies. While, like many other researchers, he attempted to explain the classic divergences between countries, Angus also devoted much effort to the understanding of important convergences in the past, in most of which China served as an important reference, e.g. Europe's rise from its nadir to overtake China, the Japanese catch-up with China in Tokugawa times, and post-war resurgent Asia, especially China, India, and the so-called tigers, which have reduced their degree of backwardness substantially relative to the advanced countries.

This was also a period in which Maddison began to work and discuss with Chinese economists. The third author of this article (Harry X. Wu) worked intensively with him for many years on the reconstruction of China's national accounts, the development of an alternative industrial output index for China (Maddison and Wu, 2008), and the Chinese translation of his three books including his China book which was updated in 2007. His criticism of the Chinese methodology used to measure output was very transparent and clear, and gained a lot of respect even from government officials. His introductory paper at the 2007 Beijing Conference on Transition Economies (which was delivered by Bart van Ark in Maddison's absence) was well received by scholars and policy makers.

On his last trip to China to celebrate the publication in Chinese of *The World Economy: A Millennial Perspective*, Angus, accompanied by the third author of this obituary and the chief translator of the book (Harry X. Wu) visited Hangzhou, the capital of China's Southern Song (1127–1279) which was then the richest country in the world according to his estimates. He was warned about the potential danger of the highway drive and that it would be a tiring day trip but he was still keen to go. Filled with excitement at stepping on the land of Hangzhou, he then realized that it was hard to find any trace of its past prosperity. He remarked that wrong policies or mistakes by the ruling elite could easily wipe out a country's accumulated wealth for centuries – an observation had motivated his long pursuit for the underlying explanation of economic growth.

During the final phase of his career, after his retirement from Groningen in 1997, Maddison concentrated on extending his macro-quantitative measures of GDP covering two millennia and all countries in the world. During the 2000s he published several updates and extension of his *Historical Statistics on World Population, GDP and Per Capita GDP, 1–2008 AD*, which is also available online from his homepage at the Groningen Growth and Development Centre website (http://www.ggdc.net/maddison/). He shook up the profession by coming up with an estimate of world GDP in the year 1. While challenged on the reliability of such an estimate, most scholars would trust Angus for giving it his best shot given his deep knowledge and broad experience. Angus lived to see the beginnings of 'The Maddison Project', aimed at creating a network of scholars to continue his work on world historical macroeconomic statistics in Angus's spirit. David Henderson, another admirer of Angus's work, summarized the special features of his macro statistics that make them so valuable – they are long, they are expressed in a standard currency unit, and breaks in series are patched up in the best possible way even when they involved changes in national boundaries. Angus's spirit was always: 'Here's my best effort. Do better.' If someone could, Angus was the first to offer his congratulations.

Angus's thinking about the dynamics of growth and stagnation are also relevant to the recent economic and financial crises. In his last major work, *Contours of the World Economy, 1–2030 AD*, he pioneered a forward looking approach to 2030, predicting a larger role for China and India in the global economy. He also had a less negative view on the impact on economic growth of a moderate increase in global warming compared to the predominant viewpoint of, for example, the Intergovernmental Panel on Climate Change (IPCC).

Angus Maddison's legacy to the profession is huge. He helped create the Groningen Growth and Development Centre (GGDC), a research group at the University of Groningen that focuses on long-term economic growth. The data-bases created and maintained by Maddison and his current and former colleagues form one of the most important sources for the analysis of long-term economic growth and are used worldwide by scholars and policy analysts.

Many of Angus's colleagues and friends have exceptionally pleasant memories of his gift for combining work and pleasure in a very natural way.

He was a scholar, mentor, colleague, and friend, all at the same time. Many will remember the great moments with him and his family at their home in France, at conferences, or wherever else in the world he would be.

Angus Maddison will be missed. But his legacy will stay, and many will continue the work in his spirit.

REFERENCES

Maddison, A. (1983), 'A Comparison of Levels of GDP Per Capita in Developed and Developing Countries 1700–1980', *Journal of Economic History*, **41** (1), 27–41.

Maddison, A. (1994), 'Confessions of a Chiffrephile,' *Banca Nazionale del Lavoro Quarterly Review*, **No. 189**, 123–65.

Maddison, A. (2005), 'Measuring and Interpreting World Economic Performance 1500–2001', *Review of Income and Wealth*, **51**(1), 1–35.

Maddison, A. (2008), 'Measuring the Economic Performance of Transition Economies: Some Lessons from Chinese Experience', *Review of Income and Wealth*, **55**(S1), 423–41.

Maddison, A. and B. van Ark (2002), 'The International Comparison of Real Product and Productivity', in Maddison, A., D.S. Prasada Rao, and W.F. Shepherd (eds), (2002), *The Asian Economies in the Twentieth Century*, Edward Elgar, Cheltenham, 5–26.

Maddison, A. and Harry X. Wu (2008), 'Measuring China's Economic Performance', *World Economics*, 9(2), 13–44.

Index